•• The Wholeness of Nature

··The

Wholeness

of

Nature

Goethe's Way

of Science

HENRI BORTOFT

FLORIS BOOKS

First published in 1996 by Lindisfarne Press and Floris Books
Third impression 2007
©1996 Henri Bortoft

British Library CIP Data available

ISBN 978-086315-238-2

Printed in Great Britain by
Cromwell Press, Trowbridge

To the memory of

DAVID BOHM

who introduced me to the
problem of wholeness

Contents

Why would anyone in the 1990s write a book on Goethe's way of science? Perhaps because of a scholarly interest—wanting to find out the truth about Goethe's scientific ideas, to discover what he had in mind. No doubt this would be a valid reason, but it is not mine. To begin with I don't speak German, so writing a scholarly book on Goethe would be, for me, equivalent to trying to climb a mountain without first having learned to walk. But what other reason could there be for writing about the scientific work of someone who died in 1832, especially when his ideas were rejected by the scientific establishment as the work of a muddled dilettante? The widespread judgment of Goethe's science seems to be just that: Great poet and dramatist he might have been, but he didn't know what he was talking about when it came to science. But times have changed since Goethe's day. Modern science had barely begun then, whereas now it has matured and we have had a chance to see its implications and consequences more clearly. Equally important, we now understand science better—the revolution in the history and philosophy of science is responsible for that.

My interest in Goethe arose as a result of working as a postgraduate research student under David Bohm on the problem of wholeness in the quantum theory, back in the 1960s. To those of us who had the privilege to participate in his daily discussions, Bohm communicated a sense of the way that wholeness is very different from how we have become accustomed to thinking of it in modern science. When I first came across Goethe's scientific ideas, I immediately recognized in them the same kind of understanding of wholeness that I had encountered with Bohm. But from the beginning I saw Goethe's way of science in practical terms, as something that was "do-able"—even though my own interest was, and is, largely philosophical. Because I had been taught exercises in seeing and visualization by J.G. Bennett in the 1960s, I was able to recognize what Goethe was *doing* instead of being limited to only what he was saying. So, thanks to this, I was not restricted to an intellectual approach. Working with Goethe's practical indications brought me to an understanding of Goethe's way of science which was not only more lively than, but also somewhat different from, what I could read in standard academic accounts. For example, by practicing Goethe's method of seeing and visualizing with plants, I came to experience the way that this turned the one and the many inside out. I later found that, using the same means, I could share this perception with students, and that we could begin to understand the whole and the part, the one and the many, the universal and the particular, in a radically new way. I would not have experienced this transformation in the mode of cognition for myself if I had done no more than read Goethe intellectually. What can only seem abstract to the intellectual mind becomes living experience when Goethe's practice of seeing and visualizing is followed. Doing this gives us a sense of a different kind of dimension in nature. It is no exaggeration to say that it turns our habitual way of thinking inside out, and I have tried to write this book in a way that will give readers a taste of this for themselves.

Over the past few decades, we have become increasingly aware of the importance of the cultural context within which modern science has developed. The new field of history and philosophy of science has shown us what is referred to now as the historicity of scientific knowledge, the way that cultural–historical factors enter into the very form which scientific knowledge takes. We have, for the most part, given up thinking of science as an autonomous activity which stands outside of history, or indeed outside of any human social context, pursuing its own absolute, contextless way of acquiring pure knowledge. In fact, now we have begun to recognize that this view of science itself first arose within a particular cultural–historical context, and that it is an expression of a style of thinking which has its own validity but does not have access to "ultimate reality." We can now recognize, for example, that the fact that modern physics is true—which it certainly is—does not mean that it is fundamental. Hence it cannot be a foundation upon which everything else, human beings included, depends. Recognizing that the foundations of science are cultural–historical does not affect the truth of science, but it does put a different perspective on the fundamentalist claims made on behalf of science by some of its self-appointed missionaries today. Looked at in the light of the new discoveries in the history and philosophy of science, such claims to have found the ultimate basis of reality look like no more than quaint relics from a bygone age.

It is astonishing to realize just how modern Goethe was in this respect. Almost two hundred years ago, he discovered the historicity of science for himself, expressing it succinctly when he said, "We might venture the statement that the history of science is science itself." He came to this understanding as a result of his struggle with the science which had fundamentalist pretensions in his own day, i.e., the science of Newton. This understanding makes Goethe our contemporary. We realize now that nature can manifest in more than one way, without needing to argue that one way is more fundamental than another. So there is the possibility that there could be a different science of nature, not contradictory but complementary to mainstream science. Both can be true, not because truth is relative, but because they reveal nature in different ways. Thus, whereas mainstream science enables us to discover the causal order in nature, Goethe's way of science enables us to discover the wholeness. I suggest that this science of the wholeness of nature is a vision much needed today in view of the limitations in the perspective of mainstream science which have now become so evident.

The three essays which appear here were written at different times and under different circumstances. "Authentic and

Counterfeit Wholes" first appeared as "Counterfeit and Authentic Wholes: Finding a Means for Dwelling in Nature" in *Dwelling, Place and Environment* (1986), a collection of essays on the phenomenological approach to the human environment, edited by David Seamon and Robert Mugeraur. It is based on an earlier work, and I am very grateful to David Seamon for encouraging me to rewrite it in this form. I would like to thank the publisher, Martinus Nijhoff, for permission to reproduce it here. "Goethe's Scientific Consciousness" is a much extended version of a paper given at a conference held by the British Society for Phenomenology in 1979. It was published in 1986 in the Institute for Cultural Research Monograph Series, and I am grateful to the Council of the Institute for Cultural Research for permission to republish it here.

"Understanding Goethe's Way of Science" was written specifically for this volume. Christopher Bamford at Lindisfarne Press asked me if I had any "further thoughts" which might be added as a postscript to an American publication of "Goethe's Scientific Consciousness." I didn't realize that I had until I started to write, and I am as surprised as he is at the result. I am very grateful to him for his initial suggestion, and for his help and encouragement in getting the book into its final form. I would also like to thank Rob Baker and Albert Berry of Watersign Resources for editing the book into a style suitable for an American readership, and for improving its general readability. I am very grateful to John Barnes, the series editor, for including this book in the Renewal in Science series, for his many helpful suggestions, and for organizing an extensive lecture tour to coincide with publication.

Finally, but by no means least, I would like to thank Jackie Bortoft, my wife, for her continued help and support. As well as word-processing my handwriting, and bringing my attention to unnecessary repetitions, she has helped me on many occasions to find how to articulate more clearly something that has been eluding me. Naturally any confusions which remain are my own responsibility.

PART 1 ..

Authentic and Counterfeit Wholes

What is wholeness? To answer this question, it is helpful to present a specific setting. Imagine someone not yet recognizing it, asking, "What is roundness?" We might try to answer by giving a number of instances, such as "The moon is round," "The plate is round," "The coin is round," and so on. Of course "round" is none of these things, but by adducing a number of such instances we may hope to provoke the recognition of roundness. This happens when perception of the specific instances is reorganized, so that they now become like mirrors in which roundness is seen reflected. In spite of what many people might think, this process does not involve empirical generalization—i.e., abstracting what is common from a number of cases. The belief that concepts are derived directly from sensory experiences is like believing that conjurors really do produce rabbits out of hats. Just as the conjuror puts the rabbit into the hat beforehand, so the attempt to deduce the concept by abstraction in the empiricist manner presupposes the very concept it pretends to produce.

I attempt the same procedure in this essay with the aim of understanding wholeness. I adduce a number of examples of wholeness, with the aim of learning more about wholeness itself by seeing its reflection in these particular cases. I distinguish authentic wholeness from counterfeit forms in terms of the relationship between whole and part. The result leads to an understanding of how the whole can be encountered through the parts. Finally, I argue that the way of science developed by the poet and student of nature Johann Wolfgang von Goethe (1749–1832) exemplifies the principle of authentic wholeness.

Goethe's mode of understanding sees the part in light of the whole, fostering a way of science which dwells in nature.

TWO EXAMPLES OF WHOLENESS:
HOLOGRAMS AND THE UNIVERSE OF LIGHT AND MATTER

The advent of the laser has made possible the practical development of a radically different kind of photography. *Hologram* is the name given to the special kind of photographic plate produced with the highly coherent light of a laser—i.e., light which holds together and does not disperse, similar to a pure tone compared with noise. Whereas the ordinary photographic plate records and reproduces a flat image of an illuminated object, the hologram does not record an image of the object photographed but provides an optical reconstruction of the original object. When the hologram plate itself is illuminated with the coherent light from the laser with which it was produced, the optical effect is exactly as if the original object were being observed. What is seen is to all optical appearances the object itself in full three-dimensional form, being displaced in apparent position when seen from different perspectives (the parallax effect) in the same way as the original object.

A hologram has several remarkable properties in addition to those related to the three-dimensional nature of the optical reconstruction which it permits. The particular property which is of direct concern in understanding wholeness is the pervasiveness of the whole optical object throughout the plate.[1] If the hologram plate is broken into fragments and one fragment is illuminated, it is found that the same three-dimensional optical reconstruction of the original object is produced. There is nothing missing; the only difference is that the reconstruction is less well defined. The entire original object can be optically reconstructed from any fragment of the original hologram, but as the fragments get smaller and smaller the resolution deteriorates until the reconstruction becomes so blotchy and ill-defined as to become unrecognizable. This property of the hologram is in striking contrast to the ordinary image-recording photographic plate. If this type of plate is broken and a fragment illuminated, the image reproduced will be that recorded on the particular fragment and no more. With orthodox photography the image fragments with the plate; with holography the image remains undivided when the plate is fragmented.

What can be seen straightaway about wholeness in this example of the hologram is the way in which the whole is present in the parts. The entire picture is wholly present in each part of the plate, so that it would not be true in this case to say that the whole is made up of parts. This point will be explored in detail shortly, but the advantage of beginning with the hologram is that it is such an immediately concrete instance of wholeness.

A second example of wholeness involves the ordinary experience of looking up at the sky at night and seeing the vast number of stars. We see this nighttime world by means of the light "carrying" the stars to us, which means that this vast expanse of sky must all be present in the light which passes through the small hole of the pupil into the eye. Furthermore, other observers in different locations can see the same expanse of night sky. Hence we can say that the stars seen in the heavens are all present in the light which is at any eye-point. The totality is contained in each small region of space, and when we use optical instruments like a telescope, we simply reclaim more of that light.[2] If we set off in imagination to find what it would be like to be light, we come to a condition in which here is everywhere and everywhere is here. The night sky is a "space" which is one whole, enfolded in an infinite number of points and yet including all within itself.

Matter also turns out to behave in an unexpectedly holistic way at both the macroscopic and the microscopic level. We tend to think of the large-scale universe of matter as being made up of separate and independent masses interacting with one another through the force of gravity. The viewpoint which emerges from modern physics is very different from this traditional conception. It is now believed that mass is not an intrinsic property of a body, but it is in fact a reflection of the whole of the rest of the universe in that body. Einstein imagined, following Ernst Mach, that a single particle of matter would have no mass if it were not for all the rest of the matter in the universe.[3] Instead of trying to understand the universe by extrapolating from the local environment here and now to the universe as a whole, it may be useful to reverse the relationship and understand the local environment as being the result of the rest of the universe.[4]

Similarly, at the microscopic level, we tend to think of the world as being made up of separate, independent subatomic particles interacting with one another through fields of force. But the view which emerges from physics today is very different. Particle physicists, as they are called, have found that subatomic particles cannot be considered to be made up of ultimate, simple building blocks which are separate and outside of each other. Increasingly, it becomes clear that analysis in this traditional way is inappropriate at the microscopic level. Thus, in the "bootstrap" philosophy of Geoffrey Chew, the properties of any one particle are determined by all the other particles, so that every particle is a reflection of all the others. This structure whereby a particle contains all other particles, and is also contained in each of them, is expressed succinctly by the phrase "every particle consists of all other particles."[5]

Just as there are no independently separate masses on the large scale, then, there are also no independent elementary particles on the small scale. At both levels, the whole is reflected in the parts, which in turn contribute to the whole. The whole, therefore, cannot simply be the sum of the parts—i.e., the totality—because there are no parts which are independent of the whole. For the same reason, we cannot perceive the whole by "standing back to get an overview." On the contrary, because the whole is in some way reflected in the parts, it is to be encountered by going further into the parts instead of by standing back from them.

··

THE HERMENEUTIC CIRCLE

A third instance of wholeness is externally somewhat different from the previous two. It is concerned with what happens when we read a written text. If reading is to be meaningful, it is not just a matter of repeating the words verbally as they come up in sequence on the page. Successful reading is not just a matter of saying the words. It is an act of interpretation, but not interpretation in the subjective sense. True interpretation is actively receptive, not assertive in the sense of dominating what is read. True interpretation does not force the text into the mold of the reader's personality, or into the requirements of his previous knowledge. It conveys the meaning of the text—"conveys" in the sense of "passes through" or "goes between." This is why readers sometimes can convey to others more of the meaning of a text than they may understand themselves.

Authentic interpretation, and hence successful reading, imparts real meaning, but the question becomes, what or where is this meaning? We often say, "I see," when we wish to indicate that we have grasped something. If we try to look at what we imagine is in our grasp, however, we find ourselves empty-handed. It does not take much experimentation here to realize that meaning cannot be grasped like an object.

The meaning of a text must have something to do with the whole text. What we come to here is the fundamental distinction between whole and totality. The meaning is the whole of the text, but this whole is not the same as the totality of the text. That there is a difference between the whole and the totality is clearly demonstrated by the evident fact that we do not need the totality of the text in order to understand its meaning. We do not have the totality of the text when we read it, but only one bit after another. But we do not have to store up what is read until it is all collected together, whereupon we suddenly see the meaning all at once in an instant. On the contrary, the meaning of the text is discerned and disclosed with progressive immanence throughout the reading of the text.

We can begin to see how remarkably similar the meaning structure of a text is to the optical form of the hologram. The totality of the text can be compared to the pattern of marks on the hologram plate. But the meaning of the text must be compared to the whole picture which can be reconstructed from the hologram plate. This is the sense in which the meaning of the text is the whole. The whole is not the totality, but the whole emerges most fully and completely through the totality. Thus, we can say that meaning is hologrammatical. The whole is present throughout all of the text, so that it is present in any part of the text. It is the presence of the whole in any part of the text which constitutes the meaning of that part of the text. Indeed, we can sometimes find that it is just the understanding of a single passage which suddenly illuminates for us the whole meaning of the text.

What we come to here is the idea of the hermeneutic circle, which was first recognized by Friedrich Ast in the eighteenth century and subsequently developed by Schleiermacher in his program for general hermeneutics as the art of understanding.[6] At the level of discourse, this circle says that to read an author we have to understand him first, and yet we have to read him first to understand him. It appears we have to understand the whole meaning of the text "in advance" to read the parts which are our pathway towards the meaning of the text as a whole. Clearly, this is a contradiction to logic and the form of reasoning which is based thereon. Yet it is the *experience* we go through to understand the meaning of the text, as it is also the experience we go through in writing a text. The same paradox for logic can be found at the level of the single sentence. The meaning of a sentence has the unity of a whole. We reach the meaning of the sentence through the meaning of the words, yet the meaning of the words in that sentence is determined by the meaning of the sentence as a whole.

The reciprocal relationship of part and whole which is revealed here shows us clearly that the act of understanding is not a logical act of reasoning, because such an act depends on the choice of either/or. The paradox arises from the tacit assumption of linearity—implicit in the logic of reason—which supposes that we must go either from part to whole or from whole to part. Logic is analytical, whereas meaning is evidently holistic, and hence understanding cannot be reduced to logic. We understand meaning in the moment of coalescence when the whole is reflected in the parts so that together they disclose the whole. It is because meaning is encountered in this "circle" of the reciprocal relationship of the whole and the parts that we call it the hermeneutic circle.

THE WHOLE AND THE PARTS

The hologram helps us to see that the essence of the whole is that it is whole. If we had begun our discussion of the whole with the statement that the whole is whole, it would have seemed to be vacuous or trivially pedantic. But the optical instance of the hologram enables us to see that, far from being a trivial tautology, this statement expresses the primacy of the whole. No matter how often we break the hologram plate, the picture is undivided. It remains whole even while becoming many.

This essential irreducibility of the whole is so strong that it seems inconceivable that there is any way in which the whole could have parts. This is very much opposite to the view we usually have of the relation between parts and whole, which is a view that effectively denies the primacy of the whole. We are accustomed to thinking of going from parts to whole in some sort of summative manner. We think of developing the whole, even of making the whole, on the practical basis of putting parts together and making them fit. In this conventional way of working, we see the whole as developing by "integration of parts." Such a way of seeing places the whole secondary to the parts, because it necessarily implies that the whole comes after the parts. It implies a linear sequence: first the parts, then the whole. The implication is that the whole always comes later than its parts.

Faced with the primacy of the whole, as seen in the hologram, we may want to reverse the direction of this way of thinking of the whole. This we would do if we thought of the parts as being determined by the whole, defined by it, and so subservient to the whole. But this approach is not the true primacy of the whole either. It puts the whole in the position of a false transcendental which would come earlier than the parts, and so would leave them no place. This approach effectively considers the whole as if it were a part, but a "superpart" which controls and dominates the other, lesser parts. It is not the true whole, and neither can the parts be true parts when they are dominated by this counterfeit whole. Instead, there is only the side-by-sideness of would-be parts and the counterfeit whole. This is a false dualism.

Inasmuch as the whole is whole, it is neither earlier nor later. To say that the whole is not later than the parts is not to say that we do not put parts together. Of course we do—consider the action of writing, for example. But the fact that we often put parts together does not mean that in so doing we put the whole together. Similarly, to say that the whole is not earlier than the parts is not to deny the primacy of the whole. But, at the same time, to assert the primacy of the whole is not to maintain that it is dominant, in the sense of having an external superiority over the parts.

We can see the limitation of these two extreme approaches to the whole if we look at the act of writing. We put marks for words together on a page by the movement of the pen to try to say something. What is said is not the resultant sum of the marks, nor of the words which they indicate. What is said is not produced automatically by the words adding together as they come. But equally, we do not have what is said fixed and finished in front of us before it is written. We do not simply copy what is already said. We all know the familiar experience of having the sense that we understand something and then finding that it has slipped away when we try to say it. We seem to understand already before saying, but in the moment of expression we are empty. What appears is not ready-made outside the expression. But neither is expression an invention from a vacuum.

The art of saying is in finding the "right parts." The success or failure of saying, and hence of writing, turns upon the ability to recognize what is a part and what is not. But a part is a part only inasmuch as it serves to let the whole come forth, which is to let meaning emerge. A part is only a part according to the emergence of the whole which it serves; otherwise it is mere noise. At the same time, the whole does not dominate, for the whole cannot emerge without the parts. The hazard of emergence is such that the whole depends on the parts to be able to come forth, and the parts depend on the coming forth of the whole to be significant instead of superficial. The recognition of a part is possible only through the "coming to presence" of the whole. This fact is particularly evident in authentic writing and reading, where something is either to come to expression or to come to be understood.

We cannot separate part and whole into disjointed positions, for they are not two as in common arithmetic. The arithmetic of the whole is not numerical.[7] We do not have part *and* whole, though the number category of ordinary language will always make it seem so.[8] If we do separate part and whole into two, we appear to have an alternative of moving in a single direction, either from part to whole or from whole to part. If we start from this position, we must at least insist on moving in both directions at once, so that we have neither the resultant whole as a sum nor the transcendental whole as a dominant authority, but the emergent whole which comes forth into its parts. The character of this emergence is the "unfolding of enfolding," so that the parts are the place of the whole where it bodies forth into presence.[9] The whole imparts itself; it is accomplished through the parts it fulfills.

We can perhaps do something more to bring out the relationship between whole and part by considering the hologram again. If we break the hologram plate into fractions, we do not break the whole. The whole is present in each fraction, but its presence diminishes as the fractioning proceeds. Starting from the other end, with many fractions, we could put the fractions together to build up the totality. As we did so, the whole would emerge; it would come forth more fully as we approached the totality. But we would not be building up the whole. The whole is already present, present in the fractions, coming fully into presence in the totality. The superficial ordering of the fractional parts may be a linear series—this next to that, and so on. But the ordering of the parts with respect to the emergent whole, the essential ordering, is nested and not linear. Thus the whole emerges simultaneously with the accumulation of the parts, not because it is the sum of the parts, but because it is immanent within them.

This process tells us something fundamental about the whole in a way which shows us the significance of the parts. If the whole becomes present within its parts, then a part is a place for the "presencing" of the whole.[10] If a part is to be a place in which the whole can be present, it cannot be "any old thing." Rather, a part is special and not accidental, since it must be such as to let the whole come into presence. This speciality of the part is particularly important because it shows us the way to the whole. It clearly indicates that the way to the whole is into and through the parts. The whole is nowhere to be encountered except in the midst of the parts. It is not to be encountered by stepping back to take an overview, for it is not over and above the parts, as if it were some superior, all-encompassing entity. The whole is to be encountered by stepping right into the parts. This is how we enter into the nesting of the whole, and thus move into the whole as we pass through the parts.

This dual movement, into the whole through the parts, is demonstrated clearly in the experience of speaking and reading, listening and writing. We can see that in each case there is a dual movement: we move through the parts to enter into the whole which becomes present within the parts. When we understand, both movements come together. When we do not understand, we merely pass along the parts. Consider, for example, the interpretation of a difficult text, say, Kant's *Critique of Pure Reason*. At first encounter, we just pass along the parts, reading the sentences without understanding. To come to understand the text, we have to enter into it, and we do this in the first place by experiencing the meaning of the sentences. We enter into the text as the medium of meaning through the sentences themselves, putting ourselves into the text in a way which makes us available to meaning. We do not stand back to get an overview of all the sentences, in the hope that this will give us the meaning of the text. We do not refer the text to some other, external text which will give us the meaning. There is no superior text which can be an authority in interpretation because there is no access to the meaning of Kant's book other than through the text itself. Even for Kant, there was no pure "meaning in itself," present as an object in his consciousness, which he then represented in language. The original text is already an interpretation, and every text written about Kant's book is itself an expression of the meaning which that book was written to make evident. The hermeneutic approach must recognize, as Heidegger said, that ". . . what is essential in all philosophical discourse is not found in the specific propositions of which it is composed but in that which, although unstated as such, is made evident through these propositions."[11] Authentic interpretation recognizes the way in which the whole, which is the meaning of the text, comes to presence in the parts, which are the sentences.

ENCOUNTERING THE WHOLE: THE ACTIVE ABSENCE

Everything we encounter in the world can be said to be either one thing or another, either this or that, either before or after, and so on. Wherever we look, there are different things to be distinguished from one another: this book here, that pen there, the table underneath, and so on. Each thing is outside the other, and all things are separate from one another. But in recognizing the things about us in this way we, too, are separate from and outside of each of the things we see. We find ourselves side by side, together with and separate from, the things we recognize. This is the familiar spectator awareness. In the moment of recognizing a thing, we stand outside of that thing; and in the moment of so standing outside of that thing, we turn into an "I" which knows that thing, for there cannot be an "outside" without the distinction of something being outside of some other thing. Thus, the "I" of "I know" arises in the knowing of something in the moment of recognition of the thing known. By virtue of its origin, the "I" which knows is outside of what it knows.

We cannot know the whole in the way in which we know things because we cannot recognize the whole as a thing. If the whole were available to be recognized in the same way as we recognize the things which surround us, then the whole would be counted among those things as one of them. We could point and say "Here is this," and "There is that," and "That's the whole over there." If we had the power of such recognition, we would know the whole in the same way that we know its parts, for the whole itself would simply be numbered among its parts. The whole would be outside its parts in the same way that each part is outside all the other parts. But the whole comes into presence within its parts, and we cannot encounter the whole in the same way that we encounter the parts. We should not think of the whole as if it were a thing.

Our everyday awareness is occupied with things. The whole is absent to this awareness because it is not a thing among things. To everyday awareness, the whole is no-thing, and since this awareness is awareness of *something*, no-thing is nothing. The whole which is no-thing is taken as mere nothing, in which case it vanishes. When this loss happens, we are left with a world of things, and the apparent task of putting them together to make a whole. Such an effort disregards the authentic whole.

The other choice is to take the whole to be no-thing but not nothing. This possibility is difficult for our everyday awareness, which cannot distinguish the two. Yet we have an illustration immediately on hand with the experience of reading. We do not take the meaning of a sentence to be a word. The meaning of a sentence is no-word. But evidently this is not the same as nothing, for if it were we could never read! The whole becomes present within parts, but from the standpoint of the awareness which grasps the external parts, the whole is an absence. This absence, however, is not the same as nothing. Rather, it is an *active* absence inasmuch as we do not try to be aware of the whole, as if we could grasp it like a part, but instead let ourselves be open to be moved by the whole.

A particularly graphic illustration of the development of a sensitivity to the whole as an active absence is to be found in the experience of writing, where we saw earlier that we do not have the meaning before us like an object. Another illustration of the active absence is provided by the enacting of a play. Actors do not stand away from a part as if it were an object. They enter into a part in such a way that they enter into the play. If the play is constructed well, the whole play comes into presence within the parts so that an actor encounters the play through his or her part. But actors do not encounter the play as an object of knowledge over which they can stand like the lines they learn. They encounter the play in their part as an active absence which can begin to move them. When this happens, an actor starts to be acted by the play, instead of trying to act the play. The origin of the acting becomes the play itself, instead of the actor's subjective "I." The actor no longer imposes himself or herself on the play as if it were an object to be mastered, but he or she listens to the play and allows himself or herself to be moved by it. In this way actors enter into their parts in such a way that the play speaks through them. This is how, their awareness being occupied with the lines to be spoken, they encounter the whole which is the play—not as an object but as an active absence.

Developmental psychology now offers considerable support for this notion that the whole is "nothing" to our ordinary awareness, as well as for the notion that we can develop a sensitivity to the whole as an "active absence." Psychologists have discovered that there are two major modes of organization for a human being: the action mode and the receptive mode.[12] In the early infant state, we are in the receptive mode, but this is gradually dominated by the development of the action mode of organization that is formed in us by our interaction with the physical environment. Through the manipulation of physical bodies, and especially solid bodies, we develop the ability to focus the attention and perceive boundaries—i.e., to discriminate, analyze, and divide the world up into objects. The internalization of this experience of manipulating physical bodies gives us the object-based logic which Henri Bergson called "the logic of solids."[13] This process has been described in detail by psychologists from Helmholtz down to Piaget. The result is an analytical mode of consciousness attuned to our experience with solid bodies. This kind of consciousness is institutionalized by the structure of our language, which favors the active mode of organization. As a result, we are well prepared to perceive selectively only some of the possible features of experience.

The alternative mode of organization, the receptive mode, is one which allows events to happen—for example, the play above. Instead of being verbal, analytical, sequential, and logical, this mode of consciousness is nonverbal, holistic, nonlinear, and intuitive. It emphasizes the sensory and perceptual instead of the rational categories of the action mode. It is based on taking in, rather than manipulating, the environment.

For reasons of biological survival, the analytic mode has become dominant in human experience. This mode of consciousness corresponds to the object world, and since we are not aware of our own mode of consciousness directly, we inevitably identify this world as the only reality. It is because of this mode of consciousness that the whole is "nothing" to our awareness, and also that when we encounter it, we do so as an "active absence." If we were re-educated in the receptive mode of consciousness, our encounter with wholeness would be considerably different, and we would see many new things about our world.

WHOLENESS IN SCIENCE

There are many hermeneutic illustrations of the active absence—speaking, reading, playing a game, and so on—which are similar to the actor playing a part in a play. These examples can each demonstrate the reversal which comes in turning from awareness of an object into the encounter with the whole. This turning around, from grasping to being receptive, from awareness of an object to letting an absence be active, is a reversal which is the practical consequence of choosing the path which assents to the whole as no-thing and not mere nothing.

It is because of this reversal that the authentic whole must be invisible to the scientific approach, as currently conceived. The paradigm for modern scientific method is Kant's "appointed judge who compels the witnesses to answer questions which he has himself formulated."[14] Science believes itself to be objective, but is in essence subjective because the witness is compelled to answer questions *which the scientist himself has formulated.* Scientists never notice the circularity in this because they believe they hear the voice of "nature" speaking, not realizing that it is the transposed echo of their own voice. Modern positivist science can only approach the whole as if it were a thing among things. Thus the scientist tries to grasp the whole as an object for interrogation. So it is that science today, by virtue of the method which is its hallmark, is left with a fragmented world of things which it must then try to put together.

The introduction of a quantitative, mathematical method in science led to the distinction between primary and secondary qualities.[15] The so-called primary qualities—like number, magnitude, position, and so on—can be expressed mathematically. But such secondary qualities as color, taste, and sound cannot be expressed mathematically in any direct way. This distinction has been made into the basis for a dualism in which only the primary qualities are considered to be real. Any secondary quality is supposed to be the result of the effect on the senses of the primary qualities, being no more than a subjective experience and not itself a part of "objective" nature.

The result of this dualistic approach is that the features of nature which we encounter most immediately in our experience are judged to be unreal—just illusions of the senses. In contrast, what is real is not evident to the senses and has to be attained through the use of intellectual reasoning. Thus, one group of qualities is imagined to be hidden behind the other group, hidden by the appearances, so that a secondary quality is understood when it is seen how it could have arisen from the primary qualities. The reality of nature is not identical to the appearances which our senses give, and a major aim of positivist science is to *replace the phenomenon* with a mathematical model which can incorporate only the primary qualities. This quantitative result is then supposed to be more real than the phenomenon observed by the senses, and the task of science becomes a kind of "metaphysical archaeology" which strives to reveal an underlying mathematical reality.

The way this approach works in practice can be illustrated by Newton's treatment of the colors produced by a prism. His method was to correlate all observations of secondary qualities with measurements of primary qualities, so as to eliminate the secondary qualities from the scientific description of the world.[16] Newton eliminated color by correlating it with the "degree of refrangibility" (what we would now call "angle of refraction") of the different colors when the sun's light passes through a prism. Thus refraction can be represented numerically, and the ultimate aim of substituting a series of numbers for the sensory experience of different colors is achieved (later the wavelength of light would replace refrangibility). Hence, something which can be measured replaced the phenomenon of color, and in this way color *as color* was eliminated from the scientific account of the world.

GOETHE'S WAY OF SCIENCE

Newton's approach to light and color illustrates the extraordinary degree to which modern science stands outside of the phenomenon, the ideal of understanding being reached when the scientist is as far removed as possible from the experience.[17] The physics of color could now be understood just as well by a person who is color-blind. There is little wonder that the successful development of physics has led to an ever-increasing alienation of the universe of physics from the world of our everyday experience.[18]

Goethe's approach to color was very different from Newton's analytic approach. Goethe attempted to develop a physics of color which was based on everyday experience. He worked to achieve an authentic wholeness by *dwelling in the phenomenon* instead of replacing it with a mathematical representation.

Goethe's objection to Newton's procedure was that he had taken a complicated phenomenon as his basis and tried to explain what was simple by means of something more complex.[19] To Goethe, Newton's procedure was upside down. Newton had arranged for the light from a tiny hole in a window shutter to pass through a glass prism onto the opposite wall. The spectrum of colors formed in this way was a well-known phenomenon at the time, but Newton's contribution was to explain it in a new way. He believed that the colors were already present in the light from the sun coming through the hole, and the effect of the prism was to separate them. It would be quite wrong to say, as is said so often in physics textbooks, that *the experiment showed* Newton this, or that he was *led to believe* this by the experiment. Rather, it was Newton's way of seeing which constituted the experiment's being seen in this way. He saw the idea (that white light is a mixture of colors which are sorted out by the prism) "reflected" in the experiment, as if it were a mirror to his thinking; he did not derive it from the experiment in the way that is often believed.

In contrast to Newton, Goethe set out to find the simplest possible color phenomenon and make this his basis for understanding color in more complex situations. He believed Newton erred in thinking colorless light was compounded of colored lights because colored light is darker than colorless light, and this would mean that several darker lights were added together to make a brighter light. Goethe looked first at the colors which are formed when the prism is used with light in the natural environment, instead of the restricted and artificial environment which he felt Newton had selected as the experimental basis for his approach. By doing this, Goethe recognized that the phenomenon of prismatic colors depended on a boundary between light and dark regions. Far from the colors somehow being already *contained* in light, for Goethe they *came into being* out of a relationship between light and darkness.

To Goethe, the prism was a complicating factor, and so to understand the arising of colors, he looked for the more simple cases, which meant looking for situations where there are no secondary factors, only light and darkness. Such a case is what Goethe first called *das reine Phänomen* (the "pure phenomenon"), and for which he later used the term *Urphänomen* ("primal or archetypal phenomenon").[20] He found the primal phenomenon of color in the color phenomena which are associated with semitransparent media. When light is seen through such a medium, it darkens first to yellow and then orange and red as the medium thickens. Alternatively, when darkness is seen through an illuminated medium, it lightens to violet and then blue. Such a phenomenon is particularly evident with atmospheric colors, such as the colors of the sun and the sky and the way that these change with atmospheric conditions. Thus, it was in the natural environment that Goethe first recognized the primal phenomenon of color to be the lightening of dark to give violet and blue, and the darkening of light to give yellow and red. He expressed this process poetically as "the deeds and sufferings of light."[21]

Once Goethe had found this primal phenomenon he was in a position to see how the colors change from one to another as conditions change. He could see how these shifts were at the root of more complex phenomena such as the prismatic colors. One result is that a dynamic wholeness is perceived in the prismatic colors—a wholeness totally lacking in Newton's account. In other words, Goethe's presentation describes the origin of colors whereas Newton's does not. The colors of the spectrum are simply not intelligible in Newton's account because there is no inherent reason why there should be red, or blue, or green, as there is no reason why they should appear in the order that they do in the spectrum. But with Goethe's account, one can understand both the quality of the colors and the relationship between them, so that we can perceive the wholeness of the phenomenon without going beyond what can be experienced.

Goethe's method was to extend and deepen his experience of the phenomenon until he reached that element of the phenomenon which is not given externally to sense experience. This is the connection or relationship in the phenomenon which he called the *law* (*Gesetz*), and which he found by going more deeply into the phenomenon instead of standing back from it or trying to go beyond it intellectually to something which could not be experienced.[22] In other words, Goethe believed that the organization or unity of the phenomenon is real and can be *experienced*, but that it is not evident to sensory experience. It is perceived by an intuitive experience—what Goethe called *Anschauung*, which "may be held to signify the *intuitive knowledge gained through contemplation of the visible aspect*."[23]

In following Goethe's approach to scientific knowledge, one finds that the wholeness of the phenomenon is intensive. The experience is one of entering into a dimension which is in the phenomenon, not behind or beyond it, but which is not visible at first. It is perceived through the mind, when the mind functions as an organ of perception instead of the medium of logical thought. Whereas mathematical science begins by transforming the contents of sensory perception into quantitative values and establishing a relationship between them, Goethe looked for a relationship between the perceptible elements which left the contents of perception unchanged. He tried to see these elements themselves holistically instead of replacing them by a mathematical relationship. As Cassirer said, "The mathematical formula strives to make the phenomena calculable, that of Goethe to make them visible."[24]

It seems clear from his way of working that Goethe could be described correctly as a *phenomenologist* of nature, since his approach to knowledge was to let the phenomenon become fully visible without imposing subjective mental constructs. He was especially scathing towards the kind of theory which attempted to explain the phenomenon by some kind of hidden mechanism. He saw this style of analysis as an attempt to introduce fanciful sensory-like elements behind the appearances, to which the human mind then had to be denied direct access. He thought Descartes' attempt to imagine such mechanical models behind the appearances was debasing to the mind, and no doubt he would have felt the same way about Einstein's picture of the impregnable watch as an analogy for the situation facing the scientific investigator.[25] Goethe did not examine the phenomenon intellectually, but rather tried to visualize the phenomenon in his mind in a sensory way—by the process which he called "exact sensorial imagination" (*exakte sinnliche Phantasie*).[26] Goethe's way of thinking is concrete, not abstract, and can be described as one of dwelling in the phenomenon.[27]

THE UR-PHENOMENON

The notion of the *Urphänomen* is an invaluable illustration of the concrete nature of Goethe's way of thinking which dwells in the phenomenon. The primal phenomenon is not to be thought of as a generalization from observations, produced by abstracting from different instances something that is common to them. If this were the case, one would arrive at an abstracted unity with the dead quality of a lowest common denominator. For Goethe, the primal phenomenon was a concrete instance—what he called "an instance worth a thousand, bearing all within itself."[28] In a moment of intuitive perception, the universal is seen within the particular, so that the particular instance is seen as a living manifestation of the universal. What is merely particular in one perspective is simultaneously universal in another way of seeing. In other words, the particular becomes symbolic of the universal.[29]

In terms of the category of wholeness, the primal phenomenon is an example of the whole which is present in the part. Goethe himself said as much when he called it "an instance worth a thousand," and described it as "bearing all within itself." It is the authentic whole which is reached by going into the parts, whereas a generalization is the counterfeit whole that is obtained by standing back from the parts to get an overview. Looking for the *Urphänomen* is an example of looking for the right part—i.e., the part which contains the whole. This way of seeing illustrates the simultaneous, reciprocal relationship between part and whole, whereby the whole cannot appear until the part is recognized, but the part cannot be recognized as such without the whole.

For example, Goethe was able to "read" how colors arise in the way that the colors of the sun and the sky change with the atmospheric conditions throughout the day. Because there were no secondary, complicating factors, this was for him an instance of the primal phenomenon of the arising of colors. This phenomenon was perceived as a part which contained the whole, and it was, in fact, through the observation of this particular phenomenon that Goethe first learned to see intuitively the law of the origin of color. Yet, the way that the colors of the sun and sky change *together* does not stand out as a phenomenon until it is seen as an instance of how colors arise. The search for the primal phenomenon is like creative writing, where the need is to find the right expression to let the meaning come forth. By analogy, we can say that Goethe's way of science is "hermeneutical." Once the primal phenomenon has been discovered in a single case, it can be recognized elsewhere in nature and in artificial situations where superficially it may appear to be very different. These varying instances can be compared to the fragments of a hologram.

Newton, in contrast, tried to divide light into parts: the colors of the spectrum from red through to blue. But these are not true parts because each does not contain the whole, and hence they do not serve to let the whole come forth. Colorless light, or white light, is imagined to be a summative totality of these colors. Newton tried to go analytically from whole to parts (white light separated into colors), and from parts to whole (colors combined to make white light). In contrast, Goethe encountered the wholeness of the phenomenon through the intuitive mode of consciousness, which is receptive to the phenomenon instead of dividing it according to external categories.[30]

CONCLUSION

The experience of authentic wholeness requires a new style of learning largely ignored in our schools and universities today.

Typically, modern education is grounded in the intellectual faculty, whose analytical capacity alone is developed, mostly through verbal reasoning. One notes, for example, that science students are often not interested in observing phenomena of nature; if asked to do so, they become easily bored. Their observations often bear little resemblance to the phenomenon itself.[31] These students are much happier with textbook descriptions and explanations, a fact readily understandable once one recognizes that most educational experience unfolds in terms of one mode of consciousness—the verbal, rational mode.

The experience of authentic wholeness is impossible in this mode of consciousness, and a complementary style of understanding could usefully be developed. This can be done, first by learning to work with mental images in a way emulating Goethe—i.e., forming images from sensory experiences. In turn, this process requires careful observation of the phenomenon. Authentic wholeness means that the whole is in the part; hence careful attention must be given to the parts instead of to general principles. In contrast, an intellectual approach to scientific education begins by seeing the phenomenon as an instance of general principles.

Working with mental images activates a different mode of consciousness which is holistic and intuitive. One area where this style of learning is now used practically is in transpersonal education.[32] Experiments with guided imagination indicate that a frequent result is the extension of feelings, whereby the student experiences a deeper, more direct contact with the phenomenon imagined.[33] In this way, a more comprehensive and complete encounter with the phenomenon results, and aspects of the phenomenon otherwise unnoticed often come to light. In addition, students feel themselves to be more in harmony with the phenomenon, as if they themselves were participating in it. This leads to an attitude toward nature more grounded in concern, respect, and responsibility.[34]

Goethe's way of science is not the only direction for a way of learning grounded in authentic wholeness. In more general terms, such a style of education and science is phenomenological, letting things become manifest as they show themselves without forcing our own categories on them. This kind of learning and science goes beyond the surface of the phenomenon, but not behind it to contrive some causal mechanism described by a model borrowed from somewhere else. A contemporary illustration of such an approach is the work of biologist Wolfgang Schad in his zoological study, *Man and Mammals*.[35] Schad shows how all mammals can be understood in terms of the way in which the whole is present in the parts. In addition, he demonstrates how each mammal can be understood in terms of its own overall organization.

Schad begins with the direct observation of the immediate phenomena, working to rediscover the uniqueness of individual animals. According to Schad's approach, every detail of an animal is a reflection of its basic organization. Thus, he does not begin by replacing the phenomenon with a stereotype, but rather searches for the animal's unique qualities. This approach does not lead to fragmentation and multiplicity. Instead, it leads to the perception of diversity within unity, whereby the unique quality of each mammal is seen holistically within the context of other mammals. With a wealth of drawings and photographs, Schad demonstrates how going into the part to encounter the whole leads to a holistic perspective. He shows that multiplicity in unity means seeing uniqueness without fragmentation.

The counterfeit approach to wholeness—i.e., going away from the part to get an overview—leads only to the abstraction of the general case, which has the quality of uniformity rather than uniqueness. Schad indicates how a biology grounded in authentic wholeness can recognize the inner organic order in an animal in such a way that its individual features can be explained by the basic organization of the animal itself. In short, the mammal "explains" itself. For example, the formation of the hedgehog's horny quills is explained in terms of the basic organization of the hedgehog itself. Other questions for which Schad provides answers include why cattle have horns and deer, antlers; why leopards are spotted and zebras, striped; why otters, beavers, seals, and hippopotami live in water; why giraffes' necks are long; why rhinoceroses are horned. Schad convincingly demonstrates that features such as these can be explained through careful observation of a particular mammal's organization in the context of all the other mammals.

Like Goethe's, Schad's way of science is phenomenological and hermeneutical. It is phenomenological because the animal is capable of disclosing itself in terms of itself. Phenomenology, said Heidegger, is the attempt "to let that which shows itself be seen from itself in the very way in which it shows itself from itself."[36] Phenomenology brings to light what is hidden at first. Schad discovers in the animal the qualities which make that animal what it is rather than some other creature. In addition, Schad's work is hermeneutical, since when the point is reached where the animal discloses itself, the animal becomes its own language. In this sense, Schad's way of seeing echoes the universal sense of Gadamer's hermeneutics, in which "being that can be understood is language."[37]

As Schad's work suggests, Goethe's way of science did not end with him. His style of learning and understanding belongs not to the past but to the future. It is widely acknowledged today that, through the growth of the science of matter, the Western mind has become removed from contact with nature. Contemporary problems, many arising from modern scientific method, confront people with the fact that they have become divorced from a realistic appreciation of their place in the larger world. At the same time, there is a growing demand for a renewal of contact with nature. It is not enough to dwell in nature sentimentally and aesthetically, grafting such awareness to a scientific infrastructure which largely denies nature. The need is for a new science of nature, different from the science of matter and based on other human faculties besides the analytic mind. A basis for this science is the discovery of authentic wholeness.[38]

PART II ..

Goethe's Scientific
Consciousness

..*1*

Introduction

Goethe does not fit easily into our categories. He was a person who was both poet and scientist, who is renowned for his poetical and dramatic work, and yet who considered that his science was the most important work he had done. We could easily accept a scientist who wrote poetry, perhaps even a poet who wrote about science, but it is difficult to accept a poet who was simultaneously an original scientist, i.e., who did science in an original way. We just cannot easily believe that what he did was really science at all.

When faced with this kind of contradiction in our cultural categories, we rationalize. One form which this takes is the accusation of dilettantism. Master among poets Goethe may have been, but as a scientist he was an amateur—and a bungling one at that in his work on color. We can compare this view with an impression of Goethe's home in Weimar as it was kept towards the end of the last century. Rudolf Magnus described how he found in it numerous specimens from Goethe's work in geology (more than eighteen thousand specimens), botany, and zoology, together with many instruments from experiments in electricity and optics. Magnus was particularly impressed with the wealth of equipment Goethe used in his optical studies, and he said: "I can testify from personal experience to the extraordinary fascination of repeating Goethe's experiments with his own instruments, of realizing the accuracy of his observations, the telling faithfulness with which he described everything he saw."[1] From this description we do not get the impression of a dilettante, nor of a person who thought of himself first and foremost as a poet. In fact,

Goethe spent twenty years of painstaking work on his research into the phenomena of color. He said himself: "Not through an extraordinary spiritual gift, not through momentary inspiration, unexpected and unique, but through consistent work did I eventually achieve such satisfactory results." Although Goethe said this specifically about his work on the metamorphosis of plants, it applied equally to all his scientific work.

Another form which the rationalization can take is the apology for the "Great Man." We can see this illustrated very clearly in the case of Isaac Newton, to whom Goethe was so opposed in his theory of color. It used to be an embarrassment that this person, who above all others set the seal on the future development of science in the West, in fact spent more of his time on occult researches and alchemy than he ever did on experimental and mathematical physics. When Newton's alchemical papers were auctioned at Sotheby's in 1936, John Maynard Keynes read through them and declared that Newton was not the first of the age of reason but the last of the magicians. The strategy was then either to ignore this "unfortunate" fact, or else to make apologies for Newton on the basis that great geniuses have their weaknesses, and we must not pay too much attention to them. But during the past two decades there has been a significant change in attitude among historians of science. It is now recognized that we cannot just ignore or dismiss approaches which do not fit in with what has become fashionable, if we want to understand how science developed historically. What later generations find an embarrassment, or otherwise objectionable, may in fact be something which needs to be taken seriously. In the case of Goethe, this means taking seriously a radically different way of doing science.

It is a superficial habit of mind to invent the past which fits the present. At the level of the individual, this takes the form of rewriting his or her own biography. This phenomenon is well known to psychologists, who recognize it as a variation of the self-fulfilling prophecy. The same mental habit can be seen operating at a more general historical level, where it takes on the form of an assumption that the purpose of the past is to prepare the way for the present. But the past, in this case, becomes no more than an extrapolation from the present. In other words, it is our invention. The result of doing this is that history can be told as a simple tale, because it seems as if there is a single, continuous line leading from the past to the present. The characters in this single-line story fall into two simple categories: forward-looking or backward-looking, depending on whether they seem to fit on the line of extrapolation or not.[2]

Now that this kind of superficial story has been exploded by studies in the history of science, it is clear that there never was a single line of development leading to the kind of science we have today. Furthermore, it has also become clear, from these same studies, that the reasons for the success, or otherwise, of a particular science are not internal to that science. It has been widely believed that science advances by the use of its own internal method for attaining the truth, so that scientific knowledge is legitimated by its own authority. However, it turns out that there is no such method, and science is best understood as a culturally based activity, i.e., as the product of a social process. Hence, the reasons for the acceptance of a scientific theory often have more to do with complex cultural factors than with the intrinsic merits of the theory in question. This has been borne out, for example, in studies of the seventeenth-century scientific revolution, where it has been shown that the success of the mechanical philosophy was due as much to external political and religious reasons as to its having been shown to be true by any internal scientific method. There are deeply rooted philosophical fashions in science, without which there would not be any science, but which stand outside the orbit of what can be verified scientifically. It is useful to remember this when looking at Goethe's way of science. For example, Goethe's physics of color contradicted Newton's, and if it is believed that Newton's physics of color has been shown to be true by "scientific method," then it *must* appear that Goethe's physics was wrong.

It now becomes clearer why Goethe's scientific work has often been received with disbelief. This does not necessarily have anything to do with the intrinsic scientific merit of his work. It has more to do with the state of mind (and what formed it) of those who reject his work as "unscientific" or "wrong." However, it is noticeable that both the rejection and the rationalization of Goethe's scientific work often come from students of the humanities, and not so much from scientists. It is often those who are primarily interested in Goethe as a poet who have the greatest difficulty integrating his scientific work into their perspective. Among scientists we often find respect for Goethe's scientific endeavors, even when there is disagreement. It is acknowledged, for example, that he was a pioneer in the study of plant and animal form—for which he coined the term "morphology." There is also some speculation that he anticipated the theory of evolution. This is a notoriously tricky point, and there have been many arguments for and against it. The difficulty is resolved when it is realized that today evolution is identified with Darwin's mechanism of random variation and natural selection. This means that there can be other ideas of evolution which are not recognized as such. For Goethe, as for his contemporaries in the philosophy of nature, there certainly was the idea of evolution. Frau von Stein wrote in a letter in 1784 that "Herder's new writing makes it seem likely that we were plants and animals. Goethe ponders now with abundant ideas over these things, and what has first passed through his mind becomes increasingly interesting."[3] The idea of evolution was certainly in Goethe's mind, but it was not *Darwinian* evolution.

Goethe's major study in physics was concerned with color. His magnum opus, *Theory of Colors*, was rejected by the establishment because of the attack on Newton which it contained. Newton had been raised on a pedestal by those who came after him, so that Goethe's physics of color rebounded on its originator because it did not look like physics. In fact, on account of this work, Goethe is now looked upon by experimental psychologists of color as one of the founders of their science. What interests the physicist today about Goethe's work on color is not so much the details, but the *kind* of scientific theory which he developed. This was very different from the kind of theory which aimed to go behind the phenomenon as it appeared to the senses, in order to explain it in terms of some hidden mechanism supposed to be more real. Goethe's approach was to avoid reducing the phenomenon to the mere effect of a mechanism hidden behind the scenes. Instead, he tried to find the unity and wholeness in the phenomena of color by perceiving the relationships in these phenomena as they are observed. The result was a theory which could be described as a phenomenology of color, rather than an explanatory model. This will be discussed in more detail below. In thus renouncing models and rooting the theory in the concrete phenomenon, Goethe now sounds very much in line with the debates about the nature of physical theory which have arisen through the development of quantum physics. His work was in fact discussed in this context at a conference on the quantum theory held in Cambridge in 1968.[4] This comparison may well be superficial, but it does mean that Goethe's scientific method, and the philosophy of science which it reflects, are taken seriously by modern physicists, who are faced with an epistemological crisis in their science.

But the value of Goethe's science is not revealed by assimilating him into the mainstream. Unfortunately, historians of science are often only interested in whether Goethe's work is a contribution to biology, or experimental psychology, or the method of physics. This approach to Goethe misses what is important, and interesting, in his scientific work. The factor which is missing from this academic approach is simply Goethe's whole way of seeing. In a letter from Italy in 1787, Goethe wrote: "After what I have seen of plants and fishes in the region of Naples, in Sicily, I should be sorely tempted, if I were ten years younger, to make a journey to India—not for the purpose of discovering something new, but in order to view in my way what has been discovered."[5] Goethe was indicating here that the discovery of new facts was of secondary importance to him. What mattered was the *way* of seeing, which influenced all the facts. His scientific work was fundamentally an expression of this way of seeing, with the result that it is present throughout all of it, immediately yet intangibly. What we recognize as the content of Goethe's scientific work should really be looked upon as only the container. The real content is the way of seeing. So what we have to aim for, if we are to understand Goethe's scientific consciousness, is inside-out to what we expect, because it is to be found in the way of seeing and not in the factual content of what is seen.

The problem for us is that we think of a way of seeing as something entirely subjective. As victims of the Cartesian confinement of consciousness to the purely subjective, we cannot believe at first that what Goethe experienced as a way of seeing could be an objective feature of the world. The difficulty here comes from the fact that a way of seeing is not itself something which is seen. What is experienced in the way of seeing cannot be grasped like an object, to appear as a content of perception. What is encountered in the way of seeing is the *organization* or *unity* of the world. Just as the organization of a drawing is not part of the sense-perceptible content of the drawing (whereabouts on the page is the organization?), so the organization of the world of nature is not part of the sensory content of that world.[6] But what "organization" and "unity" mean turns out to depend on the *mode* of consciousness—which will be discussed in the second chapter here.

To understand Goethe's way of seeing we would have to experience it for ourselves. We could only really understand it by participation, which means we would each experience Goethe's way of seeing as the way in which our own mind became organized temporarily. This brings us to another problem. If we believe that a way of seeing is only a subjective factor, then we must believe Goethe's way of seeing died with him. If this is so, then any attempt to understand it would entail the absurd requirement of trying to become Goethe! But this problem disappears when it is recognized that what is experienced as a way of seeing *is* the unity of the phenomenon. It follows immediately that any number of individuals can experience the same way of seeing without the restriction of time. A way of seeing has the temporal quality of belonging to "the present" instead of to the past. It is more like an event of perception in which we can learn to participate, instead of repeating something which once happened and has now gone. Goethe himself had to learn to see in the way which we now call "Goethe's way of seeing." We will now explore this way of seeing, as it is present first in his work on color and then in his work on organic nature.

·· 2

Making the Phenomenon Visible

oethe became interested in color during his Italian journey (1786–88). When he returned home he reminded himself of Newton's theory about color, as this was presented in the books available to him, and decided to do the famous experiment with the prism himself. However, having borrowed a prism, his interest and time were then taken up with other things. He did nothing about it until the time came when he was obliged to give the prism back. It was then too late to repeat Newton's experiments, as he had intended, and so he just took a rapid glance through the prism before handing it back. What he saw astonished him, and the energy of his astonishment was so great that it launched him into a research program on color which was to take nearly twenty years. This is what Goethe said about that experience:

> But how astonished was I when the white wall seen through the prism remained white after as before. Only where something dark came against it a more or less decided color was shown, and at last the window-bars appeared most vividly colored, while on the light-grey sky outside no trace of coloring was to be seen. It did not need any long consideration for me to recognize that a *boundary or edge is necessary to call forth the colors*, and I immediately said aloud, as though by instinct, that the Newtonian doctrine is false.[7]

What was the Newtonian doctrine, and why did Goethe believe that what he saw—or rather failed to see—indicated so strongly that it was wrong? To answer this question it will be necessary to begin with a brief account of Newton's experiments with a prism.

Newton's work on color also began with a surprise. He made a small circular hole in the window shutter of a darkened room, and passed the beam of sunlight which it formed through a glass prism onto the wall. He observed the colors which formed there, but then he noticed that the image of the aperture on the wall was oblong and not circular, as he would have expected it to have been. Other experiments were then made to explore this peculiarity. In one of these experiments he used a second small aperture in a screen, placed after the prism, to select light of one color only, which he then passed through a second prism. He found that no further colors were formed by the second prism. But he also found that the angle through which the light was deviated by the second prism depended on the color—violet being deviated the most and red the least. He called this the *Experimentum Crucis*, and on the basis of what he saw in it he made an inductive leap to propose the cause of the unexpected shape of the image which he had noticed at first.[8]

Newton's theory was that sunlight is not homogeneous, as had been supposed, but "consists of rays differently refrangible." These rays are all refracted through different angles when the sunlight is incident on the prism, and the colors which are experienced correspond with these different angles of refraction. Thus, the rays which are least refracted produce the sensation of red, whereas the sensation of violet is produced by the rays which are refracted most. It is, therefore, the separation of these rays by the prism which produces the oblong colored image of the circular aperture. Thus was born the well-known theory that colorless light is a mixture of all the colors of the spectrum, which are separated out by a prism. As such it is known to every schoolboy and repeated by every textbook writer. Yet this is not what Newton thought. In his major work on light he said:

And if at any time I speak of light and rays as colored or endowed with colors, I would be understood to speak not philosophically and properly, but grossly, and according to such conceptions as vulgar people in seeing all these experiments would be apt to frame. For the rays to speak properly are not colored. In them there is nothing else than a certain power and disposition to stir up a sensation of this or that color.[9]

The trouble is that Newton did often speak of sunlight as being composed of rays of differing colors. Goethe pointed out that this could not be so because every colored light is darker than colorless light, and if colorless light were compounded of colored lights then brightness would be compounded of darkness, which is impossible. But Newton's view that color is a sensation in the observer, and not a physical phenomenon, was quickly forgotten by his followers. One result of selecting only a part of Newton's theory is that what is said about it today is often simply nonsense.[10]

Time and again the myth is repeated that Newton showed by experiment how colorless light contains a mixture of colors, which are separated by a prism. It is presented as if this were available to the senses and could be observed directly. Yet there is no experiment in which this separation of the colors can be seen directly with the senses. Newton attempted to prove that this is what is happening by reasoning based on experiments. Originally it was an insight for him, and as such it cannot be reached directly by experiment or by logical reasoning based thereon. Subsequently he tried to present it as a consequence of following a definite method. This was the mathematical method, based on geometry, but with experiments replacing verbal propositions. Newton's presentation must be followed with care, and in the spirit in which it was intended; otherwise the unwary reader can easily fall into the trap of believing that Newton had seen with his eyes what cannot in fact be seen directly at all.

What Newton did do, by his combination of experiments and theory, was to replace the phenomenon of color with a set of numbers. In so doing, he fulfilled the aim of the program for the scientific investigation of nature developed by Galileo and others. The introduction of the quantitative, mathematical method into science led inevitably to the distinction between primary and secondary qualities. Primary qualities are those which can be expressed mathematically in a direct way—such as number, magnitude, position, and extension. By contrast, qualities which cannot be expressed mathematically in a direct way—such as color, taste and sound—are said to be secondary. This distinction was subsequently made into a dualism in which only the primary qualities were considered to be real. A secondary quality was supposed to be the result of the effect on the senses of a primary quality, being no more than a subjective experience and not part of nature. The result of this step was that some of the features of nature which are encountered most immediately in experience were judged to be unreal, just illusions of the senses. One group of qualities, the primary ones, was imagined to be behind the other group, hidden by the appearances, so that a secondary quality was understood when it was explained how it could have arisen from primary qualities alone. In other words, the secondary qualities are really primary qualities which manifest themselves in perception in a manner which is different from what they really are, so that the task of science is to reduce all the phenomena of nature ultimately to such primary qualities as shape, motion, and number.

Newton attempted to fulfill this program in two ways in his work on color. Firstly, by showing that different colors are refracted through different angles, he was able to replace the colors by a numerical measurement. Thus he could eliminate color from the scientific description of the world by correlating it with the "degree of refrangibility" (which we now call "angle of refraction"). A series of numbers could then be substituted for the sensory experience of different colors. Secondly, Newton tried to imagine a mechanical model for light, whereby the dispersion of colors by the prism was explained in terms of light corpuscles, or globules, which all moved with the same velocity in a vacuum but different velocities in glass. Thus, according to this model, Newton considered the speed of the imagined light particles to be the objective basis of our experience of color—although he also seems to have considered the size to be an important factor on another occasion, with the corpuscles which caused the sensation of red being bigger than those which caused blue. Whatever the particulars of the model, the important point is that the secondary quality of color is replaced completely by primary qualities which can be represented quantitatively. This strategy of trying to explain a phenomenon by means of a microscopic model—which is based on images borrowed from the sense-perceptible world—became standard practice in mainstream physics. Newton's own attempt to provide a mechanical model for light was not successful. The model which eventually gained acceptance was the wave model. According to this, light is a wave motion, with different colors corresponding to waves of different frequencies. Once again the phenomenon is reduced to a mathematical magnitude. The model is different, but the result is the same: color is written out of nature.

THE PRIMAL PHENOMENON OF COLOR

When Goethe saw that the prismatic colors appeared only where there was a boundary, he recognized that the theory of the colors being contained already in the light must be wrong. There must be light *and* dark for the color phenomenon to arise, not just light alone. He investigated this carefully by constructing simple boundaries from which all secondary, complicating factors were removed. Anyone who has a prism can repeat Goethe's observations. Just make a card with a straight boundary between black and white regions, and look at the boundary through the prism with the card in either of the orientations shown in the figure on the opposite page. Holding the prism so that it is oriented like the roof of a house turned upside down, with the edges parallel to the boundary, look through the slanted side facing you toward the card. You

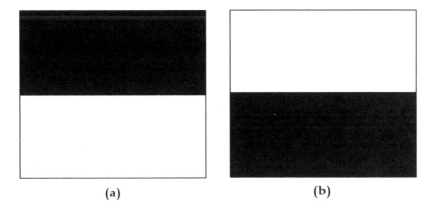

(a)   (b)

will see it displaced downward. In both cases vivid colors are seen parallel to the boundary. In orientation (a) the colors appear in the white region just below the black, with red nearest to the boundary, then orange, and yellow furthest away from the boundary. In (b) the colors also appear at first to be in the white region, but careful observation (e.g., by placing the tip of a pencil on the boundary for reference) reveals that they are in fact being seen in the black region just below the white. Again, the colors are parallel to the boundary, but with this orientation of the card the colors are blues, with light blue nearest to the boundary and violet furthest into the black. To begin with, it is best to concentrate on the central boundary and ignore the colors at the top and bottom edges of the card.

When observing the phenomenon of color in Goethe's way it is necessary to be more active in seeing than we are usually. The term "observation" is in some ways too passive. We tend to think of an observation as just a matter of opening our eyes in front of the phenomenon, as if it were something that happens to us when visual information flows in through the senses and is registered in consciousness. Observing the phenomenon in Goethe's way requires us to *look*, as if the direction of seeing were reversed, going from ourselves towards the phenomenon instead of vice versa. This is done by putting *attention* into seeing, so that we really do *see* what we are seeing instead of just having a visual impression. It is as if we plunged into seeing. In this way we can begin to *experience* the *quality* of the colors.

But Goethe's encounter with the phenomenon did not stop at this stage of observation. He would then repeat the observations he had made, but this time doing so entirely in his imagination without using the apparatus. He called this discipline *exakte sinnliche Phantasie*, which can be translated "exact sensorial imagination." In this case it would mean trying to visualize making the observations with the prism, and seeing the qualities of the different colors in the right order at a boundary as if we were producing them. This would then be transformed in imagination into an image of the colors with the boundary in the opposite orientation, and then transformed back again. The process can be repeated several times. The aim is to think the phenomenon concretely in imagination, and not to think about it, trying not to leave anything out or to add anything which cannot be observed. Goethe referred to this discipline as "recreating in the wake of ever-creating nature." Combined with active seeing, it has the effect of giving thinking more the quality of perception and sensory observation more the quality of thinking. The purpose is to develop an organ of perception which can deepen our contact with the phenomenon in a way that is impossible by simply having thoughts about it and working over it with the intellectual mind. For example, through working in this way, a relationship between the qualities of the colors may be perceived. Black, violet, and blue begin to be perceived as belonging together, as if there were a unity in these colors which is not perceived at first. The same can be found with white, yellow, orange, and red. Sometimes this relationship between the colors is perceived as having a dynamical quality, even though there is no movement in a physical sense. Thus, what is perceived by the senses as simply different colors which are separate begins to be perceived more holistically. The colors are perceived belonging together in a unity which is present in the phenomenon but not visible like the colors themselves. If there is unity in the color phenomenon at a boundary, then it is not like something which we may have simply overlooked at first. It is not like a color which we may have missed—as if we could say, "There is red, and there is yellow, and there is the unity over there." It is in fact not visible to the senses (though it may seem to be so), and yet it can be perceived—this point will be taken up in some detail later in this chapter.

Although the unity in the color phenomenon may begin to be intimated by working with the prism in the way described above, it is difficult for it to emerge clearly in these circumstances. This is because the appearance of the colors in this case depends on the peculiar shape of the piece of glass. Goethe believed that this was a complicating factor, and because of this the phenomenon of prismatic colors was not a suitable basis from which to understand the origin of colors. He also believed that there must always be some instance in nature where a phenomenon occurs in the simplest way possible, without any secondary factors to disguise what is essential. He had already recognized from his first observation with the prism that light and dark were necessary "to call forth the colors." So if he could find an instance in nature of the "coming into being" of colors out of light and dark alone, then he would have read the origin of colors directly in nature itself. He called such an instance an *Urphänomen*, which can be translated "primal phenomenon," and he described it as "an instance worth a thousand, bearing all within itself." He saw the proper task of physics as being to find the primal phenomenon for any particular field of study, and to resist the temptation to try to go beyond it by imagining a hidden mechanism as Newton and others did.

Goethe discovered the primal phenomenon of color in the colors of the sun and the sky. On a clear day the color of the sky overhead is a brilliant blue, which becomes lighter in shade as the angle of vision decreases towards the horizon. But if we were to go up a mountain, the color overhead would progressively darken until it became violet. If we could go higher still, it would darken further until it became black. When we look at the sky overhead, we are seeing darkness through the atmosphere which is illuminated by the sun. The quality of the blue we see depends on the thickness of the atmosphere through which we are seeing the darkness of outer space. The greater the thickness of the atmosphere, the lighter the shade of blue. Goethe recognized that the role of the atmosphere here is to be a light-filled medium because it is illuminated by the sun. So when we look at the sky we are looking at dark through light, and the effect of this is to lighten the dark progressively into lighter shades of blue as the proportion of the light-filled medium increases. Thus the origin of blue is the lightening of dark which occurs when dark is seen through light. In this way Goethe learned to see the "coming into being" of the various shades of blue in the phenomenon itself.

The origin of red and yellow can be discovered in the changing color of the sun. When it is overhead on a clear day the sun is yellow, and it darkens in color towards red as it moves closer to the horizon at sunset. In this case we are looking at light through the atmosphere, and the role of this medium is now to darken what is seen in proportion as its thickness increases. If we were to go higher up, the sun would become whiter as the atmospheric thickness decreased. Thus the origin of yellow, orange, and red is the darkening of light which occurs when light is seen through dark. Here also Goethe learned to see the "coming into being" of the colors in the phenomenon itself, so that from this "instance worth a thousand, bearing all within itself" he could understand how they arise out of light and dark exclusively.

Now we can read the colors of the sun and the sky in the prismatic colors. It is well worthwhile doing this by exact sensorial imagination, instead of just following it in the verbal–intellectual manner. Beginning with the color of the sky, we can visualize the change in quality of the color from black through to pale blue as the thickness of the atmosphere increases. Then we can visualize the colors formed with the prism when the boundary is in orientation (b). We can see the same order in the qualities of the prismatic colors as in the colors of the sky. The sequence from black to violet to pale blue now corresponds to an increasing thickness of cross-section of the prism which we are looking through. Since we have noticed before that these colors are seen in the black region, we can now recognize that what we are seeing here is different degrees of the lightening of dark. Repeating this exercise in imagination with the color of the sun, and the prism with the boundary in orientation (a), we can again recognize the same order in the qualities of the colors in the two phenomena. This time we are seeing the darkening of light. The colors deepen from yellow to orange and red as the thickness of the atmosphere, or the cross-section of the prism, increases. The prism plays the same dual role of the medium as the atmosphere does, depending on whether it is light which is seen through dark, or vice versa. We may not know in detail yet how it comes about that we are seeing dark through light or light through dark with the prism, and we cannot go further into this here, but what we have done is sufficient to illustrate Goethe's way of learning from the phenomenon itself in such a way that it becomes its own explanation.[11]

Although the practice of thinking the phenomenon concretely by exact sensorial imagination is irksome to the intellectual mind, which is always impatient to rush ahead, its value for developing perception of the phenomenon cannot be overestimated. It has been mentioned already how this discipline can be instrumental in perceiving a phenomenon holistically. The practice of it, as in the case just described, shows how this comes about from the demand which it makes on us to visualize the phenomenon comprehensively. It also shows how the demand to produce the phenomenon for ourselves helps thinking to enter into the coming into being of the phenomenon, instead of analyzing what has already become. What Goethe discovered in this way was a dynamical polarity in the color phenomenon. As well as the unity within the quality of the colors in each orientation of the boundary, which is a real relationship between the colors, there is also a unity between the two different color phenomena. This is the unity of a polarity, like positive and negative electric charge. Because one and the same boundary can be in two different orientations with respect to the prism, these two color phenomena are really inseparable. We may think of them separately, and in any particular case we must choose one and not the other because we cannot have both simultaneously at the same boundary. But they are not essentially separate from each other because each one determines the possibility of the other, i.e., if one is possible then the other must be too. So this polarity is essentially holistic and not analytical. We can begin to experience it as such in the colors of the sun and the sky, as well as with the prism, by working intentionally with exact sensorial imagination instead of with the verbal–intellectual mind.

Goethe described this polarity as "the deeds and sufferings of light," a poetic expression which is as precise in the science of quality as any mathematical expression in the science of quantity. But "the deeds and sufferings of light" is already a second-degree polarity. The primary polarity is the unity of light and dark. When we think of "light and dark" with the verbal–intellectual mind, we interpret it analytically—we have a mental impression of "light" and "dark," each on their own, joined together externally by "and." But this misses the fact that we cannot have the one without the other—it is as if the possibility of each one is determined by the other. There is a wholeness in the boundary itself which we usually do not notice. It is true of all opposites that they mutually determine each other, and hence that there is a unity in their opposition. Aristotle said that the knowledge of opposites is one. The trouble is that it is not one for the verbal–intellectual mind because of its analytical character. The wholeness of polarity can only be perceived when the mind works in a more holistic mode; otherwise it is only an abstraction. The practice of exact sensorial imagination is a door to this mode. This will be discussed further below.

It is possible to have both "poles" of the color phenomenon present simultaneously by making a card with a broad white band on a black background:

If we now imagine the white space shrinking in the vertical direction so that the two horizontal boundaries come closer together, a point will be reached where the two polar phenomena meet and overlap. We can find out what happens when they do by making a card with a narrow white band on a black background:

Where they meet we see green, for the first time, and there is now something like the "spectrum of light" which Newton described—the pattern of light and dark on this card being the same as for a narrow slit in a screen illuminated from behind.[12] But this has been reached in a very different way from Newton's. By following the coming into being of green in this way, Goethe was able to recognize that the idea of a spectrum of light was an error of judgment, arising from the fact that "a complicated phenomenon should have been taken as a basis, and the simpler explained from the complex." This error of judgment is a consequence of trying to understand the origin of the phenomenon in terms of the finished product. The Sufi poet and philosopher Jalaluddin Rumi described this approach in general as trying to "reach the milk by way of the cheese."[13] Following this analogy, the naive interpretation of Newton's theory of the prismatic colors, described above, amounts to the assertion that cheese comes from milk because cheese is already there in milk. The more sophisticated version, which Newton himself advocated, is the equivalent of saying that a disposition towards cheese exists in the milk, but it only becomes the cheese I experience when it enters a human digestive system. Goethe's approach, on the other hand, is the equivalent of trying to understand cheese by following through the process by which it is produced.

When the prismatic colors are understood in Goethe's holistic way, the quality of each color becomes something which is intelligible in itself and not just an accident. In Newton's account of the origin of the colors there is no reason why the color "red" has the quality of red, or why "blue" has the quality of blue, or why the colors are in the order observed and not in some other order. The intelligibility of the colors in themselves disappears in the analytical approach, and what is left seems to be merely contingent. It is no answer to be told that the order the colors appear in is the numerical order of their wavelengths, and that red has the quality of red because its wavelength is seven-tenths of a millionth of a meter, whereas violet has the quality of violet because its wavelength is four-tenths of a millionth of a meter. There is simply no way in which these qualities can be derived from such quantities. But it is very different when the colors are seen comprehensively in Goethe's way. The order of the colors is now necessary instead of contingent, and hence the quality of each particular color becomes intelligible in itself instead of appearing accidental.

A particularly vivid illustration of the difference between these two approaches to color is given by making a white card with a narrow dark strip. When this is looked at through the prism, the order of the colors is seen to be inverted compared

with the previous case. Now violet and red overlap, instead of yellow and light blue, and where they meet a ruby-magenta color appears instead of green. So the order of the colors from the top border downwards is blue, violet, ruby-magenta, red, orange, yellow. This is not mentioned by Newton. But that is not surprising, since it would have to be called the "spectrum of dark," and this would be impossible if the colors were derived from light alone in the way that Newton believed. Yet this is often the first color phenomenon a person sees with a prism, because it is the one which is formed by the bar across the middle of a window. When people see this who remember what they learned about the spectrum at school, they are naturally puzzled by what they see. In some cases, in order to reduce the cognitive dissonance of this situation, they assume that what they are seeing must be wrong! Goethe recognized that "the senses do not deceive, but the judgment deceives." In this case it is the judgment of the Newtonian theory which deceives, and it is only when this particular phenomenon is understood in terms of the primal phenomenon of color that it becomes intelligible.

GOETHE'S SCIENTIFIC CONSCIOUSNESS

It would be easy to present Goethe's work on color as if it had been done in a purely empirical manner, i.e., as if he had reached his knowledge of the origin of colors through his senses alone. It has been mentioned already that this is not true, even though it may seem to be so at first. The world which we know is not in fact visible to the senses in the way that it seems to be. We do see the world, of course. But, as the well-known philosopher of science Norwood Russell Hanson put it, "There is more to seeing than meets the eye."[14] If we want to understand what scientific knowledge is, we have to learn to recognize the extra, nonsensory factor which transforms sensory experience into cognitive perception. This means learning to recognize the fundamental incoherence of empiricism as a philosophy of science. This has to be done first, before we can understand the nature of Goethe's scientific consciousness.

Knowing the World

According to the philosophy of empiricism, and to common sense, we know the world through experience. Nobody would doubt that we do. But empiricism, and common sense, both interpret experience to mean sensory experience. So what this philosophy asserts is that knowledge of the world comes through the senses—we open our eyes and other organs of sensory perception, and what is transmitted through these channels into consciousness is knowledge of the world. Now, although we could not see the world without the senses, we also could not see it with the senses alone. Knowledge of the

world is based on sensory experience, but knowledge is not the same as sensory experience. There is always a nonsensory factor in cognitive perception, whether it is everyday or scientific cognition. Knowing even the simplest fact goes beyond the purely sensory.

The fact that there is literally more to seeing than meets the eye can be appreciated by looking at the figure on the facing page.[15] Many people at first see only a random patchwork of black and white areas; but on looking further, some people will suddenly see a recognizable figure emerge from the chaos. They suddenly see the head and upper neck of a giraffe. The effect is just as if the giraffe had been switched on, like a light. Most people who do not see it at first for themselves will do so sooner or later after being told that it is a giraffe. But what happens in this instant of transition? There is evidently no change in the purely sensory experience, i.e., in the sensory stimulus to the organism. The pattern registered on the retina of the eye is the same whether the giraffe is seen or not. There is no change in this pattern at the instant when the giraffe is seen—the actual marks on the page are exactly the same after the event of recognition as they were before. So the difference cannot be explained as a difference in sensory experience.

This conclusion is reinforced by experience with the well-known ambiguous figures used by the gestalt psychologists, such as the reversing cube or the duck/rabbit:

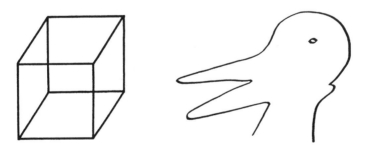

In these cases two different objects can be seen alternately, and yet the sensory experience is the same in both cases. Hanson suggests that what changes in such cases is the organization.[16] He points out that the organization is not itself seen in the same way as the lines or shapes, because it is not itself a line or shape. It is not an element in the visual field, but "rather the way in which elements are appreciated." Without this organization "we would be left with nothing but an unintelligible configuration of lines," as indeed we are left with nothing but an unintelligible configuration of shapes, a random patchwork of black and white areas, until this becomes organized in the act of seeing a giraffe. But just as the plot is not another detail in the story and the tune is not just another note, so the giraffe is not another element in the visual field. Although, when it is seen, the shapes now have a particular organization, the change cannot be shown by making an exact copy of the figure.[17] Two people, one of whom could see the giraffe and the other not, would both produce the very same copies of the figure. The difference between them lies in the nonsensory factor in perception, which is the part of seeing that is "more than meets the eye."

It is now possible to go further than this, and to understand more completely just what it is that we see in cognitive perception. The nonsensory perception of organization which has been discussed above is in fact the perception of meaning. The experience of suddenly seeing the giraffe, for example, is the experience of seeing meaning where previously there had been only a meaningless patchwork of black and white shapes. The nonsensory wholeness or unity, which we see in the instant this patchwork becomes organized, *is* the meaning "giraffe." This is not the meaning *of* what is seen, but the meaning which *is* what is seen. The marks on the page do not "have" any meaning at all, i.e., the meaning is not on the page as it would have to be if it were a sensory element. So what we are seeing is not in fact on the page, even though it appears to be there. Similarly, the alternation with the duck/rabbit, or the reversing cube, is a switch in the meaning that is seen. In fact, even to see these figures just as "a set of lines," or "a patchwork of black and white shapes," is already to see meaning. There cannot be a cognitive perception of meaningless data, because in the act of seeing the world it *is* meaning that we see.[18]

There is no fundamental difference between seeing objects and seeing facts. Seeing that a book is on the table is simply a more complex instance of seeing meaning than seeing a book, or a table, on its own would be. Spatial and temporal relationships, especially those entailing causality, which are so readily believed to be perceived through the senses, are always in fact instances of the nonsensory perception of meaning. For example, suppose that someone hears a whirring noise and, at the same time, sees a helicopter. He or she knows immediately that the one is the cause of the other, and it seems that this fact is given directly to the senses. But no such *connection* could ever be perceived by purely sensory experience. Although we cannot *know* what such an experience would be like, it is a useful exercise to try to catch a glimpse of it by suspending meaning. The attempt to do this can bring us to the point of appreciating that purely sensory experience would be a state of difference without distinction, diversity without differentiation. It would be a condition of total multiplicity without any trace of unity. In fact, the best way to describe it would be as a state of awareness without meaning. What has previously been referred to as "a meaningless patchwork of black and white shapes," is in fact meaningful compared with this state. The perception which sees "a meaningless patchwork of black and white shapes" already recognizes some unity in the multiplicity, and hence is not seeing pure "difference without distinction." Yet we know from pathological and other cases that the state of purely sensory experience does exist, and that it is a state which corresponds to the complete absence of meaning.[19] So the philosophy of empiricism, which believes that knowledge of the world comes directly through the senses, is fundamentally misleading.

The error of empiricism rests on the fact that what it takes to be material objects are condensations of meaning. When we see a chair, for example, we are seeing a condensed meaning and not simply a physical body. Since meanings are not objects of sensory perception, seeing a chair is not the sensory experience we imagine it to be. What empiricism, and common sense, miss through mistaking meaning for matter is the dimension of mind in cognitive perception. This is usually invisible to us because it is transparent in the act of cognitive perception, and hence we do not suspect that it is there. It is often only in cases where normal cognition is disrupted that the dimension of mind becomes visible.

What also hides this dimension from us is the presupposition that cognitive processes can be understood in the framework of the Cartesian divorce of subject from object, the separation of consciousness from world. This presupposition has to be brought into the light and thought through carefully, whereupon it becomes evident that it is inherently incoherent. For much of its history over the past few centuries, Western philosophy has been concerned with the problem of epistemology which arises directly out of this divorce. During this century studies in the philosophy of language and in phenomenology have both, in their different ways, led to a clearer recognition of the incoherence at the root of the Cartesian position and all that follows from its assumption. The work of Edmund Husserl, the founder of phenomenology, has been particularly influential.[20] He identified the mistake of conceiving consciousness in the manner of a natural object, as described by the physical sciences, as if it were an object among other objects in nature. He recognized that it is therefore a mistake to try to imagine an empty consciousness confronting an external world. The fundamental discovery on which phenomenology is based is that consciousness has the structure of *intentionality*—it would be better to say that consciousness *is* intentionality.[21] This is often expressed by saying that consciousness is always "consciousness of." In other words, consciousness is always directed towards an object. Hence in cognitive perception there is an indissoluble unity between the conscious mind and the object of which it is conscious. This is completely overlooked by the epistemological approach, which is based on the attempt to overcome Cartesian dualism.

The discovery of the intentionality of consciousness explains the transparency of the dimension of mind in cognitive perception and the origin of the empiricist fallacy. Because of its intentionality, consciousness is directed towards the object of cognition. It is this object which occupies attention and not the act of seeing itself. Hence the dimension of mind is invisible in the normal process of cognition, and the object which is seen appears to have been seen by the senses alone. The picture of the giraffe illustrates this clearly. When the giraffe is seen, it appears there on the page, and hence it seems to be seen by means of the senses alone. Yet in this case, as described above, we can learn to recognize that there is no picture of a giraffe on the page.

The discovery of the intentionality of consciousness also makes clear the difference between the meaning which *is* what is seen and the meaning *of* what is seen. Because of the transparency of mind in cognitive perception, arising from the intentionality of consciousness, the meaning that *is* what is seen becomes invisible as such and appears as something other than it is, namely, a sensory object. Hence we are left with only a secondary notion of meaning, namely, the meaning *of* what is seen. This is secondary because what is seen *is* meaning already. It is this primary meaning, which is constitutive of what things are, that is overlooked by the Cartesian distinction and the naturalistic attitude of empiricism. As a result of this oversight, there is a temptation on first encountering the phenomenological approach to misread the meaning that *is* what is seen for the meaning *of* what is seen. But once the primary meaning is rediscovered, then the secondary notion of meaning can be recognized as depending on what is meaning already. The difference here is really between the constitutive mind and the reflective mind. But since the former is transparent in cognitive perception, "mind" is usually identified with the latter alone. However, this is only a secondary function of the mind, which depends on there being a world which is already constituted and can therefore be taken for granted.

It is probably still true that most of us think of scientific knowledge as being somehow fundamentally different from ordinary everyday knowledge. But studies in the philosophy of

science have converged with cognitive psychology to show that
this is not true. It turns out that the differences are only superficial. There is no fundamental difference in the *process* of cognition, and scientific cognition can be understood as an extension
of everyday cognition at a more comprehensive level. Both are
concerned with condensations of meaning, and not with sense
data directly. The objects of cognitive perception at the level of
everyday cognition become the raw data for the higher-level
condensation of meaning which is cognition at the scientific
level. The transparency of mind in the act of cognition now
results in the erroneous view that scientific discoveries are made
directly by observations which are entirely sensory. This disappearance of the dimension of mind results in an understanding
of science which is upside down. It is this distorted image of scientific knowledge which is presented in textbooks and in the
media, and which is communicated tacitly by the very way that
science is taught. For example, it is reported that Galileo made a
telescope, and that when he looked through it he saw mountains
and valleys on the moon, as if this knowledge came to him down
the telescope and through his eyes. The account which Galileo
himself gave of his observations with the telescope makes it
quite clear that to begin with he saw nothing of the kind.[22] With
regard to the mountains on the moon, for example, he was at first
almost literally in a position very similar to that of looking at the
black and white blotches *before* seeing a giraffe. The discovery
that there are "mountains" on the moon was a perception of
meaning, and not the purely sensory experience it is represented
as being. This single example could be multiplied indefinitely to
illustrate the point that is being made here. It is particularly
noticeable how the "result" of an experiment may be described
as if it had been discovered through the senses. For instance,
Newton's experiment with the prism is presented as "showing"
that white light consists of a mixture of colors, as if this had been
observed. The experiment is first described in terms of the theory, which is the meaning that Newton perceived, and then this
description is mistaken for what can be seen with the senses.

When meanings are mistaken for sensory data in this way, we have what amounts to the conjuring trick account of science—the rabbit is pulled out of the hat, but only because it was put there in the first place. The difficulty with this is that the "result" of the experiment is invested with a cognitive authority which it does not have.

Discovery in science is always the perception of meaning, and it could not be otherwise. The essence of a discovery is therefore in the nonempirical factor in cognition. The recognition that meaning is a primary datum of cognitive experience brings a considerable simplification to the philosophy of science.[23] Of course, the meaning in question may be several stages removed from the meaning in everyday cognition, and at a much more comprehensive level. Such is the case, for example, with the meanings which are the most widely embracing scientific theories. But enough has now been said about the nature of scientific knowledge for us to be able to understand it more adequately.

Unity without Unification

Once it has been recognized that the unity of the phenomenon is not given in sensory experience, the question arises naturally: Is this unity simply imposed on the experience of the senses by the mind, or is it there in the phenomenon itself, with the mind functioning as an organ of nonsensory perception?

There is no doubt that, to a far greater degree than we usually realize, the mind organizes experience by *imposing* an organizational framework. This may be at a relatively superficial level, such as the social–linguistic organization of our daily lives. Or it may be at a level that is much less immediately accessible, such as the way in which we impose a temporal framework on our experience, organizing it into a linear sequence of moments. We impose this framework intellectually on nature, with the result that we imagine nature as being organized in a linear, temporal sequence, whereupon it becomes possible to describe motion and change quantitatively. Since the time of Kant's philosophy there has been a growing recognition of this active role of the mind, and of the tendency to mistake our own intellectual constructs for "the way things are."

The recognition of the active role of the intellectual mind gave rise to a philosophy of science which maintained the view that a scientific theory is only a framework which we construct for holding the facts together for our own convenience—where in this case it is believed that the facts themselves are perceived entirely by the senses, independently of the theory. At the beginning of the century this philosophy of science was developed enthusiastically by Mach, Poincaré, and Duhem. Mach, for example, believed that the laws of nature are really only our intellectual mnemonics for reproducing facts in thought, and hence are only convenient summaries of what has been experienced. This philosophy is sometimes called phenomenalism, and it clearly bears a family resemblance to empiricism. It was subsequently developed further in the late 1920s and the 1930s, by combining it with studies in mathematical logic to form the philosophy of logical empiricism, which is also called logical positivism.[24] In this form it was imported into America by Central European intellectuals; there it exerted a considerable influence on attitudes towards research, as well as on science education, during the 1940s and 1950s.[25] But even before this, several of the major figures in the development of physics had been strongly influenced by this philosophy. For example, Einstein said: "The object of all sciences is to coordinate our experiences and to bring them into a logical system"; and Neils Bohr said: "The task of science is both to extend the range of our experience and to reduce it to order." Although these may look like the independent judgments of two individual scientists, they are in fact simply reflections of a prevailing philosophy in the culture of the time.

According to the understanding of the intellectual mind, the unity of experience is produced by unification, i.e., unity *is* unification. It is the synthetic unity of an organizational synthesis. Now this is certainly true for the intellectual mind. But the unity which Goethe perceived in the color phenomenon is *not* a unity that is imposed by the mind. What Goethe saw was not an intellectual unification but the wholeness of the phenomenon itself. He came to see the wholeness of the phenomenon by consciously experiencing it, and this experience cannot be reduced to an intellectual construction in terms of which the phenomenon is organized. It is not reached by a process of intellectual thought, but by a change of consciousness—this will be discussed in the next section, "Modes of Consciousness." The unity which is perceived in this way is the phenomenon—but not the phenomenon as it is immediately accessible to the perception of the senses. The perception of this unity is an experience of seeing the phenomenon in depth. But this depth is not an extensive dimension. It can be approximated by saying that the phenomenon is experienced as "standing in its own depth." There is in fact no adequate intellectual equivalent to this experience of an intensive depth in the phenomenon—as will be discussed further in "The Depth of the Phenomenon." By contrast with the intellectual unity which is unification, this unity of the phenomenon itself can be called "unity without unification." The experience of seeing this unity *is* the theory for Goethe, for whom the term "theory" was much closer to the original Greek *theoria*—which simply means "seeing."

The difference between the two kinds of unity discussed here can be expressed in terms of a distinction introduced by Martin Heidegger.[26] He considered two different perspectives of the notion of "belonging together." These can be seen as being like the two perspectives of the reversing cube. Just as we see one of these cubes easily but have to make an effort to see the other one, so with the two perspectives of "belonging together," one comes easily to us, but we have to learn how to see the other.

Heidegger's distinction is made according to whether the emphasis is placed on "belonging" or "together." Thus, in the perspective of "belonging *together*" he sees the belonging as being determined by the together; whereas in the perspective of "*belonging* together" the reverse is the case, and the together is determined by the belonging. In the first case, he says that "to belong" means to be placed in the order of a "together," i.e., a unity which is the unity of an organized system. But in the latter case, "*belonging* together," there is "the possibility of no longer representing belonging in terms of the unity of the together, but rather of experiencing this together in terms of belonging." The perspective of "belonging *together*" clearly corresponds to the unity which is unification, and this suggests that the perspective of "*belonging* together" corresponds to unity without unification. In terms of this distinction we can say that Goethe perceived the *belonging* together of the colors, instead of trying to make them belong *together*. This is the unity which is perceived in the qualities of the prismatic colors at a boundary, and in the qualities of the colors in Goethe's "instance worth a thousand." For example, he saw the yellow sun and the blue sky *belonging* together. But, although he saw this "unity without unification" in the sensory world, he did not in fact see it by means of the senses—for which there is only the juxtaposition of these two color phenomena without any connection or relationship. This unity is within the phenomenon itself, unlike the intellectual unity of unification, but it is not visible to the senses. When we see the sun and the sky, we usually do so separately. Even if we do notice them together, we do not experience their colors *belonging* together. We experience the colors of the sun and sky in the mode of separation and not in the mode of their unity. It will be shown below that the difference between these two experiences is a difference in the mode of consciousness, from which it will emerge that "unity without unification" is the unity of the intuitive mind instead of the unity of the intellectual mind.

It helps to keep in mind the fact that consciousness is always directed toward the object and not toward itself—as described above in "Knowing the World." Hence this unity is easily experienced *as if* it were also part of the phenomenon perceived through the senses, and as if it were observed along with the colors themselves. In fact, we can observe the colors, but we *see* the unity. The unity "lights up" in consciousness—

it is an insight and not an "outsight." The phenomenon is only partially visible to the senses. The complete phenomenon is visible only when there is a coalescence of sensory outsight with intuitive insight.

Modes of Consciousness

We will now see that the difference between these two perspectives of belonging *together* and *belonging* together, corresponding to the two kinds of unity, can be understood in terms of two different modes of consciousness.

There is now a growing body of evidence to support the view that there are two major modes of human consciousness which are complementary.[27] In our technical–scientific culture we have specialized in the development of only one of these modes, to which our educational system is geared almost exclusively. This is the analytical mode of consciousness, which develops in conjunction with our experience of perceiving and manipulating solid bodies. The internalization of our experience of the closed boundaries of such bodies leads to a way of thinking which naturally emphasizes distinction and separation. Since the fundamental characteristic of the world of solid bodies is *externality*—i.e., everything is external to everything else—then this way of thinking is necessarily analytical. For the same reason it is also necessarily sequential and linear, proceeding from one element to another in a piecemeal fashion—the principle of mechanical causality is a typical way of thinking in this analytical mode of consciousness. Henri Bergson noticed the affinity between logical relations with concepts and spatial relations with solid bodies, and he concluded that "our logic hardly does more than express the most general relations among solids."[28] The principles of logic—identity (A is A), noncontradiction (not at the same time A and not-A), and excluded middle (either A or not-A)—are extrapolations from these limited circumstances which are assumed to hold universally. For this reason the mode of consciousness associated with logical thinking is necessarily analytical.

The analytical mode of consciousness is also associated with language. A basic structure of modern languages is their subject–predicate grammar, which has the effect of dividing experience into separate elements which are then treated as if they existed independently of each other. For example, "I see the tree" seems to entail the external union of a disjoint set of elements comprising subject, object, and the act of seeing which links them together. But the experience indicated by this sentence can only artificially be considered to be put together like this, because in the case of cognitive perception there is no seeing without somebody there to see and something to be seen. It has been noticed often that the effect of such a grammatical structure is to lead to a view of the world as consisting basically of a collection of detached objects, which combine in various ways to produce the different kinds of entities that we encounter.[29] In other words, the grammatical structure of language articulates the world analytically. It discloses the analytical world. But we believe this to be "the way the world is," independently of language, because language itself is transparent in the act of disclosing this world.[30] It is this analytical structure of language which has made it inadequate for describing the domains which have been discovered in modern physics.[31]

Another aspect of the analytical nature of language is seen in its linear, sequential character. For example, the mechanics of writing consists in putting one letter after another, and one word after another, in lines. But this linearity of language can be overemphasized, and there are nonlinear, holistic features of language that can easily be missed. This happens because attention becomes fixed on the level of the word instead of on the level of meaning. The meaning is not present in the same linear manner as the words, and the tension which the writer experiences is between the linearity of the words and the nonlinear meaning. Nevertheless, it is inevitable that the linear mechanism of writing, and reading, has the effect of conditioning us into an analytical mode of consciousness. Often what is called the stream of thought is in fact the stream of language, and the process of thinking is none other than the flow of linguistic associations. The analytical mode of consciousness, therefore, corresponds to the discursive thought of what, for completeness, should be called the verbal–intellectual mind.

The holistic mode of consciousness is complementary to this analytical one. By contrast, this mode is nonlinear, simultaneous, intuitive instead of verbal–intellectual, and concerned more with relationships than with the discrete elements that are related. It is important to realize that this mode of consciousness is a way of seeing, and as such it can only be experienced in its own terms. In particular, it cannot be understood by the verbal–intellectual mind because this functions in the analytical mode of consciousness, for which it is not possible to appreciate adequately what it means to say that a *relationship* can be experienced as something real in itself. In the analytical mode of consciousness it is the *elements* which are related that stand out in experience, compared with which the relationship is but a shadowy abstraction. The experience of a relationship as such is only possible through a transformation from a piecemeal way of thought to a simultaneous perception of the whole. Such a transformation amounts to a restructuring of consciousness itself.[32]

It will be shown below how Goethe's way of science leads to just such a restructuring of consciousness. But before entering into the details of Goethe's scientific consciousness, a more everyday example of what is meant by a transition from an analytical to a holistic mode of consciousness may be useful. When this idea is first introduced, it is often understood in a rather static way—which is itself a characteristic of the analytical mode of consciousness. Thus, lacking the necessary experience, or perhaps just not having noticed it, we try to imagine elements which are experienced simultaneously as if they were present together in a static way, as in a snapshot of a changing scene. In fact the experience of simultaneity and relationship in the holistic mode of consciousness is the opposite of this, inasmuch as it is inherently dynamical. Whereas we imagine movement and change analytically, as if the process really consisted of a linear sequence of instantaneously stationary states (like a sequence of snapshots), when movement and change are experienced holistically, they are experienced dynamically as one whole. The elements which are experienced simultaneously in this mode are thus dynamically related to each other, and this *dynamical* simultaneity replaces the static simultaneity of the analytical mode.

Imagine cutting an orange, for example. We see the knife and orange simply as separate entities which are brought together externally in space and sequentially in time. But another way of experiencing this is possible, which is entered into by giving attention to the *act* of cutting the orange, instead of to the separate entities which are brought together. If this is done, the process of cutting can be experienced simultaneously as one whole, as if it were one present moment instead of a linear sequence of instants. Similarly, if we watch a bird flying across the sky and put our attention into seeing flying, instead of seeing a bird which flies (implying a separation between an entity, "bird," and an action, "flying," which it performs), we can experience this in the mode of dynamical simultaneity as one whole event. By plunging into seeing *flying* we find that our attention expands to experience this movement as one whole that is its own present moment.

It becomes evident through doing this kind of exercise that the description of motion and change as a linear sequence of instantaneous states is a device of the intellectual mind, i.e., it is a consequence of being in the analytical mode of consciousness. This analytical framework is very useful for calculating motion and change, i.e., for apprehending them quantitatively, but it does not take us into the reality of movement and change as a mode of being. This can only be experienced holistically, not analytically, and hence only through a change in the mode of consciousness.[33] It is important to realize that this is not a change in the content of consciousness, as if there were some element which previously had been overlooked, but a change in the *mode* of consciousness. This means that the change is in the relationship between the elements, i.e., in their mode of togetherness.

These examples illustrate very clearly the way that the holistic mode of consciousness can be entered into by plunging into looking, which means by the redeployment of attention into sense perception and away from the verbal–intellectual mind. In the case of motion, by directing our attention into sense perception we discover an aspect of motion which is completely different from the way that motion is understood analytically, and which is therefore not included in the way that we have come to understand motion intellectually—which in fact denies the reality of motion. Arthur Deikman has identified this investment of attention in the sensory as a major step in the transition to another mode of consciousness.[34] In his experimental studies of the psychology of meditation, he discovered that "the meditation exercise could be seen as withdrawing attention from thinking and reinvesting it in percepts—a reverse of the normal learning sequence."[35] The normal learning sequence which is referred to here is called the process of automatization. This is the transference of attention from the sensory experience to the mental abstraction. After this has happened, the sensory occurrence is always experienced tinged with the mental abstraction, or even "tuned out" altogether—so that what we "experience" is only an abstraction, in which case we are completely automatized and in fact no longer different from any complex machine.[36] It is this process which contemplative meditation reverses by reinvesting attention in the sensory experience, and thus withdrawing it from the mental abstraction—and from thought in general, this being often no more than a process of associating such abstractions via the medium of language which encapsulates them. For this reason, Deikman identifies meditation as an exercise of the attention for producing *deautomatization* of the psychological structures organizing experience, especially the logical organization of consciousness—which has been identified here, following Ornstein, as the analytical mode of consciousness.

This is the key to the psychology of Goethe's way of science. He was doing science and not meditation. But if we look at the psychological process, instead of the nominal identification, we can recognize that Goethe's way of science and meditation share the common factor of deautomatization and the transformation of consciousness. In the description of Goethe's work on color, in "The Primal Phenomenon of Color," we distinguished two stages in the encounter with the phenomenon. First there is the observation stage, which is characterized by active seeing instead of the passive reception of visual impressions. This entails putting attention into seeing, plunging into seeing the qualities of the colors. Doing this takes us into the phenomenon, but at the same time it takes attention away from the verbal–intellectual mind and hence promotes deautomatization from the analytical mode of consciousness. The intellectual mind is concerned with uniformity. For example, in the case of, say, two leaves, it is concerned with only what is common to them—that they are both instances of "leaf"—and overlooks the individual differences between them. In contrast to the intellectual mind, the world of sensory experience is nonuniform and endlessly varied and rich in diversity. Hence, investing attention in the sensory inevitably promotes deautomatization from the uniformity of the intellectual mind. The second stage in Goethe's way, the stage he called exact sensorial imagination, takes this process further. It deepens both the encounter with the phenomenon and the process of deautomatization. The attempt to think the phenomenon in imagination, and not to think about it, is sensory and not intellectual, concrete and not abstract. Attention is thereby further withdrawn from verbal associations and intellectual reasoning. This, therefore, is a deautomatization exercise. But at the same time it is an exercise in trying to see the phenomenon in the simultaneous mode, i.e., all at once. Hence, as well as undoing the usual construction of consciousness by the redirection of attention—which by itself can be sufficient for the other mode of consciousness to emerge—this exercise actively promotes the restructuring of consciousness into an organ of holistic perception.[37]

    This psychological interpretation of Goethe's way of access to nature in terms of deautomatization is reinforced by considering the subjective experience of the procedure. Through trying to direct attention into the act of looking, we can experience for ourselves the gap which there is between our habitual awareness and the direct experience of what is there in front of us. It is only when this hiatus in experience is overcome that we realize how little we usually perceive directly of the concrete detail of the particular. We usually classify verbally and experience just a vague generality. A striking feature of this attempt to give attention to active looking and exact sensorial imagination is how much subjective resistance it can set up in a person. This in itself is an indication that the orientation which it calls for is towards deautomatization or dishabituation. This subjective effect is an instance of the psychological inertia which has to be matched by a person's own activity if the state of his or her awareness is to change, just as the inertia of a material body has to be matched by a force if its state of motion is to be changed.

When consciousness is thus restructured into an organ of holistic perception, the mind functions intuitively instead of intellectually. There is a lot of confusion and misunderstanding about intuition, as if it were something intangible and mysterious. But in fact it is a very clear and precise notion. Ornstein defines intuition as "knowledge without recourse to inference."[38] He links it with a simultaneous perception of the whole, whereas the logical or rational mode of knowledge "involves an analysis into discrete elements sequentially (inferentially) linked."[39] He connects the intuitive mind with the holistic mode of consciousness—as the intellectual mind is linked with the analytical mode. Thus, intuition is connected with a change of consciousness, and moreover in a way which can be made quite precise and not just left vague. It now follows that Goethe's procedures are practical exercises for educating the mind to function intuitively instead of intellectually, leading to a science which is intuitive instead of organized intellectually.[40]

It can now be seen that "unity without unification" is possible in the holistic mode of consciousness, whereas unity by means of unification is the characteristic of the analytical mode of consciousness. But because the former is literally a matter of seeing with the mind, i.e., insight, it can easily be mistaken for the sensory. This is why it was necessary to establish first that knowledge is not achieved by the senses alone. There is always a nonsensory element in knowledge, and this must be so whether this element is verbal–intellectual or intuitive. The difference is that, whereas the verbal–intellectual mind withdraws from the sensory aspect of the phenomenon into abstraction and generality, the intuitive mind goes into and through the sensory surface of the phenomenon to perceive it in its own depth. It is by first going into the full richness and diversity of sensory detail that the intellectual mind is rendered ineffective, so that we can escape from its prison into the freedom of intuition.

The Depth of the Phenomenon

Etymologically, "intuition" means "seeing into," which clearly expresses the fact that it is the experience of seeing the phenomenon in depth. But this depth is peculiar inasmuch as it is entirely within the phenomenon and not behind it—so it should be understood as an intensive dimension, and not in the manner of an extensive dimension of physical space. It is in fact the depth of the phenomenon itself. It is as if something which appears to be two-dimensional suddenly turns out to be three-dimensional, so that what had seemed flat is now seen in relief. This is the experience mentioned earlier, of seeing the phenomenon "standing in its own depth." It was said then that there is no intellectual equivalent to this experience, and the reason for this is now clearly because it is an intuitive experience which depends on a change of consciousness.

When the phenomenon is seen intuitively, it has a further dimension to it, but this does not change the particular elements in the phenomenon. It changes the way that the elements are related, and hence their significance, but they remain the same elements so far as the senses as concerned. For example, the blue of the sky and yellow of the sun are, in a clearly recognizable way, the same elements when they are seen *belonging* together in the holistic mode, as they are when seen analytically as just two separate and contingent facts. In the former case there is a depth in the phenomenon which is entirely absent in the latter. This intensive depth which is seen intuitively in the holistic mode of consciousness is the wholeness of the phenomenon. The authentic unity of the phenomenon (i.e., unity without unification) is literally a further dimension of the phenomenon itself, which is seen as such only when the mind functions in the intuitive mode of "seeing into."

The intellectual mind misses this dimension, because it is not visible in the analytical mode of consciousness, and therefore must compensate for what is missing by adding on its own thought construction to the phenomenon as it is presented to sensory experience. This has usually been done in physics by constructing an explanatory model. It has already been mentioned how Newton tried to construct such a model for light. This method of explanation by mechanical models was the classical way in physics from Descartes onwards, until its validity was called into question in this century by the development of the quantum theory.[41] It was depicted in a memorable way by Einstein and Infeld. They ask us to imagine a watch that is being examined by someone who has never encountered a watch before, and who therefore does not know what it is. They also ask us to imagine that this watch is impregnable, so that no matter what the person does he or she cannot open it and look inside. This picture is offered as a parallel to the situation of the scientific investigator with regard to the phenomena of nature. We can investigate the watch through our senses and our mind, until we discover the "law of the watch," i.e., the pattern of the movement of the hands. But an investigator of the watch cannot open it up to discover the mechanism that produces this pattern. "If he is ingenious he may form some picture of the mechanism which could be responsible for all the things he observes, but he may never be quite sure his picture is the only one which could explain his observations."[42] Like actual scientific investigators, we can discover the regularities in the phenomena of nature, i.e., the so-called laws of nature, but we cannot open nature up to look inside. We cannot go behind the scenes to discover something hidden which produces the observed regularities. So at this point we must try to construct a picture of a hidden mechanism that would give rise to the phenomenon observed with the senses.

This metaphor for the intellectual step from observation to theory is clearly very limited, and in terms of the contemporary philosophy of science it is also very naïve. But, in spite of this, it must be taken seriously because of what is communicated by its form. This communicates the view that there is another world hidden behind the world we experience with the senses, and that it is this *other* world which is the physical cause of the world that we experience directly. Now this is a very widespread assumption and, without going into detail, there are some aspects of it which need to be brought out explicitly. Firstly, this other world is conceived in a spatial manner, as if it were like the world of our bodily experience, only hidden. So here too the phenomenon is conceived as having a depth to it, but this is an *extended* depth *behind* the phenomenon. Secondly, this other world hidden behind the scenes is pictured as being like the sensory world that it explains, insofar as the kinds of things which it contains are imagined as sensory-like elements, such as light waves for example. Thirdly, there is no direct access to this backstage world, and it can be approached only by means of the intellectual mind in terms of mental constructions and representations. But, because this world also contains sensory-like elements, albeit invisible ones, there is no reason in principle why it should not be directly visible if we had developed the necessary sense organs. All of this can be summarized simply by saying that this is how the depth of the phenomenon is conceived by the intellectual mind in the analytical mode of consciousness, and hence according to the logic of solid bodies. In other words, it is a superficial projection of what the depth of the world is like, because it is literally a fanciful projection of the surface into the depth.

This helps, by contrast, to bring out more clearly the nature of Goethe's discovery. He would strenuously deny that there is another world hidden behind the sensory world in this way. Any such dualism was repugnant to him. What he saw was a depth in the phenomenon which is another dimension of *the same phenomenon* that is experienced with the senses. There is nothing backstage. There is only the phenomenon itself, but this has another dimension to it, a further aspect which is not a sensory element at all. This is the dimension of wholeness, which is the unity of the phenomenon. For Goethe, the theory *is* seeing this intensive dimension of the phenomenon. This is much closer to the original Greek *theoria*, which simply means "seeing." This dimension of the phenomenon is not seen by the senses, and not by the sightless fancies of the verbal–intellectual mind. It is seen intuitively by a change of consciousness. But it has to be remembered all the time that, when this dimension of the phenomenon is seen, the elements are the same as in the sensory phenomenon—the difference is in the way that they are related. It is the transformation in their mode of togetherness, which is experienced intuitively through a change of consciousness, that gives the phenomenon its intensive depth.

Now it is possible to understand better the meaning of some of Goethe's occasional remarks about the relationship between fact and theory:

> Let the facts themselves speak for their theory.

> Don't look for anything behind the phenomena; they themselves are the theory.

> The greatest achievement would be to understand that everything factual is already its own theory.

It is easy to misinterpret these remarks by failing to realize that they refer to the phenomenon as it is experienced by the intuitive mind, and by trying to understand them with the intellectual mind alone. For example, it would be possible to produce a rational reading of what Goethe is saying here by making an association with the discovery by the contemporary philosophy of science, which is corroborated by the psychology of perception, that scientific observation is always theory-laden.[43] It would also be possible to produce another, equally rational, reading by making an association with the kind of phenomenalism developed by Ernst Mach which was mentioned in "Unity without Unification." In this case these remarks would be interpreted as saying that the theory reduces to the facts, as if it were nothing more than merely the facts themselves. But what Goethe is saying goes in the opposite direction to this. He says this is something *to be achieved*. The facts are to be raised to the level of being theory, and not the other way round. But when this is achieved they are still the same facts. They have been transformed, but they have not been changed into something different. This can readily be seen by considering the two separate facts that the sun is yellow and the sky is blue, and the way that these are transformed when they are seen *belonging* together in the mode of unity without unification.

Goethe's remarks about the relationship between fact and theory become transparent when the phenomenon is experienced intuitively in its own depth. They simply describe what this experience is like. The theory *is* the facts when these are seen in another dimension. This perception is attained by a change of consciousness and not by a process of rational thought. Seen in one mode, the analytical, the facts are merely the facts; seen in the other mode, the holistic, they *are* the theory.

This transformation from an analytical to a holistic mode of consciousness brings with it a reversal between the container and the content. What is encountered in the theory is, for Goethe, the real content of the phenomenon, for which the sensory facts are now merely the container. This is in contrast to the analytical mode for which the sensory facts are the content of the phenomenon. In the case of phenomenalism and positivism, it has been mentioned already that the theory is considered to be only a container for the facts. Now if the theory, in Goethe's sense, is the real content of the phenomenon, then it can be said that in the moment of intuitive insight we are seeing *inside* the phenomenon. But this "inside" is very different from that which is imagined by the intellectual mind, and which is depicted by Einstein's watch analogy. The "inside" of the phenomenon which is imagined by rational thought is a fiction based on our own bodily experience in the *external* world of bodies. In this case "inside" is really thought of in an outside kind of way. Hegel saw that the world of bodies is essentially the external world.[44] He did not mean by this that it is external to consciousness in a Cartesian sense, because consciousness is not in space and therefore no thing can be outside of it. Hegel meant that the external world is a world which is characterized and permeated by externality, so that it is the world in which everything is outside everything else. So in the mode of thought which is based on our experience of this world it is inevitable that "inside" is conceived externally. Hence the "inside" of the world which the intellectual mind imagines is really an outside in disguise. Contrary to this, Goethe's intuitive way of science goes inside the phenomenon to find that it is the *same* phenomenon in another dimension. This is the intensive depth of the phenomenon, and hence the *intensive* inside instead of the extensive "inside" which is characteristic of the external world. It could therefore be said that in knowing the phenomenon, Goethe dwells within it consciously instead of replacing it with mental constructs— although equally it could be said that the phenomenon itself dwells in Goethe's scientific consciousness.[45]

The effect of this shift from the intellectual to the intuitive mind is that the phenomenon becomes its own explanation. It discloses itself in terms of itself and thereby becomes self-explanatory. In the terminology of modern philosophy, Goethe's intuitive way of science is a phenomenology of nature, where this term must now be understood in the sense in which it is used by Heidegger.[46] He returns to the Greek word *phainomenon*, which he says gives the fundamental meaning of phenomenon as "that which shows itself in itself." He emphasizes that this is not to be confused with the mere appearance of something. The phenomenon is not what is immediately visible. Combining this with his interpretation of the meaning of the Greek word *logos*, Heidegger tells us that phenomenology, as a method of investigation, means "to let that which shows itself be seen from itself in the very way in which it shows itself from itself." Clearly such an approach is the very opposite of an intellectual analysis which imposes its own categories on the phenomenon to organize it subjectively. This description of phenomenology seems cumbersome, and it is a source of irritation to those philosophers who insist that if something cannot be said simply in English then it must be muddled. Yet it describes the *experience* of Goethe's way of science precisely, and thus enables us to identify this philosophically as a phenomenology of nature.

But it is possible to be more specific about this phenomenology. The effect of this event of phenomenological disclosure is that the phenomenon becomes its own language. This is the concrete language which things are. It is important to realize that "language" is being used literally here and not metaphorically. This confusion can arise because language is usually identified with the verbal language of the intellectual mind, which is a consequence of being restricted to the analytical mode of consciousness. In fact this is really only a special case of language. As well as the meaning that belongs to the intellectual mind, which is verbal, there is the meaning that belongs to the intuitive mind, which is nonverbal and can only be perceived in a holistic mode of consciousness. Nevertheless, both of these are linguistic. While there can be meaning which is nonverbal, there cannot be meaning which is nonlinguistic, for much the same kind of reason that there cannot be a triangle which is not three-sided. Nonverbal meaning can only be perceived intuitively and not intellectually. We can only approximate this verbally, in an imperfect way, by saying that nonverbal language is the concrete language which things *are* when they are experienced as being their own language. So it could therefore be said that Goethe learned to read the language of color. It will be shown in the next section how he learned to read the plant in terms of itself, so that the plant becomes its own language, and similarly how it is possible to learn to read the language of animal form so that the animal becomes its own explanation. In view of this, Goethe's intuitive way of science can be recognized as a concrete illustration of Gadamer's principle of universal hermeneutics that "being that can be understood is language."[47] The philosophy of Goethe's science can therefore be identified more precisely as the hermeneutic phenomenology of nature.

The difference between Goethe's phenomenological way and the mainstream of mathematical physics from Newton onwards was summarized memorably and concisely by Cassirer: "The mathematical formula strives to make the phenomena calculable, that of Goethe to make them visible."[48] Taken at its face value, this would certainly seem an odd thing to say, because we would usually take it that the phenomena are visible already, and so there is no need to strive to make them visible. But now we can appreciate what is being said here. Goethe's way makes the phenomenon visible intuitively, and not just to the senses. Whereas the phenomenon is only partly visible to the senses, it is brought fully into the light by the intuition which perceives the intensive depth and not just the sensory surface. The key to this is the transformation of consciousness into the holistic mode. Then the phenomenon is seen wholly, and hence completely, instead of only partly. Of course, this does not mean that the complete phenomenon is the sum of two parts. It is an original unity which is experienced by us partly through the senses and partly through the intuitive consciousness. It was a remarkable insight of Rudolf Steiner to recognize that this is a consequence of the way that the human being is organized, and not the result of a division in the phenomenon itself.[49] In other words, there is no dualism in nature. It only appears so to us because of the way in which we ourselves, as human beings, are involved in the process of knowing. What this means is that the phenomenon as it appears to the senses is only an abstraction.

This is a reversal of our usual way of thinking, for which what is given to the senses is concrete and what is present to the mind is an abstraction—which of course it is to the intellectual mind.

The difference between the intuitive and intellectual approaches to the science of nature is illustrated metaphorically by Edwin Abbott's story *Flatland*.[50] This concerns a society of creatures who inhabit a two-dimensional surface, and what happens when a sphere appears to one of them. Of course, he is unable to perceive a sphere. All that his sensory experience tells him, as the sphere passes through the plane of his existence, is that a point appears, grows into a circle of expanding diameter until this becomes a maximum size, and then shrinks back to a point again and vanishes. Evidently, what his senses tell him is an abstraction. The sphere tells him that he must go upward. Not having any experience of "upward," he tries to interpret it at first in terms of his familiar experience with a compass as "northward." After struggling for some time with the paradox, to him, of how to go "upward, yet not northward," the sphere casts him out of Flatland into the three-dimensional world. Now he sees directly what he had previously only been able to infer by association based on his familiar experience in the two-dimensional surface. This is a transformation of his consciousness. With the difference that the further dimension in this case is extensive and not intensive, this can be taken as a metaphor for the restructuring of consciousness into the holistic, intuitive mode that is necessary for the Goethean phenomenologist of nature to be able to make the phenomenon visible.

Goethe's Organic Vision

Now that the structure of Goethe's scientific consciousness has been described, it is not difficult to begin to
understand his way of seeing organic nature. Patterns of
relationships which seem strange, even unconvincing, to the
analytical mind begin to fall into place when understood in
terms of a holistic mode of consciousness. When this is followed
through, it brings us to the point of being able to see the essence
of Goethe's organic vision for ourselves.

THE UNITY OF THE PLANT

Goethe's best-known contribution to biology is undoubtedly his
work on the flowering plant, as described in his essay *The Metamorphosis of Plants* and in some other fragmentary comments
dispersed throughout his writings. The flowering plant is usually described in elementary botany books as if it were an external
assemblage of different parts—leaves, sepals, petals, stamens,
etc.—which are separate and independent of each other. There
is no hint of any necessary relationship between them. This is
the analytical plant—the plant as it appears to the intellectual
mind in the analytical mode of consciousness. It is the plant in
Flatland. Linnaeus produced his system for organizing plants
into species, genera, etc., on the basis of comparing these parts
of the plant as they occur in different specimens. In contrast to
this, Goethe saw the plant holistically. He discovered another
dimension in the plant, an intensive depth, in which these

different organs are intimately related. In fact, he discovered that they are really all one and the same organ. When we can see the way in which he saw this, then we can understand what he meant by the idea of metamorphosis.

What Goethe discovered in the flowering plant could be described simply as continuity of form. He began *The Metamorphosis of Plants* with the statement that "anyone who observes even a little the growth of plants will easily discover that certain of their external parts sometimes undergo a change and assume, either entirely, or in greater or lesser degree, the form of the parts adjacent to them."[51] He goes on to describe the anomalous case of a plant which makes a retrograde step and reverses the normal order of growth. Thus, in the case of a double flower, petals develop in the place of stamens, and in some cases it is possible to recognize in the extra petals traces of their origin as stamens in the normal simple flower. It is in such cases, Goethe believed, that the laws of growth and transformation which are hidden in the normal course of nature are made more readily visible to intuition. What we learn in this way, and can then recognize in normal growth, is that nature "produces one part out of another and creates the most varied forms by the modification of one single organ."[52]

The question is: What is this single organ whose modifications appear as the different visible organs? Paradoxically, it is everywhere visible and nowhere visible. Goethe called it the *Urorgan*, which has been variously translated as the archetypal organ, the primal organ, or the organ type. What it must not be confused with is the notion of a primitive organ, as if the *Urorgan* was an especially simple organ out of which other organs develop materially in time. To think of the archetypal organ in this way is to look at it through Darwinian spectacles, and so fail to recognize that Goethe was seeing the plant in another way.

Cassirer recognized that a unique feature of Goethe's way of science is to be found in the relationship between the particular and the universal which it expresses. He said: "There prevails in his writings a relationship of the particular to the universal such as can hardly be found elsewhere in the history of philosophy or of natural science."[53] We are accustomed to thinking of the universal as if it were a generalization made inductively from several particular instances. In this case we imagine going from the particular instances to the universal, which, because it is now identified with the general, appears to be an abstraction. It is in fact an abstraction of the intellectual mind. But Goethe worked to awaken the intuitive mind, for which the universal is not the same as the general, and which is therefore not reached by abstracting the common denominator from several particular instances. For the intuitive mind there is a reversal of perception here. Instead of a movement of mental abstraction from the particular to the general, there is a perception of the universal shining in the particular. In this moment of reversal the particular is seen in the light of the universal, and hence it appears as a concrete manifestation of the universal. In other words, the particular becomes symbolic of the universal. So what is merely particular to the senses, and the mode of thought which corresponds to them, is simultaneously universal to an intuitive way of seeing which is associated with a different mode of consciousness.

Goethe's description of the primal phenomenon as "an instance worth a thousand, bearing all within itself" has to be understood in terms of this relationship between the universal and the particular. This is also the way that the archetypal plant organ has to be understood—which is why it can be said to be everywhere visible and nowhere visible. Goethe experienced this organ directly with the intuitive perception of the holistic mode of consciousness, and so it must not be confused with a mental abstraction—which is all that it would be for the intellectual mind. Also, as mentioned previously, the archetypal organ must not be confused with a primitive organ from which other organs have developed materially in time. The *Urorgan* is neither internally subjective (a mental abstraction) nor externally objective (a primitive organ). Both of these errors have been made from time to time, and it may even be that Goethe had to work his way through one of them himself (the primitive organ error) before he recognized that what he was looking for would never be found where he was looking for it—or rather, in the *way* that he was looking.

In his botanical notes made on his Italian journey, Goethe wrote: "Hypothesis: All is leaf. This simplicity makes possible the greatest diversity."[54] The leaf he refers to here is to be understood in the universal sense as an omnipotential form and not as a particular physical leaf. The different organs of the plant are then perceived as the metamorphic variations of this form, each of which could be derived from any of the others. There is continuity of form, but not of material substance. Thus a petal can be understood as a metamorphosis of a stem leaf, a stamen can be understood as a metamorphosis of a petal, and so on until all the organs are understood as metamorphic variations of one single organ, which nowhere appears as a physical organ but is visible everywhere to the intuition which sees the universal in the particular. Thus the "leaf" in "All is leaf" should be understood as a concrete universal, compared with which any particular plant organ is only an abstraction. Goethe tried to avoid the confusion which follows inevitably from seeing this statement in the wrong way, literally instead of intuitively, by suggesting that the organs of the plant should be visualized in metamorphic sequence backwards as well as forwards. Thus, for example, a petal should be seen as a metamorphosis of a stamen equally well as a stamen can be seen as a metamorphosis of a petal. In this way he tried to compensate for the fact that there is no general term with which to designate the diversely metamorphosed organ which *is* the flowering plant.

It is an extraordinary experience to look at a flowering plant and see it in Goethe's way. Organs which can be quite different in outer appearance are recognized as being manifestations of the same form, so that the plant now appears as the repeated expression of the same organ. Seeing the plant intuitively in this way is to experience it "coming into being," instead of analyzing the plant as it appears in its finished state.

In terms of the category of wholeness, the statement that "all is leaf" becomes an expression of the principle of wholeness that the whole is reflected or disclosed in the part.[55] We could therefore also say that in the moment of intuitive perception the leaf becomes "an instance worth a thousand, bearing all within itself." Many of the themes which have been discussed already in connection with color can also now be recognized in Goethe's way of seeing the plant. Thus, he made the plant visible in terms of itself, so that "it shows itself in itself." So the plant is seen in another dimension, standing in its own depth. This intensive depth is the wholeness of the plant, which is the unity without unification in which the various organs of the flowering plant *belong* together. Thus the factual plant is disclosed as being its own theory, so that the plant becomes its own language.

Whereas Linnaeus was concerned with making the plant manageable, for the purpose of organizing gardens, Goethe was concerned with making the plant visible. Linnaeus therefore imposed an organization on the plant so that each specimen had a place in a system, whereas Goethe let the plant speak for itself. This is the difference between the intellectual mind and the intuitive mind, which in this case can be linked very clearly with the difference between the analytical and holistic modes of consciousness. In the one way the plant which is observed with the senses is covered over, whereas in the other way it is made more deeply visible. It is only in this latter way that the metamorphosis becomes visible. This is perceived holistically as a relationship within the plant, with the quality of necessity. There are some plants where the metamorphosis of the organs is more open, whereas in others it is more hidden. It was through the pathological cases, such as the retrogressive metamorphosis mentioned earlier, that Goethe finally came to see the growth of the flowering plant in terms of the metamorphosis of a single organ. But there are also cases of regular metamorphosis where it is especially visible. A particularly good example is the white water lily, where the transformation of petals into stamens occurs in stages, so that several different stages can be seen

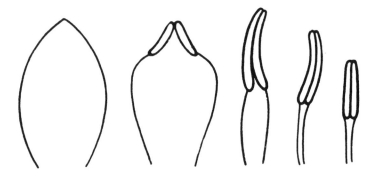

simultaneously.[56] Yet in no case does a petal materially turn into
a stamen. The metamorphosis, in Goethe's usage, is not a causal
relationship in the mechanical sense. Because our idea of continuity is often superficial—being no more than an extrapolation
from our sensory experience of material change—metamorphosis can appear at first more like a discontinuity. It is in fact a
deeper continuity, the continuity of form, which can only
become visible to intuition.[57]

The One and the Many

Goethe's intuition of the fundamental unity of the plant, as
expressed in the metamorphic variations of the archetypal
organ, was gradually extended to the plant kingdom as a whole.
He came to believe that there must be an *Urpflanze*, a primal or
archetypal plant, whose metamorphic variations are what we
see as all the many different plants. He wrote, after visiting the
Botanical Gardens at Padua, that "the thought becomes more
and more living that it may be possible out of one form to develop all plant forms." It seems that at first Goethe believed this
would be some kind of primitive plant which he could hope to
encounter if he searched diligently enough. He imagined it as
an especially simple plant out of which other plants would
develop materially in time. Eventually, as with the archetypal
organ, he understood that the *Urpflanze* would never be found
in the way that he was looking for it. He came closer to it

through the organ of imagination.[58] He described this experience in his notebooks:

> When I closed my eyes and bent my head representing to myself a flower right at the center of the organ of sight, new flowers sprung out of this heart, with colored petals and green leaves. . . . There was no way of stopping the effusion, that went on as long as my contemplation lasted, neither slowing nor accelerating.

He wrote to Herder that with the archetypal plant it would be possible "to invent plants ad infinitum; they would be consistent; that is to say, though nonexisting, they would be capable of existing, being no shades or semblances of the painter or poet, but possessing truth and necessity."

It is clear from these descriptions that when Goethe began to encounter the plant in its archetypal mode, this experience is not to be confused with a mental abstraction, as if it were a sort of lowest common denominator of all plants. But this error is just as common as the error of supposing the archetypal plant to be a primitive organism. Thus, it is supposed that Goethe started with finished plants as they were presented to him in the environment, and by comparing them externally with one another he abstracted what was common to them to produce a generalization. In this way, it is supposed, he found unity in multiplicity. To begin with he would probably have had to do this with several sets of different plants, producing a generalization for each. Then he would have produced a generalization of these generalizations until he reached the ultimate generalization, the ultimate unity in multiplicity, which would be the archetypal plant. Then perhaps Goethe made the mistake of hypostatizing this ultimate mental abstraction—in much the same sort of way that it is often believed Plato did—and imagined it standing behind the world of the physical plants in a separate world of pure Form.

The process of comparing external appearances to find what is common to them is the way that the analytical mode of consciousness tries to find unity. But the unity of this "unity in multiplicity" has the quality of uniformity, and hence it is static and inflexible. In this mode of consciousness we refer to *reducing* multiplicity to unity. This is the mechanical unity of a pile of bricks, and not the organic unity of life. But Goethe did not begin by making an external comparison of different plants. His own account shows that he worked with his mind in a different way from this. As he was able to see into the individual plant to perceive it holistically, so now he saw into all the plants holistically. He saw into the coming-into-being of the plants so deeply that he saw all plants as one plant. What he saw could be described as "the possibility of plant." A philosopher of being like Martin Heidegger would perhaps have said that Goethe reached the "to be" of plant. The archetypal plant as an omnipotential form is clearly a different dimension of the plant than what appears in the space–time dimension as many plants. To the analytical mind which is formed around experience with material bodies this must seem unreal, and hence must appear to be only an abstract thought. But phenomenologists of nature do not argue with the phenomenon they encounter! Instead, they look into their own mind to winkle out the prejudgments and presuppositions which are making them think the phenomenon is unreal. It is not the proper business of intellectual thought to prescribe what is real and what is not, because what seems unreal in one mode of consciousness may not seem so in another.

The omnipotential form which is the archetype is one plant which is all possible plants. As such it is not a blueprint for plants, a general plant, or the common factor in all plants. This, as we have seen, would have the quality of uniformity. But the archetypal plant has the quality of diversity within unity, and from Goethe's own account it is inherently dynamical and indefinitely flexible. The intellectual mind does not understand omnipotentiality dynamically in terms of the coming-into-being of the plants, but statically in terms of the plants that have already become. It conceives it as if it were a state which already contained the finished plants beforehand. This is an analytical counterfeit of something which can only be understood holistically. It is yet another instance of trying to "reach the milk by way of the cheese." Another analytical counterfeit of the omnipotential form, which is also an example of this habit of mind, is the attempt to conceive it as some kind of synthetic assemblage. A notorious instance of this is found in Turpin's attempt to depict Goethe's archetypal plant pictorially. He drew a picture of a composite plant in which he placed, on one main axis, as many different kinds of leaves as were known, and then showed examples of different kinds of flowers as parts of a single flower. Agnes Arber described this as "a botanist's nightmare, in which features which could not possibly coexist, are forced into the crudest juxtaposition."[59]

The unity of the archetypal plant is inside-out to the unity of "unity in multiplicity." The unity of this "one plant which is many" is better described as "multiplicity in unity." This has to be understood intensively, not extensively, so as to avoid implying the contradiction that unity is divided.[60] What this means is that, whereas extensively there are many plants, intensively there is only one plant because each plant is the very same one—yet without being identical in the extensive sense, i.e., like a number of copies. It is an exercise in active imagination to go from "multiplicity in unity" to "unity in multiplicity" and back again. This gives a sense of turning inside-out from the intensive dimension of the prenumerical "one which is many" to the extensive dimension of numerical multiplicity where there are many single ones. For the sake of clarity, the intensive dimension of "one which is many" (multiplicity in unity) will be written with a capital letter as the intensive dimension of One, to distinguish it from the extensive dimension of many ones (unity in multiplicity). Thus, "One" is a prenumerical intensive dimension, whereas "one" is a numerically single individual.[61]

A model for "multiplicity in unity" is provided by the hologram. There are several unusual features of the hologram, but the one which is relevant here concerns what happens if the film is divided into, say, two parts. With a conventional photograph the picture would be divided, with a different part of the photographed object appearing on each bit of the film. But when a hologram film is divided, the whole object is optically reconstructed through each part. The division of the hologram materially is an extensive operation—each part getting smaller and smaller. But the division of the hologram optically is intensive—it is divisible and yet remains whole, producing "multiplicity in unity." Whereas there are many holograms materially (many ones), there is One hologram optically (the One which is many) because each is the very same One. Instead of just following this with the verbal–intellectual mind, for which understanding can often be no more than recognizing the meaning of the words, it is better to approach this as an exercise in visualization so that it becomes more of an adventure in perception.

It is through the use of the power of visualization, as in the process of exact sensorial imagination, that the transition can be made from the analytical to the holistic mode of consciousness. We have seen already how this exercise leads to deautomatization from the verbal–intellectual mind which is associated with the analytical mode of consciousness. The unity of the plant kingdom can only appear to this mode of consciousness as "unity in multiplicity." This is the extensive perspective of unity. The intensive perspective of unity, "multiplicity in unity," can only be seen in the holistic mode of consciousness. The common failure to appreciate what Goethe meant by the archetypal plant can be traced to this difference. A lot of confusion has arisen generally in the history of philosophy through attempting to understand unity in the wrong mode of consciousness. Plato's theory of Forms, for example, is almost invariably approached analytically in terms of "unity in multiplicity." It is this which leads to the notorious difficulties with his theory of "one over many."[62] The same can be said about the medieval dispute about the nature of universals and the argument between nominalism and realism. Plato's theory of Forms, and the problem of universals, become quite different when approached holistically in terms of "multiplicity in unity" and the intensive dimension of One. Philosophers like to proceed by the way of logical argument, but it could be that it is the mode of consciousness associated with this way which is responsible for some of the conundrums which they are thereby trying to resolve.

It is now possible to clarify the difference between the general and the universal which was referred to earlier. It is clear that the general has the structure of "unity in multiplicity," since it is what is common to many particular instances. The universal has the structure of "multiplicity in unity," and is not reached by standing back from many instances to get an overview but by a change of consciousness. In this case the One is seen reflected in the many, so that the many are seen in the light of One instead of trying to evaporate one off from the many as a mental abstraction—which is sometimes referred to as reducing the many to the one. The universal is therefore the unity of the intuitive mind. The general is the unity of the intellectual mind, and so it is the intellectual mind's counterfeit for the universal. The difference can be summarized in a diagram:

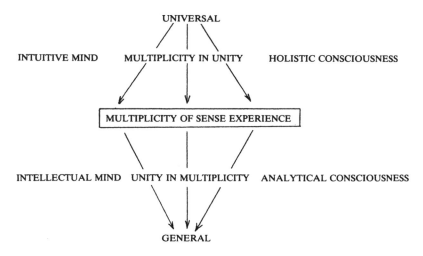

Throughout his life Goethe gradually had to emancipate himself from the idol of empiricism.[63] To begin with, he thought of his work on color empirically in the manner laid down by Francis Bacon. But he came to think subsequently that Bacon's method of inductive generalization from many individual cases was lifeless.[64] He pointed out the limitation in Bacon's approach: that complicated cases were necessarily given the same weight at first as simple cases—though, of course, there would be no way beforehand of knowing which was which. He believed that it would be impossible in practice to proceed in the way that Bacon advocated, and instead he gradually developed his own way of looking for "an instance worth a thousand, bearing all within itself." The method which Bacon advocated clearly has the form of looking for "unity in multiplicity." Goethe's way is effectively inside-out to this because it sees multiplicity in the light of unity instead of trying to produce unity from multiplicity. The important thing to remember here is that whereas extensively we see many in the form of one (i.e., uniformity), intensively we see One in the form of many. Hence in the intensive perspective each of the many is the very same One, and yet in a way which includes difference instead of eradicating it. This is the difference between a genuinely holistic perspective and the analytical counterfeit. With the distinction between "unity in multiplicity" and "multiplicity in unity" it is now possible for us to look at a statement such as "All is leaf" and understand it as the expression of a perception of the universal shining in the particular, and not as an inductive generalization reached empirically by external comparisons and abstraction. In coming to recognize the limitation of Bacon's method, Goethe was feeling his way towards understanding that he was not working with the intellectual mind. He eventually realized that he was working with the intuitive mind, but only after he had first freed himself from the illusion of naive empiricism.[65] We can now understand this precisely in terms of the psychology of consciousness, and we can appreciate why it took Goethe himself some time to begin to clarify the cognitive nature of his own way of science.

At the beginning of this section it was pointed out that Goethe's organic vision has often been misunderstood through failure to realize that he was seeing organic nature in another dimension. We can now recognize that this dimension is the intensive dimension of One. The dimension of One is the intensive depth of the phenomenon when it is organic, and Goethe's notions of the archetypal organ, the archetypal plant, and metamorphosis all need to be understood in the perspective of this dimension. He saw the plant holistically as One organ, and he saw the entire plant kingdom holistically as One plant. In the language of the hologram metaphor, the many plants are the fragments of a hologram for the archetypal plant, as the plant organs are the fragments of a hologram for the archetypal organ. Metamorphosis is essentially a "multiplication" in the intensive dimension of One, and as such it applies to the plants of the kingdom in the same way as to the organs of the plant. It is therefore an inherently holistic notion which cannot be understood adequately in the analytical mode of consciousness. When the plant kingdom is seen analytically in the extensive perspective of the intellectual mind it appears numerically as the "unity in multiplicity" of many plants. But if it is seen holistically in the intensive perspective of the intuitive mind it appears nonnumerically as the "multiplicity in unity" of the One plant. The many plants which are one (unity in multiplicity) and the One plant which is many (multiplicity in unity) are really different dimensions of the same individual. Which way it is seen depends on the mode of consciousness.

THE UNITY OF ANIMAL ORGANIZATION

Goethe coined the term morphology for the study of form in the plant and animal kingdoms. *Morphe* means "shape" in Greek, but the form which concerned Goethe was not limited to the external spatial outline of the organism. However, with the tendency to approach the organism through the intellectual mind, the form of the organism as a whole has appeared to be no more than an external aspect of the organism. For this reason, the notion of form has come to be thought of as something which does not refer to an objective feature of the organism in the way that, say, a leg or an eye is an objective feature. Compared with such organs, the form of the organism as a whole seems to be nebulous and unreal. It seems as if it belongs more to the mind of the beholder than to the organism itself. In other words, it seems that believing the "form of the organism as a whole" to be a real feature of the organism is a confusion based on mistaking a subjective experience of the observer for an objective aspect of the phenomenon itself. Of course, the form of the organism as a whole cannot be part of the organism in the same way as an individual organ. Nevertheless, Goethe was sure that the form of the organism was something real and not just a figment in the mind of the beholder. He described the task of morphology as being to recognize living forms *as such*, and "to master them, to a certain extent, in their *wholeness* through a concrete vision."[66] The German term which is translated here as "concrete vision" is *Anschauung*. Agnes Arber, who spent her long life studying plants, said that in this context it "may be held to signify the *intuitive knowledge gained through contemplation of the visible aspect*."[67] This indicates very clearly that Goethe's approach to animal form follows the same pathway that we have discovered in his work on color. The method, as described above, is active looking followed by exact sensorial imagination, plunging into the visible aspect to produce dishabituation from the verbal–intellectual mind and the analytical mode of consciousness. This exercise of redirecting attention into seeing, inwardly as well as outwardly, removes an obstacle to the holistic mode of consciousness. At the same time, the exercise of trying to see the visible aspect as a whole promotes the restructuring of consciousness into the holistic mode. This procedure therefore has the result of taking the *Naturschauer* into the phenomenon intuitively and not just sensorially, while escaping from the prison of abstractions that is the intellectual mind.[68]

It seems clear from this that the concrete quality that Goethe meant by the form of the organism as a whole can only be perceived adequately in the holistic mode of consciousness. This quality of the wholeness of the organism is another dimension of the organism itself. Goethe's morphology is thus another example of a way of science that aims to make the phenomenon visible.

The reason for doubting the objective reality of form now becomes apparent. The intellectual mind functions in the analytical mode of consciousness, and it is in the nature of this mode for the organism to be seen as a conglomerate of individual parts. Hence for this mode of consciousness, the form of the organism as a whole can only be interpreted as, at best, a mental abstraction or construction. The concrete experience of living form *as such*, the experience of the wholeness of the organism as a real quality, is only possible in the holistic mode of consciousness. To do morphology in Goethe's sense, therefore, means working with the mind in a different way from that of mainstream science today, which is dominated by the analytical power of the intellectual mind. This is why Goethe's approach to morphology has seldom been understood.

The experience of form in Goethe's way leads to an understanding of organisms that differs from seeing them in the light of either finality and purpose or causality and mechanism. He described his approach to animal form in a conversation with Eckermann, indicating how it differed from the way of understanding common at the time:

> Human beings are inclined to carry their usual views from life also into science and, in observing the various parts of an organic being, to inquire after their purpose and use. This may go on for a while and they may also make progress in science for the time being, but they will come across phenomena soon enough where such a narrow view will prove insufficient and they will be entangled in nothing but contradictions if they do not acquire a higher orientation. Such utilitarian teachers will say that the bull has horns to defend itself with, but there I ask why the sheep has none. Even when they have horns, why are they twisted round the sheep's ears so that they cannot be any use at all? It is a different thing to say that the bull defends himself with his horns because they are there. The question *why* is not scientific at all. We fare a little better with the question *how*, for if I ask the question, "How does the bull have horns?" I am

immediately led to the observation of his organization, and this shows me at the same time why the lion has no horns and cannot have any.[69]

Of course, if Goethe had been writing today he would have addressed his remarks more towards the mechanistic explanation of the animal's appearance. Darwin got rid of "natural purposes," and so he would have agreed with the first part of Goethe's statement. Instead, he explained the features of an organism, such as the giraffe's long neck, by means of "natural selection" acting over long periods of time on small, random variations in the individuals of a breeding population. The overall appearance of a species of organism is thus explained as a long-term statistical effect of the environment acting mechanically on the results of chance. The organism as a whole is not involved, since in Darwin's theory the small random variations are only in individual features of the organism, which are considered separately without any correlation between them. Darwin's organism is a thoroughly analytical organism. Goethe's way of understanding the appearance of an organism in terms of its organization is therefore different from the modern mechanistic explanation, as it was in his own day different from the purposive interpretation.

Goethe himself was only able to go so far with his approach to animal form. For example, he noticed that no animal had a complete set of teeth in its upper jaw if it had horns or antlers. Seeing this connection is an example of *significant* perception, i.e., a perception of meaning, and not just a sensory perception as it seems to the naive empiricist.[70] It was this correlation that enabled Goethe to understand "why the lion has no horns and cannot have any." The fact that he could say the lion *cannot* have horns because it has a complete set of teeth in its upper jaw, means that this connection is perceived to have a quality of *necessity*—as will be discussed in more detail in "The Necessary Connection." But there were many questions which Goethe could only touch on and not answer fully in terms of the organization of the organism itself. In the above illustration, for example, he was not able to answer why it is precisely the incisors that are missing from the upper jaws of animals with horns or antlers, and why the upper canines are missing as well from the jaws of rhinoceroses and cattle. Such details will inevitably seem very specialized, and perhaps even trivial. But in the holistic biology of animal form each feature of an animal is significant because the whole is reflected in each part. Questions about horns and antlers can only be answered by taking into account all the mammals, those that do not have these organs as well as those that do. Ultimately this requires a biology of form which takes into account *all* the features of the animal in question, not just horns and teeth, and perceives intuitively the way that they *belong* together in a natural unity without unification.

The glimpse which Goethe had of such a morphology has now been turned into a much fuller view by contemporary natural philosophers who are following his way. The most thorough work of this kind has been done on the mammals by Wolfgang Schad.[71] It is described in detail in his book *Man and Mammals*, which it would be difficult to praise too highly for its demonstration of what can be done by following Goethe's way of science far beyond the point that Goethe himself was able to reach. It also has the advantage of a clarity of exposition which makes it available to anyone who is interested. Schad begins from the recognition that there are three fundamental functional processes, or dynamical organic systems, in the mammalian organism. He designates these the nerve–sense system, the respiratory–circulatory system, and the metabolic–limb system. These three dynamical systems are balanced in the human being, in the sense that no one of them predominates over the others through being more specialized. Although each system is centered in a particular region of the organism, they should not be thought of as being separate and external to each other, lying side-by-side, but as acting simultaneously throughout the whole organism. In other words, they have to be understood holistically and not analytically, as well as dynamically and not statically. They are three processes which act throughout the entire organism, and not localized anatomical features. For example, whereas the nerve–sense system is centered in the head region, there are some features in this region which have the *quality* of the respiratory–circulatory system (the air-filled cavities in the cranium) and also some features which have the *quality* of the metabolic–limb system (the mouth region). But this relationship whereby the whole threefold functional process reenters each of its own parts—so that the whole is present in its own parts—should not be thought of in a causal-mechanical way. It is not as if the respiratory–circulatory system somehow acted physically in the head region to produce a material modification, and so on. Seeing in the holistic perspective is more a matter of learning to read qualities.

In all the mammals other than the human being these three functional processes occur in a one-sided way which emphasizes one of them over the other two. The difference between the three major groups of mammals—rodents, carnivores, and ungulates—then becomes intelligible in terms of which particular system is dominant.

The rodents (mice, squirrels, rats, beavers, etc.) emphasize the nerve–sense system. This is reflected in the small size of these animals and their restless activity. The trunk and limbs are rudimentary compared with the development of the head, although in many cases the limbs have definitely acquired a sensory function (e.g., the forepaws of a squirrel). The ungulates (horses, pigs, cows, deer, etc.) are the opposite pole to the rodents. These mammals emphasize the metabolic–limb system. This is reflected in the large size of these animals and the elongation of their limbs. Here the metabolic process is so intensified that even the nerve–sense pole of the organism shows the influence of the metabolism in the form of the various head protuberances (horns and antlers). They also exhibit a passive temperament. Finally, the carnivores (cats, weasels, badgers, seals etc.) emphasize the respiratory–circulatory system, which is intermediate between the other two. In their well-proportioned form, in which no one part of the body is accentuated over any other, as well as in their intermediate size, they represent an active balance between the two extremes of the rodent and the ungulate. Their predatory nature fits this intermediate position. A feel for the differences between these groups and the relationships between them can be developed by exact sensorial imagination.

But in any one of these major groups of mammals one of the nondominant systems can also be accentuated to a lesser degree, and this exerts a secondary influence which modifies the influence of the dominant system. It has to be remembered always that the activities of these systems should be thought of as interpenetrating qualities and not as causal mechanisms. In other words, they should not be thought of in terms which are more appropriate for the world of inorganic bodies. Thus, for example, the squirrel is a rodent. In this case the nerve–sense process dominates the other two, but there is a secondary influence from the respiratory–circulatory process which is absent in the case of other rodents like mice and rats. The beaver, on the other hand, is a rodent with the metabolic–limb process exerting a secondary influence on the nerve–sense process. Similarly, among the ungulates, where the metabolic–limb process is dominant, the horse is an animal which is secondarily influenced by the nerve–sense process, whereas the pig is secondarily influenced by the respiratory–circulatory process.

As well as considering specific mammals, it is also possible to distinguish different groups of mammals, each of which is differentiated within itself as a group according to the same threefoldness that is found in the individual. For example, the swine group as a whole is dominated by the metabolic–limb process and has a secondary influence from the respiratory–circulatory process. The pig is the characteristic member of this group because, as mentioned above, it has exactly this pattern of functional processes. But within *the swine group* as a whole there are other mammals which, while they have this pattern of processes, are also further influenced by either the metabolic–limb process or the nerve–sense process. The former is the case with the hippopotamus, and the latter with the peccary—a slender, belligerent pig from South America. This can be seen more easily by referring to the diagram below. Similarly, in the same group as the horse (the odd-toed ungulates) we find the tapir, which is influenced by the respiratory–circulatory process, and the rhinoceros, which is influenced by the metabolic–limb process— i.e., in a group which as a whole is dominated by the metabolic– limb process with a secondary influence from the nerve–sense process. Again, the squirrels form a group as a whole which is dominated by the nerve–sense process and has a secondary influence from the respiratory–circulatory process. The squirrel itself is the characteristic member of this group because, as mentioned above, it has just this pattern of functional processes. But within this group *considered as a whole*, the beaver is the mammal which is further influenced by the metabolic–limb process, and the dormouse is the mammal further influenced by the nerve–sense process—and this mammal in turn is further differentiated into different species according to the same threefold structure of functional processes.

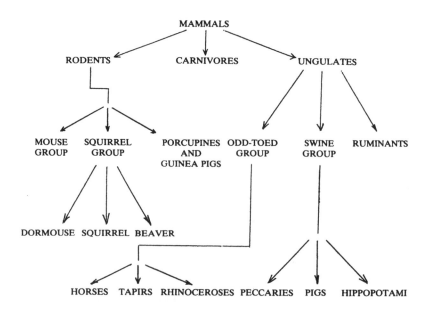

The relationships between the few mammals which have been mentioned here for the purpose of illustration can be represented in the diagram on the facing page. The convention which is adopted is that arrows pointing to the right indicate the influence of the metabolic–limb process, arrows pointing to the left indicate the influence of the nerve–sense process, and arrows which are vertical indicate the influence of the respiratory–circulatory process.[72]

In this way Schad is able to show how the threefold organization of the mammal gives rise to the entire spectrum of the mammalian form—although it is simply not possible to give any idea here of the degree of detail which he goes into with each particular mammal. He shows how the whole form of any particular mammal—including shape, size, and coloration—can be understood in terms of the animal's overall organization, so that the animal becomes intelligible in terms of itself. The same threefold organization which is found in any particular mammal is then found to be present in the various groups of mammals, as well as in the mammal family as a whole. Thus the organization of the mammals *as a whole* is understood in terms of the same organization as the individual mammal, so that the individual can then be seen as a reflection of the whole in the part. In this way Schad's holistic biology of form illustrates and extends Goethe's comment to Eckermann that he understands a particular feature of an organism by looking at the overall organization of the animal. Schad then goes even further, and shows in detail how the environment in which a particular mammal lives also reflects the functional process which is predominant within its own organism.[73] There is therefore a truly organic relationship between a mammal and the landscape in which it dwells. The connection between them has a quality of necessity, and is not simply the contingent result of an external adaptation to circumstances. Even the behavior of such anomalies as the tree-climbing dwarf goat of North Africa can be read as an expression of organic necessity instead of being explained mechanically as a contingent adaptation. Thus the mammal and the environment in which it dwells are perceived as *belonging* together in an organic unity without unification instead of just belonging *together* by force of external circumstances. This organic wholeness of the mammal and its environment is a further dimension of the phenomenon. This discovery is a further illustration of the way that the phenomenologist of nature makes the phenomenon visible.

When it is summarized like this, Schad's procedure can be mistaken for an intellectual schematization of the mammals, as if it provided a set of pigeonholes into which the mammals can be conveniently classified. If this were the case, it would be a reductionist procedure. The details of an organism would be omitted in favor of a broad generalization, resulting in the kind of uniformity which is characteristic of all attempts by the analytical intellect to find unity in multiplicity. But Schad's way of proceeding is the reverse of this. He does not try to group the mammals artificially into an ordered system. The result of his discovery, that the order among the mammals is the same as the order inherent in each mammal, is that Schad sees the mammals in the nonreductionist perspective of "multiplicity in unity" instead of "unity in multiplicity." In other words, he sees the mammals in the light of Goethe's organic vision, which permits diversity within the unity and therefore "in no way contradicts the abundant variety of nature."[74] As each detail is significant because it is an expression of an organism's overall organization, so for this very reason every difference between organisms is significant. Thus, on the one hand, Goethe's organic vision allows difference and uniqueness to be included without falling into sheer multiplicity, while on the other hand it avoids the lifeless unity of uniformity. The difference here is between the perception of multiplicity in a holistic perspective (multiplicity in unity) and the perception of unity in an analytical perspective (unity in multiplicity). It is in the nature of the latter to exclude diversity, whereas it is in the nature of the former to include diversity without fragmentation into unrelated multiplicity. Flexibility is the strength of "multiplicity in unity," as uniformity is the weakness of "unity in multiplicity."

It is through this holistic perspective of "multiplicity in unity" that Schad is able to understand the organism in terms of itself, so that it becomes its own explanation. His work is therefore a vivid contemporary illustration of what Goethe meant when he said, "The greatest achievement would be to understand that everything factual is already its own theory," and "Don't look for anything behind the phenomena; they themselves are the theory." We have seen already that Goethe's phenomenology is equivalent to what could be called the hermeneutics of nature. The aim of this natural hermeneutics is to learn to read the phenomenon in terms of itself. The holistic biology of animal form illustrates this clearly. When the mammal is disclosed in terms of itself, it becomes its own language. This therefore provides us with another concrete instance of Gadamer's principle of universal hermeneutics that "being that can be understood is language."[75]

The Necessary Connection

It was mentioned briefly in "Modes of Consciousness" that a *relationship* cannot be experienced *as such* in the analytical mode of consciousness. Since in this mode it is the elements which are related that stand out in experience, the relationship itself can only seem to be a shadowy abstraction to the intellectual mind. The perception of a relationship *as such* would require a simultaneous perception of the whole, and hence the restructuring of consciousness into the holistic mode. It has been mentioned several times in the discussion of animal form that the phenomenologist of nature perceives connections which have the quality of necessity. Goethe's recognition that an animal with a full set of teeth in its upper jaw *cannot* have horns is an illustration. The perception of a necessary connection is the perception of a relationship as a real factor in the phenomenon, instead of being only a mental abstraction added on to what is experienced with the senses. The reality of a relationship, the necessity of a connection, is not experienced as such either by the senses alone or by the intellectual mind. Hence any attempt to understand this

reality in terms of these faculties is bound to find that it vanishes from the phenomenon itself and appears to be only a subjective belief.[76]

Schad's work abounds with examples of what he calls "the
awesome inner logic of the organism."[77] For example, he
describes how the basic tripartite structure of the teeth (incisors,
canines, and molars) is a reflection of the threefoldness of the
functional processes. Hence he shows, in terms of the animal's
organization, why the rodents accentuate the incisors, the carnivores accentuate the canines, and the ungulates accentuate the
molars. There is therefore a necessary connection between the
predominant functional process in an organism and the structure
of its teeth—and this extends also to the secondary influence
from one of the other functional processes, and so on, in great
detail. Here Schad is able to go further than Goethe and understand in terms of the animal's organization why it is precisely the
upper incisors which are missing from animals with horns. But he
goes even further than this. He shows how the different layers of
skin also reflect the three fundamental functional processes, and
this enables him to go on to discover the "inner logic" of the specific forms taken by the various kinds of head appendages. So, for
example, he is able to understand in terms of the animal's organization why the rhinoceros grows a horn on its snout (and why the
canines are missing in its upper jaw as well as the incisors), why
swine grow warts in the middle of the face along their cheeks,
and why ruminants grow horns from the rear part of the frontal
bone near the back of the head. He subsequently goes on to
understand the difference between horns and antlers, showing
that, far from being random, the otherwise bewildering variety
of antlers can become comprehensible when related to the overall
organization of each of the different kinds of deer. What this
means is that the existence of each of these different kinds of
head appendage is not a contingent fact. They are not accidental
developments, but real necessities which cannot be otherwise.

Because every detail in an organism is a reflection of its basic
organization, there is an intimate correlation among all the

features of a particular mammal. With the ruminant ungulates, such as the cow for example, there is an intimate correlation between the horns and hooves and the specialization of the digestive tract at the anterior end. With rodents, on the other hand, there is an intimate correlation between the tail formation (e.g., squirrel, beaver) and the specialization of the digestive tract at the posterior end. There is therefore a necessary connection between these features. But they are not connected in a causal–mechanical way, like the parts of a watch or even a more sophisticated device with feedback, etc. They *belong* together organically:

> In life, causes and effects take place simultaneously and complement one another. For this reason the organism always presents itself as a whole. Correlations, not causes or aims, determine the order of the life that forms a single whole, because life exists only as a continuing present. The processes of life, therefore, cannot be understood by either causal or teleological ways of thinking; they must be discovered as an active connection existing necessarily among phenomena in the present.[78]

Furthermore, because Schad sees the mammals in the light of "multiplicity in unity," it is inevitable that he finds correlations between mammals in different groups. But he is not constrained to look at these correlations as being accidental, which they would be if the correlated features of the organisms in question had arisen simply as external adaptations to the environment by the mechanism of natural selection. For example, among the carnivores there are some which choose water, either wholly or partially, as a habitat. Looking at these mammals in terms of their organization leads to the discovery of a relationship of form among the mink, the otter, the seal, and the whale. It emerges that what the mink is to the weasel, and the otter is to the marten, so the seals are to the central carnivores (e.g., dogs) and the whales are to the carnivores as a whole. This correlation emerges out of the inner logic of the organisms in question, and hence it is "dictated by internal necessity."[79] So the fact that whales exist, for example, can be seen as an organically necessary expression of the fundamental constitution of the mammal itself; whereas the usual view today is to see the fact that whales exist simply as a contingency, resulting from a long process of external adaptation of a land mammal to life in the sea. Darwin himself said: "I can see no difficulty in a race of bears being rendered, by natural selection, more and more aquatic in their habits, with larger and larger mouths, till a creature was produced as monstrous as a whale."[80] In other words, the fact that whales exist is considered an accident, in the philosophical sense of the term. This misses the dimension of the animal itself. There are many other examples of correlations between mammals in different groups which help to make visible the quality of necessity in the existence of a particular mammal. But there is no need to go into any further examples here.

The assertion that the phenomenologist of nature can find real necessities, i.e., which are in the phenomena themselves and not simply in the mind of the investigator, will seem strange to anybody who is familiar with the history of modern philosophy. The idea that science could discover necessary connections in the phenomena of nature was discarded by many after David Hume's devastating analysis of the principle of causality.[81] Hume's influence on subsequent philosophy has been enormous, and there are many philosophers today who believe that his denial that there are real necessary connections in phenomena which can be known is essentially correct. He reached this sceptical position as a result of following a thoroughly empiricist approach to knowledge. He insisted that ideas are copied from sense impressions and that all impressions, and hence all ideas, are atomic—i.e., separate and independent of each other. For every idea in the mind he asked the question "From what impression is this idea derived?" Applying this to the idea of a necessary connection in matters of fact, he asked what we can observe which corresponds to the idea of necessity? He could find no sense impression from which this idea can be derived, and hence concluded that there is no justification for believing that the idea of necessity corresponds to anything real. All that we actually experience, according to Hume, is the constant conjunction of two events, and it is their habitual association in the mind which gives us the feeling of necessity. In other words, the origin of the idea of necessity is psychological, and the belief that the necessity is real is an illusion. All that the scientist can discover are contingent correlations between phenomena, which therefore might have been otherwise.

By following Goethe's way of science, it is possible to experience what Hume denied to human consciousness when he concluded "that all our distinct perceptions are distinct existences and that the mind never perceives any real connections among distinct existences."[82] Furthermore, through linking Goethe's way with the discovery of two major modes of consciousness, it is possible to see that Hume's sceptical conclusion is a consequence of an extreme identification with the analytical mode of consciousness. What he really did was to describe what knowledge would be like for a purely analytical mode of consciousness. It has already been suggested that such a consciousness could not experience the reality of relationship, since this would require the experience of wholeness. Hence for the analytical mode of consciousness, a relationship could only appear as an abstraction compared with the elements which it relates. Without the experience of the wholeness of the relationship there cannot be any experience of a *necessary* connection. This step is made by a transition to the holistic mode of consciousness, as a result of which we do have the experience corresponding to the idea of necessity, but as an intuition and not as a sense impression.

Goethe's science of nature, because it makes this transition from the analytical to the holistic mode of consciousness, is therefore a practical way of developing the experience of necessity. Hence it gives the experience which is needed to see the limitation that is the cause of a major philosophical problem. Hume was right, as far as his account went. But he was unaware of the *mode* of consciousness as a determining factor in experience, and so he did not know that another mode of consciousness was possible in which the very factor that he found to be missing can be experienced. It has been noted already (see note 49) that the condition of the knower cannot realistically be separated from what is known. It is, of course, a consequence of the analytical mode of consciousness itself to separate these two and consider them in isolation. Developments in modern physics, especially in the quantum theory, have helped to bring into question the possibility of making this kind of separation. A more comprehensive approach is needed, in which the content of cognition and the condition of consciousness for that cognition are considered as a whole.[83]

It seems to be an unexpected by-product of Goethe's way of science, when it is allied with the distinction between modes of consciousness, that it gives an insight into some of the longstanding problems of philosophy. This is therefore a means of approaching philosophy by the way of experience instead of the way of argument.[84] It has already been mentioned above how some of the difficulties over Plato's theory of Forms have arisen through approaching this theory exclusively by the way of argument, which functions in the analytical mode of consciousness and therefore in the extensive perspective of "unity in multiplicity." Yet another example of this experiential way of approaching philosophy now follows from the above discussion of necessity. As well as giving us an insight into the origin of Hume's problem, it also gives us an insight into Aristotle's view of the nature of scientific knowledge. For Aristotle, one of the conditions for something to count as being known is that what is known must be the case of necessity; it is not possible for it to be otherwise. Consequently, scientific knowledge is not knowledge of what *happens* to be true—since this would not be "knowledge" for Aristotle—but of what *cannot* be otherwise and hence *must* be true. This really does seem strange to us now that we have been deeply infected by the empirical tradition, whether we are aware of it or not. It seems to us a matter of common sense that facts are contingent. For example, it seems to be no more than a contingent fact that lions don't have horns—and this is certainly how it seems to biology in the

Darwinian paradigm. We can imagine that it could have been otherwise, or that there could be a lion with horns somewhere yet to be discovered. But we have learned from Goethe's approach to animal form, especially as developed by Schad, that there are many facts about the mammals which superficially appear to be contingent and yet turn out to be necessary when perceived with the intuitive mind. Aristotle would have understood exactly what Goethe meant when, in his remark to Eckermann, he asserted that the fact that the lion has no horns *cannot* be otherwise.[85]

Recently there has been a resurgence of interest in Aristotle's philosophy of knowledge. This is partly a consequence of the work of the American philosopher Saul Kripke, who has argued that there can be necessarily true propositions which describe essential properties of things in the world, and hence which are not merely logically necessary and therefore empty of factual content.[86] Thus he attempts to refute Hume's view that there cannot be propositions which are both necessary and give information about the world. He maintains, for example, that the fact that gold is yellow should not be taken to be contingent, as if the color yellow were an accident, but that it should be taken to be a necessary property which is true "in all possible worlds." There cannot be blue gold—anymore than there can be a lion with horns or a cow with a single stomach. So Kripke arrives at the position taken by Aristotle—and by Goethe. But because he belongs to the school of analytical philosophy, which proceeds by the way of argument, his philosophy does not bring us to *experience* necessity in the world. This remains an intellectual abstraction. Goethe's approach to science, through the holistic mode of consciousness, could therefore provide the intuitive experience of necessity which would complement what can be achieved by means of argument.

Clearly, the understanding of the animal as a whole which emerges from Goethe's organic vision is very different from the way that the animal is understood in Darwin's theory of evolution by natural selection. For the organic perspective, the different features of an animal are expressions of the whole animal and not just useful adaptations. But for Darwinism the animal is a contingency. There is no form of the animal as a whole, with necessary connections which result in an intrinsically intelligible structure. Instead, the animal is conceived as a bundle of features which are considered to be effectively separate and independent of each other, because any one of them is capable of varying independently by chance. Whether such a variation is biologically viable is then determined by the environment, and not by any factors which are intrinsic to the organism. This is the analytical organism which is implied by the mechanism of the Darwinian theory. In other words, it is a constraint of the theory that the animal comes to be seen in this way. In place of necessary connection and wholeness, there is simply contiguity and constant conjunction—it is little wonder that the Darwinian animal has been called a Humean bundle.[87]

Darwin approached the animal in the analytical mode of consciousness. So there is no perception of internal relationships in the organism—as with Newton there is no perception of relationships between the colors. Yet there is clear evidence of a more holistic approach to animal form among the breeders Darwin met. In *The Origin of Species* he refers to breeders who "habitually speak of the animal's organization as something quite plastic."[88] He recounts how in one place "the sheep are placed on a table and are studied, like a picture by a connoisseur," and how it had been said of sheep breeders that "it would seem as if they had chalked out upon a wall a perfect form itself, and then had given it existence." It is just this sense of the organism as a whole which disappeared in Darwin's theory, with the result that "the organism as a real entity, existing in its own right, has virtually no place in contemporary biological theory."[89] However, Darwin himself was not quite so dogmatic as his followers became. In focusing only on what had survival value for the individual and the species, he overlooked the purely morphological study of living organisms. Eventually he recognized this limitation in his approach and said that it was "one of the greatest oversights."[90]

The holistic biology of form shows in abundant detail how misleading the wholesale application of the theory of natural selection can be, because it eclipses those relationships which belong to the organism as a whole. Thus a dimension of the organism is lost. This disappearance of the organism as a whole is even more acute today than it was in Darwin's time, because of the alliance of Darwin's theory with genetics. The result is that the organism has now been replaced by microscopic entities hidden behind the scenes, like the mechanism in Einstein's watch. But now that there is a growing feeling of dissatisfaction with the current evolutionary paradigm, it is beginning to be recognized that an adequate understanding depends on "the reinstatement of the organism as the proper object of biological research; as a real object, existing in its own right and to be explained in its own terms."[91] This is where Goethe began.

•• 4.

The Scientist's Knowledge

In conclusion we will look briefly at Goethe's view on the nature of scientific knowledge itself. In doing so we find an understanding of knowledge which is very different from the way that we understand it today—although it would not have been so unfamiliar to Goethe's contemporaries, and especially not to such philosophers as Schelling and Hegel. We consider knowledge to be a subjective state of the knower, a modification of consciousness which in no way affects the phenomenon that is known, this being the same whether it is known or not. Goethe, on the other hand, saw the knowledge of a phenomenon as being intimately related to the phenomenon itself, because for him the state of "being known" was to be understood as a further stage of the phenomenon itself. It is the stage which the phenomenon reaches in human consciousness. Consequently the knower is not an onlooker but a participant in nature's processes, which now act in consciousness to produce the phenomenon consciously as they act externally to produce it materially. This is the meaning of Goethe's remark that the aim of science should be that "through the contemplation of an ever creating nature, we should make ourselves worthy of spiritual participation in her productions."

If "being known" is a higher stage of the phenomenon itself, then the phenomenon should not be imagined as being complete until it is known. The participatory view of the role of consciousness in knowledge is therefore an evolutionary view, in the widest sense, because the state of "being known" is an evolutionary development of nature itself. When consciousness is properly prepared, it becomes the medium in which the phenomenon itself comes into presence. We call this "knowing the phenomenon," and understand it subjectively. But in a more comprehensive view it *is* the phenomenon itself which appears in consciousness when it is known. This is the ontological significance of intuitive knowledge. The true significance of "theory" now becomes apparent. When the phenomenon becomes its own theory, this is a higher stage of the phenomenon itself. Evidently this does not apply to the kind of theory which is an intellectual framework imposed on the phenomenon by the mind. Thus the phenomenologist of nature himself becomes the apparatus in which the phenomenon actualizes as a higher stage of itself. This brings us to a more comprehensive form of the principle of the wholeness of the apparatus and the phenomenon being investigated (see note 49). In this case the scientist himself becomes the apparatus in which the phenomenon appears. Hence, for the intuitive knowledge of nature, when the phenomenon becomes its own theory, we have the ontological condition that the knower and the known constitute an indivisible whole.

What makes this particularly difficult for us to understand is the extreme separation between subject and object, consciousness and the world, which is characteristic of the onlooker consciousness. This separation is a consequence of overreliance on the intellectual mind and the analytical mode of consciousness with which it is associated. Although this extreme dependence on the verbal–intellectual mind developed over a period of time throughout Western Europe as a whole, it is demonstrated particularly clearly in the writings of Descartes. For this reason he can be taken as representative of the shift in awareness which marks the emergence of modern Western consciousness. Although he is famous for his statement "I think, therefore I am," he is best approached through his first two *Meditations*.[92] Here, in a few pages, he shows how he was led to doubt the existential status of his experience. Since he cannot tell whether he is dreaming or not, he cannot be certain that the world exists, or even that his own body exists. He indicates how he eventually came to experience a feeling of certainty that "I am, I exist" in the act of thinking itself. So he is led to identify himself as a thinking being, and as such he feels himself to be separate and independent from the world, as well as from his own body. Descartes then equated thinking with subjective experience in the widest sense—which subsequently came to be identified with consciousness.[93] Thus the famous Cartesian dualism between consciousness and the world was born, and it is inherent in this dualism that consciousness has the role of onlooker to a world which is outside itself.

It is well known that as soon as Descartes' philosophy is looked into, it rapidly becomes incoherent—and much of modern philosophy has been concerned with the attempt to break away from the Cartesian framework. For example, Descartes identified the world with the property of extension; hence consciousness *must* be unextended. But if consciousness is nonspatial, how can the world be "outside" it? As Gilbert Ryle put it: "What is the External World external to?"[94] Can we even *count* consciousness and world as "two" without thereby reifying consciousness in our imagination, as if it were a ghostly thing, and thus contradicting its essential nature? Even if we ignore these difficulties, as many have, there remains the problem of how two factors which are divorced so exclusively can ever be related. Thus it becomes a problem as to how unextended mind and extended body can interact. Similarly, it becomes a problem as to how the subject can arrive at knowledge of the external world. But any attempt to solve these problems must be self-defeating because it rests on the very assumption which generated them in the first place. Heidegger has called the persistence of the question "How does the subject arrive at knowledge of the so-called external world?" the real scandal of philosophy.[95] In fact, Hume demonstrated over two centuries ago that the attempt to take subjective experience as a starting point ultimately leads to total scepticism about the existence of a self which has that experience. In other words, Hume made the incoherence in Descartes' philosophy fully visible.[96]

Yet the fact remains that this is how we do think of ourselves in relationship to the world. We do have an impression of ourselves as being separate and independent from the world, detached from nature, which puts us in the position of being onlookers. It is this sense of separation that gives us the attitude which is necessary to be able to treat the world as an object to be operated on, manipulated, and organized. In other words, this is the condition of consciousness which is necessary for us to approach the world from our modern technological standpoint, both instrumentally and conceptually. It has been pointed out often enough that it is only by withdrawing ourselves from the world that we can feel sufficiently separate to be able to approach it in a detached way as an object. Subject and object are born together, so that a change in the mode of one necessarily entails a change in the mode of the other. It has also been pointed out equally often how this attitude developed strongly in Western Europe during the sixteenth and seventeenth centuries. It has been mentioned previously how the development of science from Galileo onward was in the direction of *measuring* nature, i.e., concerned with those aspects of nature which can be represented quantitatively. In order to do this it is necessary to organize nature with a network of concepts. The mathematically based physicist then works with these conceptual representations instead of with the perceived phenomena. We are so accustomed to this that we do not realize just how much the physicist inhabits a thought-world of his own making, and hence we identify this thought-world with nature itself. To recognize this needs a shift of attention to make the activity of the mind visible to itself. The mathematical physicist and the industrial entrepreneur are alike in that they are both concerned with the technical–conceptual organization of what they see as "the external world." Both depend on the onlooker condition of consciousness for which it is "common sense" that knowing is a subjective state of the knower and the knower is ontologically separate from the known.

This "onlooker" condition of consciousness is a consequence of emphasizing the thinking activity of the intellectual mind. We can see this quite easily by returning to Descartes. He liked to spend his mornings in bed "meditating" in a thinking kind of way. In this situation his attention was withdrawn from the world, as well as from his own body, and directed into the activity of thinking. Thus, whereas his body was inactive, his thinking activity was by comparison hyperactive. The psychological effect of doing this was to produce an awareness of the world and his body as being outside himself, together with the feeling that he himself existed in this intensified activity of his mind. Hence he experienced a strong sense of being separate from the world and even his body, which therefore seemed unreal compared with his mental activity. Through directing his attention into the thinking activity of the intellectual mind he became an onlooker consciousness. He felt himself to be identified with his thinking activity, and he expressed this feeling that *he* existed in thinking by "I think, therefore I am," or by saying "I am, I exist" as a being whose nature is to think and no more. In fact, as mentioned already, he then widened this to include all of what today we would call "conscious experience." Thus the Cartesian dualism and the onlooker consciousness are *psychological* consequences of emphasizing the verbal–intellectual activity of the mind. Descartes' philosophy is therefore a projection of the psychological state which he produced in himself. In other words, he made himself into a psychological apparatus for producing the Cartesian philosophy. Once again we find that a more comprehensive approach is needed, in which the content of cognition and the condition of consciousness for that cognition must be considered as a whole. Evidently this is just what the *onlooker* consciousness cannot do. But Descartes' philosophy must be considered even more comprehensively. It is also an expression of a cultural–historical situation, which it simultaneously helped to produce, and not merely the subjective expression of an isolated individual.

It is inevitable that when Goethe's understanding of scientific knowledge is seen through Cartesian spectacles it seems to make knowledge into something entirely subjective. Goethe's view could be called "organic" because it sees knowledge as a further development of the phenomenon itself. In point of fact, a more organic understanding of knowledge preceded the modern period, although this is often missed because of the inevitable tendency to look back towards earlier periods with the perspective of the onlooker consciousness. Owen Barfield, for example, draws a parallel between Goethe and Aristotle. Pointing out that the primal phenomenon of color and the organic archetypes are neither objective nor subjective, he says:

> They come into existence as types, or as laws, only as they are intuited by human beings. And until they have so come into being, the object itself is incomplete. Knowledge in fact, so far from being a mental copy of events and processes outside the human being, inserts the human being right into these processes, of whose development it is itself the last stage.[97]

He sees this as being parallel to Aristotle's conception in *De Anima* of the reality (*eidos*) which only exists potentially (*dunamei*) until it is known, and when it is known it has its full existence actually (*energeia*). Aristotle's understanding of knowledge was elaborated further by Aquinas in the Middle Ages.[98] But this organic understanding of knowledge, which sees it as a mode of participation in the phenomenon, was not restricted to the Aristotelian tradition. Gadamer reminds us that "this involvement of knowledge in being is the presupposition of all classical and medieval thought." So the philosophers of these earlier periods conceived "knowledge as an element of being itself and not primarily as an attitude of the subject."[99] If we look on this "involvement of knowledge in being" as a remnant of primitive animism, this in itself is an indication that we are perceiving it with the Cartesian attitude of the onlooker consciousness.

After the emergence of the onlooker consciousness as the dominant attitude of modern Western culture, the perspective of the knower as a participant in the known became an underground minority viewpoint. Whenever it came to the surface, as it did from time to time, it was usually misunderstood because it was interpreted in the perspective of the onlooker consciousness. Goethe's own period in Germany was such a time. The organic

understanding of knowledge emerged in the Romantic movement, post-Kantian philosophy, and the philosophical approach
to nature (*Naturphilosophie*). It was from his contact with the
philosopher Schelling, for example, that Goethe learned how his
own way of science exemplified a participatory way of knowing
nature. Schelling held the view that in knowing nature the scientist produces nature—which looks like an extreme form of
subjective idealism to the onlooker consciousness. It was in the
light of what he learned from Schelling that Goethe subsequently expressed the aim of his science to be that "through the contemplation of an ever creating nature, we should make ourselves
worthy of spiritual participation in her productions."[100] As the
waves of influence from these movements spread outwards in
space and time, they inevitably became more diluted, eventually
degenerating into romanticism and sentimentality.[101] It is surprising to discover how widespread the influence of the organic
understanding of scientific knowledge was—even if it was sometimes only sentimental. For example, we find the man we usually
think of as a hard-headed Victorian materialist, T. H. Huxley,
contributing Goethe's prose aphorisms on nature as the opening
article for the first number of the weekly science journal *Nature*.
Huxley commented: "It seemed to me that no more fitting preface could be put before a journal, which aims to mirror the
progress of that fashioning by Nature of a picture of herself, in
the mind of man, which we call the progress of science."[102]

As stated in the introduction, the real value of Goethe's way
of science is independent of any comparison, favorable or otherwise, with the mainstream of science. Also, the value of Goethe's
way is not to be found in whatever individual discoveries he
may have made. The real value of his original approach to science is that it is a new way of doing science, and a new way of
seeing nature as a whole. As such it belongs to the present and
not to the past. It is an original event of perception in which we
can learn to participate. By seeing how the philosophy of
Goethe's way of science is illuminated by contemporary European philosophy, and especially how the psychology of this

science is clarified by recent research into the psychology of consciousness, we can begin to recognize that this is an authentic way of science in its own right. The science which belongs to the intuitive mind and the holistic mode of consciousness can reveal aspects of the phenomena of nature which *must* be invisible to the verbal–intellectual mind and the analytical mode of consciousness. No matter how sophisticated today's institutionalized science may become, or how much further it may be developed, it will still be concerned predominantly with only the quantitative aspects of phenomena. No matter how beautiful, elegant, and harmonious the equations may be to the mathematical physicist, the fact remains that the variables in the equations represent quantities. Hence science today is concerned with only one aspect of the phenomena, and there are other aspects which cannot be reached in this way. Goethe's way of science, by contrast, can be seen as the science of quality instead of quantity—but we need to have the corresponding experience to understand what this means.[103]

At a time when, once again, some physicists are saying that the key to the universe is in sight, it may be useful to be reminded that the science in which they work is only one-dimensional, and that there are aspects of the phenomena to which it is blind. To be able to see these other aspects there would need to be a transformation of science itself. But this needs a transformation of the scientist. The result of such a transformation would be a radical change in our awareness of the relationship between nature and ourselves. Instead of mastery over nature, the scientist's knowledge would become the synergy of humanity and nature. The historical value of Goethe's work, in the wider sense, may be that he provides us with an instance of how this can be done. If this should turn out to be the historical significance of Goethe, then our present science will be only a phase in the development of science. Goethe will then be seen as a precursor of a whole new way of science, for which, to quote Goethe himself, he will be "an instance worth a thousand, bearing all within himself."

PART III

Understanding Goethe's Way of Science

.. 1

Introduction

The growth of understanding more often comes from opposition than from agreement. We feel that our views, which seem to us so evidently true and complete, meet not with the acceptance we expect, but with disagreement, rejection, caution, or simply indifference. If we take this opposition as something to be fought against, argued away, or just shrugged off, then the opportunity which it represents for the growth of our understanding is lost. We become a fixed, dogmatic kind of person. But if we encounter this opposition as a resistance to be worked with, then it becomes our point of application. Taken in a more positive spirit, opposition to our views becomes the means of development whereby our understanding is enhanced, instead of, as it seems at first, threatened. We are taken further by this opportunity in a direction which we would not have found ourselves, instead of being overcome by it. Our previous understanding, which we took at first to be the end of the story, is now seen as only a beginning, a stage on the way which is to be incorporated as part of a further, more comprehensive viewpoint.[1]

For Goethe, the development of his understanding of his own way of science took place through his friendship with Schiller, as well as through the resistance which his contemporaries showed toward his work on color. Goethe's friendship with Schiller was remarkable in that it was a friendship of opposites—Goethe spoke of them as "spiritual antipodes, removed from each other by more than an earth diameter."[2] Yet twelve years after Schiller's death, Goethe wrote about the occasion of their first meeting in an essay which he entitled "Happy Encounter." He recognized and understood that, no matter how irritating this opposition was to him at first, it was through Schiller that he began to become aware of his own "way of seeing" as such.[3] Before that time, Goethe had been epistemologically naïve. He had believed that what he saw was "just there" as he saw it, so that seeing it was a visual experience which did no more than reflect what was present already in a purely factual way. In other words, at this stage Goethe's philosophy of science was a very naïve empiricism. What Goethe discovered as a result of his encounter with Schiller, with his Kantian background, was the active role in all acts of cognitive perception of what he called a *Vorstellungsart*, a way of conceiving, or a mode of illumination, whereby the world becomes visible in a particular way. He realized that different *Vortstellungsarten* would result in the world being illuminated differently, and hence being disclosed in different modes.[4]

As Goethe became more aware of the contribution which the *way* of seeing, or mode of illumination, makes to *what* is seen, he began to understand more adequately the reason why his early "Contributions to Optics" (1791) did not have the impact on the scientific community he had expected. He had believed that physicists would simply repeat his experiments and their truth would be evident. Accordingly, they would replace Newton's color theory with a new understanding grounded in the phenomena in the way that he showed. When this did not happen, and his work was in fact either ignored or rejected, he eventually responded by undertaking a deeper investigation of the science of color, which meant following through the historical development of this science, as well as pursuing his own experimental work. It was through his historical investigations that Goethe came to recognize the role of *Vorstellungsarten*, the ways of conceiving, in the very constitution of scientific knowledge. This, he realized, was at the basis of the scientific community's rejection of his work on color. The

Vorstellungsart of this community he saw as being atomistic, mechanical, and mathematical, whereas his own way of conceiving was genetic, dynamic, and concrete. Because of this difference, he concluded that an atomistic intelligence would find nothing at all wrong with Newton's theory of color.[5] Thus Goethe came to realize that science is not empirically founded in the naïve way he had imagined it to be. He discovered that the foundations of science are historical instead of empirical, and hence that scientific knowledge is *intrinsically* historical instead of merely factual. Far from being accidental to it, the history of science *is* science. As Goethe himself said, "We might venture the statement that the history of science is science itself." This is an astonishing discovery to have made at that time! It was not until the 1960s that the intrinsic historicity of science began to be generally recognized, although not without considerable opposition from the long-established, ahistorical philosophy of science which went under the name of positivism.[6] What Goethe came to realize is that in science, as in art, truth is active and not passive, as the dogma of factualism implies. It is not the passive registration by an onlooker of what is there as such, independent of the scientist. The scientist is an active participant in scientific truth, but without this meaning that truth is thereby reduced to a merely subjective condition.[7]

What I propose to do in this part is to look at Goethe's way of science in the light of the process of cognitive perception and the organization of scientific knowledge, and then in the light of the historical development of modern science. By this means we shall come to understand Goethe's own understanding of his pathway in science, and how it differed from the understanding of science which had become the majority viewpoint. But we shall be able to go further in understanding Goethe's science than he was able to do himself at the time, because of the discoveries in the philosophy and history of science which have been made more recently. So we shall attempt to understand Goethe's science in a way which parallels his own understanding, but in the context of the new philosophy and history of science. We will find that this more comprehensive understanding brings out the relevance of Goethe's way of science for us today. In Gadamer's terms, this part, like the previous one, is intended as a contribution to the "effective history" of Goethe's pathway in science. It is not an account about what is past, but an attempt to participate in the working out of Goethe's science today.[8]

The Organizing Idea in Cognitive Perception

We begin by looking into the act of knowing the world. There are two major difficulties here. First, there is the difficulty that the process of knowing the world happens very quickly, so that it is over before we can catch it. This problem can be overcome to some degree by having recourse to situations in which the normally smooth-running process breaks down, so that the process of knowing is revealed instead of just the result of this process. This is the way that we shall proceed below. The second difficulty is much more awkward to deal with and cannot be done so directly. This arises from the fact that we ourselves are part of the process of cognition. We are participants, and not onlookers outside of the process. But also the *way* that we are participants in the process of cognition is not quite how we imagine it to be. We are participants in a dynamic and genetic way, not in a static and finished way. The inner dynamic of the process of cognition is also an inner dynamic in the process of the self. What this means is that the "self-entity" itself emerges *from* the process of cognition and is not there *as such* beforehand. To our everyday consciousness it seems evident that we are a self-entity which is present *before* cognition (to our everyday consciousness it also seems evident that the Earth is at rest). So, in trying to understand cognition, we start from what is really a result of the process of cognition.

Hence we get it all backwards. Georg Kühlewind has recognized that since we are not conscious of the *process* of cognition, but conscious only of the *result* of this process, our everyday consciousness is really "past consciousness." We are conscious at the level of the past and not the present, i.e., conscious at the level of finished perceptions and not of the process of their coming into being.[9] So our ordinary thinking is "too late": we are already the past of ourselves. Therefore any account of the cognitive perception of the world which *begins* with a self-conscious subject, conceived as a self-entity, is an account which begins from the final phase of the process of cognition. This is what we do when we describe cognition as if it took the form of a separate, independent subject confronting an equally separate, independent object, i.e., the Cartesian mode of subject–object separation.

The difficulty which this presents is not one which can easily be tackled directly—certainly not without radical innovations in grammar and style of expression, which would make the account less readable and thereby only obscure the point which it is intended to make. We shall therefore begin by simplifying—which inevitably means also distorting. Later we shall then try to correct for distortions due to simplification. This will involve some degree of circularity in the exposition, as we return to take a new view of points made previously. Cognitive perception is not a process which maps conveniently into a single line of development.

With this proviso, we can now look at cases of disrupted cognitive perception, where what is normally hidden by the smooth running of the process is now revealed by a breakdown. We have to find cases where the process of knowing the world is temporarily suspended in midflow, as it were (*in statu agendi*).

If we look at the picture on page 50, what we see at first is just a chaotic assemblage of black and white blotches.[10] But when we are told that there is the head of a giraffe to be seen here, then we soon see it. To begin with, we have to make an effort to see the giraffe, and when we cease the effort the picture reverts to its previous random appearance. Quite quickly we can reach the point where we can switch seeing the giraffe on and off. After that the stage is reached where it becomes harder to switch it off, so that we can no longer "not see" the giraffe.

But what is the difference between the two cases? Whether someone sees or does not see the giraffe, what is there on the page is exactly the same set of marks. They do not move about and reorganize physically on the page at the moment when the giraffe is seen! This means that the purely sensory aspect of the experience of seeing, the stimulus to the organism received via the light, must be the same whether the experience is of seeing a giraffe or not. What is different in the two cases is the seeing experience, and not what is on the page. There is in fact no giraffe on the page, although there seems to be one when it is seen there. When it is seen "there," we can tell the familiar "empiricist story" about seeing being the the experience of sensory impressions which are caused in the organism by stimuli from the "outside world." According to this widespread viewpoint, seeing the world is a purely sensory experience. But what happens to this story when the giraffe isn't there, and yet the array of visual stimuli is the same? The answer is that, contrary to empiricism, the giraffe is in the seeing and not out there on the page. More precisely, the giraffe *is the way of seeing* which sees the giraffe. When we see the giraffe, we are *seeing it* —think of "seeing" actively, as a mode of doing, instead of passively as a state of the organism. The page is the terminus of seeing, and so this is where we see the giraffe. But the giraffe which we see is really the *way of seeing* the random blotches. The *way* of seeing and *what* is seen cannot be separated—they are two poles of the cognitive experience. When it is said that the figure which is seen is in the seeing, and not "there" as a sensory object, this does not mean that it is present in the seeing in the manner of a mental picture or image which is being projected, as if it were a "mental transparency." To think this way is backwards. A mental image or picture is a cognitive after-image, left behind *after* the act of seeing. Such an image *is* formed by abstraction from concrete experience in the way that the empiricists imagine. But this process is *not* the origin of ideas that they believe it to be—Hume, for example, believed that ideas were faded copies of sense impressions. The empiricist starts out from the finished product, the end of the process of cognitive perception, and tries to understand the entire process in terms of its end point. This is like "trying to get to the milk by way of the cheese."[11] The dynamic approach, on the contrary, tries to catch the cognitive process *in process*, so that it flows with the coming-into-being of cognitive perception instead of starting from the finished product, i.e., from *what* is seen. For this approach, seeing is the *act* of seeing.

Look at the well-known ambiguous figure on the right on page 51, and imagine two people, one of whom can see only the duck and the other only the rabbit. Now imagine a third person who can see neither, but only a squiggly mark on the page. The duck-seeing person *sees* the duck, and the rabbit-seeing person *sees* the rabbit. Neither of them projects a mental picture of a duck or rabbit, as the case may be, onto the figure. There is no experience of having a mental picture separate from the figure, and then bringing it together with the squiggle on the page. All three are looking at the same thing, having the same pattern of sensory stimulus on the retina, and yet each is seeing differently. If asked to draw what they see, they will each draw the same shape. They can only draw the visual appearance, and not what they see even though they will each believe they have drawn what they see. The duck-seeing person *sees* a duck, and so on. The *difference* between them is in the way of seeing, from which *what* is seen cannot be separated, and they cannot draw this difference. We *see* what we see.

What we have discovered so far is that, literally, there is more to seeing than meets the eye! We usually think of seeing in a passive way, as something which just *happens* to us when our eyes are open (as if it could be reduced to mechanical causation). But seeing cannot be equated with visual experience. There is also an extra, nonsensory factor as well as the sensory stimulus when we see. It is this nonsensory factor which makes the difference between seeing a duck or seeing a rabbit, where the sensory stimulus is the same in each case. The difficulty in catching this factor, and recognizing that it is not provided by the sensory input, i.e., not part of the *visual* experience, is that when we see the giraffe, for instance, we think that we *do* see it entirely by our sense of sight. It looks to us as if it were a sensory experience and no more. Discovering the nonsensory factor in cognitive perception is like discovering the movement of the Earth: it is difficult to make it visible and easy to "prove wrong" by appealing to immediate experience. But we could go on having the same visual experience and not *see* the giraffe.[12] The *extra* factor, which turns the visual experience of random black and white blotches into seeing a giraffe, will not come (*cannot* come) from more and more visual experience. There is a qualitative change, a discontinuity, in the experience. Something new enters which can never be derived from sensory experience alone—how could anyone derive the giraffe *from* the visual experience of the black and white blotches?

The first thing we can say is that there is a change in the *organization* as we go from the visual experience of black and white blotches to seeing a giraffe. When we can see the giraffe, the blotches are organized in a characteristic way instead of randomly. There is now a *distinction* between the marks, whereas before they were all equivalent. Thus some of the marks are seen as contributing to the giraffe, and others as not doing so, instead of all being of the same value. Yet there is evidently no change whatsoever on the page—the black and white blotches do not physically rearrange themselves! The organization is not actually there on the page, even though we see it there. If it were, it too would only be part of the sensory stimulus.[13] As we have recognized already, there is no giraffe on the page, even though we see it there—we *see* it there.

The giraffe is in the seeing—it *is* the seeing (we could say that we see "giraffely"). So the organization of the black and white blotches is *in* the seeing. But "organization" here must be thought of actively, i.e., as *organizing*, as an organizing *act* (an act which *is* organizing), and not as a state of organization, i.e., the condition of having been organized. Thinking in the mode of coming-into-being, instead of in the mode of the finished product, means we have to think verbally instead of thinking in terms of the noun.

We have found a nonsensory factor—the organization—but this now leaves us with the question of *what* it is that organizes the blotches in the act of seeing. The answer is that it is an idea. It is an idea which organizes the sensory stimulus into *seeing* instead of just a visual appearance. In the illustrations above, it is the giraffe idea (*not* the idea of a giraffe), the rabbit idea, and so on. There is an *organizing idea*—this is what an idea is: *organizing*. The idea organizes because an idea is active—an idea *is* its activity, and this activity is organizing. Brentano said, "by 'idea' I mean the act of conceiving, not that which is conceived"—to which he might have added, for the sake of the empiricist, "and not a mental image abstracted from that which is conceived."[14] We could paraphrase this directly, in terms of the discussion above, as "by 'organization' we mean the act of organizing, not that which is organized," to which we should add that there is no separation *within the act* between the organizing act and that which is organized. It is clear from Brentano's statement that we should not think of an idea as if it were some kind of entity, a content of the mind, which is what we tend to do in the English-speaking tradition. An idea is active, and the active idea *is* its activity. The term "active idea" must not mistakenly be read as in any way implying a separation between the idea and the action—they are one and the same. We must not think of the active idea as if it were an idea-entity which acts. The idea *is* the action. An entity cannot act, because an entity is already too late, being the stage of "solidification" which marks the end of activity. The tendency to think this way is a particular instance of what can be called the "intellectual illusion," which imagines that an action is initiated by an entity, e.g., a self, which exists independently of, apart from, and prior to the action. The difficulty which this presents to us is that where our thinking usually begins it is already too late. We have to go to the stage prior to our usual awareness, which has the effect of reversing the direction of our thinking so that we can recognize that we usually begin from what is, in fact, the end. This refers to what was said earlier about the difficulty that arises from the fact that we are not conscious in the act but only conscious of the result: we are conscious at the level of that which is organized but not of the organizing act. To be conscious at the level of the organizing act would need a participant mode of consciousness instead of the onlooker mode. This would take us to a stage prior to our usual mode of consciousness.[15]

What has been said above, about not thinking of an idea as if it were some kind of entity, also means that we must guard against another common tendency. This is also a consequence of starting from the wrong end, with the finished product, instead of trying to catch the process "in the act." This is the error of thinking of the idea as a mental picture, as if it were a thought in our heads which we add on to the blotches, applying it to them externally, as it were. This is the error of intellectualism.[16] We don't add on the giraffe intellectually by thinking about it. The giraffe is the organizing idea in the seeing. We could almost say that it is the seeing idea, to emphasize that it is *not* the idea of what is seen (i.e., a mental picture). Equally, as mentioned before, the idea is not something we see through, as if it were some kind of "mental transparency." Here again, if we think this way, we miss the idea "in the act" and try to begin from the stage of the finished product, projecting this back in imagination to the earlier stage. This is yet another instance of trying to "reach the milk by way of the cheese."

Now the point of all this is that such organizing ideas are active in our everyday cognitive perception of the world. So this shows us what the everyday process of seeing the world is like, which we are usually unaware of because there is no disruption to the process. For example, consider seeing a chair. We imagine this is just a straightforward case of sense perception and no more. But the chair we are seeing is not a sense perception any more than the figures we have discussed above. Imagine people from a society where there were no chairs—where the very idea was missing. Such people *could not* see a chair, even though they may be looking at the very same chair we are seeing and their senses are in perfect working order. They would have a visual experience, but could in no way see what we see directly: a chair. The chair is not the sensory object we take it to be. The chair is in the seeing—it is the organizing idea. Of course, there is a material object present which has all kinds of physical properties, but these do not include a property "chair," which is experienced by sense perception. Seeing the chair is a cognitive perception, not just a sense perception, and we see the chair when we see in a chair way (when we see "chairly"). Thus "the chair" is the way of seeing. This applies to everything that we see about us.[17]

There is a strongly prevailing prejudice, usually associated with the empiricist frame of mind, in favor of the idea that "direct apprehension" of the world would be achieved by "pure sense perception." This state is taken to be one which is achieved by taking away all conceptualization—as if ideas formed a film between us and reality which stops us from seeing what is really there "in itself." Then, it is believed, we would "see reality directly." One reason for this prejudice has already been indicated above. We tend to think of an idea as a kind of mental entity, like a mental picture or image (the noun form predisposes us this way), whereas we should really think of an idea as the *act* of conceiving (cf. Brentano's statement referred to above). Mental pictures and images *can* come between us and what is there, but the *idea* is in fact the act of seeing what is there. Far from coming between us and some supposed external reality, the idea (understood as the act of conceiving) *is* the direct apprehension of what is there.[18]

To illustrate that our perception of reality *is* normally direct, David Best considers the example of looking at a chessboard.[19] This would not be seen more directly by someone from a society in which the game of chess was unknown, as the "pure perception" theorists would have us believe. Such a person could not see the chessboard more directly than a person from a chess-playing society. In fact, people from a society where chess was unknown could not see a chessboard at all! They would see only the variously shaped pieces of wood, etc. The chessboard which is seen is in the seeing and not *as such* an object of sense perception, although it seems to be so at first because we do not experience our participation in the process of cognitive perception and, as explained above, experience ourselves as if we were onlookers confronting a world which is "out there" separate from ourselves. What appears in the act of seeing is "what it is," which is the chessboard in the above example. As Best says, "Someone who suffers a total loss of memory does not, as a consequence, understand reality *directly*. On the contrary, he understands nothing. For example, he could no longer directly see a tree, since he no longer knows what a tree is." Eliminating all concepts would not therefore achieve a direct encounter with the world. On the contrary, it would only achieve the end of the world.

We have to be careful not to fall into a false dualism here. We don't experience the sensory factor separately as such, nor do we experience the organizing idea separately as such. The *experience* which is cognitive perception is the coalesence of the organizing idea with the sensory factor. We experience neither on its own—they are inseparable ingredients in the cognitive experience.[20] This coalescence is the experience of *meaning*. But we must be careful here not to think of meaning as if it were added on to what we see. The coalescence is the meaning which *is* what we see—the meaning which it is—not the meaning *of* what we see. What we see *is* meaning: we see "what it is" directly.[21] Meaning, which is the coalescence of the organizing idea with the sensory, is therefore always individualized.[22]

We take what we see in cognitive perception to be simply material objects which we encounter directly through the senses. But what we take to be material objects are really condensations of meaning. When we see a chair, we are seeing meaning and not having a purely visual encounter with a material object. The error of empiricism is that it mistakes meaning for a sensory object, a mistake which has been recognized by Owen Barfield as an instance of idolatry—it could be called "cognitive idolatry."[23] The world which we encounter in cognitive perception is really a text and not a set of material objects. They are material objects, of course—otherwise how could somebody sit on a chair! But they are more than this, and it is this "more" that we see. The material ingredient of the world is only the script. So the material chair is the script which, in the act of cognitive perception, we read as "chair." But the meaning is no more there in the material chair than the meaning of "chair" is there in the letters of the word which appear on the page.

We miss the dimension of mind which is active in our lives, and it is the job of philosophy to make this dimension visible to us.[24] The dimension of mind in cognitive perception is as invisible to us to begin with as the movement of the Earth. Just as it seems so evident to us that the Earth is at rest, so does it seem evident to us that everything we see about us is "just there," i.e., object instead of meaning, and that cognitive perception is just sense perception. We are accustomed to thinking of mind as if it were inside us—"in our heads." But it is the other way around. We live *within* a dimension of mind which is, for the most part, as invisible to us as the air we breathe. We usually only discover it when there is a breakdown.[25]

When we miss the dimension of mind in cognitive perception, we inevitably mistake the nature of ideas. Instead of beginning with the role of the organizing idea which is active in cognitive perception, we think of an idea as a mental picture, an image, drawn off or abstracted from our experience in the world. So, instead of talking about "the 'table' idea," we talk about "the idea of a table." Whereas the former refers to the organizing idea, the latter indicates much more a mental picture of a table. Now there certainly are ideas in this sense, too, but they are secondary, or derivative, and not primary. They encourage us to get everything backwards:

(1) We miss the organizing idea "table" which is active in the cognitive perception of a table;

(2)   we believe we see the table directly, by the senses alone;

(3)   then we form the idea of the table by abstraction (the mental picture);

(4)   and finally, from many such "ideas," we find what they have in common by a process of comparison and further abstraction which eliminates differences, and this is how we finally arrive at the concept "table."

But the concept "table" is, of course, the original organizing idea (which was missed at the beginning, as noted in point 1 above) that is actively organizing the perception of the table in the first place. This is therefore the "rabbit in the hat" version of the origin of concepts. We can only recognize *any* table in the first place by means of the concept, i.e., the "table" idea. To be able to see *one* table is already to be able to see all tables, i.e., all *possible* tables. So the notion that the concept comes, in the first place, from finding what is common to many tables is far too late. We do not derive concepts *from* experience.[26]

The concept "table" is *constitutive* and not abstract. It is the possibility of table. We are accustomed to thinking of possibility as abstract and less real than actuality. But when we begin to understand what the concept (the organizing idea) is, then we realize that in this case "higher than actuality stands possibility."[27] However, there is no preformation in the idea. The possibility of table—or, better, the table possibility—must not be thought of as if it were the set of all possible tables. This is "finished product" thinking, which proceeds by falsely imagining the total actualization of all tables, and back-projecting this into the idea in the vain attempt to "reach the milk by way of the cheese." But possibility cannot be derived *from* actualizations in this way. The attempt to do so gets it backwards: possibility is *higher* than actuality. Perhaps a better approach (though also ultimately inadequate) would be to think of possibility like a multivalent figure—like the duck/rabbit, or the reversing cube, but multivalent instead of bivalent. Such a figure has the advantage that each picture is wholly the figure, and not part of it, and yet no one picture exhausts the figure. Similarly, each table possibility is wholly a table, and not part of one, and yet no one table exhausts the possiblity of table. The disadvantage is that this, too, can suffer from the fallacy of preformation, as if each picture-possibility were there already formed. It tries to represent possibility in terms of actuality, and thereby misses the possibility which is higher than actuality. To avoid this we would have to imagine an indeterminate multivalent figure which spontaneously produces the different figures which it is, which means that it is intrinsically dynamic and self-productive. The form which such a multivalent figure would have, which is the same as the form of possibility, is "multiplicity in unity." This does not mean that unity is divided into parts in an extensive sense. There is diversity *within* unity, but not division *of* unity. This has been referred to in part II of this book as the prenumerical, intensive dimension of One.[28] The organizing idea, the concept, has this form of "multiplicity in unity," and not the form of "unity in multiplicity" which it would have if the concept were simply what is common to many particular instances. The concept is not a generalization, which would exclude difference. It is possibility, which includes difference in such a way that in becoming other it remains itself.[29]

The difference between these two approaches to what an idea is can be summarized schematically:

PASSIVE MIND	ACTIVE MIND
• the idea of a table	• the "table" idea
• idea as mental picture (Hume—faded copies)	• idea as act, (Brentano—the act of conceiving)
• secondary, derivative idea	• primary, original idea
• mind as a screen or space on (in) which images are formed	• mind as productive act
• we recognize this idea because we are onlookers	• we miss this idea because we are participants
• "finished product" thinking (static)	• "coming-into-being" thinking (process)

Broadly speaking (although such stereotypes can be misleading), the left-hand column is more typical of English-speaking philosophers, whereas the right-hand column is more typical of Continental philosophers. We can recognize the classical empiricism of Locke and Hume on the one hand and the phenomenology of Husserl on the other.

Finally in this section, before going on to the role of the organizing idea in scientific knowledge, we must correct a distortion which may have arisen as a result of simplifying. This concerns the meaning of "organizing" as this term is used in "organizing idea." The meaning here is not the same as when we talk about organizing a pile of bricks, say, into an ordered arrangement, or any situation where the organization is imposed on something. This way of thinking is too late. What we are concerned with here is the *emergence* of organization rather than its imposition.

The "organizing" of the organizing idea is an act of distinguishing which is *simultaneously* an act of relating. The one act *is* both of these together, whereas we usually think of them as two different acts because we start at the end, with the finished product. The primary *act* of distinguishing does not point out something which is already "there." It "theres" it! Thus the concept, or organizing idea, does not apply to something which is already present. It "presences" it. The concept delineates or defines the "something" in the first place—"It is the concept that tells us where 'something' has its boundary."[30] The concept "boundaries"—it is an act of boundarying. So the act of distinguishing is the "presencing" of what is *thereby* distinguished and does not merely separate what has effectively been distinguished already. "Distinguishing" and "separating" are often confused as a result of not following the coming-into-being of distinction, and beginning instead with the finished product, i.e., the already distinguished, in which case distinction can only appear as separation. But this is a secondary mode of distinction which presupposes (usually unnoticed) the primary, original distinction which delineates that which *consequently* can be separated.

When we follow the coming-into-being of distinction in this way, we notice that distinguishing has the effect of relating. To mark out "something," to give a boundary to "it," is *thereby* to relate it to that from which it is distinguished—i.e., to distinguish "something" is *at the same time* to distinguish what is "other" by virtue of that very distinction—and to which it is thereby related. The point here is that the relation is *intrinsic* to the act of distinguishing, and not an external connection between separate "somethings" which have already been distinguished. This means that the relation is a necessary relation, and not contingent, as it would be if it were an external connection.[31]

What we notice here is that, at this stage, the act of distinguishing is holistic and not analytical. This is surprising at first, because we are accustomed to think of distinguishing as a separating action, and hence as being manifestly "analystical" (*lysis:* "to separate"; *ana:* "from above"). So we do not expect to find a holistic quality in the act of distinction. But we only find this if we try to catch distinguishing in the act. If we do not (and we usually don't), but instead attend to *what* is distinguished, then we become aware of separation. Then we do not notice the integrating, relating aspect of distinguishing, and so inevitably we think of distinguishing analytically, i.e., as externally separating one from another. But this is really separating the already distinguished, so that the primary or original act of distinguishing is missed. Once again, this is because we are too late. "Separating" is how distinguishing appears in the plane of the past and not in the living present of the *act* of distinguishing.

There is the *one* act of "distinguishing which is relating," and not two separate acts: distinguishing *and* relating. This one act takes place in "opposite" directions simultaneously. This polar movement, intrinsic to the primary act of distinguishing, is *before* analysis and synthesis, which come later, at the secondary stage of separating and then unifying. Analysis and synthesis are two separate acts. The original "distinguishing which is relating" falls apart into analysis and synthesis as the act of distinguishing falls into "separating the already distinguished."

This is a fall from the living present of the process to the dead past of the product. It is because our ordinary consciousness is ontologically at the level of the past that we miss this simultaneous polar movement of "distinguishing which is relating," which is *before* analysis and synthesis. We are always too late.[32] However, we can experience the primary stage of distinguishing, before it becomes separating, by learning to free attention from *what* is seen, so that it shifts into the seeing activity itself. If this happens, we become aware of the *appearance* of what appears instead of *what* appears.[33]

In this study, "organizing" is used in "organizing idea" to mean the primary act of "distinguishing which is relating," and not the secondary operation of ordering what is already distinguished. It is useful to remember this in what follows.

•• 3

The Organizing Idea in Scientific Knowledge

S cience is also concerned with the cognitive perception of the world, albeit in a more comprehensive way than our ordinary, everyday cognitive perception. We could say that science is a higher level of cognitive perception. But there cannot be any fundamental difference between science and its everyday counterpart. The intrinsic features of the process of cognition must be the same wherever it occurs. So, contrary to widely held belief, science is not a special activity which is uniquely different from all other kinds of cognitive activity. It is *epistemologically* no different from the everyday process of cognitive perception, and therefore everything which has been said about this must apply equally to science itself.[34]

All scientific knowledge, then, is a correlation of *what* is seen with the *way* it is seen. When the "way of seeing" is invisible—as it is in the naïveté of what Husserl called "the natural attitude," which just takes the world for granted—then we live on the empirical level where it seems to be self-evident that discoveries are made directly through the senses. In this "natural attitude" we have no sense of our own participation, and hence we seem to ourselves to be onlookers to a world which is fixed and finished. Forgetfulness of the way of seeing is the origin of empiricism, which is still by far the most popular philosophy of science, in spite of all the discoveries in the history and philosophy of science which show that it is a philosophy of cognitive amnesia. This is certainly the philosophy of science which is usually communicated, often implicitly, by the way that science is taught in schools and the way that it is presented in popular books. What is missing from all such accounts is the active role of the organizing idea.

THE ORGANIZING IDEA IN OBSERVATIONAL DISCOVERIES

The difference between the cognitive and the empirical approaches to understanding scientific knowledge can be illustrated in the first place by observational discoveries. Typical examples are found in astronomy. An excellent one is provided by Galileo's telescopic discoveries. In this case we can compare the account which is given in popular histories of science with the one which Galileo himself gives in his book *Siderius Nuncius*.[35] We read in modern books that Galileo pointed his telescope at the heavens and saw mountains and valleys on the Moon, satellites around Jupiter, and spots on the Sun. We are told that these new phenomena were observed by him through his telescope directly, and we are naturally left wondering why there were so many who were opposed to him initially and derided these discoveries. Surely, all they had to do was to look through the telescope, and they would see for themselves. What Galileo's own account makes clear is that he did not see any of these features immediately on looking through the telescope. He only came to see them subsequently, and in each case doing so entailed a change in the way of seeing as a result of the action of an organizing idea in perception.

In the case of the Moon, what he actually saw was a larger number of spots than could be seen with the naked eye. These were small and numerous, compared with the much larger ones with which everyone was already familiar. So "what Galileo actually *saw* through the telescope was a collection of spots of two sorts."[36] This was the visual data. It is not, of course, *pure* visual data, since to see "spots" is already to have a nonsensory factor, i.e., the concept, in the perception. *This* was the visual data that anyone at the time could have experienced on looking through the telescope, not mountains and valleys. The visual data here is similar to the hidden giraffe before the giraffe appears. Eventually this visual data was transformed by Galileo into the cognitive perception of mountains and valleys (the interested reader will have to consult the accounts referred to in notes 35 and 36 for details). *This* is the discovery—which is similar to the experience of seeing the giraffe. It is evident that the discovery is a change in the way of seeing because of the intrinsic action of an organizing idea in perception. The discovery of mountains and valleys is in the seeing which *sees* mountains and valleys on the Moon, not in the reception of the visual data—"discovery is not a matter simply of accurate sensory perception."[37]

Galileo's discovery of the satellites of Jupiter is a case which is similar to the duck/rabbit. What he saw on January 7, 1610, was three stars close to Jupiter:

East   •   •   O   •   West

He believed "them to be among the number of fixed stars."[38] The following night, January 8, he found a different arrangement:

East   O   •   •   •   West

All three stars were now to the west of Jupiter, closer to each other than on the previous night, and separated by equal intervals. He tells us that he began to wonder whether Jupiter was not moving eastwards at the time, contrary to the computations of the astronomers. The next night was overcast. But the following two nights, January 10 and 11, he saw a different arrangement again:

East   •   •   O   West

East   • •   O   West

Then his cognitive perception was transformed into seeing "entirely beyond doubt, that in the heavens there are three stars wandering around Jupiter like Venus and Mercury around the Sun." He goes on to say, "This was at length seen clear as day in many subsequent observations, and also that there are not only three, but four wandering stars making their revolutions about Jupiter."[39]

It is clear from this account that the discovery is not a purely sensory experience of a visual appearance. The transformation which Galileo describes is a change in the way of seeing as a result of the action of an organizing idea—the *change* in the way of seeing *is* the action of the idea. The visual appearance remains the same, but *what* is seen, the meaning, is entirely different—this is the meaning which *is* what is seen, not the meaning *of* what is seen.[40]

Failure to notice the dimension of mind which is intrinsic to observation leads us to think we can pinpoint an observational discovery as if it were a point-event. Thus, for example, we believe that the planet Uranus was discovered by Sir William Herschel at a particular moment in 1791. But compare this with the following account of the discovery:

> On at least seventeen different occasions between 1690 and 1781, a number of astronomers, including several of Europe's most eminent observers, had seen a star in positions that we now suppose must have been occupied at the time by Uranus. One of the best observers in this group had actually seen the star on four successive nights in 1769 without noting the motion that could have suggested another identification. Herschel, when he first observed the same object twelve years later, did so with a much improved telescope of his own manufacture. As a result, he was able to notice an apparent disk-size that was at least unusual for the stars. Something was awry, and he therefore postponed identification pending further scrutiny. That scrutiny disclosed Uranus' motion among the stars, and Herschel therefore announced that he had seen a new comet! Only several months later, after fruitless attempts to fit the observed motion to a cometary orbit, did Lexell suggest that the orbit was probably planetary.[41]

So who discovered the planet Uranus, Herschel or Lexell? The textbooks and the popular history of science tell us it was Herschel. Yet he saw a comet! Once we recognize that an observational discovery is not made through the senses alone, in the way that we might imagine, then we can see the origin of the difficulty here. An observational discovery is a cognitive process, and not an instantaneous point-event. As well as the sensory aspect, there is also a nonsensory factor in cognitive perception. The discovery is the perception of meaning which is the coalescence of these two factors. If we try to catch the coming-into-being of a discovery, instead of beginning from the finished product, then we can recognize that the discovery is a structured process. But when we begin from what has been discovered, the intrinsic dimension of mind is hidden. This results in a distortion in our understanding of what a discovery is—a distortion which affects the way we read the history of science, as we have seen in the example above.[42] When the dimension of mind which is intrinsic to observation is covered over, then we get what amounts to the *Flatland* story of discovery.[43]

The role of the organizing idea in cognitive perception is of such an active kind that if the idea changes, then *what* is seen changes. In this case what is seen is changed *from within the seeing itself*, and not by the addition of a further sensory factor. The new organizing idea makes it possible to see what was not seen before. The transformation can be dramatic. An illustration of how dramatic this can be is also provided by Galileo, but this time from his work on the kinematics of projectiles. It is well known that he showed the trajectory of a projectile, such as a cannonball, to be a curve with the form of a parabola. But it is only after he had introduced the *idea* of this that people *saw* the path of a projectile, such as a cannonball or an arrow, to be curved. What is seen "lights up" as "what it is" in the light of the idea. The idea is the light which allows *what* is seen to appear as such. Before Galileo's discovery, pictures of the trajectory were drawn like the illustration at the top of the next page. This fits the theory of motion which was believed at the time.

But this does not mean that what was seen was the (post-Galilean) trajectory we would see today, and that the drawing was made to fit the theory of the time contrary to what people actually saw. The organizing idea of the Aristotelian theory of motion resulted in *this* trajectory being seen. We should also consider the fact that, for most observers, the trajectory would look like this because they would be behind the projectile and in the same line, not facing it from the side, as in the diagram.[44] But after Galileo's discovery, the organizing idea in the observation had changed, and a different trajectory was seen and drawn:

As indicated above, it wasn't that before Galileo people didn't look carefully enough. They saw what they saw in the light of an organizing idea. Galileo saw in the light of a different organizing idea, so what he saw was different. A change in the *way* of seeing means a change in *what* is seen.

In fact, whether or not something appears at all depends on the action of an organizing idea in perception. Oliver Sacks describes his experience of coming to recognize Tourette's syndrome. He was surprised, after first seeing one Touretter, to see three the next day in downtown New York within the space of an hour. He was surprised because he knew that Tourette's syndrome was said to be extremely rare. He recounts that he began to wonder if it was possible that he had been overlooking Tourette's syndrome all the time—perhaps just not seeing such cases. "Was it possible that everyone had been overlooking them? Was it possible that Tourette's was not a rarity, but rather common—a thousand times more common, say, than previously supposed?" The next day, after seeing two more Touretters in the street he supposed to himself "that Tourette's is very common but fails to be recognized, but once recognized is easily and constantly seen." Sacks then mentions the similar case of muscular dystrophy:

> A very similar situation happened with muscular dystrophy, which was never seen until Duchenne described it in the 1850s. By 1860, after his original description, many hundreds of cases had been recognized and described, so much so that Charcot said: "How come that a disease so common, so widespread, and so recognizable at a glance—a disease which has doubtless always existed—how come that it is only recognized now? Why did we need M. Duchenne to open our eyes?" [45]

The answer to this question is to be found in the process of cognitive perception itself. As we have seen, there is more to seeing than meets the eye, and the extra factor is the action of the organizing idea. Without this we cannot see what is there. However, we must not think of something which is seen *for the first time* as if it were there already *as such*, i.e., as if it had already become visible but simply was not being seen. Seeing it for the first time "there's it," so that it becomes visible. This means that it comes into the realm of the visible from the invisible, so that it appears and thus comes to be as such.[46]

The failure to notice the dimension of mind which is intrinsic to observation leads directly to the most popular misunderstanding of scientific knowledge, namely, naive empiricism—which could also be called "factism." This is the view that there are "facts," which are independent of any ideational element and to which we have "direct access" by sense perception. Such facts, it is believed, constitute the basic data ("the given") of science. The scientific procedure, according to this view, is to begin by collecting such facts by "pure observation" (i.e., idea-less observation). Only then, when the facts are known independently of any ideas, does thinking begin.

Thinking then organizes the facts and seeks to explain them by means of a theory, which can be tested by means of further observations and experiments. A view of scientific procedure which is commonly associated with this image of science is "inductivism." This purports to show that scientific laws are empirical generalizations reached by abstracting what is common to a number of observations. David Hume showed long ago that scientific laws *cannot* be derived from facts in this way.[47] This is not a possible pathway for science. But to Hume's reason for rejecting induction as a basis for discovering scientific laws from facts, we must now add that in any case facts are not what they are assumed to be by the empiricist philosophy of science. Far from there being direct access to the facts by sense perception alone, there is actually a nonsensory factor in every fact. Far from being idea-less, there is an organizing idea in every act of cognitive perception. In Feyerabend's vivid metaphor, observational terms (and hence facts) are "Trojan horses."[48] For the same reason, there cannot be an independent test of a theory, if by this is meant an idea-less, purely sense-perceptible encounter with nature, which can be compared somehow with the theory to decide whether it is true or false. The so-called correspondence theory of truth is based on a mistaken view which is still "alive and well" in the teaching of science in schools and colleges, often hiding implicitly in the way that science is taught, in spite of the belief which philosophers of science may have that it has been thoroughly discredited.

THE ORGANIZING IDEA IN THE THEORIES OF SCIENCE

Science is more than just observational discovery. It involves a much more comprehensive level than this. But at whatever level it is taken, we always find that the key factor is an organizing idea. The core of discovery is always the organizing idea and not the sensory input. At a more comprehensive level than we have looked at hitherto, for example, there are such scientific discoveries as the moving Earth and inertial motion. These are often wrongly presented as if they were simply observational discoveries (or in the latter case, observation augmented by experiment). But this is far from being the case, as we will see below. Ideas such as the "moving Earth" idea or the "inertial motion" idea organize scientific cognition and research in the same way that the "chair" idea organizes cognitive perception of a chair. Historically, they function as new organizing ideas for scientific cognition. They were not derived *from* observations (or from experiments) any more than the concepts in everyday cognition can be derived from sense experience—or the giraffe could be derived from the black and white patches. These are theoretical ideas of science, and as such they function at a higher level of organization than the organizing ideas of everyday cognition, but otherwise they are no different in kind.

Copernicus and the Moving Earth

We will begin by exploring briefly the discovery which can be placed at the beginning of modern science: the discovery that the Earth moves, rotating on its own axis and revolving around the Sun. This discovery is due to Copernicus, who made it public in his book *De Revolutionibus Orbium Caelestium*, which was published in 1543. The term "discovery" is used here in the conventional way. But this hides an ambiguity in the use of this term when we extend it beyond the kind of observational discoveries discussed so far (and even there we found ambiguity—in the discovery of Uranus, for example). The point here is that, contrary to what is so often believed, Copernicus's discovery was *not* based on observation. In fact, the observational evidence was not attained until 1838.[49] When this "discovery" was announced by the publication of Copernicus's book, not only was there no observational evidence *for* it, but there was a considerable body of evidence *against* it. On top of which, there were other weighty reasons for rejecting what Copernicus said, which came from physics, philosophy, and theology (which were by no means separated from each other at the time). But, above all, there was (and is!) the inescapable fact that the movement of the Earth is plainly contradicted by the immediate experience of the senses. There would be very few indeed at the time who would look at the proposal of a heliocentric universe, with its moving Earth, as a discovery. Yet gradually it came to be accepted, so that by the time the observational evidence became available, it was almost superfluous.[50] A scientific discovery of this kind is a complex cultural–historical process, which cannot be pinpointed at one moment in time. What comes to count as a "discovery" does not begin as such, but is socially constituted. The recognition that something is a discovery constitutes it as a discovery—it is not a "discovery" before it is recognized as such. Rather than something which happens at a particular instant, like a natural event, a discovery is a social event which seems to have an extended present moment of its own.[51]

At the time, there seemed to be very good reasons for rejecting what Copernicus said. It should perhaps be added that many of these would still seem to be good reasons today, if we did not "know" that what Copernicus said is true. Our belief system effectively renders such objections inoperable—not because we know how to answer them (unless we have studied physics), but because they would no longer be raised. First and foremost there is the evident fact that our senses inform us unequivocally that the Earth is at rest. A little thought should soon discover what would seem to be inevitable consequences of a moving Earth, none of which are to be found. In fact everything is exactly as it would be if the Earth were at rest. If the Earth moved, any object not attached to the Earth would be left behind. An object dropped from the top of a tower, or the mast of a ship, would not fall at the foot of the tower or mast. A person jumping up and down would land far away from the point he or she jumped from. But worse than these inconveniences, everything on the Earth's surface would be hurled off it by the Earth's rotation like a stone from a sling. Evidently the Earth does not move!

But there are other compelling reasons, as well as common-sense physics, for believing that the Earth is at rest and in the center of the universe. There were good astronomical reasons.

The problem of parallax, or rather the lack of it, has been mentioned already (see note 49). But correlated with this, there is the fact that the Earth's central position in the universe can apparently be derived from the observation that the horizon for any observer on Earth bisects the sphere of the stars.[52] The system of physics accepted throughout the period before Copernicus was the one developed by Aristotle. This physics provided a coherent way of seeing the phenomenon of change in the various forms that it takes in nature. Aristotle's physics is anything but speculative (in the derogatory sense). It is much more concrete and experiential than the mathematical–experimental physics which later replaced it, and once prejudices are put aside it is easy to see why it was so influential.[53] Many modifications were made to Aristotle's physics during the later Middle Ages, but none of them ever suggested moving the Earth away from the center of the universe. This notion was so fundamental to the cosmological scheme based on Aristotle's physics, that the attempt to displace the Earth from the center would require the rejection of the entire system of physics. This, of course, is what happened. However, at the time this was a very weighty objection to any proposal which entailed moving the Earth from the center of the universe.

But more than physics and astronomy were involved here. There were also strong theological reasons for a stationary Earth at the center of the universe. Albertus Magnus, followed by his pupil, Thomas Aquinas, had worked to reconcile Aristotelian physics and cosmology with the Bible. The thoroughness with which this was done resulted "in the creation of a new fabric of coherent Christian doctrine," so that "during the last centuries of the Middle Ages the setting of Christian life, both terrestrial and celestial, was a full Aristotelian universe."[54] The central, stationary Earth became a pillar of the new Church theology, and since everything in this system of thought was interconnected in an internally coherent fashion, "Moving the Earth may necessitate moving God's Throne."[55]

When we add together all these objections against a nonstationary, noncentral Earth, we may well wonder what advantage

Copernicus's innovation could have had for it to have superseded the existing account of planetary motion. The fact of the matter is that, to begin with, it had none! It is an extraordinary historical fact that a theory which had no immediate advantage, and many disadvantages, eventually succeeded in becoming the mainstream, orthodox theory of planetary motion. It is not a matter of some supposed "scientific method" deciding one way or the other; criteria of falsification/verification do not enter into it. The progress of this initially most unlikely theory can only be understood historically and not scientifically—as this term is usually understood, i.e., as referring to an ahistorical method for attaining "truths" which is autonomous and independent of all cultural factors. To take Copernicus's innovation beyond the point that he was able to reach required a commitment to his idea which went far beyond the lack of evidence for it at the time. Such commitment has no place in the standard view of the development of science.[56] The answer to the question of how the Copernican theory succeeded is a historical answer, and not a scientific one, if by "scientific" is meant the application of a self-contained methodology with its own intrinsic logic.

The scheme of astronomical computation which Copernicus replaced had enjoyed a long and successful history. The origin of the method employed is unclear, but it was at least eighteen hundred years old by the time of Copernicus. Because of the major contribution made by Ptolemy (about 150 C.E.), it is often referred to as Ptolemaic astronomy. In this system, the complex motion of the planets, as seen against the background of the stars, is calculated on the basis that, no matter how it appears, the motion of a planet is always fundamentally movement in a circle at a constant rate.[57] The geometrical techniques of major and minor epicycles on a deferent, eccentrics and equants, were all developed to show quantitatively how complex planetary motions could be understood in terms of circular motion. It was very successful: "For its subtlety, flexibility, complexity, and power the epicycle-deferent technique . . . has no parallel in the history of science until quite recent times."[58]

But gradually, as time went on, there were those to whom it seemed the system was becoming too subtle, too flexible, and too complex. Copernicus's aim was to reduce the complexity, and he tried to show how this could be done geometrically by inverting the position of the Sun and the Earth (and moving the Moon around the latter). On this basis, Copernicus was able to dispense with the need for major epicycles, because the retrograde motion of the planets was now understood as only an apparent motion, when the planets were viewed against the background of the stars from a *moving* Earth. This was his major achievement. Kuhn points out that "with respect to the apparent motions of the Sun and stars, the two systems are equivalent, and the Ptolemaic is simpler."[59] But he then goes on to say that with regard to the planets, "this apparent economy of the Copernican system, though it is a propaganda victory that the proponents of the new astronomy rarely failed to emphasize, is largely an illusion."[60] If this comes as a surprise to us, it is because we view Copernicus's achievement from the other end of the story, when the difficulties which Copernicus himself was unable to resolve had been overcome. But if we attribute this achievement to Copernicus himself, then we present his work as being unproblematic, and we obscure the *historical* nature of the development of scientific knowledge (what this means will become clearer below). The seven-circle system which Copernicus presents in the first part of his book, and which is presented in elementary treatments today, is certainly very simple. But it does not predict the positions of the planets with an accuracy comparable to Ptolemy's system. Although he got rid of the major epicycles, Copernicus had to introduce minor epicycles and eccentrics in order to achieve quantitative results comparable to Ptolemy. Kuhn draws the conclusion:

> His full system was little if any less cumbersome than Ptolemy's had been. Both employed over thirty circles; there was little to choose between them in economy. Nor could the two systems be distinguished by their accuracy. When Copernicus had finished adding circles, his cumbersome Sun-centered system gave results as

accurate as Ptolemy's, but it did not give more accurate results. Copernicus did not solve the problem of the planets.[61]

So there still remains the question of where the commitment came from which was needed to develop this system beyond the point which Copernicus himself was able to reach. At the end of the letter to the Pope which Copernicus prefixed to his book, he mentions the possibility that his work might contribute to the reform of the calendar, which was a concern of the Church at the time. He indicates that it was the need for this which had led him to consider such radical proposals. In actuality, the Gregorian calendar, adopted in 1582, was based on calculations which made use of Copernicus's work. However, this in itself does not mean that Copernicus's theory came to be accepted as a physically true theory—as it stood it couldn't possibly be physically true with all the complications he had needed to introduce just to achieve results comparable to Ptolemy. It could have been adopted simply as a computational device. Such an attitude towards schemes for calculating the planets was quite common at the time, and the unsolicited and unsigned extra preface which Osiander added to Copernicus's book said this was how the Copernican scheme could be taken.[62] But it *wasn't* accepted ultimately, or even originally, as just such a device—though no doubt this is how it was used in connection with the Gregorian calendar. It was accepted as a physically true theory, and to find the root of the commitment to the Copernican theory that made this possible against all the difficulties, we have to go a bit deeper into Copernicus himself.

We can begin by looking further at what Copernicus says in his prefatory letter about how and why he came to make such radical proposals. Apart from some specific technical and mathematical–aesthetic objections to Ptolemy's scheme, he says of the mathematicians:

> Nor have they been able thereby to discern or deduce the principle thing—namely the shape of the Universe and the unchangeable symmetry of its parts. With them it is as though an artist were to

gather the hands, feet, head, and other members for his images from diverse models, each part excellently drawn, but not related to a single body, and since they in no way match each other, the result would be monster rather than man.[63]

Now this is the very thing which Copernicus claims to be able to do as a result of his proposal that the Earth moves:

> I have discovered that, if the motions of the rest of the planets be brought into relation with the circulation of the Earth and be reckoned in proportion to the circles of each planet, not only do their phenomena presently ensue, but the orders and magnitudes of all stars and spheres, nay the heavens themselves, become so bound together that nothing in any part thereof could be moved from its place without producing confusion of all the other parts, and of the Universe as a whole.[64]

Copernicus can discover the harmony and unity of the whole as it had never been shown before, by the expedient of ascribing motions to the Earth. What this tells us is that the harmony and the unity of the whole mattered very much to Copernicus; it mattered so much in fact that he was prepared to move the Earth to achieve it. How he came to be able to do this, he tells us, was by returning to the works of earlier astronomers before the establishment of the mathematical tradition which culminated in Ptolemy. Here he discovered a number of references to the moving Earth. He mentions Heraclides, amongst others, who considered that the Earth rotated on its axis. But he fails to mention that Heraclides also considered that Mercury and Venus revolve about the Sun instead of the Earth.[65] He does not mention Aristarchus, which is very surprising, because if he "took pains to read again the works of all the philosophers on whom I could lay hand" then he could not have missed Aristarchus.[66] It is now quite customary to refer to Aristarchus as the Copernicus of antiquity because, as well as the rotation of the Earth on its axis, he added the further movement of the Earth around the Sun—in fact he seems to have had all the planets moving round the Sun in the center. But, as Marshall Clagett points out, it would perhaps be preferable to call Copernicus the Aristarchus of modern times.[67]

The new philosophy and history of science which have developed over the past thirty years have come to recognize the way that scientific knowledge is situated in historical traditions. Far from beginning with pure observation, any natural science of the modern period is constituted within a historical tradition. The new history of science makes this context visible, whereas the practice of science often covers it over and thereby distorts our understanding of science. What we discover with Copernicus is not new observations and evidence, but a new way of seeing observations and data which had themselves long been familiar. The discovery is a new organizing idea, which sets what is known into a new pattern of relationships and thereby changes its meaning. But this transformation of meaning is brought about by incorporating into science a body of ideas which are drawn from a historical school of thought, and not by any of the procedures which are today recognized as being specifically "scientific." Copernicus believed that the problem of planetary motion could not be solved by any further work within the accepted system of ideas because it was that system of ideas itself which needed to be changed. There is no way that such a change can be brought about by further observation, no matter how carefully done, and so what Copernicus did was to turn to a different historical tradition for the new organizing idea. The new theory emerged from a school of thought, not from new facts.[68]

The alternative tradition to which Copernicus turned is one which was inspired in him, and many Renaissance scientists, by the movement of humanism. The humanists were very much opposed to the Aristotelian tradition of learning in the universities, and they tended to reject the activity of natural science as being one which it was unprofitable for people to pursue while they are still ignorant of what was for them the most important thing, viz., knowledge of human nature. Yet, although the humanists were against science, through their concern with the ancient sources which were newly recovered, they introduced many ideas which greatly influenced the development of modern science. Foremost among these were the ideas which are clustered under the name of Neo-Platonism, which includes what is also called Neo-Pythagoreanism.[69] Copernicus was introduced to this school of thought by his teacher in Bologna, Domenico de Novara, who was a close associate of the Florentine Neo-Platonists—who were at a later time to influence Galileo (see "Galileo and the Moving Earth," below). Several of the main ideas of Neo-Platonism are woven through Copernicus's book. Once we recognize them, we can begin to see the extent to which the revolution in science was the result of the influence of a major school of thought, and not the work of a handful of scientists working on their own independently of any cultural, social, or historical context.

There are four main ideas of Neo-Platonism woven together throughout Copernicus's work. For convenience, we will consider them separately.

(1) *The Earth moves—and therefore is a planet.* We have seen already that Copernicus did not discover this directly himself, "from the facts," but that he found it in the ancient sources to which he turned. Now we discover that this idea of a moving Earth belongs to a school of thought, and hence that it is part of a continuous historical tradition. When we know this, it gives us quite a different perspective than when we believed that it was discovered by Copernicus on his own.

(2) *The Sun is of central importance in the universe.* It is the source of light and life, and the symbolic representative of God— and therefore is unique and *not* a planet. The only place which is compatible with the Sun's creative and symbolic role is in the center of the heavens. This is how Copernicus refers to the Sun:

> In the middle of all sits Sun enthroned. In this most beautiful temple could we place this luminary in any better position from which he can illuminate the whole at once? He is rightly called the Lamp, the Mind, the Ruler of the Universe; Hermes Trismegistus names him the visible God, Sophocles' Electra calls him the All-seeing. So the Sun sits as upon a royal throne ruling his children the planets which circle round him.[70]

(3) *The true order of the world is found by going beyond the senses, even by going against them.* Copernicus, as we have seen, does this in the way that he explains the daily rotation of the heavens (the Earth rotates), and the gradual motions of the Sun and planets around the ecliptic (the Earth moves around the Sun). These motions, so evident to common sense, are but appearances to the senses and as such are illusory and misleading for Copernicus. The true order contradicts this, and once it is discovered, many otherwise disparate observations fall into place as natural consequences of a single cause, viz., the Earth moves.[71] Galileo, who also came under the influence of the philosophy of Neo-Platonism, said this about the senses:

> I cannot sufficiently admire the eminence of those men's wits, that have received and held it to be true, and with the sprightliness of their judgments offered such violence to their senses, as that they have been able to prefer that which their reason dictated to them, to that which sensible experiments represented most manifestly to the contrary. . . . I cannot find any bounds for my admiration, how that reason was able in Aristarchus and Copernicus, to commit such a rape on their senses, as in despite thereof to make herself mistress of their credulity.[72]

Such a statement can only come as a considerable surprise to those of us who have unwittingly accepted the view that modern science began when human beings "came to their senses" and left theoretical speculation behind in favor of the evidence of the senses. Confusion here arises from realizing that the beginning of modern science came when people experienced a new awakening of interest in the world encountered through the senses, an interest in the natural world instead of religious matters, but failing to realize that the science of the "sensory world" which was developed was not derived *from* the senses. The modern science of the natural world is not a sensory science. This is in fact what Goethe tried to do. He developed a natural science which *is* sense-based, and, as such, stays close to the sensory, dwelling within it instead of going beyond it.[73]

(4) *The true order of the world, which is reached by going beyond the senses, is a mathematical harmony consisting of simple arithmetical and geometric relationships.* The unity of the universe is mathematical, and, as such, it is discovered by the intellectual mind. According to Neo-Platonism, this mathematical unity is the ultimate reality of the phenomenon itself. The influence of this aspect of Neo-Platonism on Copernicus can be recognized in several of the quotations already given above. His complaint against the Ptolemaic astronomers, that they had not "been able thereby to discern or deduce the principle thing— namely, the shape of the Universe and the unchangeable symmetry of its parts," is a good example. When he says that "the orders and magnitudes of all stars and spheres, nay the heavens themselves, become so bound together that nothing in any part thereof could be moved from its place without producing confusion of all the other parts and of the Universe as a whole," this is an expression of the attitude of Neo-Platonism towards the unity of the whole. After the statement of the role of the Sun quoted above, he goes on to say, "So we find underlying this ordination an admirable symmetry in the Universe, and a clear bond of harmony in the motion and magnitude of the Spheres such as can be discovered in no other wise,"[74] which is a clear expression of the Pythagorean stream of Neo-Platonism. This statement is followed by the long list of phenomena (see note 71) which "all . . . proceed from the same cause, namely Earth's motion," which we can see clearly expresses the Neo-Platonist emphasis on simplicity. The notion that the business of science is to discover simple mathematical relationships in nature, which will reduce many phenomena which would otherwise be merely a multiplicity to a single cause, and thereby discover simple harmony in nature, is a fundamental contribution of Neo-Platonism to the growth of modern science.

For the Neo-Platonist philosopher, the mathematical provides an intermediate realm between the imperfect and changing world of the senses and the perfect and unchanging world of pure spirit. Mathematical relations concerning triangles and circles, for example, are true independently of any particular triangle or circle. They are properties of pure triangularity or circularity and cannot be drawn as such. Yet any triangle or circle that is drawn must reflect them imperfectly inasmuch as they *are* triangular and circular. Thus each triangle or circle participates simultaneously both in the intelligible and the visible.[75] This is how Copernicus understands the mathematical harmony of the Sun and attendant planets. As we saw above, he speaks of this system as a "most beautiful temple" with the Sun which is the representative of God in the center. In 1560, the architect Paladio wrote that the beauty of a temple will result "from the correspondence of the whole to the parts, of the parts among themselves, and of these again to the whole; so that the structure may appear an entire and complete body, wherein each member agrees with the other and all members are necessary for the accomplishment of the building."[76] How remarkably similar this is to Copernicus's statement that if the motions of the planets be brought into relation with the movement of the Earth, "the orders and magnitudes of all stars and spheres, nay the heavens themselves, become so bound together that nothing in any part thereof could be moved from its place without producing confusion of all the other parts and the Universe as a whole."[77] Copernicus meant it to be taken literally when he said that the solar system is a beautiful temple. He was not just speaking metaphorically, as we might at first have supposed. It is the mathematical harmony that he discovered which makes this possible.

Copernicus's new system of the planets fits smoothly into the Renaissance aesthetic, of which it can now be seen as one expression. In discovering the distance from Earth to Sun to be the common measure, the symmetry *(sym + metria),* in terms of which the whole coalesces, he disclosed the cosmos as a temple for the living God in the same way that the Renaissance architect understood a temple and the anatomist and the artist understood the human body as a temple. By recontextualizing Copernicus in this way, we see him no longer as an isolated individual but as being of a piece with his time. Consequently, his revolution in planetary astronomy no longer appears as an isolated event, but as a development which is intelligible in the cultural–historical context of its time.

Now we can see the source of Copernicus's commitment to his theory in the face of all the objections to it, and the evident inadequacy of his scheme as far as he had been able to develop it before publishing. The Copernican universe was really a new overall organizing idea which had its roots in a school of thought, and not in new empirical discoveries. The theory is not founded on observation, but in a new way of seeing which is incorporated into science (literally) from an extrascientific source. So the foundations of the Copernican revolution are historical, and not "scientific" in the sense that they are the result of an autonomous methodology. This does not mean that Copernicus's theory should not be considered to be scientific. It means that, so far as its origin is concerned, it does not conform to what we usually think "scientific" means. We must therefore change our understanding of what science is to be in accord with what practitioners of science do, and not expect what they do to conform to what we think science ought to be. This means recognizing the intrinsically historical character of scientific knowledge, and hence coming to recognize with Goethe that "the history of science is science itself."

It was the commitment to this new organizing idea which made it possible for others to develop the Copernican scheme further. Kepler, in particular, was able to go forward in an unprecedented way because of this. His insistence that the Sun *must* be in the center, and must be the guiding power of the system of planets, entered so deeply into his work that it guided practical strategies of working right down to the details. Far from being a superficial philosophical decoration added on to Copernican astronomy, and therefore scientifically superfluous, Neo-Platonism was an effective guiding idea for a whole research program.[78]

It looks at first as if what Copernicus discovered was not new facts, but a new way of seeing the facts which were known already. Yet it is more subtle than this. Putting it this way implies that the facts are like bricks, which are just rearranged into a different structure. Rearranging a pile of bricks into a new structure does not change the bricks. But this does not hold for facts which are reorganized according to a new way of seeing. In this case the facts are changed in a subtle way. Before Copernicus it was a fact that the Sun is a planet; after Copernicus the Sun is not a planet but a unique body with special powers and significance in the universe. Before Copernicus the Earth was a unique body; after Copernicus the Earth is no longer a unique body but a planet— and hence to be counted in the same category as Mars or Venus. So the new organizing idea does not just take "astronomical bricks" and change their arrangement from a Ptolemaic one into a Copernican one. The "astronomical bricks" are changed in the process, and this is because the new organizing idea changes the concepts, so that there is a comprehensive change in meaning. Thus, the concept "planet" itself is changed, so that there is a change in the meaning of "planet." It is not simply a matter of redistributing heavenly bodies among categories with invariant meanings. So if we want to talk about reorganizing the data, we have to remember that the facts, too, are modified. The facts themselves are transformed in the new way of seeing. There is no more elementary level where we can find immutable data. As Kuhn says, "What occurs during a scientific revolution is not fully reducible to a reinterpretation of individual and stable data. In the first place, the data are not univocally stable."[79] So if we are going to talk about the new idea as "reorganizing" the facts, then we must understand this as a *creative* reorganization because it does not simply reorganize already existing elements but changes their meaning. The failure to notice this, and the consequent tendency to think in terms of an external rearrangement of already existing elements (the data), is another instance of beginning from the finished product instead of following through the coming-into-being.

When we do follow the coming-into-being, then we recognize that the new organizing idea is a new beginning—"planet,"

"Earth," "Sun," "Moon" are *new meanings*, not the same elements rearranged. Furthermore, the new meanings cannot be
derived *from* the old meanings, otherwise it would not be a new
beginning.[80] Thus we come to recognize that the new organizing
idea is a genuinely *creative* idea. So, whereas it is true that there
are no new facts in Copernicus's discovery, it is also true that the
facts are not the same facts after Copernicus that they were
before. The facts are *changed within themselves* as a result of the
new meanings, which are correlative with the new way of seeing. This change is internal to the facts, unlike the external
addition of new facts. When we recognize this transformation of
the facts, we discover for ourselves the *primacy* of meaning, and
see that meaning cannot be derived from anything which is
other than meaning (i.e., from nonmeaning).

Galileo and the Moving Earth

Galileo's work on the science of motion provides a beautiful
illustration of a change in meaning which transforms the facts
from within. Here again, there is an organizing idea which does
not simply rearrange data which are themselves invariant with
respect to the way of seeing. There is a new way of seeing—new
meaning, which in the first place entails *seeing differently*,
instead of seeing different things. Such a transformation of
meaning is a change in "the possibility of experience" instead of
an additional experience.

It has often been pointed out that, to begin with at least,
Galileo is concerned with familiar facts about motion and not
with new, previously undiscovered facts. Yet this way of putting
it can often treat the facts of motion as if they were like bricks
which are just rearranged into a different pattern, a Galilean pattern instead of an Aristotelian one. It hides the way that the facts
of motion are transformed as a result of the change in meaning of
"motion" that is at the core of Galileo's new way of seeing.
Because Galileo changed the concept "motion," his new science
of motion is a *creative* rearrangement of the facts of motion. So it
is a new beginning. We will explore this step of Galileo's briefly,

because of the way that it illustrates so clearly the development of scientific knowledge, and how this is very different from the empiricist's account of science.

As we have seen previously, the problem with the Copernican hypothesis is that, in terms of both common sense and the physics of the day, the motion of the Earth ought to be all too evident by its consequences. Objects which are not attached to the Earth should be left behind—clouds, birds, and the like. The air left behind by the Earth's rotations should result in a very strong wind near the surface of the Earth. To travel to the west the traveler would merely need to jump up and down, and the west would eventually arrive at his or her feet. Rocks, trees, animals, and people would be hurled from the rotating Earth like stones from a sling. Evidently, none of these supposed consequences of the Earth's movement are observed to happen. In fact, bodies move on the Earth in just the way that they would do if the Earth was at rest. But far from accepting this as empirical evidence that Copernicus was simply wrong, Galileo turned the problem the other way round and saw that "the crucial thing is being able to move the Earth without causing a thousand inconveniences." Contrary to the empirical evidence, the motion of the Earth was simply not in doubt for Galileo. So the problem became that of creating a radically new physics of motion, which would show how bodies move on a moving Earth in exactly the same way that they would move if the Earth itself were at rest.

In the way that he did this, Galileo exemplified Goethe's maxim that "the greatest art in theoretical and practical life consists in changing the *problem* into a *postulate*; that way one succeeds."[81] The problem for Galileo was that bodies moving on the Earth are *indifferent* to the Earth's motion, and he took *this* as the fundamental postulate of a new science of motion. Thus, indifference to motion ceases to be a "problem" and becomes instead a *new way of seeing* motion. Far from being an automatic step to take, when this inversion is first made it is an act of creative imagination. It is certainly not an inference from the phenomena, but *once* this step of creative imagination has been taken, *then* it can be re-presented retrospectively *as if* it had been deduced *from* the phenomena—in which case the dimension of mind in cognition is covered over. It seems this way subsequently because the phenomena are then being seen in the light of the new idea of motion (the conjurer's rabbit is already in the hat). Once again, we get a false impression if we begin from the finished product of cognition instead of trying to catch the process of cognition before this stage, i.e., in its coming-into-being.

Now in order to see that a body is indifferent to its motion, Galileo had to come to a further fundamental change in the way of seeing motion itself. He separated the motion of a body from the essential nature of the body, i.e., he saw the motion which a body had as being entirely extrinsic, instead of intrinsic, to the body. Before Galileo, motion entailed the essence of whatever it was that was in motion. Motion itself was considered to be a special case of change, and change was considered to be whatever it is that is changing becoming more fully itself. Thus a growing plant, the education of a child, and a body falling to the ground were all instances of change in which something comes to be more fully itself. So motion (change of place) was seen as being a *necessary* feature of what it is to be the body which is in motion. For Galileo, on the other hand (and thence for modern physics), there is no such necessary connection between the kind of motion a body has and its essential nature. A body's motion is contingent to it, and hence a body can be indifferent to its state of motion. "Motion" is now merely a *state* in which a body finds itself, and "as Galileo repeated over and over, a body is indifferent to its state of motion or rest."[82]

The key point here is that a body's motion is now seen as a state which the body is in, whereas before Galileo motion was not seen as a state but as the change *from* one state *to* another state. If motion is only a state in which a body can be, and not part of the very nature of the body, then clearly the body itself must be *indifferent* to the state of motion which it *happens* to (not must) be in. It is this idea of indifference, dependent as it is upon the new idea of motion as a state, that is the foundation of

Galileo's new way of seeing the problem of how bodies can move on a moving Earth in exactly the way that they would move if the Earth itself were not in motion—the new way of seeing which turns the problem into a postulate. Familiar phenomena of motion are now seen differently. For example, Galileo considered a ball dropped from the top of a tower. If the Earth is at rest, the ball should fall straight down to the foot of the tower. It does so. But if the Earth is moving, then according to the physics of Galileo's day, the ball should fall well to the west of the tower because of the immense speed with which the tower is traveling from west to east (rotational speed about one thousand miles per hour). The fact that it does not fall like this, but falls straight down, could easily be taken as good empirical evidence against Copernicus for a stationary earth. Most, if not all of us, would have agreed with this at the time. But Galileo turned it round: "Keeping up with the Earth is the primordial and eternal motion ineradicably and inseparably participated in by this ball as a terrestrial object, which it has by its nature and will possess forever." So, the ball is moving with the earth at the top of the tower, and it continues to do so as it is falling, with the result that it comes to rest at the bottom of the tower, just as it would have done if the Earth had not been moving. It also follows that, because a body is indifferent to its state of motion, it can have several motions simultaneously without these getting in each other's way. They will simply add together to produce a resultant motion without any of the constituent motions being modified by the presence of the others. It was in this manner, following the comprehensive change in the way of seeing motion which he introduced, that Galileo was able to reach one of his greatest achievements in the new science of mechanics. He showed that the path of a projectile must be a parabola by adding together a uniform horizontal velocity and a uniform vertical acceleration, with neither one disturbing the other. From this it followed that the motion of any body could be *analyzed,* i.e., separated into independent parts which would add together to produce the original motion. Hence motion could be investigated mathematically in the way Galileo had shown, and this provided the model for the future development of science.

The Idea of Inertial Motion

Galileo's new way of seeing the motion of a body was a key step towards the discovery of inertial motion. Although Galileo did not make this discovery (not in the sense in which it is understood in physics today), his recognition of motion as a *state* in which a body happens to be, so that a body's motion is separate from the essential nature of the body, and hence that a body is indifferent to its motion, opens the way to seeing that it can be just as natural for a body to be moving as to be at rest. So the idea dawns that there can be a motion which happens "naturally," i.e., without a cause—in which case the role of a causal agent (force) now becomes that of changing motion and not sustaining it.

Although Galileo opened the door here, he was too much concerned with the problems arising from the work of Copernicus to go through it himself. He saw everything in the context of the universe as it was betrayed by Copernicus—a finite universe bounded by the sphere of the stars, with all motions in concentric circles around the central point which was occupied by the Sun. Furthermore, as we have seen, Galileo was especially concerned with the problem of how a body on a moving Earth moves just as it would do if the Earth was at rest. So a falling body will fall straight downwards to an observer on the Earth because, once released, it continues to rotate with the Earth. Because of his concern with this kind of problem, Galileo seemed to think of the kind of motion we now call inertial (i.e., not needing a cause to sustain it) as being circular motion. Evidently this would fit in well with a universe whose basic structure was spherical, as well as with the fact that any body which rotated with the Earth would thereby execute a circle. Furthermore, there is the fact that, in emphasizing movement in a circle, Galileo was acting in accordance with the special role given to the circle (and sphere) in the philosophies of Plato and Aristotle, which had dominated thinking for about two thousand years.[83]

The person who broke with circularity was Descartes's. He seems to have been the first to conceive of inertial motion as being constant motion (i.e., unaccelerated) *in a straight line*. The question is how did he come to this conception, especially in view of the fact that it went against such a long-standing tradition? It certainly was not reached as a result of observations and experiments, as we might falsely be led into thinking from the way that science is taught. The prejudice of empiricism is impotent for understanding the discovery of inertial motion—as Herbert Butterfield expressed it: "In fact, the modern law of inertia is not the thing you would discover by mere photographic methods of observation—it required a different kind of thinking-cap, a transposition in the mind of the scientist himself."[84] This transposition came about through the influence of another school of philosophy—in this case the ancient philosophy of atomism.

The earliest atomists, Leucippus and Democritus, developed the philosophy of atomism as a response to a difficulty which seems to have beset the early Greek philosophers. It appeared to these thinkers that there was a contradiction between what our senses perceive and what our thinking tells us. As it happened, this led to a mistrust of the human senses and a belief that the true reality could only be discovered by the power of thinking. Atomism was one way which was proposed to answer the difficulties which this caused, and Platonism was another.[85] This philosophy was subsequently developed further by Epicurus and his later follower Lucretius, a Roman poet whose literary work *De Rerum Natura* had a considerable philosophical influence when it was rediscovered in the Renaissance.[86] In the first place, the philosophy of atomism was intended by Epicurus and Lucretius as a means of dissolving fear of death and the consequent attainment of a state of tranquility (*ataraxia*). The interest which the Renaissance humanists had in atomism had nothing to do with its possible use as a basis for scientific thought. But once it had been introduced, the idea of atoms began to influence the thinking of the new "scientific" philosophers, who took it as the basis of a new and very different (at the time) worldview.

One of the first to use it for this purpose was Giordano Bruno, who combined in a speculative manner the ideas of Copernicus on the heliocentric universe, the subtle vision of Nicholas of Cusa concerning the infinity of the universe, and the ancient atomistic philosophy of an infinite void populated with freely moving atoms. It was Bruno who first introduced the idea that the Sun itself is a star, one of an infinite number of stars scattered throughout an infinite space, some of which would have systems of planets like the Sun, among some of which would be planets like the Earth, where life would flourish. With this thought the ordered cosmos of the ancient and medieval world (including that of Copernicus himself), with its ontological hierarchy that included a well-defined place for humanity, conferring cosmological significance on its existence, was replaced by the vast chaos (as it seemed) of the modern universe in which Earth and Sun were nowhere in particular, insignificant specks in an endless uniformity of particles, and human beings themselves, having no particular place, came to feel that their existence lacked intrinsic meaning and was therefore cosmologically devalued.[87] Contrary to what may be imagined to have been the case, the understanding that the Sun is another star "nowhere in particular" in the immensity of space, did *not* come into our modern Western culture in the first place from observational discoveries in astronomy. It was introduced through the rediscovery and adoption of an ancient school of philosophical thought—it had been proposed by the earliest Greek atomists, Leucippus and Democritus. However, there was a certain timeliness in the virtual conjunction of the publication of Bruno's work (1584) and Galileo's publication of his telescope discoveries (1610). Among the latter was included an account of the discovery that the Milky Way, visible to the naked eye as a pale glow in the sky, was resolved into a huge number of stars. Kuhn comments that "Bruno's mystical vision of a universe whose infinite extent and population proclaimed the infinite procreativeness of the Deity was very nearly transformed into a sense datum."[88]

Atomism was introduced explicitly into physics by Galileo in *The Assayer* in 1623, an influential work in which he proposed an entirely new language of physics to replace Aristotle's physics of qualities.[89] Thereafter, throughout the seventeenth century, in one form or another, the philosophy of atomism (often called "corpuscularianism") became the dominant philosophy in the development of the new physics. The program of research became (1) to discover the laws imposed by God on the corpuscles at the Creation, which governed their motions, interactions, and possible combinations; and (2) to apply these laws to explain sense experience. It was while engaged in pursuing this research program that Descartes's first came to see what we now call the law of inertial motion. He considered how a single corpuscle would move in the infinite space of atomistic cosmology—and then how this motion would be altered by collision with another corpuscle, and so on.[90] When the motion of a corpuscle is imagined *in this context*, then, if it is moving freely (i.e., without any external influence), it seems "natural" that it can only move straight ahead—because an infinite space has no center and no intrinsic directions. In other words, when the *context* of the motion is changed from a spherical bounded space to an infinite space, then it seems "evident" to thought that a single corpuscle will *move in a straight line*. It follows from the work of Galileo, in particular, that it will also move at constant speed. So the natural motion of a body, i.e., the motion which does not need a cause, is motion at constant speed in a straight line and not motion in a circle.

What is important here is the recognition of the role played by a philosophical school of thought in this discovery. Far from being discovered *by* science, the idea of atoms was introduced *into* science. As with Neo-Platonism and Copernicus, this is a cultural–historical factor which contributes to the constitution of scientific knowledge. As we have seen previously, this means that science is not a self-grounding activity, i.e., it does not provide its own foundations by means of some pure scientific procedure that makes no references to anything outside of science. The image of science as autonomous in this way is not borne out by a study of the coming-into-being of science historically. What this shows us instead is that, as Goethe discovered, "the history of science is science itself." It is by means of the kind of illustrations given herein that we can begin to understand the meaning of this succinct statement. What it means above all is that scientific knowledge is *not* attained empirically, as the examples we have given show so clearly. There is always a nonempirical determining factor which is of cultural–historical origin. It is by recognizing this historical conditionality of scientific knowledge that we can be free from the enchantment with science which turns it into an ideology.

Newton took Descartes's formulation of the law of inertial motion and made it the cornerstone of his mathematical physics. It appears in his *Principia* as the first law of motion: "Every body perseveres in its state of being at rest or of moving uniformly straight forward, except insofar as it is compelled to change its state by forces impressed upon it." But Newton makes the extraordinary claim that this law of motion is based on countless observations and experiments done by others, most notably Galileo. He presents it as an empirical generalization reached by induction from experiments. So we can talk about the "experimental evidence" for the first law of motion, as if the law had simply been derived directly from experiments. We have seen that this is certainly not true. Yet here we recognize the standard view of science, the one which is repeated in so many books, and the one which is still taught in science education today. When we consider the enormous prestige which Newton has had, in his own lifetime as well as afterwards, then we cannot help but wonder if this statement of Newton is a major historical source of the widespread view that science is essentially empirical.[91]

If the law of inertial motion was not discovered empirically as supposed, then neither can it be confirmed empirically by laboratory measurements, because the conceptual elements entailed in it transcend experiment—for example, the notion that motion is a state which a body is in, instead of part of its essential nature. When we think through the fundamental ideas of the science of motion, we discover that they are all intertwined, and therefore that any experimental test which is proposed already *presupposes* the whole system of concepts. We therefore cannot have an independent test (i.e., independent of the very concepts we are testing) in the way that we believe we would like, although what we can do is to construct empirical *demonstrations* of the ideas.[92] What are usually passed off as "experiments" in science education are in fact really "demonstrations." The student is encouraged to think that this is how the discovery was first made. But this is an inversion which amounts to a sleight of hand ("sleight of mind" would be an appropriate term) which hides the dimension of mind in the discovery and makes it appear to be empirical. So the student thinks, wrongly, that inertial motion, for example, is a property of a body which is given in sense experience in the same way as the color of the body. The point about a *demonstration* is that it *embodies* the idea. We do not derive the idea from the demonstration (i.e., when this is mistakenly thought to be an experiment), but we construct the demonstration according to the idea. So the demonstration *shows* the idea, but it does so only to those who see it—in which case they are seeing the demonstration in the light of the idea, as if the idea is reflected in it. But when we are unaware of the process of cognition, it seems as if this is there in the physical situation in the same kind of way that color is, say, and that we are seeing it entirely by means of sense perception. It is as if someone looking in a mirror thought that what he or she saw was actually there in the mirror. The idea is the *way* of seeing; the idea of inertial motion *is* seeing in the "inertial" way. The laboratory demonstration is itself a carrier for the "inertial motion" idea because it is organized according to this idea. So it is nonsense to suppose that the idea was discovered in the first place from some such "experiment." It would be like believing that the meaning "dog" was derived in the first place from the letters d-o-g.

If the fundamental ideas of science are not confirmable by independent empirical testing, then neither does it seem that they are falsified by observations and experiments which seem to give empirical counterinstances, We have seen, for example, that the counterinstance to Copernicus of the lack of any observable parallax was not permitted to falsify Copernicus's theory. In fact, far from rejecting his theory on account of this, he used it to extend his picture of the universe and suggest that it was much larger than had been supposed. In this way he accommodated what would otherwise be a counterinstance.[93] Similarly, we saw with Galileo that all the empirical evidence provided counterinstances to the proposal that the Earth moves. But instead of rejecting this theory, Galileo set about devising a radically new physics which would accommodate these seemingly falsifying observations.

According to the traditional philosophy of science, all propositions which are meaningful fall into one of two categories. Leibniz called these "truths of reason" and "truths of fact"; in more recent philosophy they are referred to as "analytical propositions" and "empirical (or synthetic) propositions." An analytical proposition is one which is intrinsically true because the predicate is the defining characteristic of the subject—e.g., "all triangles are three-sided"—so that any counterinstance would be self-contradictory, which is another way of saying that there cannot be a counterinstance. For instance, in the above example, a counterinstance would take the form "There is a particular triangle which isn't three-sided," which is equivalent to saying "There is a three-sided figure which isn't three-sided," which is self-contradictory. As well as all definitions, the propositions of logic and mathematics are analytical propositions. So the truth of mathematics is contained within itself, and hence can be ascertained without going outside of the system of mathematics. An empirical (synthetic) proposition, on the other hand, is one which refers to something beyond itself, to which reference has to be made to ascertain whether it is true or not. For example, "There is at least one raven in Iceland" requires someone to go to Iceland and look.[94] The counterinstance, that there are no ravens in Iceland, is certainly not self-contradictory. On the contrary, it is just as possible. Analytical propositions must be true, but empirical propositions just happen to be true, and could just as well be false. So the truth of the former is necessary, whereas that of the latter is contingent.

The assertion that every meaningful proposition must fit into this dichotomy is often known as "Hume's Fork," because Hume insisted that this was the criterion for what constitutes genuine knowledge. It was a central feature of the philosophy of logical positivism earlier in this century—which dominated the philosophy of science up until the work of Kuhn and others in the early 1960s. Hume maintained that any work which did not contain these two kinds of propositions was not knowledge and should be consigned to the flames. The irony is that this would include science! The fundamental laws, principles, and theories of science are neither analytical nor empirical. Yet Hume would have been the last person to deny the validity of science, especially the science of Newton.

The propositions which express the fundamental principles of science are evidently not analytical because a counterinstance is not self-contradictory. For example, a possible counterinstance of Newton's first law of motion would be a body moving in some way other than at constant speed in a straight line without any resultant force acting on it. There is nothing logically impossible about this, as there is with the proposition that there is a triangle which isn't three-sided. What the physicist would do in such a case is to consider this as a research problem within the conceptual framework of Newtonian physics. He would work on the basis of Newton's first law of motion to try to find the force(s) which are responsible for the deviation from inertial motion. But we have seen that Newton's first law of motion is not empirical. So here is a fundamental principle of physics which escapes from Hume's Fork. Harold Brown calls such propositions, which are neither empirical nor analytical, "paradigmatic propositions."[95] They are the *organizing ideas* which organize (the primary act of "distinguishing which is relating") scientific cognition. As such they *constitute* this cognition in that they determine the form it will take, so they could also be called "constitutive propositions." Such constitutive propositions function in scientific cognition in the same way that concepts function in everyday cognition. They are "the conditions of the possibility" of scientific knowledge (using Kant's terminology). A constitutive proposition is an organizing idea which creates the possibilities of scientific cognition, as concepts create the possibilities of everyday cognition. Such a proposition gives us the *form* which scientific cognition must take, but not the specific content of the cognition. So, as with ordinary concepts, the principles and laws of science are to be understood as organizing ideas acting at the level of possibility.

The Organizing Idea of Modern Science

In fact, the change in the way of seeing which we have explored so far rests upon a further, deeper, and more comprehensive change in the way of seeing motion. Galileo was a pioneer in the *quantitative* science of motion. This does not mean that he simply applied mathematics to the world. The world is not just sitting there in mathematical form already, waiting to have mathematics applied to it—which is the image that "applying mathematics" conveys. The world has to be *mathematized*. It has to be worked over mathematically first, and *then* it appears as if mathematics were applied to the world because the world has already been mathematized. Once again, the confusion here comes from the failure to distinguish between the way of seeing and what is seen, which is itself a consequence of starting from the finished product instead of following through the process of its coming-to-be. If we do not follow through the process of mathematization by which the world comes to be mathematical, then we make the mistake of believing that mathematics is just applied because the world is mathematical. Once again, the way of seeing is eclipsed, being falsely objectified so as to appear as a feature of the world which is given directly to sense experience.

The Quantitative Way of Seeing

Aristotle defined "quantity" as that which has parts external to one another. It is an instance of what he calls a category, which is really to be understood as a mode of illumination by virtue of which the world becomes visible in a particular way. In other words, for Aristotle, "quantity" does not refer to a specific content of the world which is given materially, but to a way of seeing which constitutes the world in the *form* of "parts external to one another." As a way of seeing, quantity is not abstracted from the world as we usually imagine it to be. If we think so, it is because we have failed to notice that the world we believe we have abstracted it from is already seen, "in advance" as it were, in the mode of parts external to one another. In other words, quantity is present already in the way of seeing, so it is present as the *form* which the world takes and not as part of the content of the world. Because of this, "quantity" is manifest wherever there are parts external to one another, regardless of whether number is explicitly part of the specific content or not.[96]

The science of quantity is measurement science. The process of measurement divides whatever it is "measuring" into units which are external to one another, separate but juxtaposed. Whatever is "measured" is thereby spatialized in conception into a string of units juxtaposed along an imagined line which effectively constitutes a scale. In practice, a measurement consists in comparing whatever is to be measured with this scale, and counting the number of units which correspond. This means that wherever science is concerned with measurement, the particular aspect of nature involved has first to be prepared quantitatively. This entails dividing it into a set of homogeneous parts that are intellectually superimposed on nature like a grid or scaffolding. Nature is then seen in the perspective of the framework, *which is not part of nature at all*, but is really an intellectual rearrangement of nature that reduces it to the purely quantitative—i.e., to parts which are external to one another. The system of measurement is in no way intrinsic to nature, but the reduction of nature that it effects enables us to calculate nature and hence to manipulate it for our own ends. Such calculative thinking (as Heidegger called it), or instrumental reason, becomes possible with the quantitative way of seeing. It certainly gives us power over nature, but it has the effect of separating us from nature in such a way that we cease to *experience* nature directly. We can control and organize nature according to our will, but the price for this is that we withdraw from nature. We begin to experience ourselves as being separate and essentially different from nature, while nature in turn begins to seem lifeless and empty. The consequence was stated concisely by John Davy:

> The thoughts we embody in measurement are only applicable to dead phenomena—for measurement means dividing up into units which can be counted, and no living thing can be thus fragmented without dying. It is a form of thought entirely appropriate to the inanimate world, but quite inadequate for apprehending life.[97]

Thus science becomes rational because it "ratios" everything. Nature then appears in a conceptual *framework*, which is falsely identified with nature itself when the activity of mind ceases to be visible to itself. It is not surprising that the historical emphasis on quantity in science has led to a situation of crisis in the world today. But this was present as a possibility from the beginning of the science that measures nature.

It seems clear from Aristotle's definition of quantity that parts which are external to each other must appear as independent, autonomous units, separate existences with their own intrinsic properties. In other words, the quantitative way of seeing discloses a world fragmented into separate and independent units, and it is therefore not surprising to find that the philosophy of atomism was readily incorporated into the new quantitative science of physics. Atomism fits the form of quantity like a hand fits a glove. The two are congruent to each other, so that atomism functions as a picture of the quantitative way of seeing. It pictures the mode of conception. So when the physicist speaks about "the atomic picture," this should be taken strictly as referring to the mode of conception rather than to a material content of the world that is first given and then represented in a picture. There is a reversal of container and content here. Atomism is really a container that carries the quantitative way of seeing.[98]

When quantity is taken to be *the* fundamental category, then nature is reduced to matter and the general viewpoint that is formed corresponding to this is materialism. This is what has happened in the development of physics in the modern period, when physics became *mathematical* physics and "experiment'" came to mean "measurement." In other words, the viewpoint of materialism is a distortion that results from a one-sided emphasis on the category of quantity. It is only our failure to think through the inevitable consequences of the distortion arising from this one-sided emphasis that enables us to entertain the comforting thought that physics progresses ever further towards an ultimate understanding of nature. In fact, "nature" was replaced by "matter" long ago. Although scientists often refer to "nature," this only hides the fact that nature has been reduced to matter by modern science, so that we now think they are the same thing. But whereas there can be an atomic theory of matter, there cannot be an atomic theory of nature. This is born out by the fact that, according to modern science, most of what we attribute to nature, color for instance, is really not in nature but in human beings. It is reclassified as *only* a subjective experience (see the discussion of primary and secondary qualities in "Newton and the Mathematical Physics of Color"). When that which seems to belong to nature is relocated in human beings, what is left is matter and not nature at all. There is little wonder that the development of modern science has led to the crisis of nature!

The category of quantity is exemplified most clearly by the world of solid bodies. In fact, the world of solid bodies is the category of quantity become an object of sense. Hence there is the temptation, when the "way of seeing" is not recognized, to think that the category of quantity is derived *from* the world of solid bodies by abstraction. But this is an inversion. It cannot be stressed sufficiently that the world of solid bodies is not given *as such* to the senses, but that a specific way of seeing discloses this world. We take it for granted that the world of solid bodies is *the* world, existing as such independently, whereas it is in fact the world that appears in the light of the "solid world" mode of conception. Indeed, this very image of a separately existing world, independent as such of our knowing it (and yet appearing just as it is when we do know it), is itself an instance of the "solid world" mode of conception. What is seen cannot be separated from the way it is seen: The solid world is the cognitive correlate of the "solid world" mode of conception.[99]

The solid world could equally well be called the external world. When Hegel referred to "the external world," he meant the world for which externality, the outsidedness of part to part, is the fundamental characteristic—not the world "outside" of consciousness, which would be meaningless because consciousness isn't "anywhere." So the quantitative world, the solid world, and the external world, are one and the same world. Once we understand that this world is a way of seeing, then we can become aware of this mode of conception *as such* wherever it occurs. We cease to think of it only in the restricted context of the physical world—which is what we usually identify as the world of solid bodies.

To illustrate this, we will consider as an example the way that "mind" is constituted in the mode of this way of seeing by the British empiricists, notably Locke and Hume. These philosophers purported to be following through the genesis of our knowledge of the world, but they were really introducing the quantitative, solid world perspective into the description of mind. They begin at what is in fact the stage of the finished product, and back-project this into the process, so that effectively they are trying "to get to the milk by way of the cheese." The description that they give could well be called psychological atomism. According to this, sense experience consists of distinct and separate sensations, each of which gives rise to a distinct and separate idea in the mind. For Hume, these ideas are no more than faded copies of sense impressions. Ideas are conceived here as self-contained, mutually external mental entities, each of which exists separately and independently of the others. These simple ideas ("simple" because they are each derived from a single atomic sensation) then combine to form more complex ideas. This process of combining is by juxtaposition and association, in much the same sort of way that atoms were thought to combine. Conversely, any idea which is found in the mind can be broken apart (analyzed) into its constituent simple ideas. This, then, is how it was thought that new ideas are formed, simply by making new combinations of already existing ideas. Thinking, according to this view, is no more than this process of associating together ideas which are already there "in the mind." Evidently the mind is conceived as a space containing ideas that move about, combining with one another, just as the physical universe is thought of as a space containing material particles that collide together and combine with each other to make new arrangements. It is a finished world, in which the only movement is the *external* movement of finished products—a *thought* is a finished product. Reading Locke and Hume, it is not difficult to recognize that the Newtonian picture of the material universe was a major inspiration to them.[100]

This "solid world" way of seeing mind attempts to reconstitute thinking out of thoughts, which is equivalent to attempting to produce the living present out of the past, life out of death. Yet this externalistic way of conceiving mental activity is very common, especially the view that thinking is a process of associating thoughts which are there already, like "mental bodies," so that a new idea is no more than a new combination. There *is* such a process of association, whereby thoughts are connected externally, but far from being the basis of thinking it is precisely when we are *not* thinking that this happens. The associative mind is very superficial, and it is only in the light of the quantitative, solid world way of seeing that it can appear to be the basis of creative thinking.

We have seen already how this viewpoint is inadequate for understanding the process of scientific discovery. We have seen that the primary factor here is a change in the way of seeing, and that the effect of this is to transform the facts. So the facts are not like bricks which are just rearranged; they are transformed by the new way of seeing that reorganizes them. There are no immutable facts. As Kuhn expressed it: "What occurs during a scientific revolution is not fully reducible to a reinterpretation of individual and stable data" because "the data are not univocally stable." [101] New meanings are not just generated by rearranging the elements of a system into a different pattern, because in the "new arrangement" the elements are no longer the same but have been transformed. The facts are transformed from within by the new way of seeing, and therefore this new way of seeing itself cannot be produced by *any* external rearrangement of the facts. There is no *mechanism* for producing meaning. If there were, then meaning could be produced out of nonmeaning. But, as we have seen, this is not possible because of the primacy of meaning. So what we see here is that the authentic process of scientific discovery itself cannot become visible in the light of the solid world mode of conception. What we get instead is the after-the-fact counterfeit of this process.

Finally, we are in the habit of considering concepts themselves in an isolated manner. We consider each concept as if it were distinct and separate from every other concept, each concept being independent and having its own self-contained meaning. The quantitative way of seeing is clearly evident here. David Bohm points out that "logically definable concepts play the same fundamental role in abstract and precise thinking as do separable objects and phenomena in our customary description of the world."[102] But in fact it is not possible for concepts to be separate and external to each other in this way. Concepts are not self-contained but inherently interdependent. Hegel pointed out that an absolute distinction is impossible because it is self-contradictory. Thus, A is not distinguished just in terms of itself, because in the *act* of distinction it is ipso facto distinguished *from* B. Hence it follows that A is *necessarily* related to B by the very act of distinction itself, and therefore that B is entailed in A.

Thus A is not self-contained, and so A and B cannot be *separated* in the way that the quantitative way of seeing implies. Far from being isolated, concepts are intrinsically related and belong together in a more organic way.[103]

This inevitably leads to a reevaluation of the laws of traditional logic, namely, the principles of identity, noncontradiction, and the excluded middle:

(1) A is identically equal to itself, i.e., self-identical;
(2) not at the same time A and not-A;
(3) either A or not-A; there is no third possibility.

These principles evidently emphasize a sharp division into self-contained, mutually exclusive terms. There is no necessary entailment of not-A in A, and hence A is entirely excluded from not-A. So A and not-A are external to one another. This is clearly the logic that is characteristic of the quantitative, solid world perspective. So whenever we think "logically," and especially whenever we think in an either/or manner, the very *form* of our thinking conforms to the solid world mode of conception. It is therefore clear how apt it was when Bergson referred to traditional logic as "the logic of solid bodies."[104]

The Metaphysical Separation

The separation we have considered so far is that of quantity— parts which are external to each other. We have seen that this is congruent with the solid world. This could equally well be called the plane of separation, or the plane of quantity, inasmuch as the elements which are separate are considered to be all on the same level. In the plane of quantity, there is no "above" and "below," no "higher" and "lower." There are no ontological differences.

There is, however, another kind of separation which also functions as a fundamental organizing idea of modern science. This is the metaphysical separation. It is so fundamental to modern science—especially to mathematical physics—that this could well be called metaphysical science. It is particularly important to bring out the metaphysical separation clearly, and the way that it has been incorporated into modern science, especially in view of the widespread belief that modern science has liberated human knowledge from metaphysics. The very opposite is true: "Metaphysics finds its ultimate expression in modern, mathematical physics."[105] Because metaphysics is in the last place we would think of looking for it—"Metaphysics is alive and well and lives on in modern physics"[106]—it can function unhindered, without being recognized for what it is, as part of what we take for granted. Metaphysics is the "openly secret" presupposition of much of our thinking.

The basic point of the metaphysical separation is that the world which we experience through the senses is not the full reality, and that *behind* this world there is another, nonsensory world, which is the intelligible origin of what appears as the sensory world. This is not simply saying that the intelligibility of the world we encounter through the senses cannot be encountered by sense experience. The metaphysical attitude goes much further than this to deny that there *is* any intelligibility in the world we encounter through sense experience—not just that it doesn't appear to the senses, but that it is not there at all in the sensory world. The intelligibility of whatever we encounter in the world of sense experience is *in another world* that is *separate* from this sensory world. Metaphysics is the *two-world* theory that separates the sensible and the intelligible into two different worlds of unequal ontological status. So the sensible world is subordinated to the higher intelligible world and is dependent on it for its being. There is one-way ontological traffic in metaphysics: the lower world of the sensory particulars could not be without the higher world of intelligible universals, but the latter could perfectly well be without the former.

Although the roots of the metaphysical attitude, particularly the mistrust of the senses, are to be found in earlier Greek philosophy, it is with Plato that this first became a full-fledged philosophy embodying this mistrust in a two-world theory. Plato is the father of metaphysics, and it is from Plato that the idea of the metaphysical separation spread through historical time to be a profound influence on the Western mode of understanding.[107] The incorporation of Platonism into Christianity, to produce a Platonized Christianity, was a particularly significant step for deepening the hold which the metaphysical separation has had on the development of the Western mind.[108]

In Plato's philosophy, the true object of knowledge is in the intelligible world. This is the *eidos*, which is usually translated as Form or Idea—but the latter must not be confused with the subjective meaning which the term usually has today (to avoid this it is common to write "Idea" instead of "idea"). What we encounter in the sensible world are imperfect copies or reflections of the Form (Idea) which is in the intelligible world. This means that whatever we encounter in the sensible world does not have its own reality. In itself it is *merely* an appearance. Reality (Being) is in the intelligible world. For example, we encounter "equality" in many different ways in sense experience, as when we find one thing equal to another, and so on. But according to Plato, all these experiences of equality are imperfect because we always find the opposite of equality mixed in with them, i.e., inequality.[109] We are only able to recognize them as instances of equality in the first place because they resemble or reflect the Form, "Equality-as-it-is-in-itself," which is purely intelligible, and which a person can only approach "with the unaided intellect, without taking account of any sense of sight in his thinking, or dragging any other sense into his reckoning."[110] The Form, or Idea, is free from any contamination with its opposite and is therefore perfect. Hence it is unchanging and eternally self-identical, in contrast to the ever-changing multifarious realm of appearances. The Form belongs to the world of "Being-as-it-is-in-itself," which is pictured as being "behind" or "above" the sensible world, not within it. This *separation* of the intelligible from the sensible has the consequence that, in Plato's metaphysics, the Form, which is the essence and therefore the reality of the sensible, is *separated* from the sensible. Aristotle asked how something which is separate from the sensible *can* contain the essence of the sensible. His answer was that this showed the theory to be impossible.[111] Were it not for the fact that we have lived with this metaphysical, two-world picture for so long that it is part of the very fabric of our thought, we too would surely find this theory very strange indeed.[112]

We have already encountered the influence which Platonism had on the origin and development of modern science. We saw something of the Platonistic mistrust of the senses, coupled with the belief that only reason could discover the true order of the world. We saw also that this order was understood to be primarily mathematical. All three of these factors come together in the work of Galileo, resulting in a Platonized mathematical physics.

Mathematics, and especially geometry, seems to lend itself so readily to Platonism that it almost appears as the paradigm case. A point and a line do not exist in the visible world. They cannot be drawn because a point has no magnitude and a line has no thickness. Yet it is with the relationship between such entities that geometry is concerned. The "point" and "line" we can draw are not the *true* mathematical point and line. Given the philosophy of Platonism, it is easy so see the difference between the geometrical point and the drawn "point" as exemplifying the difference between the intelligible, which is invisible and perfect, and the sensible, which is visible but imperfect—and then to see the latter as an imperfect copy or reflection of the former.[113] Geometry lends itself easily to Platonism, and this was the way Galileo took it. He interpreted his mathematization of nature Platonistically, giving birth to what Husserl called "the physics of Galilean style."[114]

Now mathematics does not *have* to be taken in a Platonistic spirit—most mathematicians today certainly would not do so.[115] But the fact is that this *is* how it was taken by Galileo, and this has had a decisive influence on the understanding of the natural world that has grown out of the science of mathematical physics. Because of the extraordinary success of this science, the Platonistic picture, with its fundamental dualism, gradually became the philosophical paradigm for the sciences of nature. When Sir James Jeans said in the 1930s that the universe is a thought in the mind of God, he was simply echoing the Platonism of mathematical physics, and saying no more than had been said before him by Kepler, Galileo, and others.[116] Here is Kepler, for example:

> Why waste words? Geometry existed before the creation, is coeternal with the mind of God, *is God himself* (what exists in God that is not God himself?); Geometry provided God with a model for the creation and was implanted into man, together with God's own likeness—and not only merely conveyed to his mind through the eyes.[117]

Although at the time when Jeans made his remark, it was perceived by many as emerging somehow from the exciting new (twentieth century) physics of relativity and quantum theory, it was in fact simply a repetition of the inevitable confluence of *Platonized* physics and *Platonized* Christianity—although it is unlikely that this would have been recognized by many at the time because, except for a few (e.g., E. A. Burtt), the historicity of science had not then been recognized. According to Platonized Christianity, the universe is an imperfect reflection or copy of the Ideas which God thinks; according to Platonized physics, the Ideas are mathematical "laws" which organize nature. So mathematical physics is the physics of God's universe. The mathematician and philosopher A. N. Whitehead is often quoted as having said that the development of Western philosophy could be regarded as a series of footnotes to Plato. But more than philosophy, the development of the Western way of thinking in religion and science seems to have been dependent on Plato and the metaphysical separation.

What God thinks in the universe of the new physics is the mathematical laws of nature. The task of the natural philosopher, in coming to know the laws of nature which are hidden behind appearances, is therefore equivalent to knowing God's thinking.[118] The mathematical laws of nature are the intelligibles for the "physics of the Galilean style," to be found by intellectual reasoning behind the visible world of the sensible.

So, like the Platonic Forms, they are immutable and unchanging. It is these laws which are the source of order in the world of sense experience, but they belong to another, separate world from that which they order. The traffic is ontologically one-way. In classical physics, the mathematical laws act on matter to determine the order of nature, but the laws themselves are not determined by matter in any way. The laws are therefore transcendental.

Galileo's work was evidently not simply a repetition of Plato, or even of earlier Platonists. It was a Platonism which was *transformed* in accordance with the new historical context and circumstances. Gurwitsch says that "Galileo's work may be said to mark the turning-point in the historical development of 'Platonism'. . . . It was thoroughly transformed and renewed by him."[119] What Galileo did was a contribution to the "effective history" of Plato, to use Gadamer's term. Of course, the historical link with Platonized Christianity has disappeared from science, but Platonized physics remains, because the mathematical laws of physics are conceived as being *separate* from the matter they organize. Platonized physics is metaphysics in disguise. This is now just part of the fabric of scientific thought, so that for the most part we are simply unaware of it.

Galileo attempted to bring about an alliance of two ancient philosophical doctrines, Platonism and atomism, which had been totally antithetical in the ancient world. He was not able to get far with the synthesis of these two, but others developed it further. First and foremost among them was Descartes, whose entire work can be seen as an attempt to develop a new mathematical physics that will give a complete account of nature, and to give a foundation to this enterprise which would leave it beyond doubt.[120] It is with this attempt that most of what is now often taken as his purely philosophical work was concerned. Although he is widely known as the founder of modern philosophy (which is certainly justified), his work does need to be seen in its context. To abstract it from this context, and present it as being purely philosophical, is artificial. His most fundamental and influential work, the

Meditations, was far from being what it appeared to be on the surface. Descartes wrote in a letter to Mersenne:

> . . . and I may tell you, between ourselves, that these six *Meditations* contain all the foundations of my *Physics*. But please do not tell people, for that might make it harder for supporters of Aristotle to approve them. I hope that readers will gradually get used to my principles and recognize their truth, before they notice that they destroy the principles of Aristotle.[121]

The *Meditations* were written with the intention of clearing the ground for Descartes's mathematical physics, so that in it the foundations needed for the new physics are laid out almost surreptitiously. The title indicates how the work was intended to be studied: meditatively, dwelling with each meditation until it had been taken in thoroughly. Descartes believed that "if properly taken in, they would do no less than break the habit of a lifetime, the habit of taking one's beliefs about the nature of the material world and about one's own nature from one's sense experience."[122] The book was intended to persuade, but to do so by means of the reader's own effort. Readers are taken on a skeptical journey, whereby they are brought to doubt everything that their senses tell them, including their sense of their own presentational immediacy (the famous dream argument). Eventually one is brought through this skepticism to certainty. One discovers that, by the very thinking activity that one is pursuing, one can be certain that "I am, I exist."[123] Because one arrives at this certainty by means of thinking, as well as discovering with certainty *that* one is, one also recognizes *what* one is: a thinking being, i.e., a being whose essential nature consists in thinking.

One cannot be certain that there is a world, or even that one has a body, but one can be certain that one is, one exists, as a thinking being.[124] Then, having trapped himself in a corner, Descartes provides an argument which, while it does not get him out of the corner, opens a small hole in it for a lifeline to the world "outside of consciousness" to come in to him.[125] The aim of this argument is to convince readers that, as well as being certain of their own existence as thinking beings, they can also be certain that God exists. Since God is benevolent, he will not deceive us. Hence, if we have done our part and thought things through so that we can come to a clear and distinct idea, then we can be confident that this idea is true. Now we do find that we have the idea that, apart from ourselves, there is a world of nature which exists "outside of consciousness." If we have thought about this carefully enough, then we can be confident that it *does* exist because God will not deceive us. One is certainly left with feeling about Descartes that "he seeks truth in an artificial way."[126]

So, having doubted it, Descartes puts the world back. *But* the world which he puts back, which he can be certain of, is not the world he began to doubt. He switches one world for another—the world of mathematical physics for the world of everyday experience. The world we can be certain exists is not the world we see, but the mathematical world of corpuscular matter in motion. A great deal of what common sense tells us is part of the world is missing from it so far as mathematical physics is concerned. All that Descartes can admit as part of the real world is what he can form a clear and distinct idea of, because God has so arranged things (he believes he has shown convincingly) that he can be confident that such an idea is true. What he can form clear ideas of are the mathematical properties, such as size, shape, position, motion, and so on. So these must be part of the real world. Other qualities—among which he lists light, colors, sounds, smells, taste, warmth, roughness or smoothness—he says "appear in my mind with such darkness and confusion that I do not know whether they are true or false, i.e., whether the ideas I have of these objects are in fact the ideas of any real things or whether they are mere chimerical entities which cannot exist."[127] So, since he does not have a clear and distinct idea of these qualities, he cannot admit them with any degree of certainty as part of the real world. Following the pathway taken by Galileo, he therefore removes them from the world and relocates them in subjective human experience (see also "Newton and the Mathematical Physics of Color"). So, the redness of a body, for example, is not part of the body which we perceive, but exists only in human experience. It is produced in us by the impact of particles of matter on our organism—there is no color in nature. Of course this is inevitable. Descartes's criteria for clear and distinct ideas are the ideas of mathematics. So whatever cannot be mathematized cannot become a clear idea, and hence it cannot be part of the real world. There *is* only one other place to put these qualities in Descartes's picture, and so they are pushed into human experience.[128]

Thus the familiar world of sense experience is illusory, just as the appearance of the Sun going around the Earth is illusory. There are only mathematical qualities in nature, and so nature is reduced to matter which is inert, passive, mechanical, and qualitatively neutral. Mathematical physics is the physics of matter, not nature—but, of course, nowadays these are thought to be the same thing just because of this historical development. Furthermore, ideas are now entirely separate from nature (reduced to matter), belonging entirely to the sphere of human subjectivity. Richard Westfall describes Descartes's place in the historical development of modern science as follows:

> Many of Descartes's explanations of phenomena differ so widely from those we now believe to be correct that we are frequently tempted to scoff. We must attempt rather to understand what he was trying to do and how it fits into the world of the scientific revolution. The cornerstone of the entire edifice of his philosophy of nature was the assertion that physical reality is not in any way similar to the appearances of sensation. As Copernicus had rejected the view of an immovable earth, and Galileo the common sense view of motion, so Descartes now generalized the reinterpretation of daily experience. He did not intend to conduct the sort of scientific investigation we are familiar with today. Rather his purpose was metaphysical—he proposed a new picture of the reality behind experience. However wild and incredible we find his explanations, we must remember that the whole course of modern science has been run, not by returning to the earlier philosophy of nature, but by following the path he chose.[129]

In the process of doing this, Descartes subjectivized metaphysics—it is really for this reason that he is now called the founder of modern philosophy. It has often been pointed out that Descartes is part of the Platonic tradition.[130] Both mistrust the senses and deny that the senses themselves can give knowledge. Both affirm that certainty can only be found by the power of reason, which alone can reach true ideas—and both take mathematics as their model for this. But there is a difference between them. For Plato an Idea is an element of being itself, whereas for Descartes an idea is an activity of the subject. For Descartes, ideas are confined to human experience, to what was later called "consciousness," and therefore can never be more than true representations. For Plato, on the other hand, Ideas are the true being of the world. Descartes subjectivized ideas, and hence he subjectivized metaphysics. The separation is still there, but now it is the separation between the (subjective) idea in the mind of the thinker and whatever it is "outside" of the mind that the idea represents. So long as Descartes has God to hold these two together, everything is all right—albeit in a very artificial way. But once the role of God is weakened, then the idea in the mind and that which it purports to represent fall apart into the dichotomy of the so-called Cartesian dualism. This is really the subjective version of the two-world theory. It is from this that the famous problem of knowledge arises, i.e., the question: How can we be certain that a representation (idea) in consciousness corresponds to what is there "outside" of consciousness? How can we bridge the gulf between representation and reality? This "problem of knowledge" arises automatically from the Cartesian position once we cease to rely on God to guarantee things for us. Heidegger recognized that the problem of knowledge, i.e., epistemology, is really the metaphysics of knowledge. There is no answer to be found in the direction in which the problem itself encourages us to seek. The only answer is to see how it arises in the first place, out of what is really a false position. But this false position has an alarmingly strong hold on us because it corresponds so well to the characteristics of the modern "onlooker" mode of consciousness. When contemporary philosophers refer to "metaphysics," it is usually epistemology and its consequences which they have in mind, and not Plato's metaphysics.[131]

In his discussion of Husserl's phenomenological investigation into Galilean physics, Gurwitsch asks, "What logical status should be assigned to the thesis that nature is mathematical throughout?" He goes on to say:

> Obviously, it is not a formulation of empirical findings, nor is it arrived at by generalization from experience. On account of its generality, it cannot pass for a law of nature; in fact every determinate law of nature is one of its particular specifications. Because of its generality, it cannot be considered as an hypothesis in the usual sense. . . . One might speak of it as the 'hypothesis underlying hypotheses'. . . as a methodological norm which directs the formulation of scientific hypotheses and guides all scientific activities, theoretical and experimental alike.[132]

The idea that nature is mathematical throughout is an organizing idea which acts at the level of science itself, i.e., science as a whole, to constitute a whole new style of physics—the physics of Galilean style. It is neither empirical nor analytical, but constitutive in the sense that it creates the *possibility* of this kind of science. Such a science then has to be worked out. In fact this is the *only* way that such a constitutive idea, or "hypothesis underlying hypotheses," can be substantiated. No argument or observation can do this, but only the continuing success of the science based on this methodological hypothesis. As Gurwitsch says, this means ongoing, never-ending work, because "the thesis that nature is mathematical throughout can be confirmed only by the entire historical process of the development of science, a steady process in which nature comes to be mathematized progressively."[133] Goethe's statement that "the history of science is science itself" can also be read in this sense, as an expression of the insight that science is confirmed only by its own historical development.

The organizing idea for a whole new science does not come from within science itself, as if it were somehow intrinsic to science. It is grounded in historical movements of thought, which means that the science in question is based on choices and decisions which are cultural–historical and not empirical. Because it is not grounded in any intrinsic necessity, the discoveries of science are not binding *in the way they have been thought to be*. We are not compelled to follow the pathway of mathematical physics, as if it were somehow intrinsic to nature. But we may easily lose sight of this fact. Developing an awareness of the historical dimension which is inherent in scientific knowledge helps to counteract this tendency. As Hübner puts it:

> Insight into this historical conditioning prevents the progressive degeneration which so often accompanies the acceptance of scientific positions—a degeneration which moves first to the level where the position is accepted uncritically, then to a level where it is thought to be somehow self-evident, ending finally in a stage where all questionability has disappeared. In this way historical awareness possesses a critical function. Over and over again it tracks down origins that have only contingent meanings, and thus lack necessity or compelling grounds. And it is precisely for this reason that historical consciousness can reject such positions.[134]

When we recognize the irreducible historical dimension of scientific knowledge, then we can also begin to understand that the kind of science with which we are familiar may be only one possibility. This increases our flexibility and hence frees us from the idolatry of science. We can become aware that there may be other possible kinds of scientific knowledge, other possible ways of encountering nature, than that of mathematical physics. This does not mean that the science we have is somehow wrong—of course it isn't! In its own way it is complete, but it is not comprehensive—as the figure of the duck is complete in itself, but not comprehensive, because another complete figure is also possible. Modern science created one pathway, but it is only one possible pathway. Becoming aware of the historicity of scientific knowledge opens the way to the recovery of other possibilities, which were covered over by the historical decision at the origin of modern science. Goethe's pathway in science is such a possibility. To enter it is to experience another way of seeing, another way of encountering nature.

4. Understanding the
Science of Color

We will begin by focusing on Goethe's pathway in the science of color. Goethe's concern with color arose out of his interest in art (Newton's arose out of his technical interest in improving telescope images). During his first journey to Italy (1786–88) he found that artists were able to give rules for all the elements of painting except coloring. This was unsatisfactory to him because he believed that the work of art was Nature realizing herself on a higher level through the artist. Hence he believed that the same kind of lawfulness that was to be found in nature must be present in art—the division between art and science simply didn't exist for Goethe. So he set out to discover the lawfulness in the phenomena of color.

To begin with, "Like everyone in the world I was convinced that all the colors were contained in the light; I had never had the slightest reason for doubting it since I had taken no further interest in the matter." But not having seen the experiments upon which supposedly this theory was based, "I undertook at least to see the phenomena for myself."[135] The discrepancy which he experienced between the phenomena and the accepted theory led him to undertake a further series of experiments and observations. These, he believed, let the phenomena speak for themselves so clearly that it would be immediately apparent to everyone that the accepted theory was wrong. In actuality, the opposite to what he expected happened: Goethe experienced great resistance to his work, and he became isolated from his contemporaries, standing on his own on this account. So he went more deeply into the question, going into the history of earlier ideas about color and into the history of science. It was through this deeper investigation that he discovered that science is intrinsically historical.

The results of this intensive labor were eventually published as the *Theory of Colors* (*Farbenlehre*). The English translation published in 1840 leaves out the polemic against Newton, and all of the historical part. Perhaps this is why Goethe's advance beyond inductive empiricism towards understanding science as historically situated knowledge has not been recognized. Dennis Sepper describes how Goethe's thinking shifted towards the possibility that there are several ways of conceiving things, each of which has its own value. These *Vorsellungsarten* (ways of conceiving) were explored by Goethe through his historical studies, and he came to see such exploration, and the historical awareness which it developed, as a necessary part of doing science.

It has been mentioned already (in chapter 1 of this part) that Goethe contrasted the atomistic, mechanical, and mathematical *Vorstellungsarten* with his own way of conceiving, which he thought of as more inclined to the genetic, the dynamic, and the concrete. He saw that an atomistic intelligence would see nothing wrong with Newton's theory, but to limit our understanding to this one way of conceiving would be to make the science of color unnecessarily one-sided. Goethe's ideal was that science should become a many-sided activity, encompassing a plurality of ways of conceiving, in contrast to the reduction to a single way of conceiving, which had been the ideal of Newton and others in the development of mathematical science in the seventeenth century. We will now explore these different *Vorstellungsarten* in the science of color.

NEWTON AND THE MATHEMATICAL PHYSICS OF COLOR

To understand what Newton did, we must first return to Galileo. Galileo's method was to find those elements of a phenomenon which allow it to be translated into mathematical form, which means resolving the phenomenon into quantitative combinations.[136] From there onward these quantitative combinations are used in place of the phenomenon. Galileo was concerned primarily with motion, and to resolve motion into quantitative combinations he had first to reduce space and time to something which could be treated mathematically. In the process of doing this he changed the meaning of "space" and "time" in a very fundamental way.[137] Once he had done this, Galileo could treat motion quantitatively in terms of units of distance and units of time which, as parts which are external to each other, can be counted. Hence motion can be measured.[138] The quantitative perspective which makes this possible is not intrinsic to the phenomenon, but is imposed upon it as a framework. It is by this means that thinking (i.e., quantitative thinking) can calculate the phenomenon, so that it can be manipulated and controlled in a precise way. This is the primary interest of instrumental science: to control nature.

There are many "qualities of nature" which cannot be directly mathematized because they cannot be described in terms of parts which are external to one another. Color cannot be described in this way, for example. In such cases the procedure that was adopted was to correlate the quality with occurrences that could be described in spatiotemporal terms, and hence could be mathematized directly. This gives rise to a *methodological distinction* between qualities which can be mathematized directly and those which cannot and have to be mathematized indirectly by such a correlation. There is nothing wrong with this procedure in itself. For example, in Newton's famous experiment with a prism, color can be correlated with "degree of refrangibility" (i.e., angle of refraction). Different colors have different angles of refraction, which can be measured, and thereby color can be mathematized indirectly by correlating it with a factor which entails only a spatial relationship. This enables us to calculate color so that it can be manipulated precisely—e.g., in a telescopic eyepiece or in the construction of an achromatic lens for a telescope objective. But although it is suitable for such "calculative thinking," this nevertheless remains superficial. It tells us nothing about color itself as a quality. Color is rationalized by this procedure, but it does not become intelligible. We should go no further than this. In particular, we have no warrant for drawing the conclusion that the colors are already there in the light and that the prism separates them. This goes beyond the mathematical correlation of color with degree of refrangibility, which is solely for the purpose of making color indirectly quantifiable. We should be very wary of trying to draw conclusions about the phenomenon itself from the procedure for quantifying it.

It is customary to refer to qualities which can be directly mathematized as primary qualities, and those which cannot, and must be mathematized indirectly by correlation with a primary quality, are called secondary qualities. This terminology was first introduced by John Locke, and it is often thought that he was the first to make the distinction. In fact, what he did was to give a name to this distinction, which had been part of the new scientific thinking for some time. If we remember that this primary/secondary distinction is entirely methodological, then we will realize that this way of proceeding tells us nothing about the phenomenon itself when it is of a "secondary" nature. Medieval scientists, with their contemplative approach to nature, would find this very strange. While admitting that such a correlation is certainly possible, they would not see any point in it because it completely misses the phenomenon itself. They would think that to draw conclusions about the phenomenon from such a correlation would be very misleading. There is a deep change in interest in going from the medieval to the modern.[139] The new interest is in the manipulation and control of nature, and the way this is brought about is by mathematics. The quantitative perspective becomes the key to nature, and calculative thinking replaces understanding (to such an extent that these are now thought to be identical). So "quantity," which had been a minor category, one among many, for the medievals, is elevated above the other categories to be made master of them all.

From now on only quantity can be dealt with directly in science. But to begin with, this did *not* necessarily mean that all qualities other than the primary ones had to be *reduced* to quantity. It simply meant that they stood outside of the science of quantity which, methodologically, could only handle them by finding an external correlation (e.g., the correlation of the pitch of sound with the frequency of the corresponding physical vibration). Kepler had no difficulty with this. For him the secondary qualities were part of nature just like the primary qualities. However, inasmuch as he gives priority to quantity, the other qualities are not so fundamental for him—but they are still there as part of nature. We can see how a difference in degree of reality begins to emerge for Kepler as a consequence of his identification of mathematics as the key to certain knowledge of nature. However, he does not thereby doubt that color is a real part of nature, even though according to him we cannot have as certain knowledge of such qualities as we can of quantity.

This changed in a decisive way with Galileo, who went a step further than this as a consequence of his introduction of the ancient philosophy of atomism into physics. He maintained that *only* the primary qualities are part of nature, and that the secondary qualities are *entirely subjective*. This step is so important for the subsequent history of modern science that it is well worth reading Galileo's own account in *The Assayer (Il Saggiatore)*, a text which is a rhetorical masterpiece.[140] Here we can do no more than indicate Galileo's treatment by means of a quotation:

> Now I say that whenever I conceive any material or corporeal substance, I immediately feel the need to think of it as bounded, as having this or that shape; as being large or small in relation to other things, and in some specific place at any given time; as being in motion or at rest; as touching or not touching some other body; and as being one in number, or few, or many. From these conditions I cannot separate such a substance by any stretch of my imagination. But that it must be white or red, bitter or sweet, noisy or silent, and of sweet or foul odor, my mind does not feel compelled to bring in as necessary accompaniments. Without the senses as our guides, reason or imagination unaided would probably never arrive at qualities

like these. Hence I think that tastes, odors, colors, and so on are no more than mere names so far as the object in which we place them is concerned, and that they reside only in the consciousness. Hence if the living creature were removed, all these qualities would be wiped away and annihilated. But since we have imposed upon them special names, distinct from those of the other and real qualities mentioned previously, we wish to believe that they really exist as actually different from those.[141]

Now we *do* have the *reduction* of the secondary qualities to the primary ones. They alone are part of nature, whereas the secondary qualities have no objective existence. We have noted before that the quantitative perspective and the philosophy of atomism fit like hand in glove. It seems that Galileo's thinking was prompted to turn a valid methodological distinction into an unwarranted ontological dualism by his adoption of atomism. This ancient philosophy believed that "By convention [*nomas*] there is sweet, bitter, hot, cold, color, but in reality atoms and void,"[142] and that it is the movement of the atoms impinging on the human organism which causes these experiences, which are mere appearances, to arise therein. Galileo explains how the sensations of taste, smell, and sound, for example, could arise in this manner, before going on to give a similar explanation of heat. It does seem quite clear from reading Galileo that the subjectivization of secondary qualities, and hence their removal from nature, is entirely a consequence of his incorporating this ancient philosophy of atomism into physics. In other words, the origin of this ontological bifurcation (as distinct from the methodological division) is historical, and not something which science "discovered" in the way that is usually supposed. It is a consequence of a way of thinking, and not a discovery which was somehow made empirically. This was Galileo's deed, and its effect has been carried through to the present day. But it is unwarranted. The mathematical method itself does not require this subjectivization, since this method requires only that the so-called secondary qualities be correlated with occurrences which are themselves capable of direct mathematization.

This is so important for the subsequent development of the scientific understanding of the relationship between human beings and the world that it is well worth summarizing it briefly:

(1) There is a valid methodological distinction between primary and secondary qualities. This enables secondary qualities to be quantified indirectly, so that they can be calculated and thereby manipulated and controlled. This does not lead to insight into the nature of the quantities in question. We must be careful above all not to attribute causality to what is only a correlation. Such a correlation may be only superficial (e.g., the correlation of degree of refrangibility with color), or it may be more fundamental (e.g., the correlation of the frequency of vibration of a string with the pitch of a musical note), but whichever the case it is not the causal relation it is often mistaken to be.

(2) There is no basis on which this methodological distinction can also be taken as an ontological distinction. The sensory qualities which are mathematizable directly do not have any kind of priority in themselves over sense qualities which are not directly mathematizable.

(3) The pressure to make this error (which does not invalidate the methodological distinction in any way whatsoever) becomes irresistible when the ancient philosophy of atomism is incorporated into science. This has the effect of bifurcating the senses, giving priority to the sense of touch. Goethe said of this: "Democritus and most physiologists who treat the perception of the senses assert something quite inadmissible—they reduce everything perceptible to something that is *felt*."[143] But why should touch be so privileged? Why shouldn't touch also have no direct access to reality and reside only in consciousness? The answer is that it is through touch that we gain our sense of solidity, which is the basis for the conceptualization of "body." Without this, what would happen to all the primary qualities that Galileo lists: boundary, shape, position, contiguity, and number? The sense of touch is the basis of our experience of the world of solid bodies, i.e., the quantitative world. So this distinction between touch and the other senses is methodological and no

more. It fits the requirements of the mathematical method. There is no other reason why touch should be granted an access to reality which is denied to the other senses.

(4) In the hands of Galileo, this developed into the subjectivization of the secondary qualities. These were held to exist only in the conscious experience of the subject, and not to be present as such as part of the object. Thus nature was drastically impoverished. But so, too, was humanity, for these secondary qualities were thought to be of no significance compared with the primary ones which alone were part of nature—a nature which was now reduced to matter.

Burtt observes that the stage is now fully set for the Cartesian dualism of the mathematical realm of matter (denatured nature) and the realm of human nature.[144] Inevitably the question now arises as to *how* these primary qualities can give rise to the secondary qualities in conscious experience? This leads to the so-called causal theory of perception—causality itself now being reduced to mechanical pushes and pulls, as befits the sense of touch. But this attempt to understand perception in the framework of mechanical causality is incoherent. This becomes self-evident if we try to think it through, because the two sides (matter and consciousness) have nothing in common, and "of two things which have nothing in common between them, one cannot be the cause of the other."[145] It's not a question of trying to overcome the difficulty, but of recognizing how this way of thinking led us into a cul-de-sac in the first place.

With this preparation, we are now in a position to understand Newton's experiments with a prism and the interpretation which he gave to them. Newton published a first account of this work in the *Philosophical Transactions* of the Royal Society in 1672. The controversy which this youthful and enthusiastic work produced, resulted in a lengthy interchange of further papers and replies over the next four years. This response to his "New Theory about Light and Colors," as he called it, was so vexatious to him that he published no further work directly on light and color until his monumental *Opticks* in 1704. His *Optical*

Lectures, given at the University of Cambridge in 1669, were not published until 1728, after his death. It is in these lectures that he gives some indication of the background to his famous prism experiments. Furthermore, historians of science have now researched Newton's early manuscripts, written between 1666 and 1672, and have discovered that these contain indications of important factors which entered into Newton's thinking but which he omitted from the first account of his work which he gave to the Royal Society in 1672. This account presents his new theory of color as emerging straightforwardly from his experiments, and this is how we see it today. We think of it as a classic of experimental discovery, in which the conclusion follows inevitably from the experiments themselves. This is certainly what Newton encouraged his readers to think. But the controversy his work aroused (and those who objected to his conclusion were not stupid people who simply failed to understand him) indicates that there is more to it than this.

Newton began his first letter to the Royal Society by telling the reader that in 1666 he was "applying myself to the grinding of Optic glasses of other figures than Spherical." This very difficult task was undertaken by Newton in an attempt to solve the problem of spherical aberration with the objective lens of a telescope, in the manner which had been indicated by Descartes. It was in connection with this attempt to improve the quality of the image in a telescope that Newton "procured me a Triangular glass-Prisme, to try therewith the celebrated *Phenomena of Colors*."[146] As a consequence of his interpretation of these phenomena, Newton concluded that it was impossible to improve the image formed with a refracting telescope, "not so much for want of glasses truly figured" (as Descartes had thought), but because of the relationship between color and refraction. So he turned to the relecting telescope instead, which does not show chromatic aberration of the image because refraction is not involved.[147]

Newton described the steps by which he came to this conclusion in such a way that it seemed to follow directly from his experiments. To begin with, he was struck by the observation that the colored image of a small hole (through which sunlight came) which the prism formed on the wall was *not* circular, as he expected it to be according to the law of refraction (discovered by Snell and Descartes). It was oblong, and five times as long as it was broad, "a disproportion so extravagant, that it excited me to a more than ordinary curiosity of examining, from whence it might proceed." To this end he proceeded through the following sequence of questions and experiments:

(1) Does the thickness of the glass influence the result? To find out, Newton passed the beam through different parts of the prism. He discovered that the result was always the same.

(2) Is there an irregularity in the prism which causes the beam to spread out? To answer this he placed a second prism upside-down behind the first, so "that the light passing through them both, might be refracted in contrary ways." By this means any changes in the light on account of a flaw in the glass would be increased by the second prism. In fact, Newton found that the image became round again, as it would be if the light had not been passed through a prism in the first place.

(3) Is the oblong shape the result of light from different parts of the Sun meeting the prism at different angles? Careful calculation showed that it could not be.

(4) Does the light move in curved instead of straight lines after leaving the prism? Measurements showed that the difference between the length of the image and the diameter of the hole through which the light was transmitted to the prism was proportional to the distance between them. Hence, by putting a screen at different distances from the prism, he was able to show that light traveled in straight lines from the prism to the image.

(5) After proceeding through this sequence of measurements and calculations—it is this careful and detailed quantitative approach which distinguished Newton from his contemporaries, such as Boyle and Hooke, who also investigated color—Newton described what he called the *Experimentum Crucis*.[148] He made a small hole in a second screen which he placed behind the prism in such a way that a single color from

the "spectrum" formed by the prism passed through it. Then he placed a second prism behind this screen, so that the light which had passed through the hole would pass in turn through this prism and onto the wall. By slightly rotating the first prism, he was able to vary the portion of the spectrum formed by the first prism which passed through the second one. A diagram may be helpful here, although it should be remembered that this is constructed for the purpose of clarification and does *not* represent what can actually be seen.

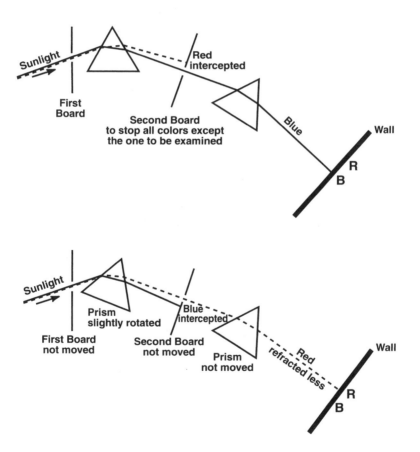

Newton found that light from the blue part of the spectrum formed by the first prism was refracted more than light from the red part, when it was passed through the second prism. Having described what he observed, he then says immediately: "And so the true cause of the length of that Image was detected to be no other, than that *Light* consists of *Rays differently refrangible*, which, without any respect to a difference in their incidence, were, according to their degrees of refrangibility, transmitted towards divers parts of the wall."[149] He then goes on to emphasize that the reason why some rays are refracted more than others is "from a predisposition, which every particular Ray hath to suffer a particular degree of Refraction," and not "by any virtue of the glass, or other external cause." Then he makes a strong correlation between the difference in the degrees of refrangibility of the rays of light (now considered to be inherent to the rays themselves) and their "disposition to exhibit this or that particular color." So he concludes that

(1) Colors are not *Qualifications of Light* derived from Refractions . . . (as 'tis generally believed), but *Original* and *connate properties*, which in divers Rays are divers.

(2) To the same degree of Refrangibility ever belongs the same colour, and to the same color ever belongs the same degree of Refrangibility.

This, then, is Newton's new theory of light and color which he maintained he had derived directly from experiment. His discovery that the colors are not produced by the prism, but are already there in the light and separated out by the prism, is now admired as the very paradigm of the scientific procedure. However, Newton's new theory was not well received in his own day. It seemed to many of his contemporaries that it contradicted the existing view about the origin of colors, without it being at all clear just how it followed directly from experiments with the certainty Newton believed it to have. Also, the account which he gave did not conform to what was expected at the time, in that it did not depend on an underlying hypothesis about the nature of light.

Over the next four years (from 1672 to 1676) ten criticisms were published in the *Philosophical Transactions* of the Royal Society, together with eleven replies from Newton. During the course of this correspondence Newton further articulated and clarified his views. It was agreed that Newton had shown that differential refraction explained the elongation of the image produced by the prism. However, before he pointed it out, not many seemed to have noticed the significance of this elongation, namely, that it appeared to contradict the newly discovered law of refraction, because it was not yet common for investigators to make precise measurements in the way that Newton did. Also, Newton's demonstration that a single color was unchanged when it passed through the prism seemed to refute a theory, often held at the time (by Hooke, for example), which proposed that there were two major colors, red and blue, and that all intermediate colors were compositions of these two. In which case, the differential color refraction produced by a prism would be expected to result in the separation of a chosen inter-mediate color into further components. But this does not hap-pen, and Newton proposed instead that each color was elementary and indivisible and that it was such colors which were separated out by the prism. This is what was unacceptable to his critics. They did not agree with him that his *"experimen-tum crucis"* *showed* that the different colors were already con-tained in the light prior to refraction, and they could see no reason why it should cause them to abandon their view that the colors were produced by the prism.

This was not the only objection to Newton's work by his contemporaries. His account of his new theory of light and color was simultaneously an account of a new methodology of science which he was keen to promote.[150] This new style of science was a fundamental departure from the style of science which was familiar at the time. This consisted of a combination of some form of mechanical philosophy (usually atomism) with the new experimental philosophy. This was the style of science devel-oped by Descartes, who was the most influential of the new philosophers. But Newton openly refused to adopt this approach. His concern was that it could not lead to knowledge which is certain, but only to knowledge which is probable. He agreed with his critics that his experiments, together with his interpretation of them, would be readily understandable in terms of a corpuscular hypothesis of the nature of light. He affirmed that he thought this hypothesis to be very probable, but that is as far as it is possible to go, and that other hypotheses might explain the observations equally well and hence also be probable. What he proposed, on the other hand, was certain because, he maintained, it was reached directly by experiment. It was not dependent on any hypothesis about the nature of light, nor did it lead to any certain knowledge of the hidden nature of light underlying the observed phenomena. As he put it in his *Optical Lectures* in 1669 (not published until 1728): "It is affirmed that these propositions are to be treated not hypothetically and probably, but by experiments or demonstratively." Because, he maintained, his theory was not dependent on any hypothesis concerning the nature of light, discussion and examination of it must be based solely on the experiments in question, or on other experiments which may be suggested. Any discussion which depended on the assumption of a hypothesis about the nature of light was therefore methodologically unsound and must be rejected.[151]

However, it seemed to others at the time that Newton *did* have a hypothesis about the nature of light, and that, contrary to what he claimed, he *did* "mingle conjectures with certainties." Hooke attributed a corpuscular philosophy to Newton in the report which the Royal Society asked him to write on Newton's work. One statement of Newton's in particular seemed to indicate clearly that he was affirming positively a corpuscular hypothesis of light:

> These things being so, it can no longer be disputed, whether there be colors in the dark, nor whether they be the qualities of the objects we see, no nor perhaps, whether light be a body.

It seems quite understandable that this passage would be a source of confusion. What did Newton really mean by the last phrase? Hooke saw it as an assertion of the corpuscular hypothesis, but Newton, in his reply to Hooke's report, denies that he *asserted* such a hypothesis while agreeing that "as to the principle parts [it] is not against me." Newton goes on to say about hypotheses:

> And therefore I chose to decline them all, and to speak of light in general terms, considering it abstractly, as something or other propagated every way in straight lines from luminous bodies, without determining, what that Thing is; whether a confused Mixture of *difform* qualities, or Modes of bodies, or of Bodies themselves, or of any Virtues, Powers, or Beings whatsoever. And for the same reason I chose to speak of *Colors* according to the information of our Senses as if they were qualities of Light *without* us. Whereas by that *Hypothesis* [i.e., the corpuscular hypothesis] I must have considered them rather as *Modes* of Sensation, excited in the mind by various motions, figures, or sizes of corpuscles of Light, making various Mechanical impressions on the Organ of Sense.

This view, i.e., that colors can be considered as qualities of light, is one which Goethe vigorously rejected. His argument was that every colored light is darker than colorless light (often mistakenly called white light). Of course, we need to remember that all light is invisible in itself; light only becomes visible when it illuminates matter. It is only in making something visible that light becomes visible itself. In empty space we see neither colored nor colorless light. Now the point of Goethe's argument against the view which Newton expressed in this passage is that any colored light on a screen is darker than colorless light on the screen. So if colorless light were to be composed of colored lights (we should say, to be more precise, color-producing lights), then the brighter light would be compounded of darker lights. Evidently this is a contradiction.

Newton's notebooks reveal a very different story than the one which he presented in his publications. They show that from the start Newton held a corpuscular hypothesis, conceiving light rays as streams of corpuscles. The important point is that this hypothesis is not an additional embellishment, an optional extra, but "formed part of his language to describe his earliest experiments on color."[152] The corpuscular hypothesis played a formative part in Newton's thinking, and it may well have been this which led him to his new theory that the prism did not produce the colors, but *separated* colors which were there already. Far from being derived *from* experiments, as indeed it could not be, and notwithstanding Newton's claim to the contrary, his new theory may have been a consequence of the corpuscular language of his early thinking. In other words, the corpuscular hypothesis functioned as an *organizing idea* in his interpretation of the prism experiments. Since the root of this idea is in a historical (philosophical) school of thought, then it seems that we would have to say that Newton's experiment, together with its interpretation, has a historical dimension as well as an empirical one. We are accustomed to thinking of an experiment as being only empirical, but this is because, as described previously, we miss the action of the organizing idea. Inasmuch as the organizing idea has its origin in a historical school of thought, then the historical dimension is incorporated into the experiment itself. A good part of the controversy aroused by Goethe's attack on Newton has come from overlooking the *intrinsic* historical dimension of scientific knowledge, treating it as if it were a purely natural or empirical kind of knowledge, as well as from taking Newton's own account at face value.

In terms of corpuscularian thinking, Newton's discovery that each color is differently refracted when passed through a prism would require a difference in some quantitative property of the light corpuscles to be correlated with each color. For example, a difference in size or a difference in velocity of the corpuscles might be associated with a difference in color. Newton considered both of these possibilities at different times. With such a correlation in mind, thinking in terms of mechanical properties of corpuscles instead of qualities of colors, it would be much easier to conclude that the colors were all present already in the light (so-called white light, which is really colorless light), since we would only need to think of corpuscles differing in some mechanical magnitude all mixed together. Similarly, it is much easier to think of the action of the prism as being to order the corpuscles into sets according to the magnitude of the mechanical property in question. Hence it seems straightforward to conclude that the prism *separates* the light into component colors.

Newton's theory looks much more plausible when it is considered in the context of the mechanical, atomistic way of thinking than it does when it is presented as if it were derived directly from experiment. We can see this particularly well when we remember that, according to this theory, there is no blue, red, or other color as such outside of the human organism. Far from being qualities of light (as Newton maintains in the quotation above), the colors as such arise only when light corpuscles interact with the human organism. If atomism is the organizing idea in the background here, then it becomes much easier to see how it would seem plausible that the different colors are present in the light already, and are separated by differential refraction as a result of a difference in some mechanical property. Color as a *quality* doesn't come into the physics at all. It is when we start to be concerned with this quality that Newton's account of color begins to appear unconvincing. This is where Goethe began: with color as a quality, instead of with the replacement of color by a measurable quantity with which it can be correlated.

One of the foremost scholars of Newton, I. Bernard Cohen, concludes that "in view of the corpuscular and mathematical presuppositions of Newton's thought . . . it would be difficult to maintain that this classic experiment and its interpretation can be understood on a simple level of experiment and observation."[153] In fact, Newton's account is far from being the straightforward exposition of his discoveries that he presents it as being. It is really a careful exercise in rhetoric, arranged to persuade the reader while at the same time leading him to believe that the conclusions come directly from experiment.[154] We have seen already that Newton did something similar in his

work on motion, where he maintained that he reached his first
law of motion (the principle of inertia) on the basis of experimental work done by Galileo, as if this could be discovered
directly by induction from experiment. But in fact he did nothing of the kind. So now, here also in his work on light and
color, we find the same misleading picture of how he proceeded. This has been a major historical source of the widely held
view that scientific knowledge is derived directly from experiment (the epistemological source of this view has been dealt
with earlier). It is the false belief that this *is* how science proceeds which stands in the way of understanding what Goethe
did in his science of color.

Newton held an *ideal* of how certain knowledge of nature
could be achieved. This seems to have been derived from the
experimental philosophy inaugurated by Francis Bacon, as
this was advocated in England at the time by Robert Boyle.
This regarded experiment as a method of making empirical
discoveries directly from nature, where the experimenter was
unencumbered by any prior assumptions of a hypothetical
nature—such as those of the mechanical philosophy proposed
by Descartes. The latter could be introduced legitimately only
after the experimental discovery had been made. Such specu-
lations, although valuable, could not lead to certainty in science. The mechanistic hypothesis was seen by Newton as
being no more than probable, and, as such, useful for conjec-
turing about causes once the primary work of discovery by
experiment had been done. This empirical approach went in
the opposite direction to Descartes' way, which was the dominant style of science at the time. He saw the mechanistic world
hypothesis as the starting point, not as something to be added
on afterwards as a plausible explanation.[155] The role of experiment for Descartes was either one of filling in the details of
the mechanistic world picture or of deciding between possible
alternative mechanical explanations. It was not the primary
route to discovery which Newton, following Bacon, claimed it
to be. Descartes' own contribution to this program of the

mechanical philosophy was so enormously influential that it was the major reason for the opposition which Newton's work met with initially.

We have seen considerable cause to doubt that Newton did in fact make his discoveries purely from experiment in the way that he maintained. But, nevertheless, he stuck to his ideal of empirical discovery in all his publications, always claiming to make his discoveries purely from experiments, and only then going on to consider possible theoretical explanations in terms of what were to him, he maintained, only plausible hypotheses. Thus he strove to keep separate what he considered could be certain in science from what could not. He was always consistent with this ideal in his publications—although to see this we have to consider them comprehensively, and not selectively as has often been done. Thus, only *after* the long correspondence in the pages of the *Philosophical Transactions*, where Newton answered each criticism by giving more experimental details, did he finally send a long paper to the Royal Society with the title (in part) "A Theory of Light and Colors, containing partly an hypothesis to explain the properties of light discoursed of by him in his former papers . . . " (December 9, 1675). He asked for this to be read, but not to be published. Before stating the hypothesis, he gives his reason for putting it forward:

> Having observed the heads of some great virtuosos to run much upon hypotheses, as if my discourses wanted a hypothesis to explain them by, and found that some, when I could not make them take my meaning, when I spoke of the nature of light and colors abstractly, have readily apprehended it when I *illustrated* my discourse with a hypothesis; *for this reason* I have here thought fit to send you a description of the circumstances of this hypothesis, as much tending to the *illustrations* of the papers I herewith send you.

He goes on to add, so there really can be no doubt as to his meaning, that he will not assume the hypothesis he is about to describe (or any other), but that to avoid repeating himself and being cumbersome he will sometimes "speak of it as if he had assumed it, and propounded it to be believed."

After this introduction, Newton plunges straight into the details of his hypothesis, which he insists is meant to be no more than an illustration to help those who cannot think without some way of visualizing in terms of the familiar sensory world. The details need not concern us here. Suffice it to mention that he supposes there to be an all-pervading ethereal medium which can undergo a vibrating motion (i.e., wave motion). Light is not the ether nor the vibrations set up in it, but consists of "multitudes of unimaginable small corpuscles of various sizes," and it is these which set up vibrations in the ether under various circumstances. Color is a subjective experience corresponding to the size of the light corpuscle—the largest particles striking the retina produce the sensation of red, for example. But, whatever the details of his hypothesis, Newton's disclaimer concerning the role it plays for him (or rather, for others, since he effectively denies that it played any role for him!) is completely at odds with what his notebooks show: that from the beginning the corpuscular hypothesis played a formative role in his thinking and an integral part in his language for describing experiments. The ideal of scientific methodology which he presented in public, and believed in, was not in fact the route by which he made his discovery.

Newton followed the same procedure, reflecting this methodology, in subsequent publications. In the various editions of his magnum opus on light, the *Optiks* (1704 onwards), he first presents what he calls propositions, followed by the proof of each such proposition by experiments. Newton is deliberately following the method of geometrical exposition here, presenting experimental science in a manner which reflects the degree of certainty he believes it to be capable of achieving. Since, he believes, this is the same degree of certainty as that achieved by mathematics, then it is only fitting that optics should be presented in the manner of geometry, for which the *Elements* of Euclid formed the paradigm (cf. Spinoza's *Ethics*, which presented a fundamental ethics in the same geometrical manner). So, Newton's *Opticks* gives a "geometrical exposition" of an experimental science. But there is a reversal in the order here which we must notice if we are not to be confused by this exposition. The experiments which Newton believes constitute proof of an experimental proposition must have come first, i.e., *before* the experimental proposition, because, according to Newton's own methodology, this must have been reached in the first place *from* the experiments. Such a reversal in the order is typical of this geometrical style of presentation, and if we are not careful it only adds to the confusion caused already (in the 1672 account of his discovery) by the misleading claim that the new theory of color was discovered directly and purely from experiments.

Only after he has completed this account of what he sees as experimental certainties, does Newton then go on to the hypothetical part of his exposition. This is given separately in the form of a series of queries containing hypotheses about light, which give hypothetical (uncertain) causes of the experimental propositions (certain). These queries increase in complexity through successive editions. However, although his presentation of them comes after the experimental propositions, in line with his general methodology, it is difficult to believe that the conjectures which the queries contain were only in the nature of auxiliary material for those who needed this kind of support in their thinking. Newton's claim that he did not need this kind of thing himself has been found to be wanting, although it does express the ideal to which he aspired.

Newton's style of science challenged the claim of the mechanistic philosophy to be *the* way to the truth about nature. But it was never completely accepted—most likely because it is not possible to separate the purely experimental from the hypothetical in the way that he wished. Eventually a new style of science developed at the beginning of the nineteenth century, especially in France, which was the reverse of that which Newton advocated.[156] Instead of keeping them apart, the attempt was made to bring together the mathematical, the experimental, and the theoretical strands of science so that they worked together in a mutually supporting way toward the achievement of scientific knowledge. This style of science, in which these three factors worked together, was very successful in physics until the developments in atomic physics in the 1920s—when the theoretical component became problematic.[157] The first major success of this style of science was in optics. It led to the emergence of what physicists still refer to as "physical optics," mainly through the work of Fresnel and Arago. This theory was particularly successful in understanding the formation of images by optical instruments and the reasons for the limit to the resolution which such an instrument can achieve. The mathematical, experimental, and theoretical components all worked together in a remarkable synthesis, but the theoretical component was provided by a wave theory of light and not by a particle theory.[158] In this case color is correlated with the frequency of the wave (as the pitch of a musical note is correlated with the frequency of the sound wave)—a suggestion which had been made already by advocates of the wave theory in Newton's day.[159] This clearly makes no fundamental difference to the viewpoint of the mechanical philosophy. Color is still understood as a secondary quality, arising from the interaction of a primary (i.e., quantitative) property with the organism, and not as a quality of nature. It is this primary, measurable property which is the objective reality according to the mechanical philosophy. The quality of color is only subjective, and is therefore not itself a fitting object of scientific knowledge. But because of the correlation, color can always be replaced by a measurable property. In the wave theory this is the frequency (or wavelength), instead of the size or speed as in the corpuscular theory. But, whichever the case, the fact remains that color itself is not conceived to be a reality of nature in mathematical physics.

The Physics of Goethean Style

It has been necessary to go into Newton's work in some detail, because the failure to understand this correctly has necessarily resulted in failure to understand the nature of Goethe's achievement. It has resulted in the misunderstanding that Goethe was a muddleheaded dilettante who did not understand science. His work on color is thought of as being, at best, a glorious failure. But when we look at this work more comprehensively, in the light of the historical dimension of science, then we begin to see *both* Newton and Goethe differently.

The origin of Goethe's work on color was very different from the origin of Newton's work. Goethe was not interested in instrumental optics—in fact he was not interested in *optics* at all. Whereas Newton had wanted to bring chromatics under optics—which was a revolutionary innovation at the time—Goethe wanted to develop a science of chromatics which was independent and free from optics. His own interest in color was aroused by his experience with paintings during his Italian journey. Far from being concerned with the improvement of optical images in telescopes, Goethe's interest was primarily in the *phenomenality* of color. He wanted to understand the necessary conditions for color to arise. Such conditions were not to be discovered by retreating from the concrete phenomena into abstractions—such as quantitative measurements or mechanistic explanations—but by going more fully into the phenomena as encountered in experience. This means, in the first place, directing attention *into* sensory experience, instead of away from it, as is the case with the theory-dominated style of physics we have discussed so far. This step into the sensory, and the mode of consciousness which it entails, has been discussed in part II of this book.[160] What we will do here is to look at the way that Goethe's approach to the phenomenon of prismatic colors illuminates Newton's approach. This has the inverse effect of making Goethe's own approach more visible to us—as the light which illuminates something is thereby itself made visible to us.

What is fundamental to Goethe's approach can be summed up in one word: attention. Goethe gives attention to the phenomena ("The Primal Phenomenon of Color" in part II) so that he begins to experience their *belonging* together ("Unity without Unification" in part II) and thereby to see how they mutually explain each other. Such a holistic explanation is an *intrinsic* explanation, in contrast to the extrinsic explanation whereby phenomena are explained in terms of something other than themselves—which is conceived to be "beyond" or "behind" the phenomena, i.e., *separate* from the phenomena in some way. Extrinsic explanation is the mode of explanation typical of theory-based science. But through *attention* to the concrete, i.e., to the phenomena as such, we begin to encounter the *qualities* of the phenomena without any concern for their supposed ontological status as dictated by a theory (i.e., whether they are secondary qualities). Attention to the phenomena brings us into contact with quality, not quantity. The latter is in fact reached by abstracting from the phenomena, which entails standing back from the phenomena to produce a head-orientated science (to use Goethe's phrase) instead of participating in the phenomena through the senses. It is when we experience qualities that the relationships among the phenomena begin to appear, and the phenomena thereby become mutually explanatory. It is when we are concerned with only the quantitative abstraction that we need to go "beyond" or "behind" the phenomena to find an external explanation. But when the explanation is intrinsic, the phenomena become intelligible in themselves. There is a subtle reversal of direction here. Instead of forcing our (quantitative) categories onto the phenomena, we are led into the phenomena through a way of access genuinely belonging to the phenomena themselves. Goethe's way of attention to the phenomena becomes the experience of reading the phenomena in terms of themselves—it becomes the hermeneutic phenomenology of nature.[161]

Such a science is a concrete science of qualities instead of an abstract science of quantities. These should be seen as being complementary to each other, not as antagonistic—Goethe saw quantity and quality as two poles of existence. The reason why this has been obscured is because of the philosophy of atomism, with its primary/secondary distinction and the subjectivizing of the secondary qualities. But a science of quantity as such does not need the carrier of atomism. When this is recognized, elements which are really foreign to the science of quantity can be removed. Since it is these elements which are responsible for the apparent antagonism, this too disappears, and the proper relationship of complementarity between a science of quantity and a science of quality can now become evident. The aim of the physics of Goethean style is to do for the qualities of nature what the physics of Galilean style, and its subsequent development, has done for the quantitative pole of nature.

The place to begin is Goethe's early work on color, *Contribution to Optics* (1791), and not with his later magnum opus, *Colour Theory* (1810). Much is to be gained by following this through practically. An excellent guide to this is now available in the work of Heinrich Proskauer, *The Rediscovery of Color*, which provides practical means for directing attention into the phenomena.[162] The first discovery is that light *and dark* are needed for colors to arise with the prism. Colors are seen only where light and dark come together, i.e., at an edge or boundary.[163] Exploration of these "edge spectra" shows that there are two contrasting colored bands, red/yellow and blue/violet, depending on the orientation of the boundary to the prism.[164] So a single boundary gives us only half the color phenomenon on any one occasion. The other half can only be obtained by inverting the boundary. To obtain the whole phenomenon we must have both orientations of the boundary together. But this can be done in two ways, as shown here:

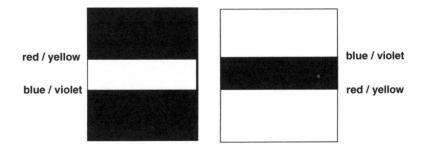

If the central band in each of these figures is made progressively narrower, the two poles of the color phenomenon (the edge spectra) are brought closer together to the point where they meet and overlap. Where this happens, a new color arises. In the one case, where yellow and blue overlap, green arises. In the other case, where violet and red overlap, the color which arises has been called "peach-blossom" or "ruby-magenta." Now the edge spectra are merged into a continuous spectrum. But since there are two such continuous spectra, with one the inverse of the other, we should call them "spectrum" and counterspectrum." In the case where green arises, we find the sequence of colors which Newton describes, and which he identifies as being there "in the light" all the while until they are separated by the prism.

But careful attention to the phenomenon shows us that the spectrum which Newton describes is *not* the basic phenomenon and that it does not arise in the way that he imagines under the influence of the (theoretical) idea which organizes his thinking. The basic phenomenon is an edge spectrum which arises at a light/dark boundary. The continuous spectrum which Newton and others observed is a compound phenomenon which appears when the two opposite edge spectra interact. The colors are not derived out of the light by the supposed separating action of the prism. On the contrary, Goethe asserts, "Light is the simplest, most elementary, most homogeneous thing we know. It is not compounded," and "The colors are excited in light, not developed out of light. If the conditions cease, the light becomes as colorless as before, not because the colors return to it but because they cease."[165]

We can now understand the origin of the phenomenon which Newton found so striking, namely, that the image of a small illuminated hole formed by a prism on a screen was not circular but oblong. When we have rectangular shapes, such as those in the diagrams above, then if the axis of the prism through which we look is parallel to the horizontal boundaries, we see colors only on these horizontal boundaries and none on the vertical edges. If we change the shape of the figure to a triangle, for example, we find colored bands on all three

edges. If the axis of the prism is horizontal, the colored band on the horizontal edge will be broader than on the sloping edges. If we now change to a circular shape, we find, holding the prism

horizontally, that there is a colored border effect all the way round, except at the points on the circle which are exactly vertical. The width of the colored border varies continuously around the circle, being widest where the circle becomes horizontal. Thus the colored figure, as seen through the prism, becomes slightly oval.

 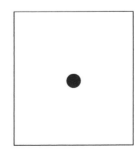

If we now shrink the size of the circles, as seen on the previous page, the broad horizontal colored bands will merge, forming green in the white circle and ruby-magenta in the black. But the vertical points on the side of the circle will not be colored, and so the width of the colored figure seen through the prism will be unchanged here—i.e., it will be the same as the width of the circle seen without using the prism. The overall result is that a very elongated colored oval is seen, with maximum width the same as the circle seen with the eye directly. In other words, we see something very much like Newton's oblong image, which he tells us was five times as long as it was broad, this being "a disproportion so extravagant, that it excited me to a more than ordinary curiosity of examining, from whence it might proceed."

We can readily verify that this is what we are seeing by making Newton's *foramen exiguum* for ourselves. To do this we simply take a piece of paper and make a small hole in it with a pin or a sharp pencil point. If this is held up to the light and looked at through a prism, the bright tiny hole is elongated into a continuous line of color: red, orange, yellow, green, blue, violet. This is the phenomenon from which Newton started—at least that is what he tells us. We can now see for ourselves that, as Goethe recognized, this is not a suitable place to begin. It is really a compound effect, which Newton mistakenly took to be simple. It is from this compound phenomenon that Newton said he eventually came to the conclusion (via his other experiments) that the colors were already contained in the light, and the action of the prism was to separate them. So this phenomenon, which is taken as basic, is now called the "spectrum of light."

But the basic phenomenon is not the continuous spectrum. It is the edge spectra which arise at the light/dark boundary. Furthermore, there is also the fact of the counterspectrum. If, instead of making a tiny hole and holding it up to the light, we make a tiny dot on the paper and look at this through the prism, we again see a continuous line of color, but in this case the colors are: blue, violet, ruby-magenta, red, orange, yellow. If we were to follow the form of Newton's thinking, we would have to say this is the "spectrum of dark." But this is impossible so far as mainstream physics is concerned. For this physics considers that darkness is only the *absence* of light, so it would be nonsense to suppose that darkness could contain colors which can be separated by a prism!

However, we should go into this a little further, because it is not quite so simple as the above account makes out. Mainstream physics does have a way of explaining how the counter-spectrum arises, and the method which it employs is the same as the one used to explain why a large white surface looked at through a prism will remain white except at the edges. It is this observation which first led Goethe to proclaim "that the Newtonian doctrine is false." He believed, wrongly, that the Newtonian doctrine that the colors are already contained in the light meant that the entire white surface should appear colored, and not just the edges. Sepper has shown that Goethe's error here was not the result of ignorance about Newton's theory, but was due to misleading presentations of Newton's theory in the German textbooks of physics available to him.[166]

The quantitative way of seeing requires that any phenomenon must be represented in terms of parts which are external to one another. Now a large white surface presents a single homogeneous appearance to the senses and does not appear in any way to be made up of a number of parts which are external to one another. So the quantitative *method* is to conceive of such a surface as if it were composed of a very large number (strictly, an infinity) of point sources. Each point source is separate from the ones adjacent to it, according to this construction, even though they are conceived purely as points of light, and hence not as having boundaries between them! This abstraction is clearly an ideal construction, which is necessary as such to accommodate the phenomenon to the quantitative way of seeing.[167]

Each such point source is now imagined to give rise to its own continuous spectrum by separation of the constituent colors in the light—each point will give rise to a continuous line of color, as described above for the case of a tiny hole. But because of the proximity of these supposed sources to each other, the continuous spectra formed by adjacent points will overlap (i.e., in the vertical direction). So the red and yellow from one point source will overlap with the blue and violet from the adjacent point source, and so on. The net effect is that the colors will recombine to give white again. The basis for this comes from a comment which Newton made in his first letter to the Royal Society:

> But the most surprising and wonderful composition was that of *Whiteness*. There is no one sort of Rays which alone can exhibit this. 'Tis ever compounded, and to its composition are requisite all the aforesaid primary Colours [N.B.: he does not mean here the colors which we call the primary colors today, but the colors which he believes are separated in the spectrum of light] mixed in due proportion. I have often with *Admiration* beheld, that all the Colours of the prism being made to converge, and thereby to be again mixed as they were in the light before it was Incident upon the Prism, reproduced light entirely and perfectly white. . . .

But at the edges the recombination must be incomplete. At one edge the red and yellow from the next point source will be missing because the "next" point source simply isn't there. So the result will be unrecombined blue and violet at the edge. The reverse will happen at the other edge, leaving unrecombined red and yellow. This explains the origin of the edge spectra, as well as explaining the persistence of the white. It is all a matter of geometry, and can be worked out in mathematical detail with an impressive degree of precision. But, even so, it is not really possible to avoid a residual feeling that there is something very artificial about a method which fills space with color only to cancel it out again.

The method by which the counterspectrum is explained in mainstream physics is the same. In this case we consider a black band sandwiched between two white surfaces. Following the same procedure, i.e., imagining the white surfaces to be made up of a very large number of point sources, each of which gives its own spectrum with the prism, we again find incomplete recombination of the colors at the black/white borders. But in this case the unrecombined colors will be blue and violet at the top border and red and yellow at the bottom one. So if they overlap in the middle (either because the black strip is narrow, or because it is viewed from a distance), the red and the violet will mix to form ruby-magenta. This explanation of the counter-spectrum was given by Helmholtz in a lecture, "On Goethe's Natural Scientific Works," in 1853.[168]

But of course there are no such "boundaryless" sources as this construction imagines. Point sources must be conceived as being without an edge to them because otherwise there would be boundaries in the white. But there cannot be a source without boundaries because it would not be delineated as a separate enti-ty. These sources are not physical but only mathematical. Atten-tion to the phenomenon itself reveals that the way the phenomenon is habitually described is wrong: colors do not come out of light, but arise only where there is a boundary. Goethe recognized that the mistake had been to miss the basic phenomenon, and to begin with what is really a compound phe-nomenon—Newton's elongated, colored image of a tiny hole. To start here and try to explain the elongation can only lead in the wrong direction, because what is fundamental *in the phenomenon* has not first been made visible. This cannot be done by measure-ment, but only by finding the laws of quality in the phenome-non, i.e., the connections which follow of necessity from the qualities of the colors themselves. It is when this has not been done that artificial constructions such as those discussed above have to be introduced. Goethe described the problem succinctly:

> The worst that can happen to physical science as well as to many other kinds of knowledge, is that people should treat a secondary phenomenon as a primordial one and (since it is impossible to derive the original fact from the secondary state) seek to explain what is in reality the cause by an effect that is made to usurp its place.[169]

Suppose we now use colored figures, instead of just black and white. Colors again appear at the edges, but not with the same degree of intensity as with black and white. The condition for the arising of color is simply that there is some distinction between a lighter and a darker region. The intensity of the colors depends on the degree of contrast (observations with different shades of grey, instead of black and white, show this clearly). But the color of the figure itself is now also a factor which has to be taken into account, and this makes the phenomenon more complicated.

Consider this figure :

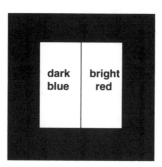

Because dark blue and bright red are both lighter than black, the colors formed here are in both cases the same as those formed with a white rectangle on a black backround. Thus at the upper edge the colors will be red, orange, and yellow— with yellow the furthest from the black. At the lower edge the colors will be blue and violet—with violet the furthest into the black. Looking at the upper edge of the dark blue rectangle, we find that the red which arises with the prism blends with the dark blue, to give a dark band which *merges with the black background*. The net effect is that the dark blue rectangle appears to be shorter at the top edge (compared with the red rectangle) by an amount equal to the "missing" prismatic red. This is easily overlooked—and indeed easily mistaken for something else, as we will see—but careful observation makes it visible.[170] Looking now at the upper edge of the bright red rectangle, we find that the red which arises with the prism adds on to the red of the rectangle to have the effect of seemingly increasing its length. The effect is the opposite of the previous case with the dark blue rectangle. But the two augment each other to increase the shift which appears to have taken place between the two differently colored rectangles at their upper edges. If we now turn our attention to the colors at the lower edges of the rectangles, we find in each case a similar effect, but the inverse of the effect at the upper edge. Thus, the violet formed at the lower boundary between dark blue and black has the effect of seeming to extend the dark blue rectangle downwards into the black. But, seen against the bright red, the blue and violet are hardly visible. So the overall effect of the colors formed with a prism when seen against dark blue and bright red backgrounds is that the blue and red rectangles appear to have been shifted with respect to each other in the vertical direction. But this appearance is only superficial. There is no such shift. But acceptance of the superficial appearance at its face value can lead to a fundamental error of judgment.

Newton offered this phenomenon as "proof by experiment" of Proposition 1, Theorem 1 in his *Opticks* (1704). This proposition states that "Lights which differ in Color, differ also in degrees of Refrangibility." However, historical research has shown that Newton was aware of this phenomenon, and that he failed to observe it correctly and hence misinterpreted it long before he first mentioned it publicly. He makes no mention of it in the letter to the Royal Society of 1672, where he focuses exclusively on the so-called spectrum of light formed with a tiny hole. But he records it in an earlier notebook:

> That the rays which make blue are refracted more than the rays which make red appears from this experiment. If one half of the thread be blue and the other red and a shade or black body be put behind it then looking on the thread through a prism one half of the thread shall appear higher than the other and not both in one direct line, by reason of unequal refractions in the differing colors.[171]

Although he does not mention this in his Royal Society paper, we can hardly suppose that he was not influenced by it. Indeed, we have noted earlier ("Newton and the Mathematical Physics of Color") that this particular paper, while appearing to be a direct account of a discovery made by experiment, is really a cleverly constructed rhetorical device. The so-called *experimentum crucis*, from which Newton claimed to have discovered differential refrangibility, does not seem to be the place where he discovered it at all. It seems more likely that he brought the idea of differential refrangibility *to* the *experimentum crucis*. So he concluded that the colors are there all along in the light *because* he already had the idea of *differential* refraction from his inadequate observation and error of judgment with the red/blue thread. It has been pointed out elsewhere (see "The Primal Phenomenom of Color") that Newton's way of thinking here amounts to trying to understand the origin of the phenomenon in terms of the finished product, instead of following through the coming-into-being of the phenomenon. He back-projects the end product (as he sees it), so that an effect is mistaken for a cause—which, in Rumi's graphic phrase, amounts to trying to "reach the milk by way of the cheese." Here, once again, a complex phenomenon is mistaken for a simple one. Indeed, the phenomenon itself is not even noticed because Newton considered only the colors themselves (i.e., the blue and red rectangles) and did not consider them in relation to their surroundings. He was too selective, considering these colors in isolation from their context (the black surrounding), instead of being comprehensive and seeing the colors and their background together. This seems to be a common habit of mind: to attend to a specific content while ignoring the context in which it occurs. This means that the content is seen analytically, as something which exists independently and can be considered on its own. But this is false to the phenomenon, which must be considered comprehensively if it is to be seen as what it is. If we do not see comprehensively, the phenomenon we encounter is not the authentic phenomenon but a counterfeit. In fact it is a pseudophenomenon because it conceals the phenomenon in a false appearance. Goethe's physics, on the other hand, is a phenomenology of nature, and as such it makes the phenomenon visible because it considers the colors in relation to their surroundings.

By this means, then, we are able to recognize that there is no differential refraction here. Newton's statement at the beginning of his *Opticks* is false. It cannot be concluded from such an experiment that ". . . the Light which comes from the blue half of the Paper through the Prism to the Eye, does in like Circumstances suffer a greater Refraction than the Light which comes from the red half, and by consequence is more refrangible." In view of the fact that, as his early notebook shows, this may well have been the experiment which convinced Newton of differential refraction from the very beginning of his work on color, it is clearly important to recognize that his conclusion, carried through all his subsequent work, is an error of judgment grounded in a mistaken observation. Proskauer points out that if Newton had observed blue and red rectangles on a *white* background, he would have found that in this case the *red* appears to be more refrangible— owing to the way that the prismatic colors at the edges merge with the colors of the background.[172] Also, as Goethe pointed out, according to the theory of differential refrangibility, the difference in refrangibility between red and violet ought to be greater than between red and dark blue. But if red and violet are placed against a black background, the violet conceals the prismatic colors formed at the edges less than dark blue does. This means that violet would seem *less* refrangible than dark blue—but, because the prismatic colors are so much more visible in this case we would have no reason to think in terms of differential refrangibility. Goethe concluded ironically:

> How it stands with Newton's powers of observation and the "exactness" of his experiments will, on the other hand, be perceived with astonishment by everyone posessed of eyes and common sense. Indeed, I make bold to say that had he not deceived himself, who would have been able to deceive a man of such exceptional gifts as Newton by means of such mumbo-jumbo.[173]

The only colors which Newton was interested in were red and blue against a dark background. It turns out that these are the only two cases where we have to look very carefully indeed to see the prismatic colors on the edges. If we do a more comprehensive experiment with a card prepared like this:

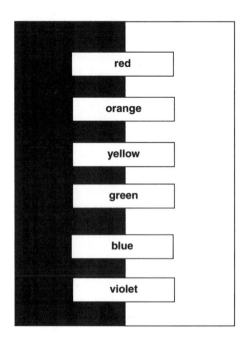

we find that the colors other than red and blue show prismatic colors at the edges clearly. When we have it all in front of us like this, then it is not difficult to see that there *are* edge colors there also with red and blue on the background. Then we can *see* that there is no differential refraction.[174]

As with the elongated image formed when light is passed through a prism after coming from a tiny hole, so here also we have reliance on an *isolated* case. It is a feature of Newton's experimental work, which Goethe criticized, that he did not attempt to see comprehensively. Just as he did not consider the prismatic colors in their context, but treated them in isolation, so also he did not consider each experiment in its experimental context—i.e., the context formed for it by all the other possible experiments with which it is related. It is a strong feature of Goethe's work, on the other hand, that he consciously tried to see comprehensively.

Goethe discussed his method explicitly in the essay "The Experiment as Mediator between Subject and Object." He wrote this in 1792, shortly after his *Contribution to Optics*, but did not publish it until 1823.[175] With Newton's *experimentum crucis* in mind, he warns that "nothing is more dangerous than the desire to prove some thesis directly through experiments" and insists that it is only when experiments are combined that we can begin to *see* the phenomena according to *their* nature, and not according to our own subjective interpretation. But this must be done in the right way:

> As worthwhile as each individual experiment may be, it receives its real value only when united or combined with other experiments. However to unite or combine just two somewhat similar experiments calls for more rigor and care than even the sharpest observers usually expect of themselves. Two phenomena may be related, but not nearly so closely as we think. Although one experiment seems to follow from another, an extensive series of experiments might be required to put the two into an order actually conforming to nature.

The question is, how can we find the natural connection (i.e., the connection according to nature) between two phenomena, appearing in two experiments, which is such as to make the phenomena more fully visible, i.e., to let them show themselves as themselves? This must be done by "working out every possible aspect and modification of every bit of empirical evidence, every experiment." The natural method is not to study a phenomenon in isolation, but to see it in the context of other phenomena with which it is closely related. If this is done adequately, an experimental sequence of *contiguous* phenomena can be arranged, which shows a natural unity in the phenomena. Goethe says that he tried to set up just such a series of contiguous experiments in his *Contribution to Optics*. The experiments in this series can all be derived from one another, so that any one experiment can be seen in the context of all the other experiments with which it is related. He says that this is the real task of the researcher into nature: to proceed from a single experiment to the one which is immediately adjacent to it, and so on. He refers to this procedure as the manifolding [*Vermannigfaltigung*] of a single experiment.[176] When an experiment is followed through its variations in this way, then the interrelationships between these variations are such that it is as if there were one single experiment. Goethe says of such a series of contiguous experiments that it "constitutes as it were just one experiment, presents just one experience from the most manifold perspectives. Such an experience, which consists of several others is obviously of a higher kind. It represents the formula under which countless single examples are expressed."[177] The Goethean "formula" referred to here is this higher experience of the One experiment which is many. We can see here the form of "multiplicity in unity," which is fundamental to Goethe's organic perspective. The series of contiguous experiments is a metamorphic sequence.

The purpose of experimentation is for the phenomenon to show itself as fully as possible. As Sepper puts it "Goethe studied the phenomenon in its phenomenality," and for him, "Comprehension does not take the form of a theory abstracted from the phenomena but rather the form of a seeing embedded in the fullness of phenomena."[178] This seeing which lets the phenomenon show itself fully, lets it appear, *is* the theory for Goethe. The theory is an experience of insight in which what is seen is the intrinsic necessity, and hence the intelligibility, of the phenomenon. We are not accustomed to this radically phenomenological approach. Evidently this is very different from what is meant by "theory" in mainstream science, which amounts to a set of propositions or an abstract mathematical model. Theory in this latter sense is almost the opposite of *seeing* in Goethe's sense, because it has the effect of covering up the phenomenon, instead of letting it appear, and of replacing it by something else. Whether this is by replacing the phenomenon with a set of numbers (i.e., formal identification of color with differences in refrangibility) or by replacing it with a mechanical model (e.g., frequency of a wave), the effect is the same. The phenomenon is explained in terms of something else, which thereby replaces it. This is an extrinsic explanation, whereas Goethe's explanation is intrinsic to the phenomena themselves.

In a statement which at first sight may seem surprising, Goethe said, "I have heard myself criticized as if I were an opponent, an enemy, of mathematics in general, which in fact no one can value more highly than I."[179] But Goethe distinguished between the *content* of mathematics and the *method of mathematics*. He asked, rhetorically, "What except for its exactitude is exact about mathematics? And this exactitude—does it not flow from an inner feeling for the truth?"[180] He saw himself doing the mathematics of the *quality* of color by following the mathematical method in the very form of his experimentation. By producing all the manifold variations of an experiment, so that they can be placed next to one another in a series, he believed he was proceeding in a mathematical way:

> From the mathematician we must learn the meticulous care required to connect things in unbroken succession, or rather, to derive things step by step. Even where we do not venture to apply mathematics we must always work as though we had to satisfy the strictest of geometricians.[181]

He said that Newton did not do this. Newton worked with the content of mathematics—i.e., quantitatively—but Goethe believed that his *method* was mathematically defective. Thus, although in his *Opticks* he tried to present his experimental work in the *style* of geometry—offering proof by experiment by arranging individual experiments like arguments—for Goethe this is defective because it is used to support a hypothesis instead of to make the phenomenon fully visible.

The consensus has always been that Goethe's work on color was entirely nonmathematical. This has been held against him as showing that he did not understand science and that he was therefore only a dilettante. But what is absent from his work (intentionally) is only concern with the quantitative aspects of the phenomena. It is thoroughly mathematical in its procedure for discovering relationships between the qualities of the colors. A parallel case in the history of science is provided by Michael Faraday's work of discovering the phenomena of electromagnetism, which gradually led to his understanding of the notion of a field of force. It is often pointed out that there is no mathematics in Faraday's work.[182] But when James Clerk Maxwell wrote his *Treatise on Electricity and Magnetism*, he said in the introduction that he had found Faraday's work to be thoroughly mathematical.[183] It was mathematical in terms of the form of its experimental procedure, not in terms of the content of mathematics. Thus Faraday's experimental procedure is mathematical in precisely the same sense as Goethe's work on color. Indeed, anyone reading Faraday's notebooks after studying Goethe's work would not find it difficult to conclude that Faraday was the Goethe of electromagnetism (or that Goethe was the Faraday of color).

It is a fundamental feature of the mathematical procedure that it does not permit the introduction of anything which is external to itself. For example, in deducing a theorem about the triangle, it is not permitted to draw a triangle and use measurements made on it in the deduction. Mathematical procedure works only with what is intrinsic to it. Goethe did just the same in investigating phenomena. He looked for relationships among the qualities of colors which have the quality of necessity. In doing this he remained entirely within the phenomena, so that the relationships are intrinsic to the phenomena, and did not introduce any elements which are external to the phenomena themselves. Any introduction of quantitative measurements, mathematical models (e.g., light rays), or mechanical models (corpuscles or waves) is utterly inadmissible because it is not in accordance with the mathematical procedure. When we do this, we begin to experience the *belonging* together of the colors (the "together" is determined by the belonging), the unity without unification, which has been described in "Unity without Unification" in part II.

We have seen that Goethe considered that a series of contiguous experiments, derived from one another in a continuous way, could be thought of as a single experiment in manifold variations. In an essay, "Mathematics and Its Abuse," Goethe gave the following quotation from the mathematician D'Alembert:

> In examining a succession of geometric propositions, each derived from the one before so that no gap exists between any adjoining tenets, one becomes aware that taken all together they constitute no more than the first proposition, which so to speak has altered gradually in the constant succession of transitions from one result to the next. It has, however, not really become diversified through these images but has merely taken on various forms.[184]

We can see that the metamorphic quality of this would appeal to Goethe. What is called the "first proposition" here is usually called an axiom in mathematics. The experience of a "higher kind," which Goethe referred to as a "formula" under which countless examples are expressed, plays a role in the science of the quality of color which is analogous to the role of an axiom in mathematics. In this case the "axiom" becomes the simplest phenomenon which can be manifolded into many closely related phenomena. He later called such an axiom of the science of qualities a "pure phenomenon," and subsequently a "primal phenomenon" (*Urphänomen*).[185]

We understand thus far that colors arise from light and dark, i.e., from their interaction, and not out of light itself by a mechanical process of separation. Goethe developed this insight further in his *Color Theory* to the point where he reached such a pure, or primal, phenomenon. He begins to do this by considering the polar opposite qualities of absolute transparency and absolute opacity. He sees these as limiting cases of the medium. The slightest restriction on absolute transparency is the introduction of the first degree of opacity. He calls this the semi-opaque or turbid condition, and there are different degrees of turbidity depending on the extent to which the transparency is diminished. Two polar situations can be distinguished:

(1) If a colorless turbid medium is placed in front of a color-less light, the light appears colored when it is looked at through the medium. The color depends on the degree of turbidity, going from yellow through orange to red, as the turbidity increases. Here the medium has a darkening effect on the light. So what we see is the darkening of light. Here we have a clear case of the arising of color out of light and dark alone, i.e., out of elements which are colorless themselves. They interpenetrate each other dynamically, and do not just modify each other in the manner of an external mechanical addition (which would produce gray). It is this interpenetration of the one by the other that Goethe meant to convey by the term *dynamic*. He said that "light and darkness united dynamically by means of turbidity generate color."[186] In no way do these colors arise out of the light—as if they were in the light already. Something *new* appears when light and dark interact dynamically: color.

(2) If a colorless turbid medium is placed in front of a black background, and the medium is illuminated from the side, then the black background will appear colored when it is looked at through the medium (i.e., from the front). The action of the turbid medium here is the opposite of what it is in the previous case. Here it holds the light, and so has a lightening effect on the dark which is seen through it. Once again, the color which appears depends on the degree of turbidity, going from violet through to pale blue as the turbidity increases. What we see here is the lightening of dark.

This is the pure phenomenon, or the primal phenomenon as he later called it. This is the "axiom" for the concrete science of the quality of color. As such, it is the "higher experience within experience" which is the "the formula" which makes all the many other possible, more complex (i.e., impure) cases intelligible. When these other, more complex color phenomena are seen in the light of the primal phenomenon, they are seen as particular manifestations of it. But Goethe understood this in a very concrete way, and it is easy to miss what he meant. To avoid doing so, we have to see unity (which is not an object, but the *way* of seeing) in an unfamiliar way. The primal phenomenon should not be taken as a principle. In other words, it should not be taken abstractly. If the primal phenomenon were simply an underlying principle, it would have the unity of "unity in multiplicity." It would be, in this case, what all the instances of color phenomena have in common. But it is much more than this, much less abstract than such an underlying principle grounded in what things have in common. Goethe described it beautifully in a letter written in 1827:

> Moreover a primal phenomenon is not to be considered as a principle from which manifold consequences result, rather it is to be understood as a fundamental appearance [i.e., phenomenon] within which the manifold is to be seen.[187]

This expresses clearly the difference between "unity in multiplicity" and "multiplicity in unity" (see "The One and the Many" in part II and "Modes of Unity" below). The manifold are to be seen within the fundamental appearance, not because they are parts of this appearance (the extensive viewpoint), but because the many are each concrete manifestations of the one (the intensive viewpoint). This concrete mode of unity is one and many at the same time. Seeing "multiplicity in unity" is the very opposite of seeing "unity in multiplicity." Unfortunately, this is often not recognized, and the uniqueness of Goethe's vision is lost. In fact, to the intellectual mind, "multiplicity in unity" and "unity in multiplicity" may even seem to be no more than two ways of saying the same thing.

What is particularly important is that there is no *separation* between the primal phenomenon and its instances. Goethe's science does not subscribe to the two-world theory. There is no underlying reality *behind* the appearances, but only the intensive depth of the phenomenon itself. We will refer to this again in connection with Goethe's organic work and his notion of the archetype. Here we will simply note that, in the domain of color, the primal phenomenon plays a role equivalent to the organic archetype. Goethe's way of understanding color is "organic" in style, instead of inorganic as it is in the mechanistic approach.

Seeing the primal phenomenon is seeing the coming-into-being of color, and every case must be an instance of the primal phenomenon, no matter how many secondary complicating factors there may be. When colors are seen archetypally (i.e., the manifold manifestations are seen within the fundamental appearance), they are seen as being intrinsically necessary. This is phenomenological seeing. In this way every color phenomenon becomes visible as intelligible in itself, i.e., without the need for any explanatory agency which lies outside the phenomenon. Colors in everyday experience—such as the colors of the sun and the sky, the color of water and the distant hills, and so on—are now seen to have such an intrinsic necessity and therefore to be understandable in themselves.

Whenever color arises, it must be a manifestation of the primal phenomenon, and this must therefore also be the case with the prismatic colors. These colors cannot be *caused* by refraction. All that matters is that the conditions for the excitation of color are brought about. *How* this is done is not relevant to the color phenomenon itself. Thus refraction must be a means for doing this, but this does *not* mean that refraction is the cause of the phenomenon. Just how the conditions for the color phenomenon to arise are produced by refraction is not easy to describe, either briefly or simply.[188] It requires that we move away from the technique of ray-optics and conceive the passage of light through the prism holistically instead of analytically. We have to see how the prism produces a differential shifting of the whole body of light which passes through it. This involves working concretely in imagination, with what Goethe called *Exakate sinnliche Phantasie*.[189] By this practice of exact sensorial imagination we can come to an understanding of what takes place *physically* (and not just geometrically) in the body of light as a whole as it passes through the prism. In this way we find that refraction itself becomes intelligible instead of just calculable. Then we have the basis for understanding

how refraction provides the conditions for the primal phenomenon, so that colors appear, without mistaking it for the cause
of color. But we cannot go further into the details of this,
which fortunately we do not need to do for the purposes of the
present work.

Goethe's insistence that "we are not seeking causes but the
circumstances under which the phenomenon occurs" led some
commentators in the nineteenth century to assert that Goethe
simply didn't understand what a scientific explanation is. They
believed that such an explanation had to be in the form of
mechanical causality. But as we have noted earlier, although this
may be satisfactory for understanding the behavior of colliding
billiard balls, it does not apply in the case of color. Spinoza's
perception—that only if two things have something in common
can the one be the cause of the other—is sufficient to show us
that mechanical causality *cannot* be applied to the *phenomenon*
of color. Goethe recognized this and therefore rejected causality
as the basis for an understanding of color. But what he was
rejecting was only *mechanical* causality, which we now recognize as being a particularly reduced mode of causality. Furthermore, we also now recognize that the adoption of this as *the*
fundamental mode of causality had its origin in a philosophical
school of thought. In other words, the idea that causality *is*
mechanical causality has no *intrinsic* scientific foundation. The
belief that mechanical causality is fundamental is another
instance of a false ontological projection of a methodological
requirement of the mechanical philosophy. In view of this, we
must now invert the judgment of those nineteenth-century
commentators who believed that Goethe's understanding of science was deficient in this respect. It now seems that it was *their*
understanding of science which was deficient. They did not
understand the historical origin of the principle of mechanical
causality in a school of thought, and so did not realize that it
functioned as a presupposition of the kind of science which
they wrongly identified as the only possible science. In this
respect, Goethe had a better understanding of causality than his

critics. He recognized, in the manner of Spinoza, the need for qualitative commensurability between cause and effect, and consequently that mechanical causality could not provide an explanation because it failed to satisfy this condition in the case of the phenomenon of color.[190]

The focus of Goethe's science is always the phenomenon itself, and this means the *phenomenality* of the phenomenon, not the phenomenon as it appears in the light of a theory. Referring to Goethe and his science, Sepper says, "The key to his perseverance and whatever success he achieved lies in the phenomenality of his science: nature and nature's phenomena, not theories about the phenomena, are its center and its center of gravity."[191] Whereas the popular view is still one which believes that modern science began when people turned to the phenomena instead of speculation, historical and philosophical studies have shown that this is not an accurate view—either of the development of modern science or of what went before it. Certainly it is true that modern science is concerned with the phenomena, but this concern is often theory-directed. This is clearly the case in mathematical physics and the quantitative approach to nature, as we have seen.

Goethe plunged into the phenomenality of the phenomena, firstly, by directing attention into sensory experience and, secondly, by practicing exact sensorial imagination. Everything is to be sought *within* the phenomenon. Working in this way brings us into contact with relationships between qualities which are intrinsically necessary—i.e., relationships which follow from the qualities themselves and cannot be otherwise. Newton, on the other hand, missed the phenomenality of color altogether. His instrumental, quantitative interest in color inevitably led him away from this. There are no intrinsically necessary connections within the color phenomena for him. He says nothing about the specific quality of any color and therefore nothing about necessary relationships between the qualities of different colors. Any connections between the colors are purely external for Newton, i.e., they do not follow with necessity from the colors themselves.[192] Similarly, with the wave theory of light which was developed later, no necessary connections between the color phenomena are disclosed by this theory—or could be disclosed by it. So everything is arbitrary: a particular color just happens to have *that* particular wavelength and not another one. Because there are no necessary connections, no internal relationships, the wave theory does not disclose any intrinsic intelligibility in the phenomena. There is no necessary connection between the quality of green and the wavelength of light which is correlated with green. Consequently there is no necessity in the fact that green lies between yellow and blue. Hence the order of the colors is without any intrinsic intelligibility. The order of the colors is therefore entirely contingent—it could equally well be otherwise so far as this theory is concerned. Necessary relationships, which disclose the intrinsic intelligibility of the phenomena, can only be discovered by focusing attention on qualities, i.e., on the phenomenality of the phenomenon. With the wave theory, it is the theory itself which is the center of attention. Consequently, instead of understanding the phenomenon, we can only explain it.

It has been customary for the most part in modern philosophy to confine necessary connection and intrinsic intelligibility to propositions, and even to only a narrow range of propositions, namely the propositions of logic and mathematics, and tautologies arising from definitions (e.g., all bachelors are unmarried). Such propositions are often referred to as analytic propositions. In distinction to these propositions, which *must* be true, there are propositions which happen to be true—but could be false. Since these entail reference to the existing world, beyond the internal relations of ideas, such propositions are often referred to as empirical propositions.[193] This bifurcation of meaningful propositions is often referred to as Hume's Fork, since he expressed the view that these and only these two kinds of propositions are genuinely meaningful. This classical division between analytic and empirical propositions became the cornerstone of the philosophy of science which was dominant in the earlier part of this century, i.e., logical empiricism, and its more extreme form, logical positivism. We have seen previously that the fundamental propositions of modern physics, such as the principle of inertia, do not in fact fall into either of these categories (see "The Idea of Inertial Motion"). Such foundational propositions function as constitutive propositions, and they have their roots in schools of thought rather than in any direct contact with nature. Their origin is cultural–historical more than it is empirical. They are comprehensive organizing ideas which constitute the possible structure of a science.

However, the necessary relationships and intrinsic intelligibility which are encountered in Goethe's way of science, while undoubtedly they do not fit onto Hume's Fork, are nevertheless not constitutive of the phenomena in the way that the foundational propositions of modern science are now recognized to be. The reason is that Goethe is concerned with necessary relationships, and hence intrinsic intelligibility, within the phenomena, and not with propositions which have the quality of necessity. In other words, the necessity and intelligibility is experienced as a reality of the phenomenon itself. It is experienced directly as a dimension of the phenomenon, not as something added to the phenomenon by the mind in order to explain it:

> His intention is not merely to bring the phenomena into a systematic structure, but to incorporate them into a system which is able to disclose a necessary connection between them. It is Goethe's fundamental assumption that a system of this kind is not confined to formal logic or, for instance, the mathematical domain of pure quantities and geometrical figures, but can also be found within the domain of qualities, e.g., color qualities.[194]

Not only did Newton miss the phenomenality of color, but, as we have seen, his work was really theory-directed. So instead of the phenomenon being at the focus of science, for Newton it was effectively the theory which occupied the central place. Newton was concerned primarily with measurement, not with the phenomenality of the phenomenon. Now measurement is possible only where things are to be found in the mode of quantity—i.e., parts which are external to each other—or where things can be rearranged in accordance with this mode. This entails the imposition of a framework upon the phenomenon, like a grid system on a map, which makes the operations of measurement and calculation possible.

Kant saw this as the prime reason for the success of natural science when it adopted the experimental method. In the preface to the second edition of the *Critique of Pure Reason* he says:

> When Galileo caused balls, the weights of which he had himself previously determined, to roll down an inclined plane; when Torricelli made the air carry weight which he had calculated beforehand to be equal to that of a definite volume of water; or in more recent times, when Stahl changed metals into oxides, and oxides into metals, by withdrawing something and then restoring it, a light broke upon all students of nature. They learned that reason has insight only into that which it produces after a plan of its own, and that it must not allow itself to be kept, as it were, in nature's leading-strings, but must itself show the way with principles of judgment based upon fixed laws, constraining nature to give answer to questions of reason's own determining. Accidental observations, made in obedience to no previously thought-out plan, can never be made to yield a necessary law, which alone reason is concerned to discover. Reason, holding in one hand its principles, according to which alone concordant appearances can be admitted as equivalent to laws, and in the other hand the experiment which it has devised in conformity with these principles, must approach nature in order to be taught by it. It must not, however, do so in the character of a pupil who listens to everything that the teacher chooses to say, but of an appointed judge who compels the witnesses to answer questions which he has himself formulated. Even physics, therefore, owes the beneficent revolution in its point of view entirely to the happy thought, that while reason must seek in nature, not fictitiously ascribe to it, whatever as not being knowable through reason's own resources has to be learnt, if learnt at all, only from nature, it must adopt as its guide, in so seeking, that which it has itself put into nature. It is thus that the study of nature has entered on the secure path of a science, after having for so many centuries been nothing but a process of merely random groping.[195]

The "secure path of science" he refers to here is the one pioneered by the Greeks in geometry, and which physics only took

much later when it was realized that "it must adopt as its guide
. . . that which it has itself put into nature." Thus nature is compelled to provide answers to the questions *we* set, which means
to be frameworked in *our* conceptual scheme. So physics underwent what Kant saw as a Copernican Revolution, namely the
transition from revolving the knower around the known to
revolving the known about the knower (which Kant himself
aimed to do for philosophy).

The Goethean approach to nature is the antithesis of this.
In the essay "Significant Help Given by an Ingenious Turn of
Phrase," Goethe refers to a favorable comment which had been
made on his work by Dr. Heinroth, professor of psychiatry at
Leipzig. Heinroth said that Goethe's approach was unique in
that his thinking works *objectively*. Goethe comments that:

> Here he means that my thinking is not separate from objects: that
> the elements of the object, the perceptions of the object, flow into
> my thinking and are fully permeated by it; that my perception itself
> is a thinking, and my thinking a perception.[196]

There is an epistemological reversal in Goethe's objective thinking which is the key to his phenomenological science of nature.
In this case the organizing idea in cognition comes from the phenomenon itself, instead of from the self-assertive thinking of the
investigating scientist. It is not imposed *on* nature but received
from nature. The organizing idea in cognition is no longer an
idea which is external to the phenomenon and which frame-
works it, but is now the intrinsic organizing principle of the
phenomenon itself which appears as idea when it is active in the
mind. Goethe called this "higher nature within nature." It does
not appear to the senses, but is discovered *within* the sensory. It
appears to the sensory imagination, when this is developed into
an organ of perception, but not to the intellectual mind which
tries to go behind the sensory. The organizing principle of the
phenomenon itself, which is its intrinsic necessity, comes into
expression in the activity of thinking when this consists in trying to think the phenomenon concretely. What is experienced is

not a representation of the organizing principle, a copy of it "in the mind," but the organizing principle itself acting in thinking. Referring back to what was said in chapter 2 about the organizing idea as "acting organizing," we see that here it is the *acting* of the intrinsic necessity of the phenomenon which produces the idea in thinking, as it is the acting of this necessity in outer nature which produces the phenomenon revealed to the senses.

This is a new kind of organizing activity in cognition. The important point here is that the organizing idea no longer comes *from* the productive mind to be imposed on nature, but is produced by the phenomenon in the activity of thinking when this can be receptive to it (which is in no way the same as being passive). When this happens, what appears is a manifestation of the phenomenon itself, not a representation. This is where Goethe's phenomenological science differs so fundamentally from mainstream science, which is intellectual rather than sensory, and where the organizing idea so often originates from the subjective thinking of the scientific investigator. With Goethe's way also, the nature of the phenomenon can only appear as a result of the researcher's thinking activity. But this activity now coalesces with the organizing activity of the phenomenon itself, which is its intrinsic necessity, so that it *is* this necessity itself which *appears* in the "container" which is provided for it by the researcher's own thinking activity. An active organizing principle in nature needs a corresponding organizing activity on the part of the scientist to be a "container" for it to come into manifestation. It is the scientist's thinking activity itself that provides the vessel in which the intrinsic, active organizing in nature can appear.[197]

However, necessary as this organizing activity is on the part of the researcher, it must be *metamorphosed* if it is not to become an obstacle (instead of a vessel) to the active organizing which is the intrinsic necessity of the phenomenon itself coming into manifestation. This is the hazard. What is needed here is a subtle reversal of will. It is the conditions for this to occur which are provided by emphasizing *attention* to the phenomenon, first through plunging into the sensory experience of the phenomenon, and then through making this inward in exact sensorial imagination. To begin with, an effort has to be made to keep attention on the phenomenon, and not to let it stray away from the sensory and allow other factors to enter the imagination. So the will is active here. But the object of attention is solely the phenomenon. So the researcher, in directing attention exclusively to the phenomenon, is in fact surrendering to the phenomenon, making a space for it to *appear* as itself. This provides the condition for the reversal of will to happen, from active to receptive will, whereupon it is the organizing principle (which is the necessity) of the phenomenon itself which can come to expression in the researcher's thinking.[198] This is the condition for the remarkable coalescence of the researcher with the phenomenon, which is objective thinking.

When the will becomes receptive, then consciousness becomes participative. It is when the will is assertive that the scientist is separated thereby from the phenomenon, and consciousness becomes onlooker consciousness. Participative consciousness means *conscious* participation in the phenomenon. Goethean scientists do not project their thoughts onto nature, but offer their thinking to nature so that nature can think in them and the phenomenon disclose itself as idea. In this way it is the being of the phenomenon itself which *appears* as idea.[199] It is not a question of a correspondence between an idea produced by the mind and the phenomenon in nature—which would be the way that our modern epistemological dualism would try to understand it.[200] On the contrary, it is an *ontological participation* of thinking in the phenomenon, so that the phenomenon can dwell in thinking. It is the phenomenon itself which appears as idea, just as, in a different way, it is the phenomenon which appears to the senses. The difficulty is that here we encounter the phenomenon inwardly in the act of thinking, and this shatters our "commonsense" materialistic assumptions. Because it is the phenomenon itself which appears as idea, knowledge for Goethe is an element of being itself, and so scientific truth is ontological and not representational as it must be for subjectivism.[201]

We are now in a position to understand what Goethe meant when he referred to his way of science as a "delicate empiricism which makes itself utterly identical with the object." He intended this to be taken literally. This delicate empiricism is a far cry from the assertive empiricism of Francis Bacon's experimental philosophy, which believed that "nature exhibits herself more clearly under the trials and vexations of art than when left to herself."[202] In Bacon's image of science, nature must undergo questioning and intervention with instruments by the investigating scientists, who thereby remain entirely external to the phenomenon that they seek to know. Here we have an indication of a prime source of the *separation* of humanity from nature which characterizes the modern attitude. This is not just a consequence of cognition (the spectator consciousness), but the result of an act of will which is assertive towards nature instead of receptive.

Francis Bacon was at one time Lord Chancellor of England, and Carolyn Merchant has noted:

> Much of the imagery he used in delineating his new scientific methods and objectives derives from the courtroom, and because it treats nature as a female to be tortured through mechanical interventions, strongly suggests the interrogations of the witch trials and the mechanical devices used to torture witches.[203]

Nature as female is compelled to answer questions when under experimentation, as a woman is compelled to answer questions when under torture with mechanical instruments. The chilling phrase "the trials and vexations of art" transposes the one situation into the other, so that they easily appear as parallel situations in what Bacon called "the truly masculine birth of time." This is the basis of Bacon's advocacy of science as power over nature, the means whereby *humankind* can achieve domination over the natural world.[204] Science now becomes an instrument, not just for knowing the world, but for changing it. We live with the outcome of this today, and we are becoming ever more aware that the *attitude* to nature which it embodies is the origin of many of the difficulties we now face. In view of this, it may well be timely to consider Goethe's alternative, "delicate empiricism which makes itself utterly identical with the object," and the very different attitude towards nature which it embodies.

Goethe did not try to find connections between phenomena by looking at them as collections of empirical facts from which generalizations could be made by induction, in the manner advocated by the traditional empiricism of Bacon (and later by Mill). On the other hand, as we have seen, he did not attempt to provide coherence in the phenomena by means of a speculative theory, especially not one which introduced elements which are outside experience. Goethe's aim was to stay *within* experience (he was empirical), but without stopping at the sense experience of particulars (he was not an empiricist). He aimed to see the *intrinsic necessity* in the phenomenon by a further encounter with the phenomenon beyond sense experience, but which is reached by going more *intensively* into the sensory instead of away from it, as in mathematical physics—or any speculative explanation. Goethe's phenomenology of nature seeks to make the intrinsic intelligibility of the phenomena visible, not to explain it.[205]

Working toward an understanding of nature in Goethe's way requires the further development of the scientist himself or herself. The scientist is required to go through what is effectively a process of evolution in order to cultivate the mode of consciousness needed for working in the Goethean way. It is in fact by working in the Goethean manner that we develop the organ of perception needed to do science in the Goethean way. "Goethe's natural science presupposes the training of new cognitive capacities or organs through the very activity of research."[206] Goethean science is highly nonlinear in this respect. It is very different from our customary view that the organs of perception are already given as part of our constitution.

Far from being onlookers, detached from the phenomenon, or at most manipulating it externally, Goethean scientists are engaged with it in a way which entails their own development. Here we have the notion of *Bildung,* which was so important to

Goethe and his contemporaries. Weinsheimer describes this as a genuine development leading to the acquisition of a potency, instead of the expression of a latency.[207] In the language of the parable, it is an "augmenting of the talent" not simply the activation of a talent one has already. The organ of exact sensorial imagination is not sitting there waiting to be activated. It has to be *developed*, and this is done by practicing exact sensorial imagination: ". . . in the present day we must be active ourselves in the development of new faculties."[208] Thus, in Goethean science the scientist himself or herself has to become the instrument, and he or she has to participate actively in his or her own development in order to become this instrument. This is quite a different matter from just using instruments externally, e.g., microscopes and telescopes, to augment the senses.

It was mentioned in chapter 1 of this part how Goethe came to recognize the role of *Vorstellungsarten* (ways of conceiving) in scientific knowledge. He contrasted the atomistic, mechanical, and mathematical *Vorstellungsarten* with his own way of conceiving, which he thought of as being genetic, dynamic, and concrete. We could characterize the difference as being between the quantitative and analytical, on the one hand, and the qualitative and holistic on the other. But we can now see that the change from one *Vorstellungsart* to another is not to be thought of as being just like a gestalt switch. The two different ways of seeing in a gestalt switch, e.g., duck and rabbit, are the same in kind. So they are simply alternatives. With Goethe, however, the change to the new *Vorstellungsart* is achieved through the development of a new organ of perception. So the new way of seeing is not just an alternative (of the same kind), but a new *kind* of seeing. If it were only an alternative, then it would be reached with the same organ of perception (as with duck and rabbit). The gestalt-switching model is misleading here. Newton and Goethe are often presented as if they were simply alternatives, with the implication that we can switch from one to the other. But this is not possible because the qualitative, holistic way of seeing requires the development of the appropriate organ of perception.

It is not just a matter of switching out of the quantitative, analytical way of seeing into this other mode. When Goethe said that an atomistic intelligence would see nothing wrong with Newton's theory, the reason is not only that such an intelligence is attuned to Newton's theory, but also that another organ of perception would be needed to see differently.

5. The Goethean One

The key to understanding Goethe's work in the science of the organic world is to recognize the specific quality of his *way of seeing* living organisms. It is as if Goethe turned our customary way of seeing inside-out. If we do not understand this by experiencing it for ourselves, then we will be trying to understand Goethe from a perspective which looks in the wrong way. Many of the pronouncements about Goethe's work on plants and animals do just that. As a consequence, a "standard interpretation" of Goethe has emerged which, while seeming plausible, takes us in the wrong direction. In fact, it totally misses Goethe's way of seeing, substituting for it a more familiar way of seeing which is appropriate for the *inorganic* world.

The factor which matters particularly here is the way of understanding unity. This is not an object of sense perception, which can be seen as such. Unity consists of the way that things are related, and hence it is experienced as the *way of seeing*. It is certainly a real factor of nature, and not something subjective, but it is encountered as the way of seeing and not as a specific content of perception. For example, we can show a picture of a particular plant, but we cannot show a picture of the unity of the plant. This is something we *see* but cannot depict.[209]

Whereas the customary way of seeing unity eliminates differences and promotes commonality, Goethe's organic unity is a way of seeing which includes differences. It avoids reducing multiplicity to uniformity. On the other hand, it also avoids fragmenting reality into sheer multiplicity. It allows the uniqueness of the particular to appear within the light of the unity of the whole. It is when this occurs that we encounter the intrinsic intelligibility of the organism. So multiplicity is seen in the light of the unity, instead of trying to derive unity from multiplicity. As we saw in part II, the difference here is between the perception of multiplicity in an holistic perspective (multiplicity in unity) and the perception of unity in an analytical perspective (unity in multiplicity). How these two modes of unity are inside-out with respect to each other (and how one corresponds to authentic wholeness and the other to the counterfeit) will be considered below. We will consider this first in a fairly general way before going on to consideration of the living organism.

Modes of Unity

Consider a set of objects of one kind, e.g., chairs. The visual appearance of the individual chairs may be very different. There may be an antique chair, a standard utility chair, a modern designer chair, and so on. Furthermore, they may be made from different materials. So they do not necessarily have anything in common in terms of visual appearance or materials of manufacture. Yet, in spite of their evident differences, we do recognize each one of them as being a chair. This is what they have in common, what is the same in each case. We have seen in chapter 2 that concepts are *not* derived by abstraction *from* sense experience. The concept "chair," which is the chair idea, is not some kind of mental picture with all particular features left out, retaining only what is the same in all possible chairs, i.e., what is general. In other words, the concept is not a generalization abstracted from particulars:

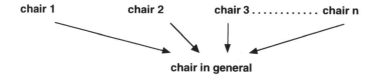

In fact, we saw in chapter 2 that there had to be the chair idea already for even one chair to be seen, and therefore to be able to see one chair is already to be able to see all possible chairs.

Nevertheless, this process of generalization by abstraction, to reach what many have in common, does occur. Although we are mistaken in our belief that the concept is such a generalization, this does not mean that such a process does not take place—it just means that this process is not the *origin* of concepts. We tend toward generalizing by abstraction whenever we begin with the finished product instead of with the process of coming-into-being. In this case we confront the finished product—the set of chairs—as an onlooker: there is a set of different objects, and what they have in common is that each one is a chair. So the process of generalization takes the form of finding unity in multiplicity, identity in diversity. The unity is abstracted from the multiplicity, drawn off it externally by standing back from the multiplicity as an onlooker to find what is common. In seeking for what is common in this way, all difference is excluded. Hence there can be no diversity within unity when unity is understood this way, and all that remains is uniformity.

Our everyday cognitive perception often tends toward this condition. In the state of habituation we notice only generalities and not particularities, what things have in common and not how they differ. For example, when we see the leaves of a plant we just see the generality "leaf" and do not notice the particularity of any one leaf or the differences between leaves. Attention does not go into sensory experience, but remains on the level of mental abstraction. This is the condition of automatization, in which the particular is "tuned out" and only the general form of what things have in common is registered. This is our habitual state of passive awareness, which is reversed by the process of *active* seeing in Goethean science (see "Modes of Consciousness" in part II).

Whenever we think about unity consciously, we usually conceive it in the mode of "unity in multiplicity." This is because we begin from a mental picture of what has been cognized, i.e., from the onlooker stage of the finished product. If we could begin with the concept, the organizing idea, we could be conscious participants in the coming-into-being of cognition, and this would lead us to conceive unity in a very different manner (to be discussed below). But beginning at the stage of the mental picture which is formed from the already cognized particulars, the only direction in which we can go is to abstract from the mental picture of the particulars what they have in common. Thus we reach the onlooker perspective of unity as "unity in multiplicity."

A model for this activity of finding unity in multiplicity seems to be presented in the early dialogues of Plato—at least in the way that these are understood according to what Flew calls "the traditional established interpretation."[210] In these dialogues Plato presents Socrates as being concerned with understanding what moral virtues are—i.e., temperance, piety, courage, justice, and so on. In each case, the unfortunate "expert" whom Socrates questions brings forth one or more particular instances of the virtue in question. But Socrates says that he doesn't want many acts of piety or courage or justice. He wants what *all* acts of piety, say, have in common, and which alone makes them specifically acts of piety. He calls this the *eidos* of the virtue in question—which in the early dialogues can be translated as "character" or "characteristic" ("pattern" is also used). From the way in which this is presented (in the traditional established interpretation), it clearly has the form of "unity in multiplicity." Socrates is shown as looking for the one "pious" which all the many pious acts have in common with each other, and evidently this is not a numerically single "one" because that would make it another particular instance.

This search for what many instances have in common, which proceeds *from* the many *to* the one, is often referred to as looking for the "one over many." The notion that there must be such a one for every many is continued further in the *Meno*, a dialogue in which Plato (through the mouthpiece of Socrates) asks what all the virtues have in common. "Well now tell me this, Meno, what do you say this is in respect of which there is no difference at all but they are all the same?"— since "even if they are many and various they all have one common character whereby they are virtues. . . ."[211] In the way that it is presented here, the one common character is understood as having the form of "unity in multiplicity."

If there is a one for every many, then we can proceed with this process of looking for what things have in common to further levels of abstraction. So, for example, we can proceed in this way from chairs to items of furniture, to objects, to matter, and ultimately to being. This conceives the category of being in the mode of "unity in multiplicity" as the ultimate commonality. This leads to the conclusion that being is the most general, abstract, and empty notion, the reduction to the final uniformity.

The term "one over many" implies a separation between the one and the many which is not implied by "unity in multiplicity." Aristotle remarked in a famous passage in his *Metaphysics* that Socrates did not make this separation, but that others who came later did:

> But, whereas Socrates made neither the universal nor definitions exist separately, others gave them a separate existence and this was the sort of thing to which they gave the name of Forms.[212]

The identity of the others is left open here, but it is taken to be a reference to Plato and his school. Aristotle says here that when a separation is conceived between the one and the many, instead of being referred to simply as character, the *eidos* is given the name of Form. This is Plato's famous theory of Forms. The important point here is that "separation" means a separate existence (whereas "distinction" does not). This step is seen by many contemporary Western philosophers (following Heidegger) as the origin of metaphysics—which is simply taken to be another name for the two-world theory. [213] The many are now conceived as being in one world, and the one as existing separately in a world of its own. But these two worlds are not of equal status. The world of the one is superior to, or more fundamental than, the world of the many. This means that the sensory (the many) is downgraded in metaphysics in favor of the intelligible (the one).

The metaphysical tradition in Western philosophy is seen today as the story of the attempts to overcome the problems to which the two-world theory gives rise—e.g., What is the nature of the one? How is the separation bridged? How can there be many in the first place? We have already noted the formative role of the two-world theory of metaphysics in the development of mathematical physics, according to which the (mathematical) laws of nature are conceived as the unity underlying the multiplicity of phenomena. This science continues to the present day to reflect the two-world theory of metaphysics: the intelligible (mathematical laws) is separate from the sensible (observable phenomena). For the science of physics, what is "really real" is hidden *behind* empirical appearances. What appears to be real is "merely appearance." So the senses cannot be trusted (remember Galileo and Descartes): they do not reach the true reality, the unity which lies beyond the sense-perceptible multiplicity. In its inversion of reality, physics shows clearly that "metaphysics is alive and well and lives on in modern physics."[214]

When unity is conceived in the mode of "unity in multiplicity," sometimes it may be considered as being no more than an idea in the nominalist's sense (as for William of Occam or the later British empiricists). As such it may be considered to be an ideal pattern, or a common plan, which is useful for the purpose of understanding, but which should not be hypostasized into a common plan that actually exists in the phenomena. In other words, the common plan should not be thought of as being constitutive of the phenomena in any way. But of course it need not be taken in this nominalist sense. Thus the nineteenth-century transcendental anatomists, for example, believed that the common plan was really part of nature and not just an explanatory idea. Certainly, when "unity in multiplicity" is understood metaphysically, as the ultimate ground underlying appearances, it is thought to be real and not just an

explanatory idea in the mind of the person who thinks it. But
whether it is taken nominalistically or realistically, since this
mode of unity is reached by the *exclusion* of difference, it is
very difficult to see how such a common plan, or underlying
ultimate ground, could ever give rise to multiplicity. In fact it
is impossible. Having extinguished difference to reach uniformity, it is clearly not possible for difference then to be produced out of this kind of unity. This mode of unity is sterile.
Brady points out how the notion of an underlying unity in the
form of a common plan, or idealized scheme, is unfruitful in
morphology because it *cannot* explain how difference arises.
He shows just how much Goethe is misunderstood if his morphological work on plants and the vertebrate skeleton is interpreted in terms of the notion of a common plan—which is in
fact how his work has usually been interpreted.[215] So the common plan is both impotent as the constitutive origin of diversity and useless as an explanation of how diversity comes about.

Copleston points out that "Speculative metaphysicians have
always tended toward the reduction of multiplicity to unity."[216]
Having done this, they then go on to try to explain how this
unity can give rise to multiplicity. There is a simple answer to
this: it cannot. The reason is contained in the term "reduction."
This is an impoverished unity, and as such it cannot possibly
accommodate the richness of diversity. Indeed, as we have said,
the unity is formed by the very process of excluding diversity.
The metaphysical attempt to see how multiplicity can come
from unity, as well as the attempt to explain difference in terms
of a common plan, are foredoomed to failure because they are
wrongly conceived. The very movement of thinking which
throws them up renders them impossible.

There is, however, another mode of unity which is very
different from "unity in multiplicity." This is a mode of unity
for which the existence of multiplicity does not present the
problem which it does when unity is conceived as what is common. Many of the so-called fundamental problems of metaphysics simply disappear when we switch to this alternative

mode, because it is the mode of unity that gives rise to these problems in the first place. The alternative is a mode of unity which, far from excluding difference, includes diversity within itself and yet remains unity. There is multiplicity *within* unity without breaking the unity. There is no longer the apparent need to understand how unity can give rise to multiplicity (which it cannot), because in this mode of unity the multiplicity is already there within the unity. Evidently this mode of unity—which we shall call "multiplicity in unity"—is very different indeed from our customary way of seeing unity. But it is the key to Goethe's way of seeing living organisms.

We can approach this by considering again the case of the hologram, in which the property of wholeness can be seen very clearly. As we saw in part I, if we were to break a hologram plate, say, into two halves, each half would give a full optical reconstruction of the original scene, compared with a photographic plate which would give separate fragments of the original scene if treated similarly. Even if the hologram plate were to be broken into a number of bits, each such bit would give an optical reconstruction of the entire original scene. The *mechanical* result of fragmenting the plate is the same whether it is a photograph or a hologram. But *optically* the result is totally different in each case. If the plate is a photograph, then we simply have a number of fragments of the original. But if the plate is a hologram, we find that as we divide it so the original hologram multiplies. With each division there is another fragment of the plate but the same picture unbroken. So here we can divide without losing the whole— the plate is fragmented but the picture is undivided. By dividing we multiply, and yet the whole itself is neither increased nor decreased. Evidently this is a very different process to mechanical repetition, as when we produce a number of copies of a photograph for example. Whereas the copying process is the repetition of a unit, producing "unity in multiplicity," the process of hologram division has the structure of "multiplicity in unity."

We tend to overlook this structure of "multiplicity in unity" because it does not correspond to the logic of solid bodies. In the case of repetition we have the multiplication of a unit to produce another one, and another one, and so on. Each one is another one. But with the division of the hologram each different fragment is optically the original One, the very same One and not another one. So the answer to the question "How many holograms are there?" can only be that there is One. Mechanically there are many, but optically there is One. So what we have is One in the form of many and many which are One. This is "multiplicity in unity," and the distinction here is *intensive* since each of the many is the very same One, the original One, and not another one. This constitutes an intensive dimension of One. Evidently this dimension does not fulfill the requirements of our familiar logic. Thus, according to the principle of noncontradiction, something cannot be both one and not one (many) at the same time. The extensive dimension of one—many separate, numerically different ones—fulfills this requirement, because in this case one is singular and therefore excludes many. This clearly fits the world of bodies which are external to each other, and therefore separate, i.e., the world which is the realm of quantity. We can see here that the mode of "multiplicity in unity" is not limited to the determining condition of the logic of solid bodies, and hence recognize that this logic is really only a restricted case.

At this point we shall introduce a simple terminology—which we have in fact already used in the previous paragraph and in the section "The One and the Many" in part II. When we refer to One in the form of many, "multiplicty in unity," we shall use a capital letter. Otherwise, when we refer to the numerically single one, we shall use a small letter. Thus we have nonnumerically One hologram in our example, whereas the writer (or reader) is sitting on numerically one chair. Clearly One is not a number since it includes many, whereas one is a number and excludes many. One is a nonnumerical, prenumerical *dimension*.

This dimension of One can be seen very clearly in the plant world. In fact, the process of "multiplication in unity," which we obtain only artificially with the hologram by breaking the plate into bits, occurs naturally in the life of the plant as the very principle of growth and vegetative reproduction. It is familiar to every gardener when she attempts to grow a new plant by taking a cutting from the plant which she wishes to propagate. From such a cutting, which may be only a branch, a twig, or a stalk, an entire new plant will grow in time. The tendency for the whole plant to grow out of each bit is very striking with plants such as gloxinia and begonia, which have the power to grow a new complete plant from each of their leaves, so that the whole plant is present in the growth of each single leaf into a plant. This process of vegetative reproduction is clearly similar to that of dividing the hologram plate—except that the *growth* of each plant is like a hologram in time.

If we take a fuchsia plant and divide it into as many pieces as we can, they will all grow until they flower—unless impaired by other circumstances. We are so accustomed to looking upon this in an ordinary way, as the multiplication of a unit to produce "unity in multiplicity," that we do not realize that here we are witnessing something which is quite extraordinary. What we are seeing is an action of a quite different kind, producing the "multiplicity in unity" which is the unity of wholeness. Thus, no matter how many times we divide the fuchsia plant, it remains whole. When we divide the hologram plate, it is always the original "picture" but never the same piece of glass. So when we divide the plant, it is always the original plant but never the same specimen. We see many plants extensively but they all belong together as One. Each *is* the original One in the organic order of the whole, but not in the numerical order of material bodies—whereas it is this latter order which is reflected in our ideas. How often we strike a new cutting is of no importance. The plant is divisible and yet remains whole, so the plant is One even when it is divided and the "parts" have become independent.[217] The plant is One and many at the same time because its individuality is independent of number. This is "multiplicity in unity."

Another such illustration of this mode of unity is provided by John Seymour in his account of the growth of potatoes:

The potato is not grown commercially from seed, but from sets, which are just potatoes, and so all the potatoes of one variety in the world are *one plant*. They are one individual that has just been divided and divided.

To produce a new variety it is necessary to fertilize one plant with the pollen from another. When a satisfactory new variety is produced:

... the breeder arranges for their new variety to be multiplied by setting the actual potatoes from it—and if it proves a popular variety the original half dozen or so potatoes on the first-ever plant of that variety may turn—by division and subdivision—into billions and billions of potatoes—all actually parts of that first plant. It would be interesting to know how many billion tons that first King Edward plant has developed into during its life![218]

As in the case of the hologram, the answer to the question "How many potato plants of a single variety are there?" can only be that there is One. Materially there are many (numerically) but organically there is only One plant. We do not recognize the One plant because it is many. We do not see One in the form of many because the empirical mind sees the single one which is the numerical unit—one plant but not the One plant. Thus we do not find the nonnumerical One which is the whole plant, and it is the failure to distinguish clearly between these two kinds of unity which gives rise to the problem of understanding organic wholeness. This failure to see how the many are One leads us to try to produce some kind of synthesis of the many, i.e., to make One from one. But the "One" which we try to reach from the many can only be the counterfeit made by an external synthesis of many ones or the abstract uniformity of what many ones have in common. The One *is* the many—we could say it is "hidden" in the many, hidden by our customary way of seeing.

The creeping buttercup (*Ranunculus repens*) is a plant which propagates vegetatively. It sends out creeping runners (horizontal stems or "stolons") along the ground. Where the tip of a runner touches the ground, it grows roots and a new buttercup plant shoots up and flowers. But it is only numerically (materially) a new plant. Organically the "new" plant is *the very same One.* This plant, in turn, will send out its own runners, and the process of reproduction will be repeated. The spreading network of plants which forms in this way is in fact One plant. So where we see two buttercups as two plants which are the same, there is really One plant which is two. This is the difference between the extensive perspective of "unity in multiplicity" and the intensive perspective of "multiplicity in unity." The former is the perspective of the onlooker, who begins from the finished product and hence finds only an external mode of unity, whereas the latter perspective is evidently a more participant mode of unity which corresponds to the coming-into-being. We could equally say the one mode is inorganic, considering the plant simply as a spatial body, whereas the other is genuinely organic, approaching the plant as a living organism. We notice that organic unity cannot be mapped onto the empirical plane, i.e., the external world of spatially separated bodies. So if our ideas are too bound to this plane, as in the logic of solid bodies, then the organic unity of the plant—in which each is the very same One and not another one—will seem to be impossible.

We can practice going from one perspective to the other. Working in imagination, we can try to form an image (which is not, of course, a sensory image in the bodily spatial manner) of "each is the same One." Then, after making the attempt to do this, we can relax and spontaneously fall back into the familiar image of "they're all the same." The one image needs an effort, whereas the other happens automatically. We don't have to be able to succeed for this to be valuable. The attempt to do it functions as a practical exercise for developing the organ of perception for seeing "multiplicity in unity." When we really catch the difference between "It's the very same buttercup!" and "These buttercups are the same," then we get a clear sense that it's not just a reversal—in the same plane, as it were—but a movement of turning inside-out in going from one mode of unity to the other. From "multiplicity in unity" to "unity in multiplicity" is a movement into

outsidedness, i.e., the side-by-sidedness which is the condition of the bodily world.[219]

A strawberry plant propagates vegetatively in a similar way
to the buttercup. We could imagine a strawberry bed which
contained many strawberry plants which were in fact organically all the very same plant. Such a strawberry bed would really
be One plant in the form of many, "multiplicity in unity," and
not the many separate plants it appears to be externally. A very
striking illustration of this is provided by bamboo, which also
propagates vegetatively by producing new shoots from underground rhizomes. It is a fascinating experience to stand in a
small forest of bamboo, surrounded by what appears externally
to be many bamboos, and to participate imaginatively in the
fact that the entire forest is One plant. This is a graphic illustration of One in the form of many. But the bamboo is remarkable
in another way as well. Plants of the same species flower simultaneously, even when they are transplanted far from their original habitat. Sometimes the period between successive flowerings
can be very long. For one species, *Phyllostachys bambusoides*, it
is about 120 years. Yet wherever this species lives, it flowers
simultaneously! In the late 1960s, plants flowered together in
places as far away as China, Japan, England, Russia, and America.[220] "The whole plant species, not a single plant, is the unity;
it is responsible for the life of the individual plant."[221] The whole
plant species is One plant which appears in the form of many
plants. But the species is not to be thought of as a unity underlying the individual plants, as if it were superordinate to them.
In other words, it is not to be thought of metaphysically. Each
particular plant is a self-presentation of the species. It is therefore a concrete manifestation of the species. The unity of the
species is concrete and not abstract—it is not separate from the
manifoldness of the phenomena but identical with it.[222] In the
language of philosophy, organic unity is not an abstract but a
concrete universal. Cassirer says of this universal that it "is not
conceived as a self-contained reality, as the abstract unity of a
genus juxtaposed to its individuals, but as a unity which exists

only in the totality of specific individuals."[223] Furthermore, this totality is inherently indeterminate because it is ever-unfinished. The important point in reading this statement of Cassirer's is to make an effort of imagination to read it in the perspective of "multiplicity in unity." If we don't, then its radical significance is lost, and it seems to say little more than that unity is all the parts taken together (like the pieces of a jigsaw puzzle). But the whole is present within its parts, imparting itself within each part but never coming into presence totally and finally in any one part.[224]

Clearly the plant world does not correspond to the world of bodies. It does not come under the category of quantity because it is one and many at the same time. Why should the laws of the organic fit the logic of solid bodies? We are surprised that they do not to the extent that we believe the realm of spatially separated bodies to be what is fundamental, and hence that the concepts appropriate to this realm constitute the basic framework for all correct understanding. But there is nothing inherent in the bodily spatial world, and the concepts appropriate to it, which justifies taking it as the yardstick of reality to which everything else, life included, must conform.[225]

The nonreductionist perspective is simply seeing the dimension of One instead of the empirical dimension of many. Here the One and the many are not exclusive, as they are numerically, because they are in fact the very same. Thus we do not attempt to *reduce* the many to the One, as is so often said, but instead we see that the many *are* One. The effect of this nonreductionist perspective is that of looking into a dimension *within One itself*. Compared with this dimension of One, the notion of "unity in multiplicity" appears as the Flatland attempt to understand unity. "Flatland" here is the extensive perspective of the empirical mind, which sees only the sheer multiplicity of the many. Beginning here means taking multiplicity as basic. So unity can only be understood in the light of the many, and consequently it is conceived as if it were drawn off the many—i.e., as "unity in multiplicity." But the real unity is another dimension—as the sphere is another dimension compared with the circle which is its cross-section in Flatland. Seen in this perspective, the many as such is only a cross-section of the One. As it appears on the plane of the empirical mind, the sheer multiplicity of the many is an abstraction from the One. If we now try to find one in the form of "unity in multiplicity," by abstracting what is common to the many, then what we achieve is an abstraction of an abstraction. Thinking we are reaching the true unity in this way, we have in fact gone in the opposite direction, away from the authentic unity of living wholeness to the counterfeit unity of abstract uniformity.[226]

Seeing the Dynamic Unity of the Plant

The key to Goethe's understanding of the organic is that he saw it in the perspective of "multiplicity in unity," i.e., the intensive dimension of One, because this is the idea which is appropriate to the organic. If we cannot make this step for ourselves, then we can only misrepresent Goethe's work by seeing it in the mode of "unity in multiplicity." This is the source of the failure of so many accounts of Goethe's work. The common Plan, the Platonic ideal, or the explanatory idea all miss this point, and therefore miss Goethe. The One is not separate from the many, and therefore juxtaposed to the many, but actually manifests in each single one of the many. But it does not manifest in its entirety in any single one. So its manifestation is never complete but ever unfinished. The One is not fixed and static, like one, but is inherently dynamic.

When the multiplicity of the many is seen in the light of unity, there is diversity without fragmentation into unrelated plurality. The One avoids both extremes: the lifeless uniformity which excludes difference, on the one hand, and on the other hand the fragmentation into the sheer multiplicity of many separate and independent entities. We can also consider this in terms of the category of wholeness (as discussed in "Authentic and Counterfeit Wholes"), whereby the whole is present in the parts. When the whole is seen within the part, this has the effect that the part is seen in the light of the whole. So, seeing the whole through the part has the effect of an inversion whereby the part is seen as an expression of the whole. If the whole is in the parts, so that each part is an expression of the whole, then the parts *cannot* be separated, i.e., external to each other as in the inorganic realm of inert bodies (the realm of quantity). Furthermore, the parts do not have to be homogeneous in kind. As a consequence of the way that each is seen as a (partial) expression of the whole, parts which appear heterogeneous when seen only in the plane of many can be seen in the light of the whole as each being the same One, and yet different, i.e., as constituting "multiplicity in unity." Hitherto we have illustrated "multiplicity in unity" with homogeneous examples—e.g., the hologram, the potato, and so forth—but this restriction is not necessary.

The Unity of the Plant Kingdom

When Goethe left Weimar and traveled in the Alps and Italy, he saw many plants with which he was already familiar, but modified in accordance with the change in external circumstances. In the Alps, for example, he noticed that, in general, branches and stems were more delicate, buds farther apart, and leaves narrower than they were in the same species in southern Germany. In Venice he found a coltsfoot by the sea which had spikes, leatherlike leaves, and a fat stem—very different in appearance from the coltsfoot he was familiar with in Weimar.[227] But he recognized that in such cases he was seeing different modifications of the same plant and not different plants. What he encountered empirically was many plants. But the step in perception which took him beyond this was more than just seeing these as many plants of one kind. Such a step would be equivalent to seeing in the mode of "unity in multiplicity" and no more. The step in perception which Goethe made by concrete imagination brought him to see the modifications of a species in the perspective of the intensive dimension of One. When the modifications are seen in the mode of "multiplicity in unity," then what is seen is One plant which is many, and not many different plants which are basically the same. The One plant is not divided and shared between the many, but actually manifests in each single one—it manifests wholly in each but not completely. It is inherently dynamic and consequently ever unfinished in its manifestations. It is only by always becoming other that it can remain itself.[228] This is the condition of livingness—if it manifested completely in any one single organism, then it would be fixed, i.e., dead. Furthermore, the plant which is One does not include the many in a preformed manner—which would be equivalent to projecting cheese into milk as an explanation of how cheese comes from milk. When the plant is seen in this way, in the perspective of the One plant which manifests in each plant but is ever unfinished, Goethe refers to it as the plant Type.[229] He does not mean by this anything like an average plant, or a common plant—as the term "type" is often taken to mean. What Goethe means by the Type requires us to see in the inside-out way of "multiplicity in unity." It is an organic reality, not a mental abstraction.

From his observations and contemplation of the different appearances of the same species of plant under different circumstances, Goethe went on to consider the entire plant kingdom as One plant. When the entire plant kingdom is seen in the perspective of "multiplicity in unity," so that it is seen in the intensive dimension of One instead of the extensive dimension of many, then there is only One plant. What appears is *the* Plant, not *a* plant, which manifests in each of all the many different plant Types. The name which Goethe gave to *the* Plant is the Archetype. The precise term he used was *Urpflanze*, which is usually translated as "archetypal plant" or sometimes as "primordial" or "primal plant." All these terms invite misunderstanding. "Archetypal" is easily identified with one-sided Platonism, to mean a plant which is "one over many," separate from and superior to the many (two-world theory). "Primordial" or "primal" on the other hand, invites the misunderstanding that it is a primitive organism, i.e., a single phenomenal form from which all other phenomenal forms subsequently developed in a material way. Of course, the other mistake—which is the error of nominalism/empiricism—is to assume that the archetypal plant is only a mental abstraction, as if it were no more than a unifying idea constructed by the intellectual mind. All of these interpretations have been attributed to Goethe. But they all miss Goethe because they do not *see* in the Goethean way.

The One is neither abstract nor real and separate from the many material plants encountered by the senses. It manifests *concretely* in the many, being present in each single one so that each such single one is the very same One. In the organic realm of the Plant, the One brings the many out of itself, so that the One comes into concrete manifestation simultaneously with the many with which it is identical. But it is only possible to see this concrete unity of the organic if we can shift into the mode of "multiplicity in unity" and see that each of the many which the One brings out of itself is the One itself. If we fail to do this, remaining instead in the extensive perspective, we cannot begin to recognize the archetypal plant as the intensive dimension of the plant kingdom, and can only conceive it in terms of one of the common misunderstandings mentioned above.

There are two extreme, one-sided cases which Goethe avoids:

(1) Nominalism/empiricism, which says that there is only the many—the one is no more than a mental abstraction derived from the many, so the one is less real than and dependent on the many, and

(2) One-sided Platonism, which says that the one is separate from the many—the one has a reality independently of the many, and the many are less real than, and dependent on, the one.

These two views are effectively opposite ways of losing our epistemological balance. Each represents a pathological case which results from falling too much in one direction, either toward the many or toward the one. Goethe's way of seeing, on the other hand, attempts to keep an epistemological balance between the one and the many, but without this being only a compromise. So Goethe's way of seeing is the basis for a science which is nonmetaphysical and yet which avoids the nominalism of classical empiricism and positivism.

As we have approached it so far, the archetypal plant may seem to be no more than a speculative idea reached by thinking intellectually. We can see how once Goethe had recognized the Type, his thinking would be led by its own logic toward the notion of the Type of Types, i.e., the Archetype. Goethe's writings show the development of his thinking in this direction. But they also show that he went much further than this, beyond the intellectual intuition that there must be an archetypal plant, to *experience* this plant directly in thinking. Goethe's way toward the living experience of the archetypal plant illustrates once again the importance of *Bildung*, the cultivation of capacities. Goethe prepared himself for this encounter, cultivating the capacity for it, over some time. We can sense the archetypal mode of being coming to birth in him from the very way in which he writes. In the summer of 1786, he writes: "It is a growing aware of the Form with which again and again nature plays, and, in playing, brings forth manifold life." Then, in the botanical garden at Padua, in the early autumn of the same year: "The thought becomes more and more alive that it may be possible to develop all plant forms out of one form." We should take it literally when he says that "the thought becomes more and more *alive*" in him, and avoid the tendency to interpret this vaguely, as being no more than a metaphorical way of speaking. On the contrary, it describes precisely the concrete experience which was developing in him. We can see this when we recall Goethe's description of his imaginal encounter with the plant. He described this as an effusion of flowers which sprang out of the organ of sight (which means here the imagination functioning as an organ of perception), new flowers which went on "neither slowing nor accelerating" as long as his attention lasted (see part II, p. 83). Having worked for so long observing plants and then recreating them in the flexible picturing of exact sensorial imagination, Goethe had cultivated in himself the organ of perception needed for conscious participation in the archetypal plant. Consequently this *Urpflanze* could come into appearance in Goethe's imagination not as a representation but directly, as an ontological manifestation of itself.

We can understand Goethe's brief description if we can recognize that this manifestation of the archetypal plant is the dynamic dimension of One within itself. It is to be understood in the intensive perspective of a multiplicity in which each different plant is yet the very same One. It must not be interpreted extensively, as if there were just many separate plants one after the other. The multiplicity must be seen in the light of unity if it is not to fall into side-by-sideness. We could conceive it in the manner of an ambiguous figure, like the duck/rabbit, but extended into an indeterminate number of perspectives instead of only two. In the duck/rabbit each figure is the whole. One figure does not occupy only part of the picture, while the other figure occupies the other part:

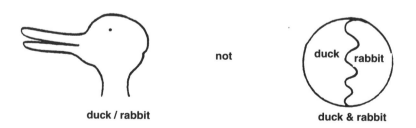

duck / rabbit   not   duck & rabbit

There are no lines left over, unused, by either figure—and no extra lines need to be added in either case. Each figure is complete in itself but not comprehensive. For any one case, there is another complete possibility. The duck and the rabbit are nested intensively. Either can come into manifestation explicitly, but not both together, side by side, because they are not component parts which add together to make a whole. Each is a complete but noncomprehensive expression of the whole—an intensively partial expression instead of an extensive part. Each is the whole, the very same One and not another one.

The manifestation of the archetypal plant in conscious experience, as described by Goethe, can be understood to some extent in an analogous way. What he encountered was not a plant which was composed of many component plants added together. The mode of being present of the archetypal plant in consciousness is more in the nature of an indeterminate multiperspectival figure. Each individual plant which "sprung out of this heart"—he is referring to "the centre of the organ of sight"—*is* the archetypal plant. Each individual plant which appears is a one-sided manifestation of the archetype, which can therefore appear only as one plant after another—but where each different one is yet the very same One, and not another one, as each different figure is the same One. Each plant which appears is therefore complete but not comprehensive. What manifests here is the *dynamic* metamorphosis of One within itself.

It would be wrong to think of each individual form which the archetypal plant takes as if it were somehow already present before manifesting. Each particular development out of the archetypal plant comes into being in its manifestation and is not preformed before appearing. To think in this way is too mechanical. It pictures all the forms which appear as already present beforehand, waiting to spring out like seeds from a pod. This is the finished-product thinking of the onlooker consciousness, which is more appropriate to the nonliving realm. It is not appropriate to the organic world, which instead requires a much more *intrinsically* dynamic way of thinking. We have noted above that if the archetypal plant is considered as analogous to a multiperspectival figure (a limited analogy), then it must be an *indeterminate* figure. This is intended to hint at the intrinsic dynamic. It is not intended to suggest, as in the manner of finished-product thinking, that the number is merely unknown, but that there is no definite number because it is dynamically unending. This is where the analogy breaks down, because we would have to imagine a multiperspectival figure which was self-productive, i.e., producing new perspectives of itself out of itself.

What we come to here is remarkable. Something which is intrinsically dynamic and indeterminate cannot be other than self-determining. The ever-metamorphosing archetypal plant gives form to itself, instead of being formed by external influences. This "forming itself according to itself" was called the "entelechy" by Goethe.[230] This was hinted at a few paragraphs above when we wrote that "the One brings the many out of itself"—which goes beyond what was strictly justified at the place where it was said.[231] We can recognize now that what is implied here is the self-determining entity which is the entelechy. This can only be understood in the perspective of the intensive dimension of One, where it appears as the metamorphosis of One within itself. The self-determination is the factor which takes the archetypal plant beyond any mechanical representation. Here we come to the irreducible difference between living and nonliving. The latter can *always* be understood as being determined by something other than itself. But the former can *never* be understood completely in this way. There is always something left over, unaccounted for, and this is the self-determining which *is* livingness. We are so habituated to thinking in an external, mechanistic manner that it is difficult to grasp at first just how extraordinary this self-determining is, and too easy just to take it in a vague, abstract kind of way. But this self-determining, i.e., "forming itself out of itself," *is* living. This *is* life itself. When we do recognize that this is what the organic is, as such, then we know that we cannot go from nonliving to living, from other-determined to self-determining. So we know that the living could not have emerged somehow from the nonliving, as much current thinking supposes it must have done. Also, for the same reason, we know that the living cannot be "explained" in terms of concepts which are appropriate to the nonliving.

In the previous paragraph, the entelechy was referred to as a self-determining *entity*, and whenever we refer to "the archetypal plant," it is almost inevitable that we tend to conceive it as if it were an object. We do so on account of the grammar of the language. The subject–predicate form of our language emphasizes the noun, and thereby encourages us to think of "objects" as the basic element, in other words, to see *beings* as fundamental— Heidegger has famously remarked that the history of Western philosophy since Plato has been the attempt to understand Being as if it were "the Being of beings." We habitually think in terms of a being, conceived as a self-enclosed, objectlike bodily entity. We think of matter, for example, as consisting of atoms which we conceive in this way, and we extend this further to the notion of fundamental particles (physicists themselves do not really think in this way—although they disguise the fact whenever they write popular books). We talk of "society," or "God," as if they were beings—e.g., the Supreme Being—and there are countless other such examples. We talk of "a plant" in the same way, without pausing to think that "the plant" we see in front of us as an object is in fact a limited, temporal cross-section of a differentiated process which constitutes a time-whole. It has been emphasized by many philosophers and scientists in this century just how inappropriate it is to conceive entities as the basic mode of being. But it has also been recognized that it is not easy to escape from this view because it is embodied in the form of our language. However, as well as this, there is what seems to be an intrinsic direction in the process of cognition itself. We have seen in chapter 2 above, as well as elsewhere in this essay, how difficult it is to see action as primary instead of object, to follow the coming-into-being instead of beginning from the finished product, to go back upstream from "past consciousness" to "present consciousness," not to try to reach the milk by way of the cheese, and so on. These are all indications of the inevitable movement of consciousness toward "solidification."

Goethe's way of seeing goes in the opposite direction to this. The archetypal plant is *not* an objectlike entity—it is not a being, in the way that we usually understand this. Lehrs says that Goethe studied the *doing* of the plant by his procedure of active seeing followed by exact sensorial imagination.[232] What he means is that the plant itself *is* doing, and not that the plant is an entity which does—i.e., the "doing" of the plant is not the "doing" of an entity. Once again, our habitual thinking is too late, too far downstream, and has to be reversed. This reversal was aptly described by J. G. Bennett when he said that we have to give up thinking in terms of beings that do, and think instead in terms of doings that be.[233] Doings that "be" can be called "formative doing," as distinct from the "operative doing" of a being, which is the operation of one already formed being (entity) on another. This is the reversal of thinking which is needed for understanding the archetypal plant. It is not a being but a doing—a formative doing that "be's" and not the operative doing of a being. Being needs to be understood dynamically, not statically, as being and not as a being. Linguistically we have to shift the emphasis from the noun to the verb—which is not easy to do in English.

The archetypal plant, the entelechy, is the be-ing of the plant. It is the formative doing which "be's" plants—and we must always remember that this doing does not have the support of an underlying being, because this is the stage before there is such a thing as "a being." So when Goethe encountered the archetypal plant consciously, in his imagination, it "be'd" plants in imagination because the archetypal plant is the formative doing which "brings into being." In this encounter the archetypal plant "be's" plants in the light of consciousness instead of in outer nature. Thus the archetypal plant becomes visible, i.e., it *appears*, whereas otherwise it would have remained invisible—"appearance" must be read verbally here, i.e., as the *event* of appearance.[234] This is why Goethe's experience of the archetypal plant took the dynamic form which it did. What occurs in consciousness in this encounter *is* the archetypal plant itself and not a representation of it. Even if it appears, as it did for Goethe, in pictorial form, this is not a copy of the archetypal plant (which would therefore be separate from the picture), but the archetypal plant itself be-ing pictorially instead of naturally. The archetypal plant *manifests* in consciousness. The epistemology of this ontological event is evidently non-Cartesian! Here the knowing is ontological instead of representational because it is a conscious participation in nature, instead of the spectator consciousness looking at a finished nature from which it feels separated. This is Goethe's "delicate empiricism which makes itself utterly identical with the object," which was discussed at the end of "The Physics of Goethean Style." As we saw there, this does *not* mean being absorbed into the object—in the present case the "object" is formative doing. The Goethean scientist does not lose himself or herself in nature, but finds nature *within* himself/herself in fully conscious experience. Rather than a dimming of consciousness, which absorption would imply, the scientist is utterly awake—in fact, more awake than in ordinary everyday consciousness. Conscious participation means just that—*conscious* participation, and therefore not absorption. It is a synergistic condition in which humanity and nature work together in such a way that each becomes more fully itself through the other. Both are enhanced, but only within their working together, because there is *one* occurrence which is the mutual enhancement of *both*.[235]

As it occurs in nature, a plant is not purely a manifestation of the self-determining entelechy, but is also subject to the conditioning influences of its physical environment. So any actual plant which we see is the consequence of accidental factors which are external to the organic as such, as well as the self-determining entelechy which is *purely organic*. So any actual plant is influenced by factors which are not part of the intrinsic dynamic of the plant—Goethe thought of the observed form of an individual plant as "a conversation" between the entelechy and the environment.[236] This means that the archetypal plant *cannot* manifest naturally in a manner which is fully in accord with its own nature.[237] Now this restriction is removed when it manifests imaginatively instead of naturally. So the self-determining, formative doing which "be's" plants that Goethe encountered as the archetypal plant is a higher or purer manifestation of the phenomenon than occurs in outer nature. The archetypal plant as it is thus "participated" consciously is more fully itself than it can be as it expresses itself naturally. Hence what manifests in consciousness in such an encounter is a higher stage of the phenomenon itself. This means that it is only through *cognition*, and hence through humanity, that the phenomenon can reach the highest stage of itself. Otherwise it would remain incomplete. This is clearly a synergistic activity: the phenomenon depend on our human cognitive activity, as we in this activity depend on the phenomenon (c.f. the account of the reversal of will at the end of "The Physics of Goethean Style"). What a far cry this is from Francis Bacon's image of putting nature on the rack!

When Goethe said there is a delicate empiricism which makes itself utterly identical with the object, he added "thereby becoming true theory." Because the archetypal plant *is* the higher stage of the plant kingdom itself, in the sense described above, then it *must* be true. Here there is no "problem of truth" as there is with the representational epistemology of the onlooker consciousness, which inevitably has the question of how adequately the representation corresponds to that which it represents. What appears in cognitive experience in participative consciousness does not represent what appears already as such outside of consciousness—which is how it would seem to the onlooker consciousness. The archetypal plant *must* be true because it is the phenomenon itself—not the phenomenon as it occurs in the external world, but the climax of its development which occurs only in humanity.[238] Because it is ontological instead of representational, the archetypal plant *cannot* be otherwise than true, for if it were not so then it could not even be. The self-contradiction entailed in trying to conceive the archetypal plant as being false would be ontological and not just propositional—i.e., the necessity is not simply logical.

Since the plant kingdom reaches its highest stage of development in the appearance of the archetypal plant, which can happen only with conscious participation, we must not make the mistake of projecting the archetypal plant into outer nature as if it were there in the manner in which it appears in imagination. What appears in conscious participation is, as it were, the highest and final flowering of the plant kingdom—which it could not reach without humanity. The formative doing which is the self-determining entelechy "be's" plants naturally, subject to the restrictions of the environment, but it only "be's" plants appearingly in the light of conscious participation. We could say that it "be's" plants nonappearingly in nature.[239] So we can now recognize that the term "archetypal plant" refers strictly to the self-determining entelechy as it manifests in consciousness. This does not mean that the entelechy is separate from or behind the archetypal plant in some way (the two-world theory), because the manifestation of the archetypal plant *is* the entelechy (but imaginatively instead of naturally). However, it does mean that the archetypal plant *as such* comes last and not first. It is important to bring this out explicitly because, within the viewpoint of the onlooker consciousness, we cannot avoid projecting the archetypal plant as something which is real *as such* separately from humanity, self-contained and complete in itself, and hence both independent of and prior to the human understanding of it—which understanding consequently seems to be no more than a subjective experience. When we move from onlooker consciousness to conscious participation in the phenomenon, we find that we have a very different kind of understanding. We see that the phenomenon itself comes into a higher stage of manifestation *in the very act of knowing*, without it becoming, thereby, something which is only subjective.

We can now summarize this section:

(1) Beginning from the outside, with the many plants which already appeared phenomenally, Goethe worked his way into

their coming-into-being until he was able to experience the plant dynamically. This is the intensive dimension of the plant, which is now experienced to such a degree that it is stronger in experience than the extensive dimension of many plants. When this happens, the plant is experienced much more directly in the intensive mode of One as a dynamic "multiplicity in unity." But this encounter is a manifestation, not an abstract idea. It is how the plant manifests in the prepared imagination—we could call this the imaginal–phenomenal form, in contrast to the material–phenomenal form. This is the archetypal plant; it is the entelechy as it manifests imaginally instead of physically. As such it is a higher product of nature which is possible only through a human being's conscious participation in the process of nature. Here human beings enter into participation with nature *consciously* in the act of cognition itself. This is the "delicate empiricism which makes itself utterly identical with the object, thereby becoming true theory." The significance of the final phrase, "becoming true theory," is now clear. Goethe said of this stage of knowledge, which is beyond dualism, that the enhancement of our mental powers which it requires "belongs to a highly evolved age." In other words, we have to develop the capacity for this to take place.

(2) It follows from all that has been said above about conscious participation in the phenomenon that we must not make the mistake of thinking that the archetypal plant is present *as such* in the material–phenomenal plant kingdom. To do this would be to project the imaginal–phenomenal manifestation of the entelechy into nature as if *this* were present outwardly in the plants.

(3) It also follows from all that has been said above that, with participative consciousness, there is simply no need to postulate anything hidden behind the phenomenon. What would otherwise have been projected behind the phenomenon (as in the two-world theory) is now experienced as being the intensive dimension of the phenomenon itself. Hence there is no need for metaphysics, which therefore becomes redundant. The development

of participative consciousness takes us beyond the metaphysical attitude, i.e., one-sided Platonism, and allows us to see that this is simply a consequence of the onlooker mode of consciousness. Conscious participation is nonmetaphysical, and therefore Goethe's science of conscious participation in nature is a non-metaphysical science. The way to overcome (dissolve) the illusion of metaphysics is therefore by the development (*Bildung*) of a new mode of consciousness, because this illusion is a consequence of the restriction of consciousness to the onlooker mode. So participative consciousness is the practical way beyond metaphysics, as onlooker consciousness is the way into it. Positivism (and prior to that, nominalism), on the other hand, which wants to say that there is no need for metaphysics, wants to do so without change in the mode of consciousness. Positivism remains in the onlooker mode, and consequently it denies metaphysics but does not dissolve the need for it.

The Unity of the Organism

As with the plant kingdom as a whole, so with the individual plant. Goethe saw the successive organs up the stem of a flowering plant in the mode of "multiplicity in unity." He did *not* see them in the mode of "unity in multiplicity," as is implied when it is said, wrongly, that Goethe saw these organs as being formed according to a common plan. When he said, "All is leaf," the term "leaf" was not intended to be taken as referring to an ideal leaf-schema, or to some organ intermediate between other organs, as if somehow "equidistant" from them, and from which they can all be derived. Brady has shown in some detail the untenability of this interpretation. By careful description he has shown that the observed variation *cannot* be produced, either from a common plan or from some supposed intermediate organ, because in neither case can a movement be generated between forms. In other words, the common plan doesn't enable us to go anywhere because the unity which excludes diversity is a cul-de-sac.[240]

Goethe used the term "leaf" to designate no organ in particular. He wrote in a letter to Herder that "it had occurred to me that in the organ of the plant which we ordinarily designate as *leaf*, the true Proteus is hidden, who can conceal and reveal himself in all forms. Forward and backward the plant is always only leaf. . . ."[241] As with the type and the archetype, this organ which he calls leaf *is* each organ up the stem—foliage leaf, sepal, petal, stamen—because it is one and many at the same time. The unity is not separate from the manifoldness but identical with it. The One manifests concretely in the many, so that each organ is the same One and yet only a partial manifestation. When the manifold of plant organs up the stem is seen in the light of unity, the plant appears in the mode of "multiplicity in unity" so that there is diversity *within* unity. This "brings the diversity back into the unity from which it originally went forth."[242] So we see the plant in the intensive dimension of One instead of the extensive dimension of many. In this dimension we see the quality of the petal reflected in the stamen, for example, without thereby supposing that the stamen is derived from the petal in a causal–mechanical way. The petal is not the cause of the stamen, nor does a petal turn into a stamen in some way. These outward ways of looking, belonging to the onlooker mode of consciousness, are not appropriate for the *living* plant.

We can take a plant and detach the various organs up the stem and lay them out side by side. If we do so, they appear to us as separate objects, i.e., as external to one another. But we do not have to do this in fact; we can just do it theoretically. We often do so without noticing, when it is the very mode of our thinking. We do not even need to imagine the organs as being physically separated, because the *possibility* that they can be manipulated in this manner is included in the object-mode of this analytical thinking to which we are habituated. When we see an organ of the plant as an object, then we are seeing it purely in the mode of outsidedness (this is what "object" really means). And so it is inevitable that we try to understand the unity of several such perceived organs in terms of what they have in common. "Unity in multiplicity," the onlooker unity, is the unity of outsidedness. But this way of seeing is fundamentally inappropriate for the *organic* nature of the plant, which is therefore excluded from this point of view, because the organs up the stem of the plant are *intrinsically* related—whereas objects can only be related externally.

At the beginning of his essay *The Metamorphosis of Plants*, Goethe writes about the laws of transformation by means of which nature "produces one part out of another and creates the most varied forms by the modification of one single organ."[243] He goes on to say that what he means by the metamorphosis of plants is "the process by which one and the same organ presents itself to us in manifold forms." This gives a clear indication that his description of the plant is to be read in the mode of "multiplicity in unity" so that each different organ is seen as being the very same organ, and consequently the plant is seen as One organ. The metamorphosis to which Goethe refers has to be seen in the right perspective if it is to be understood. The *experience* of seeing in this way has the *quality* of "It's the same organ!" and not "These organs are the same." The latter sees it externally, as if the organs were objects which can be related by external comparison. But evidently the plant organs cannot be "objects" because they are mutually entailed in one another inasmuch as they are all related intrinsically through being manifold forms of "one and the same organ." If each organ is organically the very same One, then the organs of the plant cannot be considered as if they were separate. In the growth of the plant the whole is present in each part—each organ is an expression of the One organ—and hence we *cannot* separate (analyze) the plant into *external* parts as if it were an object.

The first paragraph of *The Metamorphosis of Plants* can easily be misunderstood if it is not read in the right perspective:

> Anyone who observes even a little the growth of plants will easily discover that certain of their external parts sometimes undergo a change and assume, either entirely, or in a greater or lesser degree, the form of the parts adjacent to them.

This does not mean that one part changes into another one—as if, say, a petal were to change physically into a stamen. Furthermore, there is no causal determination of the later by the earlier—e.g., the petal is not the cause of the stamen. There is in fact no external sequence *from* one organ *to* the next one up the stem. Goethe makes it clear in the next few paragraphs that he is referring here to abnormal growth sequences, which have the effect of making visible the metamorphosis which is "the process by which one and the same organ presents itself to us in manifold forms." For example, a flower can form in which petals appear in the place usually occupied by stamens—as in the case of the cultivated rose. In another abnormal case, green foliage leaves may appear in the position usually occupied by sepals.[244] The fact that different organ forms can appear at one and the same position on the plant, together with the correlative fact that one and the same organ form can appear at different positions, is thus seen as the visible expression of the organic unity of the manifest organ forms. The visible parts of the plant—foliage leaf, sepal, petal, stamen—are seen in the light of "multiplicity in unity" as manifestations of "one and the same organ." This One organ, which ever appears and never appears, changing into different modes of itself, is what Goethe designated "leaf" when he proposed that "all is leaf." But he was aware that this is not satisfactory and could invite misunderstanding. For example, it invites the misunderstanding that what is meant here is a common plan ("unity in multiplicity"). It can also be misunderstood as intending an extensive process of physical change instead of the subtler, intensive movement of metamorphosis—which seems like a movement in a different dimension to the process of physical change in which one thing materially turns into another. To counteract such misunderstandings, Goethe comments toward the end of the essay:

> It is self-evident that we ought to have a general term with which to designate this diversely metamorphosed organ and with which to compare all manifestations of its form. At present we must be content to train ourselves to bring these manifestations into relationship

> in opposing directions, backward and forward. For we might equal-
> ly well say that a stamen is a contracted petal, as that a petal is a sta-
> men in a state of expansion. . . . (par. 120)

By practicing such an exercise in imagination, we build for ourselves a sense of the nonphysical, yet real, movement which is
metamorphosis.

There are some instances where the movement of metamorphosis is so evident in the floral organs that it seems as if we see
it directly with our eyes. The white water lily is such a case. In
this plant the transition from petals to stamens takes place in
stages, so that between the two there are several intermediate
stages progressing from organs which are more petal-like to
ones which are more stamen-like. All of these stages are present
together in the flower, and the effect of this is that we see the
passage from petals to stamens as one continuous movement.
There is a reversal of perception: individual organs now appear
as instantaneous snapshots of this movement, instead of the
movement being made up of a sequence of organs. The movement itself appears as primary, whereas individual organs now
appear as secondary. Instead of the movement being constituted
out of the individual organs, these organs serve as markers
which make the movement visible.[245]

However, we must be careful not to make the naive empiricist's mistake here, and wrongly suppose that seeing is simply a
matter of sense perception. We found in chapter 2 above that
"there is more to seeing than meets the eye." Seeing is not simply visual experience. There is no pure "what" which is seen by
a pure "spectator," i.e., a detached observer who merely regis-
ters a "what" through the senses. Observation is more than
sense experience: it is *seeing*. This does not make it into something purely subjective unless we insist on putting it into a
Cartesian framework of subject–object dualism. If we suspend
this attitude—which Husserl called the "natural standpoint"[246]—
then we are free to explore seeing without this presupposition
(which is what Husserl meant by his assertion that phenomenology is "presuppositionless"). When we do so, we discover

that it is a fundamental structure of experience that "what" is seen and "how" it is seen are always, *necessarily*, correlated. Husserl refers to this necessary correlation of what is experienced with the way it is experienced by the term "intentionality."[247] What is experienced, as experienced, Husserl calls the *noema* or noematic correlate, and the way it is experienced he calls the *noesis* or noetic correlate. So the correlation of the *way* it is experienced with *what* is experienced is called the noesis-noema correlation:

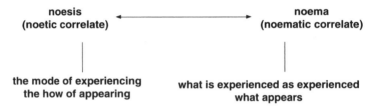

noesis　　　　　　　　　　　　　　　　　**noema**
(noetic correlate)　　　　　　　　　　(noematic correlate)

the mode of experiencing　　what is experienced as experienced
the how of appearing　　　　　　　what appears

This is an internal correlation within experience. It must not be mistaken for a correlation of experience with something which is supposedly outside of it—as in traditional, i.e., prephenomenological, philosophy. The distinction between "what" is seen and "how" it is seen is a *relational* distinction. Don Ihde expresses the quality of this relational distinction as follows:

> . . . every experiencing has its reference or direction towards what is experienced, and, contrarily, every experienced phenomenon refers to or reflects a mode of experiencing to which it is present.[248]

The *experiential* noesis–noema correlation replaces the subject–object separation of Cartesian dualism. In the latter case it is supposed that subject and object are independent of each other, each having its own separate existence and becoming related in an external way only in the act of cognition. But this leads to the well-known difficulties of epistemology, which have already been referred to herein on several occasions. The polarity of the noesis–noema correlation, on the other hand, does not entail these difficulties—e.g., the difficulties of the representational (causal) theory of perception. In this case the relation is internal:

> Acts of consciousness and objects of consciousness are essentially interdependent: the relation between them is an "internal" not an "external" one. That is to say, one cannot first identify the items related and then explore the relation between them; rather one can identify each item in the relation only by reference to the other item to which it is related. Acts of consciousness are directed upon objects such that one cannot investigate the acts independently of their objects; and the objects are always objects *for* consciousness such that one cannot investigate objects independently of investigating the conscious acts of which they are the objects.[249]

What is said here concerning the noesis–noema correlation is hinted at in the remark of Brentano's referred to in chapter 2 above: "And I understand here by 'idea' not that which is conceived but the act of conceiving." While there cannot be that which is conceived apart from the act of conceiving it, equally there cannot be a conceiving act which does not conceive something. The two sides belong together inseparably.[250] This statement of Brentano's contains the germ of the noesis–noema correlation, and it also indicates the possibility of shifting attention from what is conceived to the act of conceiving itself—which does not mean turning this act itself into a new "what" which is conceived. There has to be a refocusing of attention from what is conceived to the act of conceiving, *while engaged in the act of conceiving that which is conceived*. The important point is that this does *not* entail constituting the seeing as a new "seen," i.e., as if it could become an *object* of perception. What is entailed is really an intensive step within consciousness, so that we are conscious in the *seeing* of the seen instead of the seeing of the *seen*.[251]

We are now in a position to understand better the nature of Goethe's discovery of metamorphosis. Shifting attention from what is seen into the seeing act enables us to recognize that this is not an empirical discovery in the naïve sense. As Galileo's fundamental discovery about motion was not an empirical discovery of some new fact about motion, but a change in the whole way of seeing motion, so Goethe's discovery of the movement of metamorphosis in the plant is not the discovery of a new fact about the plant but a change in the whole way of seeing the plant. Because of the correlation of what is seen with the way of seeing, there cannot be a change in the way of seeing without there also being a change in what is seen. But the important point is that here, as in the case of Galileo, the change in what is seen comes from a change in the way of seeing. It does not come from the addition of some new factual content which previously had not been noticed. The change in what is seen is subtler than this. *The movement of metamorphosis is in the way of seeing,* and a change in the way of seeing *transforms* what is seen without *adding* to the content.

This is how Goethe's discovery of metamorphosis must be understood. It is a transformational discovery, not a factual one. For example, we have mentioned the metamorphosis which can be seen in the white water lily. But when we see this there is a sense in which nothing has changed—there is no additional content in what is seen—and yet everything is different. There is an overall transformation of what is seen because the way of seeing changes. The discovery of metamorphosis in the water lily is evidently not on the same level as the discovery of a particular fact about the water lily. But if we think that discovery in science is all of the latter kind, then we will not understand the *kind* of discovery Goethe made. We look for metamorphosis as a fact, when it is to be found in the way of seeing. In doing so we are like the Mulla Nasrudin, who lost his key in the dark, but was looking for it in the light because, he said, "there is more light here."[252] Scholarly accounts of Goethe's science often attempt to understand what Goethe says about metamorphosis without undergoing the change in the way of seeing which is necessary. If we want to understand Goethe's way of science, then we must do so in Goethe's way.

It is this movement of metamorphosis which distinguishes flowering from nonflowering plants. In flowering plants even the foliage leaves show the influence of metamorphosis, whereas the leaves of nonflowering plants do not. It seems as if, in the flowering plants, the floral quality so permeates the plant that it even modifies that part of the plant which precedes the flower. It is the absence of the floral quality, therefore, which results in the leaves of nonflowering plants showing no modification in form up the stem. In these plants there is merely repetition without change of form.

The movement of metamorphosis in the foliage leaves of a flowering plant can be seen by arranging the leaves as they appear up the stem in a series, from the leaf nearest the ground to the one nearest the flower.[253] Although doing this presents each individual leaf as a separate object, we nevertheless find that we see a movement of transformation from one leaf to another along the series. This can be seen in the case of the leaves of delphinium, for example, as shown by the following silhouettes:[254]

Each leaf form may be repeated several times on the plant before it transforms into the next form. This diagram is therefore a simplification because it includes only one instance at each stage. The sequence begins with the most highly elaborated leaf, which then simplifies as we move up the stem, until what is left nearest the flower is the barest indication of what was present in the first leaf. The overall impression is of a gradual with-drawal of the form which is present fully in the first leaf. Yet we can nevertheless see a connection (in quality) between the first and the last leaf. (We should also follow Goethe's instruction, mentioned previously, to go through a metamorphic series backward as well as forward.) When we do this we get the sense that we are seeing one dynamic form here—without falling into the trap of thinking of this as a unity underlying the multiplic-ity of visible forms. We see the separate leaves as united by a movement—which is the dynamic form. Indeed, we can see this so strongly that we begin to see in a reversed way. We have the impression that the *movement* (which is not a physical move-ment) is the reality, and that the individual leaves we see with the senses are no more than single snapshots of this move-ment—as if they were transitory markers making the movement visible. This movement is certainly not made out of the visible foliage leaves, as if it were a material sequence of these leaves—what is evident to the senses is discontinuity, not continuity. Yet it is surprising how easy it becomes to see the movement in this reversed way, with the leaves which are visible to the senses appearing as abstractions from a movement which is not visible to the senses as such but which we can see.

The movement of metamorphosis is encountered as the way of seeing and not what is seen—although what is seen is thereby modified in a subtle way, such that we can say that "nothing has changed, but everything is different."[255] This is demonstrated in a simple perceptual experiment described by Brady.[256] Given a series of leaves (or silhouettes), the question of whether an addi-tional leaf belongs or not is decided by whether it enhances or weakens the movement. We see the series of leaves in the *context* of the movement. So it is this movement, which is not visible to the senses but which we can see, which is the criterion by which we decide whether an additional leaf form is to be accepted or rejected as part of the series. The individual leaves which we see are taken out of context when they are considered separately. They are really the text for which the movement is the con-text.

What is real is the movement itself, not any single form. It is this movement which is the unity. Those who look for the unity in a single form which all leaves have in common (i.e., as a "unity underlying multiplicity") are looking in the wrong direction. However, there *is* a single form which is the unity, and this is the movement itself. The single form which is the unity is not to be found by seeing what is the same in all the leaves, but by seeing the unity which is the *movement* of the whole series. So the single form of the series as a whole is mobile, and not static as it would be if it were simply what all the leaves have in common. Instead of the movement being generated from such a single underlying form—which would be impossible—the movement itself generates individual forms. Brady concludes: "Thus the movement is not itself a product of the forms from which it is detected, but rather the unity of those forms, from which unity any form belonging to the series can be generated." So to understand Goethe's way of seeing the plant, we must "shift from static to mobile form."[257] This is what Goethe did when he emphasized the need to shift from *Gestalt* to *Bildung*, in his essay *Formation and Transformation*:

> The German has the word *Gestalt* for the complex of existence of an actual being. He abstracts, with this expression, from the moving, and assumes a congruous whole which is determined, completed, and fixed in its character.
>
> But if we consider *Gestalts* generally, especially organic ones, we do not find anything permanent, at rest, or complete, but rather everything fluctuating in continuous motion. Our language is therefore accustomed to use the word *Bildung* both for what has been brought forth and for what is in the process of being brought forth.
>
> If we would introduce a morphology, we ought not to speak of the *Gestalt*, or if we do use the word, should think thereby only of . . . something held fast in experience but for an instant.
>
> What has been formed is immediately transformed again, and if we wish to arrive at a living perception of Nature, we must remain as mobile and flexible as the example she sets for us.[258]

If the single form is the movement—which generates forms—then clearly we must not think of the movement as a sequence of forms—which are the traces of the movement! We cannot produce the mobile from the immobile in this way. Thinking in this way is really transferring the thinking appropriate for bodily movement—i.e., the movement of solid bodies as studied in the science of mechanics—to the organic realm, where it does not apply. The difficulty with understanding motion, and the habit of trying to do so in a way which is backward, was the subject of much of the work of the philosopher Henri Bergson at the end of the last and the beginning of this century. Bergson saw the impossibility which is concealed in the habitual way of conceiving motion as a sequence of states— e.g., the way that the movement of a projectile is conceived as a sequence of positions $x_1, x_2, x_3 \ldots . x_n$ occupied at successive times $t_1, t_2, t_3, \ldots . t_n$. This is the impossibility of constituting movement out of the immobile, which we attempt to do when we fail to see that the "states" or "positions" are in fact *possible stops* of the movement. In other words, they are derived *from* the movement, and therefore the movement cannot be considered as being constituted out of them. Bergson saw the newly invented cinematograph as a mechanical illustration of our "mechanical" way of thinking of movement. He emphasized the *usefulness* of this way of thinking—the science of mechanics, for example, enables us to manipulate and control the movement of bodies in a mathematically determined way. But it does not enable us to understand movement, change, and *becoming* generally: "Instead of attaching ourselves to the inner becoming of things, we place ourselves outside them in order to recompose their becoming artificially."[259] The cinematographical method may encourage the mind to think that "by straining itself to the point of giddiness, it may end by giving itself the illusion of mobility," but a different approach is needed in which we are participant instead of onlooker:

> In order to advance with the moving reality, you must replace yourself within it. Install yourself within change, and you will grasp at once

both change itself and the successive states in which *it might* at any instant be immobilized. But with these successive states, perceived from without as real and no longer as potential immobilities, you will never reconstitute movement. Call them *qualities, forms, positions*, or *intentions*, as the case may be, multiply the number of them as you will, let the interval between two consecutive states be infinitely small: before the intervening moment you will always experience the disappointment of the child who tries by clapping its hands together to crush the smoke. The movement slips through the interval, because every attempt to reconstitute change out of states implies the absurd proposition, that movement is made of immobilities.[260]

The attempt to do this is an illustration of what Bergson meant when he said that philosophy consists in reversing the habitual direction of thought.[261] This entails thinking intuitively instead of intellectually:

Intelligence starts ordinarily from the immobile, and reconstructs movement as best it can with immobilities in juxtaposition. Intuition starts from movement, posits it, or rather perceives it as reality itself, and sees in immobility only an abstract moment, a snapshot taken by our mind, of a mobility. Intelligence ordinarily concerns itself with things, meaning by that with the static, and makes of change an accident which is supposedly superadded. For intuition the essential is change: as for the thing, as intelligence understands it, it is a cutting which has been made out of the becoming and set up by our mind as a substitute for the whole.[262]

What is important here is the perception of movement *as reality itself*. This cannot be perceived *as such* by the analytical intellect, but only by a faculty which can experience the wholeness of the movement. Bergson associates this faculty, which he calls intuition, particularly with what is living—and the intellect with what is dead. He makes it quite clear that the intuition of movement and change as reality—"All real change is an indivisible change"—is something to be experienced. When we do experience this, we find:

There are changes, but there are underneath the change no things which change: change has no need of support. There are movements, but there is no inert or invariable object which moves: movement does not imply mobile.[263]

What makes this difficult to understand at first is our identification of change with change of bodily position. Here it seems
that the movement is just added on to the body, as if it were
accidental to it (cf. "Galileo and the Moving Earth"). In the
world of solid bodies, movement certainly entails a something
which moves. But this world is associated with the senses of
touch and sight (in fact only one apect of the sense of sight).
Bergson points out that we have less difficulty in perceiving
movement and change as independent realities if we consider
the sense of hearing instead. Thus, in music for example:

> . . . do we not have the clear perception of a movement which is not
> attached to a mobile, of a change without anything changing? This
> change is enough, it is the thing itself.[264]

Now this is just how it is with the movement of metamorphosis in the plant. This is not a physical movement—not a
change in which, in the physical sense, one thing turns into
another. As we have seen, the movement of metamorphosis in
the foliage leaves (as well as in the floral organs) requires us to
take the movement itself as primary. The individual organs
appearing to the senses are but temporary snapshots (possible
stops) of this movement, and the movement itself cannot be
conceived as being constituted out of them. There has to be an
inversion of our habitual direction of thinking here. So,
Goethe's movement of metamorphosis evidently instantiates
Bergson's change that needs no thing which changes. Conversely, Bergson's philosophical work helps us to understand
Goethe's discovery of metamorphosis in the plant. It helps us to
recognize the *kind* of movement that metamorphosis is—the
example of music is particularly illuminating in helping us to
see how there can be another kind of movement than the movement of bodies.

The single form is the movement of metamorphosis when
this is seen as a whole. So the single form which is the unity is
really a time-form.[265] What is seen in the foliage leaves is only a
trace of the movement of metamorphosis, which really belongs

to the whole flowering plant. Friedemann Schwarzkopf gives a graphic image of this metamorphosis:

> If one could imagine a person walking through the snow, and leaving the imprints of its feet, but with every step changing the shape of its feet, and if one would behold not the trace in the snow, perceptible to the sense-organs of the physiological eyes, but the *living being* that is undergoing change while it is walking, one would *see* with the inner eye the *organ of the plant* that is *producing* leaves.[266]

This is the One organ which *is* the plant—which Goethe called "the true Proteus" and designated "leaf." Because this organ is one and many at the same time, there is no need to posit anything "more fundamental" *behind* or *underlying* the plant. When we see the plant in Goethe's way, we discover that the unity is a dimension of the phenomenon. Hence there is no need to postulate a "one over many" as in the two-world theory of metaphysics. We do go beyond the phenomenon as it first appears, but we do not thereby go *behind* the phenomenon to some *underlying* reality. What we discover is that the unity is a depth *within* the phenomenon, so that "the appearances go all the way down."[267]

When we try to think concretely with the plant we participate in the doing of the plant. This doing, which *is* the plant, is the very being of the plant, as we can discover for ourselves when we think *with* the plant, instead of looking *at* it and thinking *about* it.[268] In this way the movement of our thinking participates in the formative movement of the plant, so that the plant "coins itself into thought" instead of into material form as in outer nature.[269] This is the way of Goethe's "delicate empiricism which makes itself utterly identical with the object."

6. Seeing Comprehensively

The greatest difficulty in understanding comes from our long-established habit of seeing things in isolation from each other. This is seeing things as objects—the bodily world in which separation, and hence material independence, is the dominant feature. No doubt this viewpoint is one which is encouraged by our own bodily experience of manipulating material bodies. But things are not only objects which can be taken in isolation from one another. In fact they are not *primarily* such "objects" at all. They only seem to be so when their context is forgotten. What this habit of selectivity overlooks is the way in which things already *belong* together. Because it overlooks this, the analytical mind tries to make things belong *together* in a way which overlooks their belongingness. It tries to put *together* what already *belongs* together. Thus the intrinsic relatedness is not seen, and instead, external connections are introduced with a view to overcoming separation. But the form of such connections is that they, too, belong to the level of separation. What is really needed here is the cultivation of a new habit, a different quality of attention, which sees things comprehensively instead of selectively.

When things are seen in their context, so that intrinsic connections are revealed, then the experience we have is that of *understanding*. Understanding something is not the same as explaining it, even though these are often confused. Understanding lies in the opposite direction to explaining. The latter takes the form of replacing a thing with something else. Thus, for example, gas pressure on the walls of the vessel containing it is explained by means of atomic collisions, between gas and wall atoms, and the consequent changes in momenta of the gas atoms. Explanation tends to be reductionistic inasmuch as diverse phenomena are reduced to (explained in terms of) one particular set of phenomena. Thus, for example, in the classical phase of modern physics (i.e., prequantum physics) all the various sensory qualities are reduced to (explained in terms of) mechanical interactions of material particles. Such an explanation evidently takes the form of saying that something is really an instance of another, different thing. Understanding, on the other hand, by seeing something in the context in which it belongs, is the experience of seeing it more fully as itself. Instead of seeing it as an instance of something else, it becomes more fully itself through being seen in its context. Thus, understanding is holistic whereas explanation is analytical.

The single phenomenon on its own is an abstraction. The aim must be to see the *belongingness* of the phenomena, and so to encounter the phenomena in the mode of wholeness instead of separation. This wholeness, which begins to be experienced through seeing comprehensively, is then recognized as being a higher dimension of the phenomena. It is only on this more comprehensive level that we encounter the concrete phenomenon ". . . in which the single phenomena become, as it were, one large phenomenon. . . ."[270] The aim is to *enhance* seeing so that "by overcoming the isolation of the single observation, it accomplishes the transition to a higher level of experience." [271] It is evident that the movement of mind which this entails is the opposite to that entailed in explaining something.

We have seen in "The Physics of Goethean Style" how Goethe's experiments on color cultivate a way of attending to phenomena which sees them comprehensively instead of selectively. We have also seen how Newton, under the influence of a hypothetical model, approached the phenomena selectively and was thereby led to his proposal of differential refraction as an explanation for the origin of spectral colors. Goethe, on the other hand, by looking at all the color phenomena comprehensively, was able to see just how this error of judgment arose as a result of selecting what is really only a single case and making that the basis for an *explanation*. In contrast to this, Goethe's comprehensive way of seeing *understands* the origin of the colors. We have seen how Goethe considered all the experiments as if they were "the manifolding of a single experiment." Seeing a series of contiguous experiments comprehensively, as a single experiment in manifold variations, is evidently very different from selecting one experiment from the series as a basis for explaining the others—which is what Newton did with his *experimentum crucis*.

In "Seeing the Dynamic Unity of the Plant," we have seen how Goethe cultivated a way of attending to the plant which sees the individual plant comprehensively and how he extended this to the plant kingdom as a whole to see this comprehensively as One plant. The movement of metamorphosis becomes visible when the sequence of organs up the stem—from the first stem leaves through to the stamens—is seen comprehensively. In this way a transition is made from seeing the individual organs to seeing the formative movement which is the plant. But as well as seeing the *belonging* together of the organs of the plant, we can also see the *belonging* together of the different plants within a family if we see them comprehensively and do not try to reduce them to a system.[272] In each case there is a metamorphosis, whether vertically up the stem of a plant, or "horizontally" between different members of a family, or between different families.

Seeing comprehensively is not be confused with seeing generally. The essential point about this is that it is the capacity to comprehend differences as a unity in a concrete way, whereas seeing generally is abstract and looks for unity by removing differences. Seeing comprehensively is a higher cognitive function than abstracting what is common. It goes in the opposite direction to thinking abstractly. Imagine abstracting what is common to "c," "a," and "t" instead of *reading* "cat." Seeing comprehensively is like reading, and this is the "higher level of experience" to which Goethe refers in the quotation above (see note 271). Looking for what things have in common, i.e., seeing generally, is an attempt to see comprehensively *without* going to a higher level of experience—which is like trying to read without going to the higher level which is the experience of meaning.

A brilliant example of seeing comprehensively instead of selectively is provided by Wolfgang Schad's study of the wholeness of the mammals.[273] This major contribution to a holistic biology has been discussed in part II. Schad sees each kind of mammal comprehensively, seeing the *belonging* together of its various features (such as size and color) in a natural whole, so that the animal becomes understandable in itself without needing to be explained in terms of something else. But the individual mammal kinds are not seen in isolation from one another, as if they could be understood separately. Each kind of mammal is seen in the context of the other mammals in the group to which it belongs, while these groups in turn are seen in the context of the larger families of mammals, and so on until (with a few exceptions) all the mammals are seen in the context of the larger orders of rodents, carnivores, and ungulates. Each level is nested within a more comprehensive one in the perspective of "multiplicity in unity." A concrete organic order emerges—not a system and not an abstract schema—which includes diversity instead of neutralizing it in favor of what is common. The effect of seeing comprehensively in this way is that diversity appears as self-difference, so that at each level which is considered, the concrete organic order appears as the manifolding of a single organism. Thus the rodents appear in the light of the intensive dimension of One as One rodent. This is not to be thought of as a rodent which is composed of many component rodents added together. It can be understood intensively in the manner of a multiperspectival figure—like the duck/rabbit, but extended to many perspectives instead of just two. Each one *is* the One rodent, but every one is only a one-sided manifestation. Similarly, there is One carnivore and One ungulate. These are in no way to be confused with a common plan for carnivores or what all ungulates have in common. The unity of "multiplicity in unity" is comprehensive, whereas that of "unity in multiplicity" is abstract. Ultimately there is One mammal, with the rodent, carnivore, and ungulate as one-sided manifestations.

When the mammals are seen comprehensively in this way, intrinsic relations begin to become visible, and we *see* connections between organisms which otherwise are perceived as being separate from one another. The separation is overcome, but not by introducing a connection externally between the organisms—such an external connection is like linking two things with a third, and therefore itself belongs to the level of separation. When we *see* the connection, instead of introducing one, then it has more the character of a nonlocal connection (to borrow a term from quantum physics). When their *belonging* together is perceived, the organisms do not have to be linked *together*. The separation is overcome, but not on the same level as the separation—which therefore remains as separation on its own level. The intrinsic belongingness of the organisms is a more subtle aspect of the phenomena than their separation.

There is a helpful analogy with language here (which will be explored further below). When we read a text, the meaning we perceive is different in kind from the letters which we see on the page. In the act of reading, the sensory and the nonsensory are perceived differently and yet simultaneously. This gives us the impression that the marks and the meaning are experienced as being on different levels. We could say that the separation of the letters is overcome in the act of reading the meaning of the word, but this does not mean that the letters on the page have become joined together. The overcoming of the separation is not an external connection, at the level of the letters on the page. The meaning we read is a connection of a more subtle kind than the connection which belongs at the level of separation. The separation is not overcome on its own level, and therefore it does not disappear when the letters are read comprehensively as the meaning of the word. In the act of reading we have the experience of two *different* levels *together*. We can understand what a mistake it would be in this case to try to overcome separation on its own level: a subtler, different kind of connection would be lost, and with it the possibility of reading. The higher cognitive function which is experienced in seeing comprehensively in Goethe's science is analogous to reading. The sensory particulars are equivalent to the letters, and the intrinsic connection which is their *belonging* together is equivalent to the meaning. We called this a nonlocal connection in the previous paragraph to emphasize that it is different from the local connection which introduces external links on the same level as the separation to *make* things belong *together*, and thereby misses the subtler possibility which is the equivalent of reading. What the experience of the Goethean way of science brings us to is the realization that this subtler kind of connection is a dimension of the phenomenon itself, and not something which is just added to it by our minds.

As has been mentioned above, this requires an *enhancement* of seeing and cannot be attained with the kind of seeing which is attuned to the bodily world. Goethe's way of science is itself a practical training for such an enhancement of seeing. Schad's book itself can be used for this very purpose. If it is read slowly and thoughtfully, and we work in our imagination to enter into the connections and relationships he describes, then this activity of reading will itself contribute to the formation of a new organ of perception in us. We begin to get the taste of the subtler kind of connection described above, as well as to exercise the capacity for seeing in the perspective of "multiplicity in unity."

Toward the end of his book, Schad indicates how seeing comprehensively can lead to a different idea of evolution from the one which has become established in science since Darwin.[274] He does this by seeing the mammals in the context of all the other vertebrates, specifically with regard to their relationship to the environment. To do this he considers the vertebrates from the fishes through to the mammals in terms of the three fundamental functional processes, or dynamic organic systems, which form the basis of his whole approach: the nerve–sense system, the respiratory–circulatory system, and the metabolic–limb system.[275]

The lowest group of vertebrates—strictly, the chordates—has a primitive hollow nerve chord (the forerunner of the true spinal chord). The anterior end of this is developed in the fishes to form the brain. It is this possession of a central nervous system which distinguishes the fishes from the invertebrates. The fishes breathe through gills, whereas the next higher class, the amphibians, transfers breathing to the interior of the body by replacing the gills with lungs. However, the amphibians depend on moisture from the environment. The next class, the reptiles, becomes free from this particular dependence on the environment by developing a closed fluid system. Nevertheless, the reptiles remain dependent on the external environment for warmth. The birds are the first class to become free from this dependence, developing an independent system of warmth which keeps their body temperature constant. The further step of independence from the environment, which is taken by the placental mammals, is when the development of offspring takes place within the uterus of the mother—whereas with all the classes of vertebrates before the placental mammals (i.e., including monotremes and marsupials), the offspring are developed externally in the environment.

This sequence, from fish to mammal, discloses an increasing degree of independence from the environment by the progressive internalization of the different life functions. Schad summarizes this in the following chart at the top of the next page. He draws attention particularly to the *sequence* in which this emancipation of the organic systems from the environment takes place. It is the nervous system, located primarily in the brain, which develops independence first. So we can see from the chart that the emancipation of the higher animals from the environment develops from the head downwards.

But the placental mammals as such do not represent the end of this process of emancipation. They are bound to their environment

FISH	AMPHIBIAN	REPTILE	BIRD	MAMMAL
Central nervous system	Breathing system	Fluid system	Warmth system	Repro-ductive system
Brain	Lungs	Heart	Visceral organs	Uterus

by means of their limb system. For example, moles have shovel-like claws, seals have flippers, horses have hooves, apes have hanging arms, and so on. All these adaptations mean that they are not independent of their environment in their limb systems. Emancipation from this dependency is the step taken by man. What emerges at the end of the sequence, the human being, is the organism which is the least specialized biologically, i.e., least adapted to, and therefore dependent on, a specific environment. Indeed this is really the characteristic difference between the human being and the other mammals, and it puts human beings in a class of their own biologically. Human beings are organisms which are unspecialized—as Schad puts it, "Humankind's perfection is its imperfection." We can see this in the case of the human hand, which is not adapted to any particular purpose and is therefore not limited to one particular function. Compared with the highly developed limb organs of the mammals, the human hand is undeveloped biologically. But this very fact frees it to perform an indefinite number of different functions, by the use of tools, without being tied to any particular use and therefore depending on a particular environment. Any tool can be used and then put down, another one taken up and used, and so on indefinitely. In contrast, we could say that the mammal is tied to the tool which its limbs have become.

What is also particularly important about the arms and hands is that these limbs take no part in the movement of the body. This is undertaken entirely by the lower limbs, which are specialized in order to do so. However, Schad shows that this specialization is not an environmental adaptation, but one which grows out of the organism itself. In the mammals, specialization takes place in the part of the limb nearest to the surroundings (e.g., the specialization of the horse's hoof), whereas the upper part of the limb, which is furthest from the surroundings, remains unaffected. The opposite happens in the human being. Here the foot remains unspecialized and therefore biologically underdeveloped, but the upper part of the leg (the femur) is greatly developed compared with the other animals. It is by this means that the legs become specialized so that human beings can stand erect—but the important point is that this uprightness can be recognized to be an expression of the organism itself, and not an external adaptation. Not being *externally* adapted to the environment, human beings are free to walk where they choose. So their habitat covers the Earth.

Such a bare sketch does not do justice to these facts. We need to approach them dynamically, seeing the development of the lower limbs (legs) in man as a movement in the opposite direction to the development of these limbs in the mammal. This is itself an exercise in seeing comprehensively. Similarly, we have to see how this development of the lower limbs, the liberation of the upper limbs (arms) from the need to participate in the movement of the body, and the consequent withdrawal of limb activity from the head, all belong together in producing the appearance of human beings. We have to work in imagination—but not fancifully—to see these factors belonging together as a whole. If we only work intellectually, in an analytical way, then we have one fact next to another, but without seeing them together—think of the way biology textbooks often describe the upper and lower human limbs without seeing them together in the context of the organism as a whole.

The chart given above, showing the progressive liberation of organic systems from the environment, can now be extended to include humanity. Schad gives it in this extended form as seen

INVERTEBRATES	FISHES	AMPHIBIANS	REPTILES
Sense system	Central nervous system	Breathing system	Fluid system
Body	Brain	Lungs	Heart

BIRDS	MAMMALS	HUMANS
Warmth system	Reproductive system	Limb system
Visceral organs	Uterus	Legs and particularly the feet

above, which includes the invertebrates at the opposite end to humanity, these being the animals which were the first to develop sensory organs. When these classes of animals are seen comprehensively in this manner, and not just separately, or even just one after the other, then this "higher fact" of progressive emancipation appears. It is with reference to this that John Davy says that "there is a particular characteristic of 'biological progress' which has not yet been granted any fundamental evolutionary significance."[276] One reason for this may well be that the mechanism of evolution proposed by Darwin seems to lead in the opposite direction to emancipation from the environment. Darwin's mechanism (as he thought of it) of random variation and natural selection means that organisms which are favored for survival are those that have a specific adaptation to an environment which gives them an advantage. in other words, natural selection leads to an increased *dependence* of the organism on its environment. But the organism to emerge last in the sequence, the human being, is the one which is least specialized. Compared with all the other groups of mammals, the human being is biologically underdeveloped in this sense. So the question is, how can a process which proceeds by increasing the fit between an organism and the environment, thus making it more dependent and specialized, lead to progressive emancipation from the environment and finally to an organism which is the least specialized of all? It seems that Darwin's mechanism must lead in the opposite direction to that which emerges when we see the sequence comprehensively. It is because the established theory requires us to look in the opposite direction that the sequence of emancipation has not been granted any fundamental evolutionary significance.[277]

When this sequence of animals is seen in Goethe's way, it is seen *metamorphically* in the perspective of "multiplicity in unity." This means that the sequence is One organism, and not a sequence of different organisms connected in an external way. They are different manifestations or actualizations of the same organism, not different organisms which have evolved from a common ancestor as in the standard theory of evolution. Once again, we have to turn our way of seeing inside-out. As one leaf does not transform into another one in the growth of the plant, so one kind of animal does not turn into another kind. They are not descended from one another, either directly or from a common ancestor, by procreative connection. As with the plant, what we are seeing here is the development of One organism out of itself, which has the dynamic unity of self-difference. So the sequence is really the progressive expression of the whole itself, and not one stage turning into another one.[278] This is evolution in the perspective of the intensive dimension of One.

Thus the Goethean approach gives us the possibility of a different kind of evolution from that envisaged in Darwin's theory.[279] There is no procreative descent whereby one kind of organism gradually turns into another kind of organism, and the large-scale differences between organisms are considered to be the accumulated result of very many small-scale differences. This different idea of evolution was current in Germany in Goethe's time under the concept of *Entwicklung*, which can be translated as "development." But because this is very different indeed from the procreational idea of evolution embodied in the theory of natural selection, this alternative view of evolution as development has been overlooked on account of the dominance of the former in the scientific establishment.[280]

THE TWOFOLD

We have seen that when we experience the belonging together by seeing connections, the separation is overcome but not at the level of separation. This is the experience of what Wittgenstein called "that understanding which consists just in the fact that we 'see the connections'."[281] His way of achieving this was to try to see comprehensively by following Goethe's procedure of giving a synoptic presentation (what Wittgenstein called an *übersichtliche Darstellung*), which is the kind of presentation of phenomena we have seen him give with plants and color. When such a presentation is seen comprehensively, the experience becomes that of seeing the connections, i.e., seeing the way that things already stand in connection with one another without needing to be joined. This experience of seeing that things connect directly—that to connect two things, we do not always need a third[282]—is recognized by Wittgenstein as a new *kind* of understanding, different from an explanation or a theory. Because *seeing* is what matters here, and this is attained by means of a synoptic presentation, Wittgenstein also refers to this as a "perspicuous presentation."

Arranging things in such a way that their relationships with each other can be seen, i.e., the internal connections, as distinct from connections which are added externally (like a rope connecting them), is a very different activity from looking to see what things have in common. Wittgenstein says that his approach—which is Goethe's—is the opposite to the traditional approach in philosophy of looking for something that all things subsumed under a general term have in common. He says, in connection with Plato's dialogues, that his method could be summed up by saying that it was the exact opposite of that of Socrates.[283] He particularly detested "the craving for generality" which he saw as the preoccupation of science. Wittgenstein's way of proceeding, and his comments on it, are of interest to us here because of the way that they confirm and illuminate the Goethean approach. But his remarks are particularly interesting because of the way that he appreciated just how radically different Goethe's mode of seeing is from that of the mainstream in science and philosophy. This is very often not appreciated by those who approach Goethe in an intellectual manner, and who therefore interpret him as searching for a common plan. Wittgenstein avoided this mistake because he was concerned with finding his way toward a new *kind* of understanding, which requires an enhancement of seeing. As has been noted in the previous section, seeing comprehensively is a higher cognitive function than abstracting what is general. It is by developing the capacity to do this that the error above is avoided.

It is practice in seeing comprehensively which leads to the *direct* seeing of connections, so that the wholeness is experienced directly as part of the phenomenon. By seeing comprehensively we come to experience the *belonging* together of the phenomena, instead of introducing connections which make them belong *together*. This is the difference between Goethe's approach to wholeness and the counterfeit approach of "systems." In the Goethean way this *experience* of wholeness is achieved by attention to concrete detail through working with the senses, followed by the practice of exact sensorial imagination. By working in this way, the tendency toward generality is avoided and at the same time the conditions for seeing comprehensively are promoted. The very nature of attention to sensory detail is that it is an act which directs the attention away from generality. But it is the nature of imagination to be holistic, because when we try to imagine something we try to see it all together, as a whole. When we see a series of leaves in imagination, for example, we try to build an image of each leaf in its concrete detail as a whole, and we also try to see the series as a whole. Attention to the sensory detail and the holistic power of imagination work together in comprehensive seeing. The important thing to remember is that seeing comprehensively is very different from generalization—it is concrete and holistic, whereas the latter is abstract and analytical. The mode of mentation which "the craving for generality" entails, effectively prohibits seeing comprehensively and hence the seeing of connections which is the experience of the wholeness of the phenomenon. These two different modes of cognitive functioning go in opposite directions to each other, so if we have the one then we cannot have the other. To become free from generality it is necessary therefore to work in the appropriate way—which is the way that Goethe provides.

When we see the intrinsic connections, the phenomenon is experienced as a whole, and it is part of this experience that we recognize the wholeness of the phenomenon to be part of the phenomenon itself and not added to it by the mind—even though it is experienced through the mind instead of the senses. But when the wholeness is experienced, the separation does not disappear—it remains as separation for the senses.[284] We have both together: the separation and the wholeness. They are not of the same kind—if they were, then we could not see them both simultaneously because they are opposite to each other. It is when we don't experience the wholeness as a real factor, i.e., as part of the phenomenon, that we try to understand everything at the level of separation and have to introduce external connections. Because these connections are on the level of separation, they are of the same kind as the elements they link together. This is the approach taken by the philosophy of mechanism.

In some of his later work, Wittgenstein is particularly concerned to try to make clear the nature of this kind of understanding which consists in *seeing* connections, and especially the way that this is different from the kind of seeing which consists in seeing a physical object.[285] He approaches this by focusing on what he calls aspect-seeing, i.e., seeing something as something, and asks what it would mean for someone to be aspect-blind. For example, consider someone who is unable to see a human head, or the giraffe, discussed in "The Organizing Idea in Cognitive Perception." They can see the random black and white blotches, but they cannot see the figure because they are aspect-blind. Wittgenstein asks what is lacking in this case, and he says." It is not absurd to answer: the power of imagination."[286] The point of this for Wittgenstein is that we *see* a connection in the same sense that we see an aspect or a gestalt. Hence this shows us that the kind of seeing which *sees* connections is *imagination*. Imagination is the kind of seeing which is also a kind of understanding (a kind of thinking). For imagination *seeing and understanding are one*. Hence there is no need for explanation. Seeing replaces theory—but not the same kind of seeing as that which sees separate objects. This is the kind of seeing which Goethe referred to when he remarked about himself that "my perception itself is a thinking, and my thinking a perception."[287]

We can now appreciate the difference between Goethe and Schiller which became apparent in their famous encounter, referred to in the introduction to this part. When Goethe remarked about science that "a different approach might well be discovered, not by concentrating on separate and isolated elements of nature but by portraying it as active and alive, with its efforts directed from the whole to the parts," Schiller was doubtful about the epistemology of this approach.[288] Doubt turned into disagreement when Goethe described the metamorphosis of plants and tried to indicate the *Urpflanze* to him "with a few characteristic strokes of the pen." When Schiller objected, "That is not an observation from experience. That is an idea," Goethe replied, somewhat annoyed, "Then I may rejoice that I have ideas without knowing it, and can even see them with my own eyes." For Schiller, the Kantian, seeing could only mean sensory seeing. This was supplemented by an idea, which entailed abstract conceptual thinking. The separation of the elements of nature was overcome by the addition of such an idea, and not by seeing. For Goethe, on the other hand, there is another kind of seeing, which sees connections instead of separation. This is the seeing of imagination. Now this is certainly not the same as having an abstract idea, as in analytical thinking, but neither is it the same kind of seeing as that which sees physical objects. Imagination sees connections directly, so there is wholeness where for sensory seeing there is separateness. The mode of togetherness is different. Wittgenstein emphasized that what is seen in the seeing of connections must not be thought of as if it were an object—because that belongs to sensory seeing. Because the connection overcomes the separateness, the connection itself cannot have the quality of separateness—which means that it cannot be like a physical object. Hence, the seeing of connections *cannot* be like the seeing of physical objects. So when the connection is seen, nothing new is added in the sense of a new object which can be seen by the senses. In this respect, everything stays the same. What is different is the mode of togetherness, not the addition of an extra object called a "connection." The way of seeing changes, and with it the mode of togetherness of the elements which are seen.[289] Goethe, in his response to Schiller quoted above, tried to indicate that what he was concerned with is an experience of seeing, but in doing so he too readily implied that this is sensory (". . . with my own eyes"). Schiller, on the other hand, by his objection, brings out that this is not a sensory experience as such. There is truth in what both of them say, but each errs in his own way. As mentioned in the introductory chapter to this part, it was through the resistance he experienced in this encounter with Schiller that Goethe began to become more aware of the epistemological dimension of his approach to science, instead of being naïvely empirical in his attitude.

Whereas these two kinds of seeing are different (it is their *difference* that Wittgenstein was concerned to establish), this does not mean that they are exclusive. We can and do have *both* sensory and imaginative seeing together. Imaginative seeing does not replace sensory seeing but is present along with it. Instead of going from one kind of seeing to another, we have what Owen Barfield refers to as a faculty of "double vision." He considers that imagination and the faculty of "double vision" are inseparable:

> Imagination, in fact, presupposes "double" vision and not simply
> the substitution of one kind of single vision for another. It requires
> a sober ability to have the thing both ways at once.[290]

Unlike ordinary double vision, which sees the same thing twice, this extraordinary "double vision" of imagination sees in two different ways simultaneously. The sensory vision sees the separateness of distinct parts, and the imaginative vision simultaneously sees their connection and wholeness. So each part of the double vision sees differently instead of the same, and yet when they occur together they are not separable. This is the kind of vision which William Blake referred to as "twofold"—a term which conveys better than "double vision" that what it refers to is double and yet irreducibly one, divided and yet integral.[291]

What Goethe's way of seeing is concerned with is the development of this twofold vision, not the substitution of one kind of single vision for another. It is not concerned with providing an alternative explanation of phenomena, but with an *alternative to explanation*. This alternative is the seeing which is twofold. Then we see connections directly. These are connections of another kind to the mechanical, material connections which are introduced at the sensory level by single vision. The latter are of necessity external connections, and so in contrast we call the connections of another kind which belong to twofold vision, internal or intrinsic connections. For example, think of the sequence of organs up the plant. We see the individual organs, which are separate for the senses, and at the same time we see the metamorphosis which is their connection. The individual organs, which are discrete, are visible to the senses; their intrinsic connection, which is the wholeness of metamorphosis, is visible to the imagination.[292] When we see the metamorphosis, the individual organs don't vanish—just as the letters of a word do not vanish when we read the meaning of the word. But neither do the individual organs (or the letters of the word) merge into one another, or join together in some way, when we see the inner connection. They remain distinct from each other at the sensory level. So in the seeing which is twofold, the different parts and the wholeness or unity of these parts are simultaneously present together. We may have the sense that they are on different levels, as it were, and it is often convenient (though it might be misleading) to talk in this way. But this is more likely a reflection of the way that we ourselves are involved in the act of perception. We are involved in a double way, simultaneously through the organ of sensory sight and the organ of imagination.

It has been pointed out by Owen Barfield that this role of imagination in science is specific to Goethe's way of science.[293] Whereas imagination certainly enters into all scientific work, it does so usually in devising hypotheses to explain facts which are known, or in producing an organizing idea to guide the overall activity of research. In such cases imagination is used to augment what is encountered by the senses, whether in advance or afterwards. But it does not become an organ of perception in the way that it does in Goethe's approach, where imagination is involved in the act of observation itself. This results in the experience of the seeing which is twofold, instead of the seeing of single vision supplemented by imagination—in which case the imagination is added on, externally, to the observation. It is because of this that the practice of Goethean science leads us to *experience* the wholeness of the phenomenon, so that we recognize it as part of the phenomenon itself and not something which is added on to it by the mind. Furthermore, we also recognize that there is no longer any temptation to look for anything beyond the phenomenon, behind the appearances, because the appearance itself has now expanded to include an intensive depth. There is now a further dimension to the appearance, which is the dimension of wholeness. So the phenomenon becomes more fully visible, whereas it is only partially visible to the senses. The twofoldness of the phenomenon as it thus appears removes the temptation to introduce a two-world theory. There is simply no need now to postulate something behind the appearances in order to explain them. Twofoldness is *not* dualism. We have seen that Goethe's way of science is nonmetaphysical (nondualistic). Now we can begin to see what it is that replaces metaphysics: the twofold.

We are already familiar with the twofold to some extent. We encounter it all the time, even if we are not aware of it, in the activities of language: reading and writing, speaking and listening. In fact, we have drawn on this familiarity on more than one occasion above to illustrate the notion of the twofold. The fact that we can do this so readily itself illustrates just how familiar we are with the twofold, even though we do not realize it. When we read a word there are several distinct letters but one meaning. Similarly, when we read a sentence there are several distinct words but one meaning. We can go on to consider paragraphs, chapters, and in some cases whole books, in a similar way. The letters are seen as a word, the words are seen as a sentence, when the distinct elements are seen comprehensively. What is seen then, the meaning, is evidently very different in kind from the individual, discrete elements. Yet these two aspects belong together as one in the twofold unity which is the experienced word or sentence— i.e., when it is read, written, spoken, or heard. Although they are so different in kind, physical manifestation, and meaning, we do nevertheless experience them both together, but each in a different way. The physical manifestation is experienced through the senses, whereas clearly the meaning is not. When reading a sentence, for example, we see the meaning and yet we know perfectly well that what we are seeing with our physical sense of sight is not the meaning but the physical marks on the page in front of us. We certainly know that the physical marks which we see with the sense of sight do not disappear when we read the meaning. Although the focus of our attention shifts from the marks to the meaning, the marks on the page are still there for us—otherwise we simply could not read! Yet when we read, we are seeing something which is very different in kind from the marks on the page. Nevertheless, we can only come to this, i.e., the meaning, by means of the physical manifestation (marks) through which it is expressed. So, in reading, we see the meaning at the same time that we see the physical marks, but differently.[294] Yet it would never occur to us to suppose that the meaning was *behind* the letters of a word or the words of a sentence, as if the letters needed to be *explained* by reference to something behind the word, or the words by something behind the sentence.[295] It is quite clear to us that *both* letters *and* meaning belong to the word at the same time, but that each is experienced in a different way. This is the twofold of physical manifestation and meaning with which we are familiar in an everyday way, but which we do not recognize explicitly as such.

Twofoldness is the fundamental characteristic of language: sensory manifestation and nonsensory meaning present together as one. Language is the primal phenomenon of the twofold, and as such it can provide us with a model to replace the dualism of the two-world theory (metaphysics) which requires us to look behind the phenomena for their explanation. This is a fundamental key to understanding Goethe's way of science: the two-world dualism of metaphysics is replaced by the twofold for which language is the model. Goethe understood this when he spoke of his way of seeing as *reading* the phenomena of nature. It may often have been assumed too readily that this is "merely a metaphor," but from the account given above it will now be clear that it is a very precise figure of speech, and one which is intended to be taken literally. Furthermore, it encapsulates the key ontological difference between Goethe's way of science and that of the mainstream. It also gives us a vivid image of the difference between Goethe's approach and the quantitative science of measurement:

> The fundamental difference of his approach is his attempt to learn to *read* in the *Book of Nature* rather than to *analyze* its constitutive parts. "Reading" means to treat the sense-perceptual aspects of Nature like letters of words, or words of a text: as signs for meaning. The analytic procedure of modern science has a tendency to dissect natural substances in order to understand them; this would be comparable to measuring the shape of the letter "B," analyzing the printer's

> ink, paper consistency etc. in order to understand its role in the
> word "Book."[296]

Continuing this image further, mathematical physics would be
comparable to producing an equation relating the letters of the
word, such that the solution of this equation would generate
the sequence of letters "Book." But this way, while it does have
its uses (manipulation and control), misses the possibility of the
more comprehensive understanding, which is reading.

There is, however, a widespread prejudice about language
which blocks the way to understanding fully the significance of
the twofold. This is the prejudice of nominalism—or the representational theory of language—which has the effect of introducing dualism into the way that we understand language. The
inevitable consequence is that the twofoldness is lost. So we
must now recognize and overcome this dualism in our attitude
to language.

Although this dualism can appear in several forms, one of
the most evident is the notion that a word is a sign which stands
for what it means. So a word functions as a token which represents the thing meant (hence the "representational" theory of
language), and from which it is therefore separate. Concomitantly, the thing meant is independent of the sign which represents it. A word names something, but names are just like labels
attached to things, according to this view (hence "nominalism"). For example, the word "table" can be used to represent a
table in conveying information from one person to another—as
in "the book is on the table." But this is taken to be the *only*
function of words. Now whereas words can have this function,
it is not their only function, nor indeed is it their fundamental
function. The difficulty with this view of language is that it
assumes we have direct access to things independently of language. So we already recognize and know something *before* we
apply language to it—this is also called the instrumental theory
of language, because it sees language as a tool to be picked up,
applied, and put down again. But we have seen in "The Organizing
Idea in Cognitive Perception" that all cognitive perception

entails not only sense perception but also an organizing idea, a concept. The problem of the origin of concepts was noted there, i.e., that a concept cannot be formed by generalization from several instances because it is only by means of the concept that we can recognize an instance in the first place. So this empiricist account of the origin of concepts presupposes the very concept whose origin it seeks to explain! For example, to be able to see a table is to have the capacity already to be able to see *all* tables— i.e., all *possible* tables, including those that don't look like tables, such as an upturned box, the surface of a rock, a cloth on the ground, and so on. It is recognized now that it is language which gives us concepts. The origin of concepts is in the dawning of language, and we would never acquire concepts if language did not dawn in us. So the commonsense view that we see and know something *before* we *apply* words to it—which are therefore merely labels—clearly does not take into account the role of language in giving the concept which enables us to see and know something *as* something in the first place. It is only by the grace of language in giving the concept that we can see a table, for example, and therefore language is intrinsically involved in the table that we see. Without it no table would appear—no *table* could be. Hence the commonsense view of language (nominalism), that the thing meant is seen and known independently of the word—which is therefore only a sign that represents it—is fundamentally inadequate and misleading.

It is language which teaches us concepts as children, and hence it is language which first gives us the ability to see the world, so that the world can appear.[297] But our first experience of language, the dawning of language, is different from our experience of language as adults. A vivid illustration of the original disclosive power of language—as distinct from the secondary representational function of language, as when it is used for conveying information—is given by the remarkable story of Helen Keller. As a very young girl, Helen Keller had a severe attack of measles, which left her deaf and blind. This happened to her before the dawning of language, and it was only due to the extraordinary work of her dedicated governess that these extreme difficulties were eventually overcome. The moment when this finally happened is described in her own words:

> We walked down the path to the well-house, attracted by the fragrance of the honeysuckle with which it was covered. Someone was drawing water and my teacher placed my hand under the spout. As the cool stream gushed over one hand she spelled into the other the word "water," first slowly, then rapidly. I stood still, my whole attention fixed upon the motion of her fingers. Suddenly I felt a misty consciousness as of something forgotten—a thrill of returning thought; and somehow the mystery of language was revealed to me. I knew then that "w-a-t-e-r" meant the wonderful cool something that was flowing over my hand. That living word awakened my soul, gave it light, joy, set it free!. . . I left the well-house eager to learn. Everything had a name, and each name gave birth to a new thought. As we returned to the house each object that I touched seemed to quiver with life. That was because I saw everything with the strange new light that had come to me.[298]

She is blind but describes herself as *seeing* with a new *light*. The word "water" does not represent or stand for water here; it is not a label to be attached to water for the purpose of communicating information. Helen Keller does not already know water, to which she then adds the word. No, in this case everything is reversed. The word "water" *shows* her water; it brings it to light so that she *sees* it. Here the name calls water into appearance; it calls water into being as *water*, instead of the indistinct sense percept which there had been before. (N.B.: the first few sentences in the quotation describe the situation before the dawn of language as it could only appear to her after language had dawned in her. This is inevitable, because she is giving an account, but we must consciously allow for it.) Thus the word here is not a sign in the sense that it designates something already known, because the thing designated by it would first have had to be seen independently of language—and evidently it had not been.

She speaks of her soul being awakened, given light, and set free. What awoke in Helen Keller is the light of the world. This is not the (formless) physical light, but the light of meaning which is the appearing of what things are.[299] Without language no things could be, and therefore there would be no world. So the dawning of language is the dawn of the world—as we can see so clearly here in the experience of Helen Keller. This sets her soul free because to be human is to live in the world. Only human beings have a "world"—which is entirely different from inhabiting an environment in the way that animals do.[300] Until this experience of the dawning of language, Helen Keller had been unable to be in the world, which is proper to human beings, and had inhabited a wordless environment. A human being not able to be human—and now she is freed from the darkness of this condition to enter the light of the human world.

Heidegger distinguishes between language as disclosure and language as representation—the former being primary, and the latter being derivative and therefore secondary.[301] He says that "the essential being of language is Saying as Showing," and that "saying is in no way the linguistic expression added to the phenomena after they have appeared." A sign is to be understood fundamentally as "showing in the sense of bringing something to light." Heidegger emphasizes the transformation which takes place when we do not understand the sign in this way (because we do not *experience* it this way), but think of it instead as something that designates. When this happens, "The kinship of Showing with what it shows" is lost and becomes "transformed into a conventional relation between a sign and its signification." When Heidegger says that the essence of language is *Saying*—i.e., Saying which *is* Showing—he does not mean this to be taken in the sense of a being which says, but more in the sense of Saying which "be's." This is the Saying which *is* language—when Heidegger says the essence of language is *Saying* he means just that and no more (the trouble is we always add more). Similarly with Showing—since Saying *is* Showing—this is not the showing of a being (like shining a flashlight on an object in a dark room), but the showing which is its self-appearance wherein it "be's." In Helen Keller's experience, the word "water" *says* water in the sense that it *shows* water (*not* points to it), whereby *water* appears. The word does not designate water *after* it has first appeared. But after it has appeared we take it that this is what the word does. This is the stage of dualism, when word and thing are separated and language becomes representational. Language as disclosure is saying–showing–seeing. This must be read holistically and not analytically, i.e., each of the three aspects is not a component part of the event of disclosure but the whole: saying *is* showing, and showing *is* seeing—like a threefold multiperspectival figure. When language is representation—which is re-presentation as well as functioning as a representative—it merely "stands for." Disclosure is primary because representation can only present again what has already been presented. If we try to understand language in terms of representation, then we begin too far "downstream," at the end, and we therefore miss the primary function of language which makes representation possible in the first place—it's another instance of trying to get to the milk by way of the cheese.

Helen Keller's experience illustrates what Wilhelm von Humboldt called the energetic phase of language, and Kühlewind calls the monistic phase:

> Children learn their first language, their mother tongue "monistically." They do not just impose "names" on objects and meanings, as nominalistic and naive thinkers imagine. Rather, language—and the concepts it provides—structures inner and outer worlds into objects, phenomena, and meanings.[302]

We do not learn our first language as children in the way that we *subsequently* imagine when we are adults. We imagine that we learn our first language in the way that we may subsequently acquire a second language. But what we forget here is that the second language names meanings created in the first language, and does not name things which are given independently of language:

> The first language *creates* the meanings that are then "named" in the second language. In fact, this process reinforces the impression that

the world is built up nominalistically because we easily forget that we perceive a thing only if it has a meaning, only if it is already defined by a concept. *Before* the first language or mother tongue, there is nothing that could be named."[303]

It is this forgetfulness which results in the entry of dualism into our understanding of language, whereby we think the word merely names the thing meant, which itself is given independently of language. Thus we treat *all* language as if it were like our second language—this is the mistake of nominalism.[304]

In the monistic, or energetic, phase of language word and meaning belong together indissolubly. The sensory part (sound) and the nonsensory part (meaning) cannot be separated, so that it would be impossible to say that the sensory part "stands for" or represents the meaning. The experience is that the word is one, whole, and therefore that the *word means itself*. When the word is experienced as self-meaning, then it is evident that it does not stand for something other than itself. This is the experience of the twofoldness of the word, whereby the meaning is encountered as being intrinsic to the word and not apart from it. This is what we all undergo as growing children (and which Helen Keller describes), and later lose:

> Language is unique in that it is not just perception but *meaningful* perception. Children must grasp both perception and meaning *at the same time*.[305]

What is encountered in such an experience is a unique mode of being. This is later lost sight of as the twofoldness which is characteristic of the monistic phase of language falls apart into the dualism of signifier and signified—whereupon the word is no longer experienced as self-meaning, but as standing for (representing) something other than itself which is given independently.

In the monistic phase the word *says* the thing, shows it, so that it appears and is seen.[306] The word does not label something seen already, before the word. If we were to experience the word in this living, energetic way—as we did when we were young children (and can glimpse again through our own children)—we would encounter *saying* directly and thereby *know* that the word says itself, and hence that it is self-meaning and does not derive its meaning from something beyond itself. The word "table" gives us the concept "table," and *this* enables us to see *any* table. In fact it enables us to see "table-ly," so that we can *see* (read actively) a table in any shape or form. This reverses the popular view that words receive their meaning by ostensive definition—i.e., that we give meaning *to* words instead of receiving meaning *from* words. According to this view, for example, we give meaning to the word "table" by pointing to a table and saying "table." This attaches the name to the thing (nominalism). Children, it is supposed, learn their first language in some such way (any observant parent can see that they don't). Now it is certainly the case that we can and do learn a second language in this manner—but this is because the concept which alone enables us to see a thing has been given in our first language. Just imagine the attempt to attach meaning to the word "table" ostensively. How would we know what to attach the label to if we could not already *see* a table? Without the concept, which comes in the first place from language, how would we know *what* was being pointed to? It is only the concept "table" which creates a *boundary* in the perceptual field so that a table is distinguished and can be pointed to. Someone who did not have the concept would not know *what* was being pointed to, because it is the concept which makes the distinction whereby there is some thing to point to. This comes from the word in the first place, and therefore pointing to the thing *cannot* be the means whereby meaning is given to the word. Although it may appear that ostensive definition is the way that nouns and verbs get their meaning, this clearly would not be possible for other kinds of words, such as "if," "because," "and," "but," and so on. Added to which there is the structuring of grammar—how could this be arrived at ostensively? However, without even considering such cases, as we have seen it turns out that even simple nouns cannot be given meaning by ostensive definition in the way that the popular view supposes. The word is self-meaning at the monistic (energetic) stage of language, and it is this which is presupposed in making ostensive definition even seem possible. Thus the popular view of how words get their meaning—the view which belongs at the level of dualism—presupposes language itself. In other words, this explanation of language presupposes language!

At the fundamental level of language we are concerned with here, a word means itself and is therefore the appearance of what it says (e.g., the word "water" for Helen Keller). Thus language is the medium of the *appearance* of "the world." There is therefore no "world" outside language—and especially is there no world-in-itself hidden behind language which is forever inaccessible.[307] Language takes on the role of a veil in such a dualism, whereas it is within language that things appear and are. It is only within the perspective of dualism that this can be mistaken for an assertion of relativism and subjectivism—i.e., that all we can know is the way we ourselves look *at* the world, what our picture of it is like.

A word means itself and we cannot refer it to something other than itself which bestows meaning on it. Thus, at the primary level we are concerned with here, the word is self-presenting. So the meaning of "table" is understanding "table," the meaning of "if" is understanding "if," and so on.[308] If a word is something that means, then concomitantly it is something that can be understood—we cannot talk about "meaning" without *thereby* entailing "understanding." Thus language is being that can be understood—which brings us to Gadamer's fundamental insight that "*Being that can be understood is Language*"[309] If it were otherwise, then understanding would not be possible. The representational theory of language, which is dualistic, misses the unique being of language and consequently tries to imagine understanding as arising out of nonunderstanding. This is impossible. It is therefore not surprising that, as we have noted already, the representational theory depends upon the prior assumption of language as disclosure—what Helen Keller (and ourselves once) experienced. It is only because language is already there in the first place that the representational theory even *seems* to make sense.

We have discussed the philosophy of language in some depth here because of the widespread prejudice about language which blocks the way to understanding the significance of the twofold. The habit of dualism in our thinking must be dissolved if we are to see the radical significance of the twofold unity of sensory word and nonsensory meaning, and hence the way that language provides us with an alternative to the metaphysical two-world theory for understanding the phenomena of nature. As there is nothing behind the word, and yet the word is not limited to its sensory aspect, so there is nothing behind the phenomenon and yet the phenomenon is not limited to its sensory appearance. As with the word, so with nature in Goethe's way of science. The twofold replaces both two-world metaphysics and the single world of positivism—which are usually seen as the only alternatives. Goethe provides us with a genuinely new way of understanding, and one which is grounded in something which is very familiar to us all. Language provides the "model" for this alternative to both metaphysical dualism and positivism, but only when we can go beyond the idea of language as communicating the already disclosed, i.e., the level of information, to the disclosure itself. Only then can we encounter the uniqueness of language and come to what Heidegger calls the experience of language:

> Instead of explaining language in terms of one thing or another, and thus running away from it, the way to language intends to let language be experienced as language.[310]

This is something we have to work toward, so that we develop the capacity to experience the uniqueness of language for ourselves. This too becomes an aspect of *Bildung*, the schooling of a faculty which is adequate to a higher experience of language. Such a development cannot just be done intellectually, but necessarily entails a transformative step which shifts consciousness from the plane of the past into the living present—from the said into the *saying* which *is* language itself. Otherwise, in our attempt to understand language, we cannot escape from the habit of trying to get to the milk by way of the cheese.

Goethe's way of seeing goes against the dogma of modern science that the phenomena of nature are to be interpreted in terms of cause and effect. We are so familiar with this now that we take it for granted that this is the *only* way to understand nature. It is certainly invaluable for manipulating and controlling nature, but this is not at all the same as *understanding* nature—even though, under the influence of the dogma, we now think that it is. Considering nature exclusively in terms of cause and effect leads us to search for a mechanism for every phenomenon. But when we succeed in finding a mechanism it does not mean that we understand the phenomenon. We can then manipulate and control the phenomenon, but we do not know *what* it is. Eventually, under the influence of our success with the principle of mechanical causality, we begin to think that the question of what the phenomenon is has no meaning— whereas it is we who have lost sight of the possibility of knowing this. We will come to feel that if we know the causal mechanism of the phenomenon, then we do know what it is.

The quest for explanations in terms of causal mechanisms eventually leads to the notion of a field of force. This is a subtler notion than mechanism, but not fundamentally different in kind. The field concept is one which has found widespread application, and there is sometimes a tendency to try to explain everything in terms of the notion of a field, without it being noticed that a field is a physical cause and therefore does not introduce anything fundamentally new. Thus, if we are considering the wholeness of nature, there will be those who want to conceive of this as if it were some kind of field—which it is not. Goethe commented that we like to think mechanistically about things which are of a higher order *because it is easier*.[311] The wholeness of nature is not to be understood as some kind of field, which would reduce it to a causal agent, but as being akin to meaning in language. Thus language becomes the model instead of mechanism. This entails a fundamentally different ontology of nature: the ontology of the twofold. This is the truly radical step which Goethe took in science. He introduced a fundamentally new ontology of nature, and we cannot understand Goethe's way of science unless we recognize this and can begin to take this step for ourselves. Understanding nature as language forms the foundation of Goethe's way of science, as metaphysics forms the basis for the mainstream scientific enterprise. But whereas the latter is now well developed, Goethe's way of science is by comparison as yet not much more than a possibility—just as mainstream science itself was once.

7. The Possibility of a New Science of Nature

Until we have discovered the role of the organizing idea in scientific knowledge, we are in a position similar to a person who believes the Earth is at rest. It seems evident to the senses that the Earth does not move, and the difficulty here is to make the movement "visible" somehow—which, of course, cannot be done directly. Similarly, it seems evident to common sense that knowledge of the world is given to us directly, by observation or experiment, through the senses. Seeing seems to be a sensory experience—as the Earth seems to be at rest. But in both cases it *seems* this way because we do no recognize the way in which we ourselves are involved in the situation. We are part of it, not outside of it, and have to adjust our perspective to take this into account. In the case of cognition, this means discovering the role of the organizing idea, whether this be at the level of the concept in everyday cognitive perception or at the level of a comprehensive organizing idea in scientific knowledge. It is only when we have discovered the role of the organizing idea that we can begin to understand science.

This is a liberating step. It frees us from our enthrallment with the science which has been established, by making us aware that such science does not have the absolute (i.e., self-standing) foundations that we customarily assume. Such a step makes us aware that "in our scientific–technological world, or, more precisely, in the a priori presuppositions of this world, we have opted for one particular possibility, grounded in one particular situation."[312] There could, therefore, be other possibilities. Historically, the origin of modern science is to be found in what Hübner calls "spontaneous acts"—because there is nothing which compels or determines the choice which is made. For example, Copernicus's choice of a Sun-centered cosmos enabled him to find the symmetry and harmony of the whole, in a way that had escaped the Earth-centered scheme. But the motivation for this was principally aesthetic. In wanting to find symmetry and harmony in the cosmos, Copernicus was adopting the Renaissance ideal in architecture and painting as a precept for astronomy.[313] So the foundations of the Copernican theory do not lie only in astronomy as such, but in the entire cultural–historical situation. Another example of such "spontaneous acts" in the origin of a scientific theory is provided by Darwin's theory of evolution. Darwin transformed the idea of evolution which was prevalent at the time, and which had become associated with social unrest, riots, and revolution in England in the 1830s. In its place he eventually introduced a new idea of evolution which was attuned much more to the new competitive, free-market, entrepreneurial, industrial capitalism than it was to the demands of the underclass for self-organization. Darwin did not see evolution as life lifting itself up from below, as the social revolutionaries wanted to think, but as arising from competition among a group of associates. His was an evolution which was suitable for the bosses of industry.[314] So, as with the Copernican theory, we can say that the foundations of the Darwinian theory do not lie only in biology as such, but in the entire cultural–historical situation. If cultural–historical factors enter into the constitution of scientific knowledge, i.e., into the very *form* which this knowledge takes, then evidently science cannot be understood apart from its cultural–historical context—as if it were self-standing, generated by its own intrinsic "scientific method." Scientific knowledge is intrinsically historical. As Goethe said: "The history of science is science itself."

The fundamental organizing ideas of science act at the level of possibility. They create what Hübner calls, using Kant's terminology, "the conditions of the possibility" of the production of experiences.[315] In other words, they give us the *form* that what counts as *scientific* experience can take. But, far from being immutable (as they would have been for Kant), their origin is cultural–historical and hence they can change. As well as applying to organizing ideas within specific domains of science, this applies also to science as a whole, i.e., to the very idea of what counts as "science." We have noted already, for example, at the end of "The Metaphysical Separation," that the idea that nature is mathematical is an organizing idea for science as a whole which constitutes a new style of physics. When Copernicus incorporated the Renaissance ideal of symmetry and harmony into a new theory of the structure of the cosmos, he did more than just this. In so doing he was at the same time incorporating this ideal into science itself as a new precept for how science should be done, and hence for what science is. This is the precept that science is to be done by looking for mathematical harmonies which are hidden from the senses. When this was transferred from astronomy to physics by Galileo, it became the precept for mathematical physics—and this is the style of physics we work with to this day. But what we can now recognize is that this style of physics does not emerge intrinsically from science itself, but is of cultural–historical origin. There is therefore nothing absolute about it, and therefore nothing which compels us to accept it *exclusively*. The recognition that this is true clearly brings with it an awareness that there may be other possibilities—not only other possible theories, but also other possible *kinds* of science.

This is the step that Goethe took. He went through a different doorway to nature than the one which had been taken in the scientific revolution. He developed a new kind of science, the science of Goethean style, which can be called the science of the wholeness of nature. In his discussion of Husserl's phenomenological investigation of what he called the science of Galilean style, Aron Gurwitsch says that "instead of stating that nature is mathematical, it is more appropriate to say that nature lends itself to mathematization." The important point about this formulation is that it brings out that "mathematization does not necessarily mean the disclosure of pre-given, though yet hidden, reality" but that "it suggests an accomplishment yet to be achieved."[316] It is the natural assumption of the onlooker mode of consciousness to believe that science is discovering a pregiven reality, which exists as an "object" prior to and independently of any scientific investigation. Hence the discovery of the mathematical structure of the world appears as the discovery that nature *is* mathematical as such. With this understanding, it seems that once science has discovered what is taken to be *the* truth, then there could not conceivably be any alternative. This is the view that "true" means "correct," i.e., corresponding to the object. Any suggestion that it could be otherwise leads to the accusation of relativism and subjectivism, since this seems to imply (when seen against the background of objectivism) that truth depends on factors which are not part of the object alone. The result of this is, at best, skepticism—and at worst, nihilism. But there is no need for this when we recognize that the truth of mathematical physics, for example, does not mean that nature has been found to be a mathematical object corresponding to the assertions of mathematical physics. On the contrary, the truth of mathematical physics is to be found in the progressive appearance of nature in its mathematical aspect, which is a consequence of the ongoing work of those committed to this particular project. The truth of mathematical physics is something which has to be *realized*, i.e., achieved, not just uncovered, as the term "discovery" is so often taken to mean. The important thing here is that nature *can* appear mathematically—and what appears *is* the mathematical aspect of nature. But this is not exclusive, and nature may be capable of appearing in other aspects if approached accordingly. What Husserl recognized is that the truth of mathematical physics is established through the ongoing work which is the never-ending fulfillment of the research program initiated by the proposal that nature is mathematical.[317] What this means is that the truth of science, is *realized historically*, not actualized by the discovery at some point in time of a correspondence between theory and reality. Goethe's statement that "the history of science is science itself" can now also be read in this sense, as an expression of the insight that a science is confirmed only by the historical process of its development—i.e., that the nature of science is that it is always an accomplishment to be achieved—as well as in the sense that cultural–historical factors enter into the form which scientific knowledge takes.

Once we recognize the historical nature of a science—mathematical physics, for example—then we can detach from it because we can see that it has no absolute claim on us. The science in question is temporarily "suspended." It is in this moment of freedom that we can recognize that there could be other possible kinds of science, which would also be accomplishments to be achieved. Thus, the Goethean proposal of the science of the wholeness of nature can be confirmed only by the historical process of the development of the science of the wholeness of nature. As it was once with the then new science of mathematical physics, so it is now with the new science of the wholeness of nature: it is an accomplishment waiting to be achieved.

This new science of the wholeness of nature is not in any way in competition with mainstream science. It does not seek to show that mainstream science is wrong or to replace it in any way. It is evident to anyone but a fool that mainstream science is correct—who could realistically doubt that mathematical physics, for example, is true? There is no way that the science of quantity and the science of wholeness could be compared to see which one is "correct." This is not for the reason that, regrettably, no way can be found *in principle* by which such a comparison could be made, so that we cannot find out what nature is "really like." Even to think that such a comparison *cannot* be made is, nevertheless, to think of a *comparison*, and this is already the wrong way to think. The science of quantity and the science of wholeness are incommensurable, but this is no reason for epistemological pessimism. Their incommensurability does *not* mean that we cannot know "what nature is really like." The being of nature can be revealed in different ways by different kinds of science, none of which has any claim to be more basic or fundamental. What becomes visible in each case *is* nature itself, but only one possible aspect of nature. Thus, nature can be quantity, or causal mechanism, or wholeness, for example. Each of these perspectives reveals nature as it is in itself (i.e., nature itself is not "hidden" behind these perspectives), but not exclusively. So the science of quantity and the science of wholeness are both true, but nature is revealed differently in each of them. Each is complete in itself, but neither is comprehensive. We can think here again of the duck/rabbit. Each one *is* the figure itself, but not exclusively. The important point is that each one is the whole figure and not part of it. Similarly, the science of quantity, for example, reveals one aspect of nature and not part of nature. The same can be said about the science of wholeness. However, in making this analogy with the duck/rabbit we must be careful not to fall into the error of thinking of different kinds of science as no more than different ways of illuminating nature, as if they were only different worldviews. The difference is that different kinds of science can reveal different aspects of nature itself—different ways that nature can be—so that each can be true even though they are incommensurable.

What we need here is the perspective of "multiplicity in unity," the intensive dimension of One which is the dimension of self-difference. Each different aspect of nature which is revealed is the same One. The difference here is the self-difference which is within unity. Hence different kinds of science reveal different aspects of nature, but not different parts of nature. So both the science of quantity and the science of wholeness can be true, and yet incommensurable, and therefore *cannot* be in competition with one another. Again, the science of physical cause and effect and the science of the wordlike quality of nature can both be true because each reveals a different aspect of nature. What is revealed in each of these sciences is an aspect of nature itself. When we understand this we can see that we have no grounds for accepting one and rejecting the other, or even for thinking that one is more fundamental than the other—let alone that one could be reduced to the other. The truth of science is not single, in the external objective sense, but neither is it plural. The fact that there is not only one truth does not mean that there are many separate truths. There is another possibility beyond the alternative of one and many. These appear as alternatives when taken in the numerical, quantitative sense, which corresponds to the world of solid bodies. But if we can leave this restricted case behind, we discover the higher possibility of the diversity which is within unity itself. Then we can see how truth can be neither singular nor plural, but One truth which is multiple. This is a higher perspective which has the effect of turning the one and the many inside out There is no longer a choice between objectivism and relativism, but a new way of understanding which transcends this dichotomy by seeing the one and the many in a new way. But this is a transformation of seeing, not just a strategy of the intellectual mind. From this transformed perspective, we can recognize how the so-called problem of objectivism and relativism arises from the way that the external perspective, corresponding to the logic of solid bodies, influences the form of our thinking. When we become free from this constraint, we can recognize that Goethe's organic perspective of "multiplicity within unity" can itself become the means by which Goethe's style of science can be seen to be justified in its claim to be scientifically true. Furthermore, it does so in a way which expands our understanding of the nature of scientific truth.

The quantitative aspect of nature reveals nature as quantity; the causal aspect of nature reveals nature as cause. But if we stop at the quantitative, or the causal, aspects of nature we have limited science and our understanding of nature unnecessarily. There is also the wholeness of nature, and the science of the wholeness of nature complements these other kinds of science in the manner indicated above. Recognizing this opens the doorway to making science more comprehensive, so that exaggerations and distortions in our understanding of nature resulting from the one-sided development of science can now be seen as such. This makes a more balanced understanding possible. Hitherto the science of the wholeness of nature has not been developed to anywhere near the same extent as the sciences of other aspects of nature. As we have seen, Goethe was a founder of such a new science. But we have also seen how Goethe has often been misunderstood, so that the real nature of his contribution has not been recognized. We can read in many places that Goethe was looking for an underlying unity behind the diversity of nature. No doubt when Goethe is approached only by means of the intellectual mind it does seem that he is looking for unity underlying diversity. But to understand Goethe we have to enter into his way of seeing, so that we go beyond the intellectual mind into the realm of experience. This means that we experience the way of seeing from within, instead of trying to approach it from the outside— which is the way of the abstract intellect. We become participants in the way of seeing instead of being onlookers. Goethe's science of the wholeness of nature can *only* be understood by participation in the way of seeing because this science can only be understood in its own terms. It cannot be understood by comparing it with something else. So, for example, we have had Goethe the Baconian empiricist, Goethe the Neo-Platonist, even Goethe the German idealist. But Goethe is none of these—and certainly not a mixture of them. As in the story of the elephant and the blind individuals, Goethe cannot be understood by this superficial habit of making comparisons.[318] Indulging the associative habit of the mind can only stop us from entering into the *perception*, so that we cannot experience the way of seeing and come to know it by means of itself.

The distinguishing characteristic of modern science is that it is analytical. The movement of thinking is one which separates into mutually external elements—the unit is the ideal expression, or embodiment, of this way of thinking. The countermovement to this, then, is to connect and combine externally to produce a synthesis. We see this clearly in the incorporation of the philosophy of atomism into science, and the way that this developed in physics, chemistry, and biology to become the dominant approach. Because modern science embodies the analytical way of seeing, it functions at the cultural level as a "carrier wave" for this way of seeing (as a radio wave carries an audio signal). The specific content is not important; what matters is the way of seeing which is carried by it. For example, atomism takes the form of separately existent elements which are external to each other, and it is this which gets communicated by sciences which embody atomism, regardless of what the specific content may be. In fact, there is a reversal of container and content here which we have encountered before. What we think of as the content is really only the container for the higher-level content which is the way of seeing. The message that we get is that everything is made up of parts which are independent and outside of each other, and which therefore can be connected by external relationships. But we are not aware of this because our attention is focused on whatever happens to be the specific content, and not upon the way of seeing which it embodies. Thus the analytical way of seeing is transmitted through the agency of modern science, especially through the emphasis on quantity, far beyond the domain in which it first arose and for which it is appropriate. The wider, cultural function of modern science is in the way that it has been instrumental in the cultivation of an analytical mode of consciousness.

Now it is usually supposed that this is the only kind of science which is possible, and hence that any alternative to the analytical perspective can only come from outside science. But another possibility is that there could be a transformation of science itself, which would be the development of a different kind of science which is not analytical. We have seen how Goethe showed the way toward such a science, and that this is not an alternative, in the sense of seeking to replace analytical science, but a way of being complementary to it. The point is that analytical science is really a one-sided development, and it is this one-sidedness which needs to be removed. So the aim is not to replace one science with another, but to overcome a one-sided development that is historically founded and not intrinsic to nature in the way that it is imagined to be. This new kind of science, which is holistic instead of analytical, is the science of the wholeness of nature. Such a science clearly could perform the same cultural function as analytical science, which would mean in this case being instrumental in the cultivation of a holistic mode of consciousness. No matter what the specific content may be, the higher-level content that this science carries will be the holistic way of seeing. Hence this way of seeing could be transmitted culturally by the science of the wholeness of nature, as the analytical way of seeing has been transmitted by the science of quantity. This could be the cultural significance of the way of science pioneered by Goethe.

Notes

Part I: *Authentic and Counterfeit Wholes*

1. T. Leith and H. Upatnieks, "Photography by Laser," *Scientific American* 212 (1965): 24–35. Note that the process of fragmentation described does not work with the kind of hologram that can be seen when illuminated with ordinary light, instead of with a laser. So if a holographic film gives an image with ordinary illumination, cutting it in half will only result in two different halves, as with an ordinary photographic film.

2. David Bohm, *Wholeness and the Implicate Order* (London: Routledge and Kegan Paul, 1980), 149.

3. C.W. Kilmister, *The Environment in Modern Physics* (London: English University Press, 1965), 36.

4. Jayant Narlikar, *The Structure of the Universe* (Oxford: Oxford University Press, 1977), 250.

5. Fritjof Capra, *The Tao of Physics* (London: Wildwood House, 1975), 313.

6. Richard E. Palmer, *Hermeneutics* (Evanston: Northwestern University Press, 1969), chap. 7.

7. P.H. Bortoft, "A Non-reductionist Perspective for the Quantum Theory," Department of Theoretical Physics, Birkbeck College, London University, 1982, chap. 5.

8. The difficulty with talking about part and whole is that a distinction is made which is extensive, and this leads to dualism. The difficulty disappears with the recognition that there can be an intensive distinction; see Bortoft, "Non-reductionist Perspective."

9. See the notion of unfolding (*explicatio*) and enfolding (*complicatio*) in the work of Nicholas of Cusa, discussed in Karl Jaspers, *The Great Philosophers*, vol. 2 (London: Rupert Hart-Davis, 1966), 129; see also, Bohm, *Wholeness and the Implicate Order*, chap. 7.

10. The terminology of "presence" and "presencing" is adopted from Heidegger as an attempt to escape dualism. See G.J. Seidel, *Martin Heidegger and the Pre-Socratics* (Lincoln: University of Nebraska Press, 1964), chap. 3.

11. Martin Heidegger, *Kant and the Problem of Metaphysics* (Bloomington: Indiana University Press, 1962), 206.

12. Arthur J. Deikman, "Bimodal Consciousness," in *The Nature of Human Consciousness,* ed. Robert E. Ornstein (San Francisco: W.H. Freeman, 1973).

13. Henri Bergson, *Creative Evolution* (London: Macmillan,1911), *ix*; see also, Milič Čapek, *Bergson and Modern Physics* (Dordrecht, the Netherlands: Reidel, 1971), 56, 69, 72–74.

14. Immanuel Kant, *Critique of Pure Reason*, trans. Norman Kemp Smith (London: Macmillan, 1964), 20.

15. E.A. Burtt, *The Metaphysical Foundations of Modem Science* (London: Routledge and Kegan Paul, 1980), 83.

16. Michael Roberts and E.R. Thomas, *Newton and the Origin of Colours* (London: Bell, 1934), 60, 110.

17. Idries Shah, *The Sufis* (New York: Doubleday, 1964), *xvi*.

18. Aron Gurwitsch, "Galilean Physics in the Light of Husserl's Phenomenology," in *Phenomenology and Sociology*, ed. Thomas Luckmann (Harmondsworth: Penguin Books, 1978); see also, Aron Gurwitsch, *Phenomenology and the Theory of Science* (Evanston: Northwestern University Press, 1974), chap. 2.

19. Ernst Lehrs, *Man or Matter,* 3d ed., revised and enlarged (London: Rudolf Steiner Press, 1985), 314.

20. H.B. Nisbet, *Goethe and the Scientific Tradition* (University of London: Institute of Germanic Studies, 1972), 39.

21. Lehrs, 317.

22. Nisbet, 36, n. 149.

23. Agnes Arber, *The Natural Philosophy of Plant Form* (Cambridge: Cambridge University Press, 1959) 209 (italics in the original).

24. Quoted in A.G.F. Gode von Aesch, *Natural Science in German Romanticism* (New York: Columbia University German Studies, 1941), 74.

25. Nisbet, 54; Albert Einstein and Leopold Infeld, *The Evolution of Physics* (Cambridge: Cambridge University Press, 1947), 33.

26. Lehrs, 94,109.

27. The difference between these two kinds of scientific thinking illustrates, and is illustrated by, the distinction which Heidegger makes

between "belonging *together*" and "*belonging* together" (Martin Heidegger, *Identity and Difference* [New York: Harper and Row, 1969], 29). In the first case, "belonging" is determined by "together," so that "to belong" means to have a place in the order of a "together"—i.e., in the unity of a framework. But in the case of "*belonging* together," "together" is determined by "belonging," so that there is "the possibility of no longer representing belonging in terms of the unity of the together, but rather of experiencing this together in terms of belonging" (ibid). Thus, we could say that Goethe experienced the *belonging* together of the yellow sun and the blue sky, and that he did not try to make them belong *together*. This experience of *belonging* together is reached by dwelling in the phenomenon instead of replacing it with conceptual representatives.

28. Lehrs, 123.

29. Ernst Cassirer, *The Problem of Knowledge* (New Haven: Yale University Press, 1974), 146.

30. Goethe followed the same approach in studying living things in nature. His insight into the growing plant, which he expressed as "all is leaf," is an instance of an encounter with the wholeness of the plant whereby he saw the whole coming into presence in the parts. Goethe did *not* mean by this that the various organs of the flower—sepals, petals, stamens—grew out of the stem leaves in a material sequence. His perception that all is leaf is an instance of the intuitive perception whereby the universal is seen in the particular, so that the particular appears as a living manifestation of the universal—and hence, in the moment of seeing, is symbolic of the universal. See Lehrs, chap. 5. Goethe's essay *The Metamorphosis of Plants* appears in Douglas Miller, ed., *Goethe: Scientific Studies* (New York: Suhrkamp, 1988).

31. R.G. Stansfield, "The New Theology? The Case of the Dripping Tap," paper presented to the British Association for the Advancement of Science, September 1975.

32. Gay Hendricks and James Fadiman, *Transpersonal Education* (Englewood Cliffs: Prentice-Hall, 1976).

33. Ibid.

34. See David Seamon, "Goethe's Approach to the Natural World: Implications for Environmental Theory and Education," in *Humanistic Geography: Prospects and Problems*, ed. D. Ley and M. Samuels (Chicago: Maaroufa, 1978), 238–250.

35. Wolfgang Schad, *Man and Mammals* (New York: Waldorf Press, 1977); see also, Mark Riegner, "Horns, Hooves, Spots and Stripes: Form and Pattern in Mammals," *Orion Nature Quarterly* 4, no. 4 (1985).

36. Martin Heidegger, *Being and Time* (New York: Harper and Row, 1962), 58.

37. Hans-Georg Gadamer, *Truth and Method*, 2d rev. ed. (London: Sheed and Ward, 1989), 474.

38. See Henri Bortoft, *Goethe's Scientific Consciousness* (Tunbridge Wells: Institute for Cultural Research Monograph, 1986). This monograph is incorporated as part II of this edition.

Part II: *Goethe's Scientific Consciousness*

1. Rudolf Magnus, *Goethe as a Scientist* (New York: Collier Books, 1961), 22.

2. English-speaking historians often refer to this as the Whig interpretation of history, using a particular instance to designate a general historical outlook. See Hugh Kearney, *Science and Change 1500–1700* (London: Weidenfeld and Nicholson, 1971), 17–22.

3. Rudolf Steiner, *Goethe the Scientist* (New York: Anthroposophic Press, 1950), 15, 31

4. Ted Bastin, ed. *Quantum Theory and Beyond* (Cambridge: Cambridge University Press, 1971), 321–34.

5. Steiner, 1.

6. Norwood Russell Hanson, *Patterns of Discovery* (Cambridge: Cambridge University Press, 1958), 13.

7. Ernst Lehrs, *Man or Matter* (3d ed., rev. and enlarged, London: Rudolf Steiner Press, 1985), 131.

8. Isaac Newton, "The Origin of Colours," in Michael Roberts and E.R. Thomas, *Newton and the Origin of Colours* (London: Bell, 1934), 71–91.

9. Isaac Newton, *Opticks* (New York: Dover, 1952), 124.

10. For example, a science report in *The Times* (London, December 4, 1984,16), begins: "In much the way that beams of ordinary light comprise a mixture of colors of the rainbow, . . . "

11. A much more detailed treatment is given in Lehrs.

12. The spectrum described by Newton, and repeated in physics books, contains seven colors: red, orange, yellow, green, blue, indigo, and violet. But most observers find they can only distinguish six colors—indigo is missing. Newton's choice of seven colors has been traced to his interest in musical theory and the

Pythagorean division of the octave into seven intervals. See I. Bernard Cohen, *The Newtonian Revolution* (Cambridge: Cambridge University Press, 1980), 205.

13. Idries Shah, *A Perfumed Scorpion* (London: Octagon Press, 1978), 25.

14. Norwood Russell Hanson, *Perception and Discovery* (San Francisco: W. H. Freeman, 1969), 61.

15. Designed by Jackie Bortoft.

16. See note 6.

17. Ludwig Wittgenstein, *Philosophical Investigations* (Oxford: Blackwell, 1968), 169.

18. The view that the proper objects of perception are meanings has been presented with considerable clarity and cogency by the philosopher of science Harold. I. Brown, in *Perception, Theory and Commitment* (Chicago: University of Chicago Press, 1977), chap. 6.

19. Merleau-Ponty, for example, considers the case of someone whose perception is abnormal, because of an injury, as a means of understanding normal perception. This is discussed in detail in M. Merleau-Ponty, *Phenomenology of Perception* (London: Routledge and Kegan Paul, 1962). Because the proper objects of perception are meanings, Merleau-Ponty is led to say: "Because we are in the world, we are condemned to meaning" (*xix*), which expresses dramatically in the language of existentialism what has now been said more soberly in the philosophy of science. Other cases are provided by the experience of persons who, having been blind from birth because of cataracts, eventually receive their sight as a result of an operation. Their experiences are described in M. von Senden, *Space and Sight* (London: 1960). A particularly clear discussion of the state of purely sensory experience is given by Rudolf Steiner in *A Theory of Knowledge Based on Goethe's World Conception* (New York: Anthroposophic Press, 1968), chap. 5.

20. A fairly straightforward account of Husserl's phenomenology is given in David Stuart and Algis Mickunas, *Exploring Phenomenology* (Chicago: American Library Association, 1974), chaps. 1 and 2. See also the introductory essay by Peter Koestenbaum in Edmund Husserl, *The Paris Lectures* (The Hague: Martinus Nijhoff, 1975).

21. The notion of intentionality was introduced by Husserl's teacher, Franz Brentano, who incorporated it into modern philosophy from the pre-Cartesian philosophy of the Middle Ages.

22. Galileo described his observations in *Siderius Nuncius* (Chicago: University of Chicago Press, 1989). See also the discussion in Cohen, section 4.7.

23. The priority of meaning in scientific discovery is shown clearly by
     Bernard Cohen's discovery that the celebrated Newtonian synthesis
     was not a synthesis of elements which already existed beforehand.
     They did not fly together like fragments in a reversed explosion, in
     the way that Koestler maintained in *The Sleepwalkers* (Har-
     mondsworth: Penguin Books, 1964, 517), because the elements were
     transformed in their meaning in the so-called synthesis. Newton's
     discovery is a whole way of seeing, and as such it influenced all the
     elements which it incorporated. An original perception of meaning
     transforms the meaning of the individual elements which it uses, so
     that they reflect the new meaning. Cohen has researched this trans-
     formation of ideas in detail in *The Newtonian Revolution*.

     Recognition of the priority of meaning in scientific discovery was
     made earlier by Paul Feyerabend in his essay "Explanation, Reduc-
     tion and Empiricism," which is now republished in Paul K. Feyer-
     abend, *Realism, Rationalism and Scientific Method* (Cambridge:
     Cambridge University Press, 1981). He realized that meaning is not
     an invariant in scientific knowledge and that there are no "estab-
     lished facts" because a fact can be altered by a change of meaning.
     The facts of science are inherently mutable. This is not because there
     are more yet to be discovered, but because the facts which have been
     discovered already can change in themselves. This is illustrated
     beautifully by Galileo's discovery that a body is indifferent to its
     state of motion. He did not discover this empirically, as if it were a
     fact which hitherto had been overlooked. The discovery was a
     change of the meaning in the facts of motion, which transformed
     these facts themselves so that they became coherent with a Coperni-
     can universe instead of with an Aristotelian one. To take a cinemato-
     graphical analogy, we can change what is on the screen by changing
     the film in the projector, but somebody who was unfamiliar with the
     cinema—an "empiricist"—might think that the change had hap-
     pened on the screen. Galileo's cognitive procedure is also discussed
     by Paul Feyerabend in *Against Method* (London: Verso, 1978) in a
     way which illustrates the priority of meaning in scientific knowl-
     edge—although Feyerabend uses this valuable study to support his
     own colorful interpretation of science in terms of an anarchistic
     epistemology.

     Thomas Kuhn's seminal essay *The Structure of Scientific Revolutions*
     (Chicago: University of Chicago Press, 2d ed., 1970) can also be seen
     retrospectively as disclosing the priority of meaning in science. See,
     for example, his discussion in chap. 6 of the difference between
     Priestley and Lavoisier over the discovery of oxygen. Here again is a
     study which shows that there are no "established facts" in the way
     the empiricist imagines and that what the facts are depends on the
     perception of meaning.

In view of these developments in the contemporary philosophy of science, it now seems somewhat strange that the priority of meaning in scientific discovery was not recognized explicity for so long. It seems as if the meaning of "meaning" was not recognized. This could simply be because philosophers of science have traditionally worked in a different philosophical paradigm from one in which "meaning" was recognized as a primary element of experience.

24. Phenomenalism is described in R. Harré, *The Philosophies of Science* (Oxford: Oxford University Press, 1972). Positivism, in all its various forms, is discussed in Leszek Kolakowski, *Positivist Philosophy* (Harmondsworth: Penguin Books, 1972).

25. The impact of positivism on science education is clearly reflected in the textbooks. A typical example is provided by a well-known textbook in physics: Gerald Holton and Duane H.D. Roller, *Foundations of Modern Physical Science* (Reading, Mass.: Addison-Wesley, 1958), especially chap. 13.

26. Martin Heidegger, *Identity and Difference* (New York: Harper and Row, 1969), 29.

27. Robert E. Ornstein, *The Psychology of Consciousness* (New York: Harcourt Brace Jovanovich, 1977).

28. Henri Bergson, *Creative Evolution* (London: Macmillan, 1911), 169.

29. For example in Benjamin Lee Whorf, *Language, Thought, and Reality* (Cambridge, Mass.: MIT Press, 1964). Also in David Bohm, *Wholeness and the Implicate Order* (London: Routledge and Kegan Paul, 1980), chap. 2.

30. It is because of this transparency of language that we think the function of language is representational—to represent what is already present—whereas the primary function of language is to disclose. Language, in this fundamental sense, *is* the event of the appearance of what becomes present—"appearance" is used here in the verbal sense of "coming forth into view." This disclosive function of language is encapsulated in the well-known question: "How do I know what I think until I see what I say?" The commonsense view of language misses this, and imagines instead that language is simply a tool which is applied to what we already know (i.e., in advance of language) for the purpose of communication. The difference between the representational and the disclosive functions of language is fundamental to the modern philosophy of language, especially as it has been developed by Hans-Georg Gadamer out of the work of Martin Heidegger. A lucid general introduction is given in Richard E. Palmer, *Hermeneutics* (Evanston: Northwestern University Press, 1969). The way in which language itself disappears in its living operation is discussed in Hans-Georg Gadamer, *Philosophical*

Hermeneutics (Berkeley: University of California Press, 1976), 64 ff. It should be noted that Whorf's account, referred to in note 29, is in one way too analytical itself. He refers, for example, to dissecting nature, cutting it up, and organizing it along lines laid down by our native language (213). This presupposes that the primary function of language is instrumental, i.e., that language is imposed externally on a preexisting world. Although this is an advance on the naïveté of common sense, which reduces language to a triviality, it nevertheless leads to a form of subjectivism which is ultimately a cul-de-sac. It is this cul-de-sac which the modern philosophy of language aims to avoid.

31. See Bohm, in note 29. See also, David Bohm, *Quantum Theory* (Englewood Cliffs, N.J.: Prentice-Hall, 1951), chap. 8. The problem of wholeness in quantum physics is also considered in connection with the structure of language in P.H. Bortoft, "A Non-reductionist Perspective for the Quantum Theory," Birkbeck College, London University, 1982.

32. Robert E. Ornstein, *The Mind Field* (London: Octagon Press, 1983), chaps. 2 and 3.

33. The discovery was made early on in Greek philosophy that motion and change appear as something paradoxical when the attempt is made to understand the world through the rational mind. Although they were not originally intended for the purpose, Zeno's famous paradoxes of motion can be taken as indicating the kind of self-contradiction we get into if we try to grasp motion by rational thought, i.e., with the analytical approach of the intellectual mind. In the paradox of the flying arrow, for example, it seems that the arrow must be stationary at any instant of its flight, because at any instant it must be at a definite location, and hence the moving arrow cannot be moving because it is everywhere instantaneously at rest. Thus the attempt to analyze motion has the effect of stopping motion and reconstituting it in the mind as a succession of states of rest. The inherent absurdity of this procedure, whereby motion is produced out of rest, as if it were some kind of optical illusion, has been discussed very fully in more recent philosophy by Henri Bergson in *Creative Evolution* and other works. He recognized that this reflected an intrinsic limitation of the rational mind itself, and he considered the possibility of a transformation of the mind into an intuitive mode whereby the reality of change itself can be experienced directly. What this amounts to is a transformation in the mode of consciousness, It will be mentioned subsequently that, whereas the analytical mode is the mode of consciousness for the intellectual mind, the mode of consciousness corresponding to the intuitive mind is the holistic mode.

The peculiar difficulty which motion and change present to the understanding was considered very thoroughly in antiquity by Aristotle. The foundation of his physics was the reality of change as a *mode of being*. Etienne Gilson said that "no one has ever better discerned the mystery that the very familiarity of movement hides from our eyes" (*The Spirit of Mediaeval Philosophy* [London: Sheed and Ward, 1950], 66). But Aristotle's philosophy of change often seems to be enigmatic. His statement that "change is the actuality of the potential *qua* such" (*Physics*, book III) seems particularly obscure. It is usually possible to perform an intellectual sleight of hand on Aristotle's philosophy of change and present it as being either platitudinous or just good common sense. But these intellectual reductions miss the point. For example, the statement above is not a definition of change, as is often supposed, but the expression of an insight into the reality of change as a way of being. The intellectual mind itself cannot grasp this because of the analytical mode of consciousness. It may be the case that Aristotle's philosophy of change can only be appreciated adequately in the holistic mode of consciousness, when it will be seen that, far from being just good common sense, Aristotle is trying to indicate something extraordinary. In other words, the so-called obscurity in Aristotle's philosophy of change may be a consequence of the mode of consciousness in which we try to understand it, in which case the difficulty could be removed by extending our experience instead of relying on verbal arguments.

It is also worth noticing that the perception of motion and change in the holistic mode of consciousness leads to a new understanding of causality. In the state of dynamic simultaneity, cause and effect are simultaneous. But in the analytical mode of consciousness, cause and effect are considered sequentially in a linear way: the cause precedes its effect, as the effect follows the cause. This will be discussed further in "The Necessary Connection," where David Hume's investigation of causality in terms of juxtaposition and succession will be examined in the light of the difference between analytical and holistic modes of consciousness. For the moment we will simply note that what Goethe said about causality fits in very well with dynamic simultaneity and the holistic mode of consciousness: "Who strives after cause and effect makes a great mistake. They are together the indivisible phenomenon."

34. Arthur J. Deikman, "Bimodal Consciousness" and "Deautomatization and the Mystic Experience" in *The Nature of Human Consciousness*, ed. Robert E. Ornstein (San Francisco: W. H. Freeman, 1973).

35. Ibid., 76.

36. Ornstein, *The Mind Field*, 52 ff.

37. Ornstein, *The Psychology of Consciousness*, 184.

38. Ornstein, *The Mind Field*, 24.

39. Ibid., 26.

40. It is interesting in this connection that Goethe described himself as a *Naturschauer* (nature looker) instead of the more usual *Naturforscher* (nature investigator).

41. Niels Bohr, *Atomic Theory and the Description of Nature* (Cambridge: Cambridge University Press, 1961).

42. Albert Einstein and Leopold Infield, *The Evolution of Physics* (Cambridge: Cambridge University Press, 1947), 33.

43. Hanson, *Patterns of Discovery*, chap. 1.

44. See R.G. Collingwood, *The Idea of Nature* (Oxford: Oxford University Press, 1960), 126.

45. This will be discussed further in "The Scientist's Knowledge."

46. Martin Heidegger, *Being and Time* (New York: Harper and Row, 1962), 51, 58.

47. Hans-Georg Gadamer, *Truth and Method*, 2d rev. ed. (London: Sheed and Ward, 1989), 474.

48. A.G.F. Gode von Aesch, *Natural Science in German Romanticism* (New York: Columbia University German Studies, 1941), 74.

49. Rudolf Steiner, *The Philosophy of Freedom* (London: Rudolf Steiner Press, 1964), especially chap. 7. Philosophically, this leads to a nonreductionist monism in which many of the traditional problems associated with the philosophy of knowledge simply do not arise. It is interesting that modern physics has made a significant step towards this viewpoint, but it has not yet gone as far as Steiner. Thus, in the quantum theory, Niels Bohr proposed the new fundamental principle that the physical system being investigated by an experiment could not be separated from the apparatus being used to investigate it. He proposed that, because of the indivisibility of the quantum, the system and the apparatus constitute an indivisible whole and must be considered as such. David Bohm suggested that this should be extended to include the theory as well, since the apparatus in question is a concrete expression of the theory. We shall see in "The Necessary Connection" and "The Scientist's Knowledge" how Bohr's principle needs to be extended further still to include the state of consciousness of the knowing observer, so that it now becomes the wholeness of the content of cognition and the condition of consciousness for that cognition. Each of these steps represents a movement away from the subject–object dualism, which selects only a portion of the whole for attention and imagines

that the other portion is merely a spectator. This movement towards a more comprehensive viewpoint was taken further still by Steiner. He considered that the human being is part of the total situation by virtue of his or her organization as a human being. Far from being merely a spectator who looks on, the human being is now understood to be an integral factor within the process of cognition, which is seen to be a nonsubjective expression of the process of actualization of the universe at a higher stage than the material level. This will be discussed briefly in connection with Goethe in "The Scientist's Knowledge."

50. Edwin A. Abbott, *Flatland* (New York: Dover, 1952).

51. J.W. von Goethe, "The Metamorphosis of Plants," in *Goethe: Scientific Studies,* ed. Douglas Miller (New York: Suhrkamp, 1988).

52. Ibid.

53. Ernst Cassirer, *The Problem of Knowledge* (New Haven: Yale University Press, 1974), 145.

54. Magnus, *Goethe as a Scientist*, 45.

55. Henri Bortoft, "Counterfeit and Authentic Wholes" in *Dwelling, Place and Environment: Essays Toward a Phenomenology of Person and World,* eds., David Seamon and Robert Mugerauer, (The Hague: Martinus Nijhoff, 1986). (This essay, retitled "Authentic and Counterfeit Wholes," constitutes part I of this edition.)

56. The diagram is taken from Gerbert Grohmann, *The Plant,* vol. 1 (Kimberton, Pa.: Bio-Dynamic Literature, 1989), 43.

57. For an account of how metamorphosis can be described in terms of Bohm's distinction between implicate and explicate orders, see P. H. Bortoft (note 31).

58. The role of imagination in this context is referred to in Seyyed Hossein Nasr, *Science and Civilization in Islam* (Cambridge,Mass.: Harvard University Press, 1968), 257. See also Lehrs for a discussion of the faculty of imagination as an organ or perception. See also Elémire Zolla, *The Uses of Imagination and the Decline of the West* (Ipswich: Golgonooza Press, 1978), 29. Goethe described his experience of dynamic imagination in the case of the unfolding flowers in his review of Purkinje's *Sight from a Subjective Standpoint* (1824); see Douglas Miller, ed., *Goethe: Scientific Studies* (New York: Suhrkamp, 1988), *xix*.

We can also understand this dynamic vision in terms of the hologram metaphor. It is possible to form several different images on one and the same hologram without them becoming confused—as would happen with a photograph if it had been multiply exposed. If each exposure is taken at a slightly different angle, then if the head is moved slightly, when the hologram is looked at, a series of images unfold, one after the other, in such a way that it seems as if each one turns into the next one. The similarity with Goethe's imaginal experience as described here is very striking. But, of course, we must not overlook the equally important difference that, in the case of the hologram, we can see only as many images unfold as were stored initially. Stanislav Grof has used the hologram as a metaphor or model for some aspects of visionary experiences. Although he does not mention Goethe in this connection, referring to the multiple images which can be stored on one and the same hologram, and then retrieved sequentially, he says, "This illustrates another aspect of visionary experiences, namely, that countless images tend to unfold in a rapid sequence from the same area of the experiential field, appearing and disappearing, as if by magic." See Stanislav Grof, *Beyond the Brain* (Albany, New York: State University of New York Press, 1985), 79.

Understanding Goethe's organic vision "holographically" helps us to recognize a fundamental feature of the organic which will be discussed in some detail below and again in part III. Each different image in the hologram is the whole hologram, and not part of it in the extensive sense. The dimension of wholeness can contain many within it in such a way that each one *is* the whole, but differently. This is an intensive dimension. It is the same with Goethe's vision of unfolding plants. Each plant which he saw in his imagination should be understood as being *the very same plant,* but differently, and not "another plant" in the familiar extensive sense. Holographically, difference is included *within* unity, without the unity thereby being broken—this will be referred to below as "multiplicity in unity" and the "the intensive dimension of One." This extraordinary feature of wholeness, that it allows something to be different from itself (self-difference instead of self-sameness), is a necessary condition for something to be "living." It opens the door to an extraordinarily rich vision which transforms our understanding of "the one and the many" in a fundamental way.

59. Agnes Arber, *The Natural Philosophy of Plant Form* (Cambridge: Cambridge University Press, 1959), 209. Arber is quoting Wilhelm Troll, Professor of Botany at the University of Mainz, who developed a new plant typology working from Goethean foundations earlier this century. A picture of Turpin's ideal plant is given in Jochen Bockemühl, *In Partnership with Nature* (Wyoming: Bio-Dynamic Literature, 1981), 4.

60. The dictionary gives the meaning of "intensive" in terms of intensity, but the meaning in mathematics (which comes from medieval philosophy) is not the same as this. It can be illustrated most easily

by way of examples. In logic, for example, "the king is dead" and *"le roi est mort"* are two different statements but a single proposition. The proposition is the intension of the statements, and the statements are the extensions of the proposition. The mathematical notion of a set is closely related to this. For example, a set of tables is defined by the concept "table." The extension of the set is the tables, and the intension is the meaning "table." It has been recognized in modern philosophy and mathematics, as it was in medieval philosophy, that the intension cannot be reduced to the extension. See Ernst Cassirer, *Substance and Function* (New York: Dover, 1953), chap. 1.

61. The difference between "unity in multiplicity" and "multiplicity in unity" can be approached in a more mathematical manner. Clearly, One is not a number in the quantitative sense because it includes many, whereas one is such a number and therefore it must exclude many. The arithmetic of quantity is the arithmetic of one. It is the calculus of the extensive dimension of unity in multiplicity. Is there an arithmetic of One, which would therefore be the calculus of the intensive dimension of multiplicity in unity? At first sight it seems that this question is based on a contradiction. We identify arithmetic with the quantitative calculus of numbers. This is what we mean by arithmetic. So it would appear that it is impossible to have a nonnumerical arithmetic. Nevertheless, such an arithmetic was discovered by Spencer Brown in the 1960s, in the context of an investigation into the design of switching circuits in electronic engineering. It has been described in his book *Laws of Form* (London: Allen and Unwin, 1969), where he provides an interpretation of the basic operation in this arithmetic in terms of the act of making a distinction. Thus, the nonnumerical arithmetic which Spencer Brown discovered is seen by him as the calculus of distinction, analogously to the way that ordinary arithmetic is the calculus of number. It calculates with the form of distinction instead of with the form of quantity. Since the act of distinguishing is prior to counting, the calculus of distinction is a prenumerical arithmetic.

The kind of distinction which Spencer Brown considers is the extensive distinction whereby one region is distinguished from another, one object from another, and so on. It has been shown by the writer that Spencer Brown's nonnumerical arithmetic can also be interpreted as the calculus of the intensive distinction of multiplicity in unity. See P.H. Bortoft, chap. 5. Thus it becomes the nonnumerical arithmetic of the intensive dimension of One. It is therefore the arithmetic of wholeness. It can also be seen as the arithmetic of the quality of One instead of the quantity of one.

There are two primitive "equations" of this arithmetic:

The right-hand side of the second equation is blank intentionally—zero is counted as a number in mathematics, and therefore cannot appear as an element in a nonnumerical arithmetic. When it is interpreted in terms of the intensive form of distinction, the first equation is the arithmetic of the whole which can be divided and yet remain whole. Thus, for example, when a hologram is divided there are two pieces of film numerically, but One hologram nonnumerically. So the arithmetic of hologram division is:

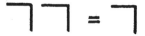

This is also the arithmetic of plant division when plants are propagated by vegetative reproduction. For example, if a fuchsia plant is divided into many pieces, they will all grow until they flower, unless they are impaired by other circumstances. But each of these new plants are "parts" of the first plant. They are really one plant which has been divided and divided, and yet which remains whole even when the "parts" have become independent. The plant is One and many at the same time—like the fragments of a hologram. We do not recognize the One plant in this case because it is in the form of many. The analytical mode of consciousness is tuned towards seeing many ones, and not to seeing One in the form of many. It requires a transformation of consciousness to the holistic mode to be able to see the One that is the many—we could say that it is "hidden" in the many, hidden by our customary mode of consciousness. Similarly, this equation is also the arithmetic of the growth of the individual plant—vegetative reproduction is only a special case of growth, i.e., growth accompanied by separation. This enables us to see the growing plant organically as a hologram in time, with the whole emerging within the whole instead of unit adding to unit as if the plant were like a pile of bricks or the accretion of a crystal. By actively looking at plants, plunging into the plant visually, followed by exact sensorial imagination, it is possible to learn to see the plant world in this way. This develops an organ of perception which is tuned towards the organic, and does not represent it conceptually in terms of the logic of solid bodies. Goethe said that "every process in nature, rightly observed, wakens in us a new organ of perception."

The second equation is the arithmetic of the relationship between the whole and the part. This relation can be expressed approximately by saying that the whole is "within" the part. This can be seen in the hologram, as well as in the relation between the archetypal organ and the organs of the plant, and between the archetypal plant and the different members of the plant kingdom. But the whole cannot be within the part extensively, because then either there would only be a single part or else the whole would be divided into pieces. This also means that the relationship between whole and parts cannot be numerical. The whole is within the part intensively. There is an intensive distinction between the whole and the part, but without any extensive difference between them. The nonnumerical arithmetic of this distinction is:

where the blank space represents the fact that there is no difference between the whole and the part in the intensive dimension of One. This relationship between the whole and the part is inside-out to how it appears in the extensive perspective—where we would say that the part is within the whole. The phenomenon of vegetative reproduction from cuttings can also be seen in the light of this intensive relationship between whole and part. Goethe recognized that this shows not only that the plant can be divided and yet remain whole but also that the whole plant is potentially present in each part of its organism. He was particularly impressed when he saw a proliferated rose, i.e., a rose from the center of which an entirely new plant had grown in place of the seed pod and organs of fertilization. He recognized in this phenomenon a vivid expression of the way that in the organic world the whole is within the part.

These two equations of the nonnumerical arithmetic of wholeness are really two different aspects of the same thing, and they can therefore be combined. Thus, the nonnumerical arithmetic of the process of dividing a hologram, or growing a plant from a cutting of itself, is given by combining:

This is the arithmetic of the process in the intensive dimension of One, instead of in the extensive dimension of many ones. In this prenumerical dimension the whole is within each part because the whole can be divided and yet remain whole.

It helps if these equations are themselves looked at in an intensive perspective, as if there is only one ⌐ in each equation because each ⌐ is the very same ⌐. This is a suggestive notation which can function as a symbolism, i.e., as a mirror in which the idea can be seen—although the "idea" here is not an image but a way of seeing. Although Spencer Brown gives a name to the sign ⌐, there is no need to do so, and it can be approached in a purely visual way. Such an approach in itself helps to stimulate the transition to a holistic mode of consciousness. It is interesting that sometimes people become uneasy and annoyed if asked to do this. They demand to be told what it is called, so that they can read it verbally, and they show signs of relief if they are told. Since the analytical mode of consciousness is associated strongly with verbal behavior, this could be an indication that the analytical mode is being inhibited by this simple device.

62. Plato called a Form "one over many" and maintained that such a Form was more real than the many particulars in which it is reflected. It has often been supposed that Plato made the mistake of hypostatizing a mental abstraction and then separating it from the things from which it had been abstracted. For example, according to this view, the Form which is Beauty is the result of abstracting what is common to many particular instances of beauty, and then imagining that Beauty itself is somehow supposed to exist apart from these instances. In other words, it seems as if Plato had made the mistake of duplicating the world unnecessarily—the resulting dualism is often called the two-world theory. However, careful reading of Plato soon makes it clear that this confusion exists in the minds of those who attribute it to Plato, and not in that of Plato himself. Nevertheless, there does remain the problem of how the Forms are to be understood. In various places Plato brings out many of the difficulties himself. It may be that in so doing his aim was to show that the Forms cannot be understood by means of a way of thinking that is ultimately based on our experience in the world of bodies, i.e., on the logic of solid bodies. In other words, there is an ironic intention in Plato's "self-criticism." The major difficulty is with understanding how something can be simultaneously one and many. It is this difficulty which arises through imagining the Form in an extensive perspective, and which disappears in the perspective of multiplicity in unity which is the intensive dimension of One. Similarly, it is the extensive perspective which is the source of the two-world theory which separates the Form from the particulars, and appears simply

to duplicate the familiar world. It seems evident that Plato cannot be understood by verbal reasoning alone, because of the analytical mode of consiousness that is associated with the discursive intellectual mind.

63. See Owen Barfield, *Saving the Appearances* (New York: Harcourt, Brace and World, 1965), for an investigation into the attitude of empiricism as a form of idolatory .

64. Lehrs, l25. Also H.B. Nisbet, *Goethe and the Scientific Tradition* (University of London: Institute of Germanic Studies, 1972), 39.

65. In an essay written towards the end of his life, Goethe said that he had achieved in practice the power of intuitive reason which Kant had declared to be beyond the scope of the human mind. Kant believed that, although intuitive knowledge was possible in principle, it was not possible in practice for human beings, who were restricted to the power of discursive intellectual reason. See Lehrs, 73–76.

66. Erich Heller, *The Disinherited Mind* (Harmondsworth: Penguin Books, 1961), 12.

67. Arber, 209.

68. See note 40.

69. Rudolf Steiner, *Riddles of Philosophy* (New York: Anthroposophic Press, 1973), 183.

70. See "Knowing the World"; also Harold I. Brown, chap. 6.

71. Wolfgang Schad, *Man and Mammals: Toward a Biology of Form* (New York: Waldorf Press, 1977).

72. Schad's book abounds with such diagrams, which help to make it readable without getting lost in all the details that have to be taken into account.

73. Ibid., chap. 11.

74. Ibid., 30.

75. Gadamer, *Truth and Method*, 474. The recognition that the objects of cognitive perception are meanings and not sense data shows us that "the world" is not an object, or set of objects, but a text. Cognitive perception is not simply sense perception, in which material objects are encountered through "the windows of the senses." It is literally, and not metaphorically, reading the text of the world. Brown (88) compares the perception of meaning in observation with the more familiar case of the perception of meaning in reading a text. In the cognitive perception of, say, the objects in a room, the aspect of the objects which we encounter through the senses is equivalent to the material script of a text without the meaning. For sense perception alone, the

material objects would be just like the meaningless squiggles of a script which we had not learned to read. Cognitive perception is the equivalent of reading the text directly, in which there is the immediate perception of meaning without focusing on the script itself.

The reader can use his or her own experience of reading to explore this. It is also a useful exercise to read a text in English and then to look immediately at a text written in a script with which one is unfamiliar—say Arabic or Chinese. This makes the point quite clearly. The nonfamiliar script is an approximation to what our experience of the world would be like without the perception of meaning—what we recognize as the various objects in the world would be just like the elements of this script. The error of empiricism is now particularly clear: what it takes to be material objects are really a text, and what it believes to be sense perception is really an experience of reading.

This discovery that the world we perceive is not an object, but a text which we read, can be applied to scientific cognition in a way which makes the hermeneutic nature of Goethe's way of science particularly clear. Scientific cognition is one level up from everyday perception, in the sense that the individual meanings of objects at the everyday level now themselves become like a script which we cannot read at first. Thus, in the case of the mammals, we recognize individual mammal types, and thus perceive meaning on this level, but we do not at first perceive the overall organization of the different mammals. This organization, which is revealed through the discovery of relationships of form, is the perception of meaning at the level of scientific cognition. The relationships of form which Schad discovers are the meanings for which the observed mammals are the script. Before these relationships are perceived, we are in the position of a person who is in front of a script which is totally unfamiliar. The temptation is to sidestep the contemplation of the phenomena at this point, and instead rely on the verbal–intellectual mind. The result of doing so is that we read meanings into the phenomena by our own intellectual activity, instead of learning to read the phenomena directly. The phenomenologist of nature really is the *hermeneutic* phenomenologist, and Goethe's way of science is therefore quite properly described as the hermeneutics of nature. Goethe meant it literally when he said that nature is a text which he was learning to read.

76. This is precisely what happened to David Hume in his attempt to understand the relationship of causality. Hume's philosophy will be discussed further below.

77. Schad, 118.

78. Ibid., 11. If "life exists only as a continuing present," it clearly cannot be described in the framework of analytical time, i.e., the

sequential instantaneous snapshot idea of time which belongs to the analytical mode of consciousness. The kind of temporality which is characteristic of life itself, i.e., a continuing present, is hinted at in the perception of change and motion in the holistic mode of consciousness. Compare also Goethe's comment on causality (note 33) with the assertion here that "in life, causes and effects take place simultaneously and complement one another."

79. Ibid., 153.

80. Charles Darwin, *The Origin of Species* (Harmondsworth: Penguin Books, 1968). The sentence appears only in the first edition. Darwin dropped it in the subsequent editions.

81. David Hume, *A Treatise on Human Nature*, book 1 (Glasgow: Fontana/ Collins, 1962).

82. Ibid., 331.

83. Cf. the story of Mulla Nasrudin and the donkeys, which encapsulates the problem here succinctly, in Idries Shah, *The Sufis* (New York: Doubleday, 1964), 59.

84. Roger Bacon distinguished these two ways in the thirteenth century. Idries Shah points out that the way of experience became interpreted narrowly in the sense of experiment, and this "has prevented the scientific researcher from approaching knowledge by means of itself" (ibid; *xxvi*).

85. Aristotle is usually thought of as an arch-rationalist who proceeded by deductive reasoning from first principles. In fact, he was a master observer of nature. He was an experientialist but not an empiricist, because he did not limit experience to the senses. On the other hand, he was not an analytical rationalist who limited the mind to logical thought and denied it the possibility of experience through perceptive insight. His scientific work involved detailed sensory observation and insight into what is not visible to the senses as such by what he called intuitive induction. It has now been suggested that the ideal of deductive reasoning, with which Aristotle has been identified, may have been meant to apply to the way in which scientific knowledge should be presented and taught, and not to how such knowledge is discovered in the first place. See Barnes, Schofield and Sarabji, eds., *Articles on Aristotle, Vol. 1: Science* (London: Duckworth, 1975), 77. Because Goethe worked by observation and intuition, it may well be that his way of science can provide the kind of experience which is needed to understand this philosopher, who has usually been interpreted exclusively in terms of the analytical mode of consciousness, which is associated with the logical mind.

86. Saul Kripke, *Naming and Necessity* (Oxford: Blackwell, 1980). See also John Cottingham, *Rationalism* (London: Granada, 1984), 115–20, for a simplified account. Since the time of Leibniz, philosophers have distinguished between "truths of reason" and "truths of fact." The former are necessarily true because they do not depend on anything outside their own meaning. For example, it is impossible for the proposition "all triangles are three-sided" to be wrong, and we can know this with certainty without ever needing to refer to anything beyond our own minds. But this kind of proposition does not tell us anything about the world. The proposition "it is raining," on the other hand, does tell us something about the world. But such a proposition can be false, and therefore, if true, it is only contingently true and not true of necessity. This division became a dogma of modern empiricism. Kripke's suggestion, that there can be propositions which are about the world and yet necessarily true, needs to be seen against this background to be appreciated. This is not the only way in which the traditional division into truths of reason and truths of fact has been called into question. For reasons which are different from Kripke's, the contemporary philosophy of science also rejects this dogma. See Brown, chap. 7, especially 105.

87. See G. Webster and B.C. Goodwin, "The Origin of Species: A Structuralist Approach," *J. Social. Biol. Struct.* 5 (1982), 29.

88. Darwin, 90.

89. Webster and Goodwin, 16.

90. Cassirer, *The Problem of Knowledge*, 167.

91. Webster and Goodwin, 42. This theme is developed further in Brian Goodwin, *How the Leopard Changed Its Spots* (London: Weidenfeld and Nicolson, 1994). Goodwin recognizes the contribution which Goethe made toward what he calls "organocentric" biology, and draws attention to the way that Goethe's understanding of organisms as dynamic forms in transformation is in agreement with new approaches being taken in biology today (122–23).

92. Descartes, *"Discourse on Method" and the "Meditations"* (Harmondsworth: Penguin Books, 1968).

93. Ibid., 107, for example. In letters to various correspondents, Descartes showed just how widely he intended "thinking" and "thought" to be taken. Although at the beginning of the *Meditations* he is clearly concerned with the act of thinking, he soon includes many other functions under the heading of thought, which we would not usually describe in this way. Even a toothache becomes a thought for Descartes, from which it is evident that he eventually came to mean by "thought" nothing more than subjective experience.

94. See Antony Flew, *An Introduction to Western Philosophy* (London: Thames and Hudson, 1971), 300.

95. See Gadamer, *Philosophical Hermeneutics*, 119.

96. See Roger Scruton, *A Short History of Modern Philosophy* (London: Routledge and Kegan Paul, 1984), 132. Hume was not able to recognize the significance of his achievement at the time; consequently he was only able to experience it in its negative aspect.

97. Owen Barfield, *Romanticism Comes of Age* (London: Rudolf Steiner Press, 1966), 36.

98. According to Aquinas, the *species intelligibilis* is the mode of being of the perceived object in the observer, so that when this is created by the *intellectus agens* the object is, in a sense, within us and we are the object. See E.J. Dijksterhuis, *The Mechanization of the World Picture* (Oxford: Oxford University Press, 1969), 148; see also Barfield, *Saving the Appearances*, chap. 13.

99. Gadamer, *Truth and Method*, 416. The quotation as given here is from the second edition (1979). The edition which is referred to throughout this work is usually the second, revised edition (1989). The wording differs slightly in this edition (456).

100. Steiner, *Goethe the Scientist*, 179. Now we can reverse the direction of influence here and use Goethe's way of science to provide the experience which is needed to understand the philosophy of Schelling.

101. Historians of science now recognize that *Naturphilosophie* influenced the development of mainstream physics in a number of ways. For example, the idea of a single unifying force for all natural phenomena, which has influenced physics in a profound way, came from *Naturphilosophie* initially. The discovery of the conservation of energy in thermodynamics, and the discovery of electromagnetism, were both influenced directly by this philosophical guiding idea. See Thomas S. Kuhn, "Energy Conservation as an Example of Simultaneous Discovery," in *The Essential Tension* (Chicago: University of Chicago Press, 1977), 97–100. See also L. Pearce Williams, *The Origins of Field Theory* (New York: Random House, 1966). The influence of *Naturphilosophie* on the growth of biology (in the areas of embryology, evolution, and the cell theory) is described in Stephen F. Mason, *A History of Science* (New York: Collier Books, 1962). The role of such a priori guiding ideas in scientific discovery is discussed widely in the literature of the history and philosophy of science. See particularly Kurt Hübner, *Critique of Scientific Reason* (Chicago: University of Chicago Press, 1983).

102. *Nature* 1, no. 1 (Nov. 4, 1869): 10.

103. See Jeremy Naydler, "The Regeneration of Realism and the Recovery of a Science of Qualities," *International Philosophical Quarterly* 23 (1983): 155–72.

Part III: *Understanding Goethe's Way of Science*

1. In Goethe's day, this movement of understanding was part of the cultural concept of *Bildung*. This is the specifically human way of coming into one's own by finding oneself in what is experienced, at first, as other than oneself. In seeking to understand something which is alien to us, we become more fully ourselves in the process. See Hans-Georg Gadamer, *Truth and Method*, 2d rev. ed. (London: Sheed and Ward, 1989), pt 1, section 1.1.B.(i), for an account of the dynamics of *Bildung*, See also Joel C. Weinsheimer, *Gadamer's Hermeneutics* (New Haven: Yale University Press, 1985), 67–72.

2. Ernst Lehrs, *Man or Matter*, 3d ed., rev. and enlarged (London: Rudolf Steiner Press, 1985), 100.

3. Rudolf Steiner, *Goethe the Scientist* (New York: Anthroposophic Press, 1950), 48.

4. We could say that the whole world is multiperspectival, where each perspective is wholly the world, as each perspective of the duck/rabbit figure is wholly the figure, and not only part of it. Yet, just as any one perspective does not exhaust the figure, so no one mode of disclosure exhausts the world. This will be discussed in several places below in some detail.

5. Dennis L. Sepper, *Goethe Contra Newton* (Cambridge: Cambridge University Press, 1988), 94. Sepper has done a thorough investigation of Goethe's recognition of the role of *Vorstellungsarten* in the constitution of scientific knowledge, and the way that his understanding of this changed. Sepper says that "the evolution of Goethe's understanding of the *Vorstellungsarten* apparently has escaped notice" (96).

6. The emergence of historical consciousness in the philosophy of science can be dated conveniently from the publication of Thomas S. Kuhn's *The Structure of Scientific Revolutions,* 2d ed., enlarged, (Chicago: University of Chicago Press, 1970). A thoroughly historicist philosophy of science has been given in Kurt Hübner, *Critique of Scientific Reason* (Chicago: University of Chicago Press, 1983).

7. Kuhn realized that the discovery of the historicity of scientific knowledge would require our very conception of truth and reality to change. He remarks that the philosophical paradigm initiated by Descartes has been very fruitful in the development of modern science (especially mathematical physics, which it fits like a glove to a

hand because it was tailored to fit). However, "Today research in parts of philosophy, psychology, linguistics, and even art history, all converge to suggest that the traditional paradigm is somehow askew. That failure to fit is made increasingly apparent by the historical study of science. . . . " (Kuhn, 121). He goes on to say that "none of these crisis-promoting subjects has yet produced a viable alternative to the traditional epistemological paradigm. . . ." Nevertheless, Kuhn was also unable to extricate himself from this paradigm.

8.   For the notion of "effective history," *Wirkungsgeschichte*, see Gadamer, 300 ff; see also Weinsheimer, 181.

9.   Georg Kühlewind, *Stages of Consciousness* (Hudson, NY: Lindisfarne Press, 1984).

10   Designed by Jackie Bortoft.

11.   A saying of Jalaluddin Rumi discussed on p. 47 of this book. See Idries Shah, *A Perfumed Scorpion* (London: Octagon Press, 1978), 25.

12.   Although it is difficult to imagine this happening with the figure of the giraffe, there are other "hidden figures" which it is not always so easy to see.

13.   A similar point can be made about the organization of notes in a tune. The tune *is* the organization—it is not another note. See Norwood Russell Hanson, *Patterns of Discovery* (Cambridge: Cambridge University Press, 1958), chap. 1, for a thorough discussion of the role of organization in cognitive perception.

14.   Franz Brentano (1838–1917) had a major influence on the development of philosophy in this century. He returned to the Aristotelian sense of empirical as experiential, and revived the notion from medieval philosophy of "intentional inexistence," which he called "immanent objectivity." This notion became fundamental for Husserl, who studied with Brentano, and it appears in a modified form as the key idea of "intentionality" in phenomenology.

15.   The term "prior" here should not be read in the usual temporal sense of "before" and "after." It should be understood ontologically instead of just temporally in this way.

16.   Philosophers of very different persuasions, from Heidegger to Wittgenstein, have been concerned with understanding and pointing the way beyond the fallacy of intellectualism. This is a major theme of twentieth-century philosophy.

17.   There is a distortion in this account which arises from the power of attention to partition focus and periphery. When we attend to something, such as a chair, we focus on this in such a way that it appears as an independent and separate entity—a chair-by-itself. But this is

not actually what we see. What we describe as "seeing a chair" is really much more than that. We see something more like a chair-by-a-table-in-a-room-in-a-house . . . in-the-human life-world. There is a halo of meaning of decreasing intensity of presence as we go further away from the physical chair. But this halo, which is peripheral because of the specific act of attention, forms the context for whatever is the focus of attention. Ultimately, an object such as a chair is seen within a contextual totality (which Heidegger refers to as a referential totality). It is really only within this context that it has its meaning, and hence the meaning is not intrinsic but relational. There is no chair-by-itself in our experience, but we forget this whenever we think of the world as if it were a totality of separate objects.

18. One of the difficulties here, which encourages us to be mistaken, is the tendency to understand the cognitive perception of the world in the context of subject–object dualism, in which subject and object are conceived as separate entities, existing as such prior to, and independently of, cognitive perception. This is how it seems when we start at the end and back-project the final state into the beginning. It is inevitable that the idea of a direct, conceptless pure perception of what is "really there" should arise in this context. But if what we are concerned with is seeing the world, then it can be recognized that this is mistaken.

Consider the description "I see a tree." We read and understand this in an analytical manner. Thus, there is an I-entity and a tree-entity which first exist by themselves, separate from and independent of each other, which are then subsequently joined together (albeit in an external way) by the intermediate link "see." What is mistaken here is the assumption that there is such an I-entity *preceding* cognition. Such an "entity" is in fact the self-consciousness, or I-consciousness, which arises *as a result* of the process of cognitive perception. The derivative nature of the I-consciousness is discussed very thoroughly in Rudolf Steiner, *The Philosophy of Freedom*, trans. by Rita Stebbing (London: Rudolf Steiner Press, 1988). Once this is understood, then it becomes clear that the descriptive statement "I see a tree" should be read in a quite different, more holistic way. The act of seeing is primary, not secondary as the analytical reading supposes. The seeing-subject and the seen-object condense simultaneously and co-relatively out of this primary act. Hence it is "subject" and "object" which are secondary, and by virtue of their origin they are necessarily correlated within cognitive perception. They are therefore a polarity—like north and south poles of a magnet; there cannot be one without the other. We usually do not notice this, and think of subject and object as being separate and independent of each other. Thus we have dualism instead of polarity.

Husserl recognized clearly that the "how" of appearing is correlated with "what" appears, and he held that such a correlation is an invariant structure of experience (without which it would not be "experience"). In Husserl's phenomenology, this correlation (for which he uses the technical terms *noesis* and *noema* or noetic and noematic correlates) replaces the subject–object separation which has been the basis of epistemology since Descartes. This correlation is a *necessary* correlation for Husserl, and there is no equivalent to this necessity in Cartesian-based epistemology.

19. David Best, *Feeling and Reason in the Arts* (London: George Allen and Unwin, 1985), 23–24.

20. There are well-documented cases of breakdown, because of organic disorder, where this coalescence is no longer maintained. In such cases the condition of the purely sensory without an organizing idea is evident. A good example of this is provided by the experience of people suffering from congenital cataracts. Eventually this could be treated by operation, since the "blindness" resulted from physical occlusion and was not physiological in origin. The results of some of the earliest such operations to be performed are described in M. von Senden, *Space and Sight* (London: Methuen, 1960). The results were very startling to all those involved. It was assumed that, when the bandages were taken off, a person whose sight was restored would simply see the world which we all see. But, in the event, the patients could *see* nothing of the kind. What they experienced instead was something like the chaotic black and white blotches before the giraffe is seen, only *everything* was like this, as well as being brightly colored and mobile. The experience was far from the immediate liberation from blindness which had been hoped for. Many patients asked to have the bandages put back again! It was only after some time, and a lot of effort, that they were able to *see* the world which we take for granted. This is a very clear demonstration that seeing the world is not the purely sensory experience we usually imagine it to be. Merleau-Ponty refers to several cases of breakdown as a result of organic disorder, in connection with their relevance to understanding perception. See M. Merleau-Ponty, *The Phenomenology of Perception* (London: Routledge and Kegan Paul, 1962). However, the most accessible account of such cases is given in part 1 of Oliver Sacks, *The Man Who Mistook His Wife for a Hat* (London: Pan Books, 1986).

Yet further evidence that purely sensory experience is something very different from the experience of seeing the world is given by the experiences which people have sometimes with anesthetics. Aldous Huxley describes such an experience in *The Art of Seeing* (Seattle: Montana Books, 1975), 20.

A particularly clear discussion of the state of purely sensory experience is given in Rudolf Steiner, *A Theory of Knowledge Based on Goethe's World Conception* (New York: Anthroposophic Press, 1968), chap. 5. Kühlewind emphasizes the importance of *attempting* to remove all concepts artificially, as an exercise, if we want to understand our normal cognitive experience—see Georg Kühlewind, *The Logos-Structure of the World* (Hudson, N.Y.: Lindisfarne Press, 1991), 15.

21. It has been familiar for a long time from phenomenology that the objects of cognitive perception are meanings. This goes back to Husserl's *Logical Investigations*, which were published at the turn of the century. The view that the objects of cognitive perception are meanings has been presented in the context of the philosophy of science in Harold I. Brown, *Perception, Theory and Commitment* (Chicago: University of Chicago Press, 1977), chap. 6.

22. To revert to an earlier philosophical language, the sensory is raised to the universal, and the universal is particularized. Gadamer (90) refers to Aristotle in this connection:

> It is worthwhile to recall Aristotle here. He showed that all *aisthesis* tends towards a universal, even if every sense has its own specific field and thus what is immediately given in it is not universal. But the specific sensory perception of something as such is an abstraction. The fact is that we see sensory particulars in relation to something universal. For example, we recognize a white phenomenon as a human. (Aristotle, *De anima*, 425 a 25.)

23. Owen Barfield, *Saving the Appearances* (New York: Harcourt, Brace and World, 1965). It could also be called cognitive enchantment.

24. Philosophy is a movement of thinking which takes us nowhere except into where we are already but do not yet recognize. Such a movement of thinking could be described as an intensive movement, as distinct from an extensive movement, which would take us somewhere other than where we are already. An intensive movement of this kind is a movement in the dimension of mind itself. See also Gadamer's remarks on *Bildung* and coming into one's own referred to in note 1.

25. But this need not be the only way. It is also possible by means of exercises which concentrate thinking. See Georg Kühlewind, *Stages of Consciousness*, chap. 3, and the same author's *From Normal to Healthy* (Hudson, NY: Lindisfarne Press, 1989), 166–170.

26. There remains the question of what *is* the origin of concepts, if it is not experience? The answer is that it is language. That this is so is obscured by that inverted philosophy of language which is called nominalism. According to this philosophy, language is simply a

matter of labeling things. A word is a label, and when a child learns to speak it is simply learning which labels go with which things. Thus, according to nominalism, language is representational. It has, therefore, an entirely secondary function, as the means by which "something which is known" can be communicated from one person to another, who will thus know it in turn (this is the "pass the parcel" view of communication). This could also be described as the commonsense view of language inasmuch as it is the one which is very commonly held. Indeed, it seems obvious that it is true. Our everyday experience seems to confirm it so readily—as it does the fact that the Earth is at rest.

Language *does* have a representational function, but this is a secondary, derivative function and by no means primary. The primary function of language is *disclosure*: to show things forth as what they are, to let things appear. The nominalist philosophy of language assumes that things have already appeared as what they are, that they are already there, delineated and circumscribed as such. Language then applies labels to these entities which are already distinguished as themselves. But, contrary to this view, it is only through the primary function of language as disclosure that there *are* entities distinguished in the first place. Thus the representational theory of language depends on the disclosive function of language, which it does not recognize. In effect it tries to explain language by presupposing language! Nominalism makes the same mistake in the philosophy of language that empiricism makes in the philosophy of science. It *begins* at the wrong end, with the finished product, instead of trying to follow (participate in) the coming-into-being. Instead of trying to catch language in the act (i.e., "language-ing") it begins with the "already-languaged." This is another instance of trying to "reach the milk by way of the cheese," which results in what amounts to the conjuring-trick philosophy of language. The philosophy of language and the origin of concepts will be discussed in detail in "The Twofold" in chap. 6.

27. Heidegger, *Being and Time* (New York: Harper and Row, 1962), 63.

28. See "The One and the Many" in part II for discussion of "multiplicity in unity" and how this differs from "unity in multiplicity." See also chap. 5.

29. The dynamic form of "multiplicity in unity," which we find to be characteristic of the organizing idea, is very much the mode of unity which is characteristic of life—and also of art. It is *organic*. Brady refers to "this peculiar potency of organic form" that *"it is becoming other in order to remain itself."* He says, "The *becoming* that belongs to this constitution is not a process that finishes when it reaches a certain goal but a condition of existence—a necessity to

change in order to remain the same" (italics in original). See Ronald H. Brady, "Form and Cause in Goethe's Morphology'" in *Goethe and the Sciences: A Reappraisal*, ed. Frederick Amrine, Francis J. Zucker, and Harvey Wheeler (Dordrecht, the Netherlands: Reidel Publishing Company, 1987), 282, 286, 287.

This "reappearance of the same in difference" is also fundamental to Gadamer's philosophical hermeneutics. In *Truth and Method*, Gadamer presents what Weinsheimer describes as "a way of thinking about art, truth and interpretation that will explain, first, the fact of multiple interpretations; second, that multiple interpretations can all be true to the work; and third, that the work can be multiply interpreted, multiply true, without disintegrating into fragments or degenerating into an empty form." Understanding an artwork is not reproductive but productive. But the interpretations, if true, belong to the possibilities of the work—"True interpretations are interpretations *of the work itself*"—and are not merely subjective, i.e., imposed on the work by the interpreter. Thus "The work is the multiple possibilities of its interpretation." This "means—despite the multiplicity of its true interpretations— it is nevertheless one work which is many," and ". . . the continuing life of the artwork . . . embodies itself, its own possibilities, in the variety of its interpretations." The work is wholly there in each interpretation, and yet no interpretation is the whole work. The unity of the work is "multiplicity in unity," and not "unity in multiplicity" as it would be if there were a single, correct interpretation. There is no "meaning in itself" behind the work. Instead the work lives in its interpretations, which are its own possibilities, so that "an artwork's way of being is: to be different; and only thus does it remain itself." Comparing this with Brady's description of organic form—"*it is becoming other in order to remain itself*"—it becomes clear that Gadamer's philosophical hermeneutics is truly organic. See Weinsheimer, *Gadamer's Hermaneutics*, 100, 111, 112, 114 for the above quotations.

30. Kühlewind, *The Logos-Structure of the World*, 37.

31. This is fundamental to Hegel's philosophy. Hegel recognized that, because thinking is distinction and relation at the same time, the so-called laws of logic would have to be seen as relative. Thus, the principle of noncontradiction (not at the same time A and not-A), the principle of identity (A is A), and the principle of the excluded middle (either A or not-A) could not be upheld in an absolute sense. He did not deny these laws (which are really three aspects of one law, since each entails the other two), but simply asserted their relative nature. Thus, since A is intrinsically related to not-A, we cannot maintain the rigid separation of A and not-A, which these

statements of the laws imply. These would amount to a "logic of solid bodies," as Henri Bergson discerningly called it, since it is in the world of such bodies that separation is the predominant feature. Eastern thinking seems to be more familiar with the intrinsic interdependence of everything, whereas Western thinking has often tended to emphasize independence (but see note 17).

32. See also Kühlewind, *The Logos-Structure of the World*, 36. In a workshop on this theme (held on June 2, 1990, at the Rudolf Steiner House, London), Dr. Kühlewind said that this simultaneous movement of distinguishing which is relating is the power of the *logos*. Examples of the primary distinction in the act of *discovery* enable us to catch the holistic quality. An illustration is readily provided by Luke Howard's act of distinguishing and naming the clouds (stratus, nimbus, cumulus, cirrus), which Goethe responded to with such enthusiasm—see Lehrs, *Man or Matter,* 113–23. What at first looks like an analytical classification system, imposed on observations of the clouds, in fact has the effect of organizing the clouds in this sense of the "distinguishing which is relating" which comes before separating. The holistic quality of the primary act of distinguishing can be recognized quite easily in this case.

33. Kühlewind indicates such a possibility in *The Logos-Structure of the World*, 93. In such an experience we would find ourselves in a monistic state of consciousness, prior to the subject–object separation, in which the *appearance* of what is seen and the *seeing* are the same. To catch this, "appearance" must be read verbally as the act of appearing. Heidegger was particularly concerned with this subtle experience, which defies description because it is so simple— the difficulty arises from the fact that the categories of language introduce separations which are just not there in the experience.

34. This does *not* mean that science is just common sense, far from it. There is nothing commonsensical about Newton's first law of motion, for example. In fact, often science could be described as being anti-common sense—which is especially true in the case of physics. The point which is being made here is that *epistemologically* there is no difference *in kind* between cognitive perception in science and everyday cognitive perception. In both cases there must be an organizing idea. Whether or not this idea is in agreement with common sense is irrelevant.

35. Galileo Galilei, *Siderius Nuncius*, trans. by Albert Van Helden (Chicago: University of Chicago Press, 1989).

36. I. Bernard Cohen, *The Birth of a New Physics*, rev. and updated ed. (New York: Norton, 1985), 188. See also Cohen, *The Newtonian Revolution* (Cambridge: Cambridge University Press, 1980), 212.

37. Best, *Feeling and Reason in the Arts*, 25.

38. Galileo, 64.

39. Ibid., 66. The term "planet" is derived from a Greek word meaning "wanderer."

40. The perception of cave paintings illustrates in a graphic way that meaning is the object of cognitive perception. Two very different interpretations of cave paintings have been put forward. The most well-known one, by the Abbé Breuil, is that the artists painted the pictures in the caves from memory and imagination. According to this view, the paintings depict animals in action, and accordingly such titles as "the bellowing bison" and "the trotting boar" are given to the pictures. But an alternative view was offered by Leason. He had made drawings of a cat which had been recently killed, and he had been struck by how vigorous the cat still looked. So, when he first saw pictures of cave art it struck him as being remarkable that people so long ago had made pictures of dead animals! He did not, at the time, know that another interpretation of the pictures had been made, and so this did not interfere with his perception. He just saw pictures of dead animals lying on the ground. He saw this *directly*. The meaning was part of the perception, not added on to the perception afterwards to try to make sense of it—"Perception always includes meaning," (Gadamer, 92). In fact, it is clear that in this example the object of perception *is* the meaning. See M. L. Johnson Abercrombie, *The Anatomy of Judgment* (London: Hutchinson, 1960), 35–38.

41. Kuhn, 115.

42. Kuhn gives several other excellent examples in *The Structure of Scientific Revolutions*. See, for example, the discussion of the discovery of oxygen, 53–56. Concerning the question of whether it was discovered by Priestley or Lavoisier, Kuhn says:

> Though undoubtedly correct, the sentence "Oxygen was discovered " misleads by suggesting that discovering something is a single simple act assimilable to our usual (and also questionable) concept of seeing. That is why we so readily assume that discovery, like seeing or touching, should be unequivocally attributable to an individual and to a moment in time.

43. Edwin A. Abbott, *Flatland* (New York: Dover, 1952). See the final paragraph of "The Depth of the Phenomenon" in part II.

44. Morris Berman, *The Reenchantment of the World* (Ithaca: Cornell University Press, 1981), 62. Berman also makes the point that cannons were not fired at long range until the end of the sixteenth century, and the short range would make it easier to see the Aristotelian trajectory.

45. Sacks, *The Man Who Mistook His Wife for a Hat*, 89.

46. The tendency to think of the invisible as if it were visible but just not seen, is another consequence of beginning from the finished product instead of following through the coming-into-being. When we encounter the *appearance* (i.e., the appearing itself), then we realize the difference between the invisible as such and what is not visible simply because it is not being seen at the particular moment in question. Perhaps we need to distinguish the latter from the former by using a term such as "nonvisible," instead of using the one word, "invisible," to cover both (ontologically very different) cases.

47. Hume's discovery of the failure of inductive generalization to provide the basis for scientific laws is described at length in *A Treatise of Human Nature*, first published in 1739/40 (Glasgow: Fontana/Collins, 1962). A simplified version appeared later in *An Inquiry Concerning Human Understanding*. It is discussed in every introductory book on the philosophy of science.

48. Paul Feyerabend, *Against Method* (London: Verso, 1978), 75. Hume was not aware of this. He thought that ideas were derived from sense impressions.

49. This is when the parallax of the stars, due to the Earth's motion about the Sun, was finally observed by Bessel. Because of this motion, every star should appear to change its position, relative to an observer on Earth, during the course of a year. The effect is very small because of the huge distances of the stars (0.3 arc seconds for 61 Cygni, the star which Bessel used), and is very easily masked by other, much larger, changes in position due to the proper motion of the stars (5.2 arc seconds per year for 61 Cygni). The possibility that there were such parallax effects associated with the Earth's motion around the Sun had been raised right from the start—in fact the Greeks also raised it. So observational confirmation of Copernicus's theory came to be identified with detecting parallax—so much so that it often passes unnoticed that evidence of the Earth's motion was available a century before parallax was finally detected. In 1725, Bradley discovered small shifts in stellar positions during the course of a year. These were too big to be due to parallactic shift, and the changes in position did not fit what would be expected for such a shift. By 1728, Bradley had recognized that the phenomenon he had seen was the effect of the velocity of the light from a star combining vectorially with the orbital velocity of the Earth. This phenomenon is called the aberration of light. The point is that there would be no aberration of light if the Earth were at rest, so this does constitute evidence for the movement of the Earth around the Sun. It may seem more indirect than the detection of parallax, because it depends on a new act of cognitive perception, entailing a new organizing idea.

50. But this is because the observational evidence *did* confirm the Copernican view. It would have been a different matter altogether if, after diligent searching with ever-improving instrumentation, the expected parallax had not been revealed. The search for parallax was important, therefore, not because it confirmed the Copernican view, but because failing to find it would, at some point, have called the Copernican view into question.

51. See Augustine Brannigan, *The Social Basis of Scientific Discovery* (Cambridge: Cambridge University Press, 1981), for a thorough discussion of "discovery" as a social category and the significance of this for understanding science. The assertion that something is not a discovery before it is recognized as a discovery, so that the act of recognizing it as a discovery constitutes it as a discovery, could be compared with Tauler's maxim that a man who was a king and did not know it would not be a king (quoted by Georg Kühlewind, *From Normal to Healthy*, 62).

52. Thomas S. Kuhn, *The Copernican Revolution* (Cambridge, Mass.: Harvard University Press, 1957), 157.

53. See, for example, Kuhn's account of how he came to appreciate the naturalness of Aristotle's physics in Thomas S. Kuhn, *The Essential Tension* (Chicago: University of Chicago Press, 1977), *xi-xiii*.

54. Kuhn, *The Copernican Revolution*, 109.

55. Ibid., 114.

56. See Brown, *Perception, Theory and Commitment*, for a discussion of the role of commitment in the development of science.

57. Details will be found in chap. 2 of Kuhn, *The Copernican Revolution*.

58. Ibid., 73.

59. Ibid., 163.

60. Ibid., 169.

61. Ibid., 169. See also Arthur Koestler, *The Sleepwalkers* (Harmondsworth: Penguin Books, 1964), 195.

62. Koestler, 170.

63. Kuhn, *The Copernican Revolution*, 139.

64. Ibid., 142.

65. Marshall Clagett, *Greek Science in Antiquity* (London: Abelard-Schuman, 1957), 90.

66. Arthur Koestler maintains:

> There can be no doubt that Copernicus was acquainted with Aristarchus's idea, and that he was following in his footsteps. The

proof of this is to be found in Copernicus's own manuscript of the
Revolutions, where he refers to Aristarchus—but, characteristi-
cally, this reference is crossed out in ink. (*The Sleepwalkers*, 208).

67.　Clagett, *Greek Science in Antiquity,* 91–92.

68.　The role of schools of thought in the development of scientific
knowledge has been emphasized by Joseph Agassi in *Towards a
Historiography of Science* ('S-Gravenhage: Mouton, 1963). Agassi
maintains, with a wealth of examples, that the inductive philosophy
of science (according to which scientific theories emerge *from* facts)
"blinds historians of science to the chief factors in the history of science—contending schools of scientific thought" (23).

69.　Details of this school of thought insofar as it affects the development of Copernican astronomy are given in Kuhn, *The Copernican
Revolution,* upon which the following account is based.

70.　Ibid., 131 and 179.

71.　This is what Copernicus says:

> So we find underlying this ordination an admirable symmetry in
> the Universe, and a clear bond of harmony in the motion and
> magnitude of the Spheres such as can be discovered in no other
> wise. For here we may observe why the progression and retro-
> gression appear greater for Jupiter than Saturn, and less than for
> Mars, but again greater for Venus than for Mercury; and why
> such oscillation appears more frequently in Saturn than in
> Jupiter, but less frequently in Mars and Venus than in Mercury;
> moreover why Saturn, Jupiter and Mars are nearer to the Earth at
> opposition to the Sun than when they are lost in or emerge from
> the Sun's rays. Particularly Mars, when he shines all night,
> appears to rival Jupiter in magnitude, being only distinguishable
> by his ruddy color; otherwise he is scarce equal to a star of the
> second magnitude, and can be recognized only when his move-
> ments are carefully followed. All these phenomena proceeded
> from the same cause, namely Earth's motion. (Quoted in *The
> Copernican Revolution,* 180)

72.　E.A. Burtt, *The Metaphysical Foundations of Modern Science* (London: Routledge and Kegan Paul, 1980), 79.

73.　"The Physics of Goethean Style" below; see also parts I and II of
this book.

74.　Kuhn, *The Copernican Revolution,* 180.

75.　Plato, *The Republic,* pt. VII, sec. 6; pt. VIII, sec. 2, in Penguin edition.

76.　Brian Easlea, *Witch Hunting, Magic and the New Philosophy* (Sussex:
Harvester Press, 1980), 59.

77. See note 64.

78. See Hübner, *Critique of Scientific Reason*, chap. 5; see also Arthur Koestler, *The Sleepwalkers*, pt. 4, chap. 6. Kepler set out to treat the Earth fully as a planet governed by the Sun. Copernicus had attributed several special functions to the Earth—e.g., he preserved the Ptolemaic feature that the planes of all planetary orbits intersected at the center of the Earth by drawing them so that they intersected at the center of the Earth's orbit, which was *not* in the same place as the Sun in Copernicus's scheme (which was therefore not strictly heliocentric). Kepler said that the Earth had no special status, and that the Sun governed all planets, so that the planes of the planetary orbits *must* intersect in the Sun. His determination to do this was an expression of his Neo-Platonic belief that the Sun is the visible representative of God, and must be in the center and nowhere else. Only by sticking strictly to this demand derived from his philosophical standpoint did Kepler eventually discover that the orbit of a planet is not circular, as had always been assumed, but is in fact slightly elliptical. This is why Copernicus had needed to use so many minor epicycles—trying to make the orbit fit a circle—for which there was no longer any necessity.

    Kepler was so convinced of the primary role of the Sun that he came to think of it as the source of all movement as well as the source of light and heat. His philosophical viewpoint led him towards the notion of a physical cause for planetary movement originating in the central body. This acted as a guiding idea in his search for the form of the planetary orbit, which finally resulted in what we now know as Kepler's first and second laws. Details can be found in the works referred to above (see especially Koestler), showing how Kepler made hypotheses and decisions, grounded in his philosophical viewpoint, which guided his thinking towards the discovery of the laws of planetary motion. This is very different from the story which is usually told of how Kepler discovered these laws empirically by searching the observational measurements until he found the right mathematical relationships. This "story" is a reconstruction according to the empiricists' myth of how science ought to proceed rather than how it actually does.

79. Kuhn, *The Structure of Scientific Revolutions*, 121. Harold Brown points out that "the thesis that the meaning of scientific concepts changes as a result of a scientific revolution has been regarded . . . as one of the most outrageous claims of the new philosophy of science" (*Perception, Theory and Commitment*, 116). At the same time that Kuhn's major work was first published (1962), another philosopher of science, Paul Feyerabend, also published an essay in which he denied the fundamental assumption of the traditional philosophy of science that

meanings are invariant with respect to the process of explanation. Feyerabend suggests in this essay that, instead of a theory explaining facts which are established independently, adopting a new theory alters the concepts, and hence alters the facts. So, as he puts it elsewhere, the facts are mutable. See P.A. Feyerabend, "Explanation, Reduction and Empiricism" in *Minnesota Studies in the Philosophy of Science*, vol. 3 (1962). See also I. Bernard Cohen, *The Newtonian Revolution*, pt. 2.

80. It is not a *formal* replacement of the Earth by the Sun which is of concern here, but a change of *meaning*. A computer could make the formal change, but not the change in meaning. The primacy of meaning enables us to avoid several common misunderstandings about science. For example, every student of physics learns that Einstein's mechanics (relativity) reduces to Newton's mechanics when the velocity of a body is very small compared with the speed of light. Formally this is true, as is evident from the mathematical equations, but otherwise it is *not* true because the *meanings* of the key terms in the two theories are very different. The theory of relativity does not reduce to Newton's theory for small-enough velocities because the meanings of "mass," "energy," "time," and so forth, are different in the two theories. The meaning in one theory is not reducible to the meaning in the other theory, because meaning is not a formal element and only formal elements can be transposed in this way. One consequence of this is that *science* cannot be developed by a computer—a "syntactic engine" cannot make changes in meaning, and therefore cannot make scientific *discoveries*. A corollary of this is that the computer cannot provide a model of *human* thinking, as so many today wish to believe. No doubt it may provide a model for those aspects of thought which have been reduced to the formal, mechanical level. But this excludes those aspects which have to do with meaning, and hence with creativity. So, the very fact that human beings do science is sufficient to show that a human being is not reducible to a computer.

81. Quoted in Ernst Cassirer, "Einstein's Theory of Relativity Considered from the Epistemological Standpoint," supplement to *Substance and Function* (New York: Dover Publications, 1953), 371.

82. Richard S. Westfall, *The Construction of Modern Science* (Cambridge: Cambridge University Press, 1977), 19.

83. See Cohen, *The Birth of a New Physics*, 117–25, and supplement 8 (210), for a more detailed discussion of Galileo's difficulties and achievements with regard to the law of inertial motion.

84. H. Butterfield, *The Origins of Modern Science* (London: Bell, 1957), 4.

85. For a very good account of atomism, in both its earlier and later phases (and also for a discussion of Platonism in connection with

this problem), see Terence Irwin, *Classical Thought* (Oxford: Oxford University Press, 1989). See also Rudolf Steiner, *Goethe's World View* (Spring Valley, New York: Mercury Press, 1985), chap. 1, for a discussion of the effect which this mistrust of sense experience has had on the development of Western science to this day. We have already mentioned the distrust of the senses, in favor of reason, when discussing Copernicus and Galileo.

86. The manuscript of *De Rerum Natura* was discovered in 1417. See Alexandre Koyré, *From the Closed World to the Infinite Universe* (Baltimore: Johns Hopkins University Press, 1968), 278, n. 5. The complete text is given in *The Epicurean Philosophers,* ed. John Gaskin (London: Everyman, 1994).

87. Here we have the beginning of the modern view that humans find themselves in a meaningless universe, which eventually works itself through historically to become philosophical nihilism. But there is another, positive side to this, which often goes unnoticed. Faced with a meaningless universe, as it seems to us, we can create meaning, and in so doing we takes a step of freedom, which is a developmental step for us. We have to do this for ourselves—otherwise it would not be freedom—and herein lies the difficulty, which necessarily accompanies any developmental opportunity.

88. Kuhn, *The Copernican Revolution*, 220.

89. It has been suggested by Pietro Redondi, in *Galileo: Heretic* (Princeton: Princeton University Press, 1987), that the introduction of the philosophy of atomism into physics was the real basis of the disagreement between Galileo and the Church, because this posed an extreme difficulty for understanding the transubstantiation of the Host in the Mass.

90. Kuhn, *The Copernican Revolution*, 238.

91. Errol Harris, *Hypothesis and Perception* (London: Allen and Unwin, 1970), 120. We may also find here the historical root of one of the most famous problems in Anglo-Saxon philosophy, namely, the problem of induction as this was encountered by David Hume. He wished to apply the style of the Newtonian science of matter to the science of human beings. But considering the origin of scientific knowledge to be empirical, he found to his dismay that he could not justify the principle of induction. So it seemed to him that he could not find a justification for scientific knowledge, and he was led into a reluctant skepticism as a result. Much has been written about the "problem of induction," but, in fact, it is not really a problem at all because scientific laws are *not* the empirical generalizations reached by induction that Hume believed them to be. But it never occurred to him that they could

be otherwise, and here we can see the influence of Newton. If Newton had said that this is what scientific laws are, then it would have seemed to Hume that this is indeed what they must be. It is perhaps for the same reason that Hume's "failure" has seemed to many to present such a monumental problem to the philosophy of science. It is, in fact, not a problem because science isn't what the "problem" supposes it to be.

As well as its historical root in the influential pronouncements of Newton, there is also an epistemological source for the view that science is essentially empirical. This is a consequence of beginning from the finished product, instead of following through the coming-into-being of cognition. In this case the active dimension of mind in the constitution of knowledge is missed, i.e., the organizing idea, and instead it seems that ideas are mental copies and abstractions for idea-less sense perceptions. But, as we have seen, cognitive perception is not idea-less.

92. See A. Rupert Hall, *The Revolution in Science, 1500-1750* (London: Longman, 1983), 183 ff. for further discussion of this point.

93. The failure to observe parallax *could* have been taken as a falsifying counterinstance to Copernicus's proposal. In fact it was taken this way when the same proposal was made in ancient times by Aristarchus. Sir Karl Popper takes falsifiability as the hallmark of scientific propositions. What he means by this is simply that to be scientific a proposition must be falsifiable *in principle*. He does not mean that a scientific theory *is* falsified by a counterinstance, only that it *could* be. Popper's emphasis on falsifiability arose out of his concern to distinguish science from nonscience. For example, he was concerned about the claim which was often made at the time (earlier this century) that psychoanalysis and Marxism were scientific. His principle of falsifiability is therefore to be understood as a criterion of demarcation, and not as a prescription for how science ought to proceed.

94. We must not fall into the trap of thinking that in doing so we are comparing a verbal meaning, "there is at least one raven in Iceland," with an actual situation to which we somehow have access apart from meaning, as if meaning could be checked against some purely sensory, meaningless "given." This is the picture which the so-called correspondence theory of truth encourages. We have seen in detail in "The Organizing Idea in Cognitive Perception" how this is absurd. If we see a raven in Iceland, then what we experience is meaning and not anything else. If what we experienced was without meaning then we could not *see* it, and therefore could not ascertain that there is a raven in Iceland. When it is said that an empirical proposition refers to something beyond itself, this does

not mean something which is outside of meaning, but that the truth of the proposition can only be ascertained by comparing the meaning of the proposition with the meaning in an actual situation. It is meaning which is compared with meaning ("Like is known only by like"—Goethe), and not meaning with something that is outside of meaning to which we have direct access, as naïve versions of the correspondence theory of truth imply. See the very good discussion of this in David Mitchell, *An Introduction to Logic* (London: Hutchinson, 1964), 113–15.

95. Brown, *Perception, Theory and Commitment*, 105. He acknowledges borrowing the term "paradigm" from Kuhn. The entire chapter 7 of Brown's book is an excellent account of the topic being discussed here.

96. Some illustrations of the quantitative way of seeing will help to make this clearer. As a first example, consider the way that letters are composed by computer in the modern office. The manager has a manual of separate paragraphs from which he or she can put together a letter simply by selecting the paragraphs which he or she wants, and these are printed out by the computer from the disk on which they are stored. The letter is thus an external assemblage of parts. This operation is entirely within the category of quantity, but without quantity appearing specifically in the content. The quantity here is the form: it is the mode of conception and not the content. It is not difficult to go on from this kind of example to the realization that the world of Western industrialized society in which we live is structured throughout in the quantitative mode. We live quantitatively today, as anyone can verify for themselves by becoming aware of the "way of seeing." We live in this world, not because it is already there, waiting for us, but because *we live it* and thus it is realized. We do not find the quantitative world; we mean it.

When we do not give attention to the way of seeing, focusing instead on what is seen, we fail to notice the *form* of cognitive perception. The result is that we are easily misled. An illustration of how this happens is found in the often-made claim that "systems theory" is the science of wholeness, which is made on the basis that systems thinking takes into account relationships. Well, it does do this, but only by first *separating* the elements which it then interrelates. A typical description of systems thinking refers to "breaking down reality into *elements* and identifying *linkages* between them." Such a "system" of elements and their linkages is clearly entirely external, because it is in the form of separation into parts which are outside of each other. Both the elements and their linkages are conceived in such an external way—each element is external to the other elements, and the linkages between them are external to the elements they link. In other words, a "system" is conceived in the form of quantity. Hence systems theory cannot be the basis of a science of wholeness, as is often claimed.

When this kind of thinking is applied to life it results in an absurdity. The notion of a living system, as opposed to one which is nonliving, is a contradiction in terms. It may *look* like something has been said, but in fact "living system" has about as much meaning as "black white." If it is a system, as defined above, then it cannot be living because what is living cannot consist of parts which are external to one another, i.e., which are separate. If we treat what is living in this way we kill it. Systems theory is no more than systems *analysis* (*lysis*: to separate). A *living* organism cannot be analyzed, whereas what is nonliving can be, since the possibility of analysis is the very characteristic of the inorganic—cf. Galileo's discovery that the motion of a projectile can be analyzed into horizontal and vertical components and conversely can be synthesized from such components. A mechanism, such as a clock, is an excellent illustration of the form of quantity. There is little wonder that the development of the science of quantity came together with the adoption of the machine as a basic metaphor for nature. We can now see that, far from being a new way of thinking, systems theory has its roots in the mechanical philosophy of the seventeenth century. Thus we are able to avoid the mistake of believing that systems thinking is the way to understanding the organic.

A further illustration of the quantitative way of seeing is provided by Darwin's theory of biological evolution by chance variation and natural selection. By its very form, this theory implicitly conceives the organism quantitatively because it considers it as if it were composed of separate parts, each of which is capable of undergoing variation independently of all the other parts. Darwin's organism is a quantitative organism, notwithstanding the fact that number is not explicitly involved. The *whole* organism loses its meaning as such, being effectively reduced to a collection of separate characters. Graham Cannon pointed out that this "regarded the characters of an organism like so many marbles in a box and, just as individual marbles may be changed at random and substituted, so might the characters undergo isolated independent random change"—H. Graham Cannon, *The Evolution of Living Things* (Manchester: Manchester University Press, 1958), 116. It is worth emphasizing that Darwin may not have deliberately conceived of an organism as composed of characters which are effectively separate, but this is the way that the organism is constituted by the very form of the theory.

We can compare this with the very different description of an organism given by Kant in his *Critique of Judgment*. Kant saw an organism as a *self-organizing* whole of mutually constitutive parts. Each such part enters into the constitution of every other part, so the parts are certainly not external and separate, and hence Kant's organism is not a quantitative organism. It is a machine, not an organism, which exemplifies the form of quantity, for with a machine the parts are clearly external to one another. In a machine, such as a clock, the parts exist *for* each other, and so a machine is a functional unity. In an organism, however, the parts exist not only for each other but also by means of each other. We can see now that Darwin's theory conceives the organism as if it were a machine. So Darwin's organism is effectively nonliving!

As a final example of seeing in the mode of quantity, we will consider briefly the way that we understand time. We commonly conceive time as a linear series of separate instants, a string of "nows" placed next to each other in an indefinitely long line. Some of these instants we imagine to have gone, some not to have arrived yet, and only one to be actually present. In this way we try to make a distinction between past, present, and future. But we imagine the instants which are "past" as if they were present, and similarly with the instants we imagine to be "future." In other words, this is a peculiarly timeless way of conceiving time! We can look at it the other way around. It is a consequence of the quantitative mode of cognition that time is separated into parts which are external to one another. Hence, in this mode of cognition, the past and the future are withdrawn from the present, so that this becomes merely the present, i.e., "now." So we have a string of "nows," all of which are identical, like units, and therefore time appears to be homogeneous. We can easily recognize this as the time of the clock, by which we organize our lives in the world today. We can also recognize it as the abstract time of mathematical physics, which is the framework in which we imagine the physical universe. It is, in fact, the way that we constitute "time" by our concern to measure it. But homogeneous time—time in the mode of quantity—is timeless. So the irony is that the time of physics is timeless! Physics, therefore, makes no contribution to our understanding of time. What physicists discover about the universe does not show us anything about the nature of time—it simply presupposes "time" in the quantitative sense. It follows that books such as Stephen Hawking's best-selling *A Brief History of Time* (New York: Bantam, 1988*)*, admirable though it is in its own way, does not tell us anything about time. To approach a deeper understanding of time, we could begin, not with the pronouncements of physicists, but with the work of philosophers such as Bergson, Husserl, and Heidegger on this subject. At least this would help us to recognize the limitation of what we ordinarily understand by "time."

97. John Davy, *Hope, Evolution and Change* (Stroud: Hawthorn Press, 1985), 8.

98. The failure to realize this eventually gave rise to the difficulties in understanding which came in this century with the development of the quantum theory. Only then did it begin to become clear that atoms should not be invested with *sensory* qualities. But by this time it seemed that this was a failure of science itself, indicating an inherent limitation of scientific knowledge. In fact, it was a release from a misunderstanding which confused the container with the content. So what seemed at the time to be a failure was really a release from imprisonment in a restricted viewpoint.

99. See "The Organizing Idea in Cognitive Perception." It is because cognition itself is seen in the light of the "solid world" way of seeing, i.e., in the form of quantity, that this correlation is missed, and instead we find the familiar picture of Cartesian dualism: separate and independent subject and object and the representational theory of knowledge which makes knowledge a property of the subject. It is helpful to remember that there can be distinction *without* separation. Of course, there cannot be in the quantitative mode, as can be recognized from Aristotle's definition. It is because this mode of illumination is the dominant one for us that we automatically assume that distinction and separation are the same. To put it another way, we think of "distinction" as being separation. In fact, the condition of distinction without separation is prior to separation, into which it subsequently falls. See Owen Barfield, *The Rediscovery of Meaning* (Middletown, Conn.: Weslyan University Press, 1977), 162. See also the end of the chapter just mentioned.

100. Isaiah Berlin, *The Age of Enlightenment* (New York: New American Library, 1956), 18.

101. Kuhn, *The Structure of Scientific Revolutions*, 121.

102. David Bohm, *Quantum Theory* (Englewood Cliffs, N.J.: Prentice Hall, 1951), 170.

103. See *Hegel's Logic* (Oxford: Oxford University Press, 1975), section 119. This is the first volume of Hegel's *Encyclopedia of the Philosophical Sciences*. A very clear account of this aspect of Hegel's philosophy is given in chapter 7 of *Hegel* by Edward Caird. This work, first published in 1883, was republished in a facsimile edition in 1972 by AMS Press, New York. I am indebted to Dr. Andros Loizou for drawing my attention to this work.

104. Henri Bergson, *Creative Evolution* (London: Macmillan, 1960), *ix*. Yet it is interesting to note that the three laws of logic are not really three laws at all, i.e., not in the sense that each is self-contained and separate from the others. Each one of these statements entails the

other two, so that in an implicit sense each one contains or includes the other two. Hence there is really only "one" law which can be seen in three partial perspectives. In other words, there is here a conceptual whole, which appears *in the quantitative way of seeing* as three separate laws of logic. So these statements comprising the logic of solid bodies themselves seem to conform to the solid world perspective—i.e., three separate, independent statements. Yet we see that something escapes from these statements—or, to put it the other way, something is excluded from them. This is the very thing which is excluded by the solid world perspective: intrinsic interdependence and therefore nonseparability.

105. G.B. Madison, *The Hermeneutics of Postmodernity* (Bloomington: Indiana University Press, 1990), 129.

106. Ibid., 130.

107. The term "metaphysics" was coined by Aristotle, who nevertheless did not use it himself in the specific way that it is used here—which is in accordance with the way that the term is used in European philosophy today.

108. Nietzsche referred to institutionalized Christianity as "Platonism for the people." See Martin Heidegger, *Introduction to Metaphysics* (New Haven: Yale University Press, 1959), 106.

109. *Phaedo*, 74c ff. For a discussion of Plato's theory of Forms, see, for example, David J. Melling, *Understanding Plato* (Oxford: Oxford University Press, 1987), chaps. 10 and 11; Terence Irwin, *Classical Thought*, chap. 6; Frederick Copleston, *A History of Philosophy*, vol. 1, pt. 1 (New York: Doubleday, 1962), chap. 20.

110. *Phaedo*, 66a (Penguin edition). This is a key passage, which is often misunderstood. It refers to *the possibility of sense-free thinking*. Yet it has often been taken to mean no more than thought which takes place without the senses for the simple reason that it is all taking place "in our heads." This is *not* sense-free thinking, because the kind of images entailed in this activity are thoroughly sense-dependent. Thinking is not sense-free because it takes place without the senses, but only if there is no trace of the sensory in thinking itself, so that it is "pure and unadulterated." (*Phaedo*, 66a).

111. *Metaphysics*, 991 b 1-3. Aristotle's objections to Plato's theory are discussed in Frederick Copleston, *A History of Philosophy*, vol. 1, pt. 2 (New York: Doubleday, 1962), 35 ff. See also Terence Irwin, *Classical Thought*, 124.

112. There does, however, remain a question over whether, and to what extent, Plato himself *separated* the sensible and the intelligible into two worlds so that a chasm (*chōrismos*) was created between

appearance (now downgraded to *mere* appearance) and idea. In other words, to what extent was Plato a Platonist? For the most part, philosophers and others have taken it that Plato *did* introduce a chasm, and hence held a two-world theory. Aristotle said that he did, but what Aristotle himself was trying to do by means of his criticism may not necessarily be as obvious as it is usually taken to be (cf. Copleston, *A History of Philosophy*, vol. 1, pt. 1, 195). Certainly today it is believed almost universally (but not quite) that Plato was the source of the metaphysical separation—a view which was strongly emphasized by Heidegger. However, Gadamer has pointed out that, in his treatment of the beautiful, Plato shows how the two realms of the sensible and the supersensible are reconciled in a way which does not admit separation. He takes this to be crucial for understanding Plato himself, as distinct from the later development of Platonism—see Gadamer, *Truth and Method*, 481-82. Elsewhere Gadamer emphasized that the view commonly attributed to Plato is really pseudo-Platonism, and added that Hegel understood this (in a seminar on "Heidegger, Hermeneutics and Interpretation" held at the Goethe Institute, London, in April 1986). Steiner attributed the origin of what he called "one-sided Platonism" to the way in which Plato presented the fact that "in *human perception* the sense world becomes a mere semblance if the light of the world of ideas is not shone upon it." *Through the way he presented this fact*, Plato "furthered the belief that the sense world, in and for itself, irrespective of human beings, is a world of semblance, and that true reality is only to be found in ideas." (Steiner, *Goethe's World View*, 17). He goes on to say that it is against *this* that Aristotle protested (22). It is this one-sided Platonism, or pseudo-Platonism, which is a major historical–philosophical root of mathematical physics.

113. Speaking about mathematicians, Plato says:

> . . . they make use of and argue about visible figures, though they are not really thinking about them, but about the originals which they resemble; it is *not* about the square or diagonal which they have drawn that they are arguing, but about the square itself or diagonal itself, or whatever the figure might be. The actual figures they draw or model, which themselves cast their shadows and reflections in water—these they treat as images only, the real objects of their investigation being invisible except to the eye of reason. (*Republic*, 510d, Penguin edition).

114. Edmund Husserl, *The Crisis of European Sciences and Transcendental Phenomenology* (Evanston, Illinois: Northwestern University Press, 1970), 23–59. Aron Gurwitsch, *Phenomenology and the Theory of Science* (Evanston: Northwestern University Press, 1974), chap. 2; see also Aron Gurwitsch, "Galilean Physics in the Light of

Husserl's Phenomenology" in *Phenomenology and Sociology,* ed. Thomas Luckmann (Harmondsworth: Penguin Books, 1978).

115. There are exceptions. See, for example, Roger Penrose, *The Emperor's New Mind* (Oxford: Oxford University Press, 1989).

116. Sir James Jeans, *The Mysterious Universe* (Cambridge: Cambridge University Press, 1930), chap. 5. The same can be said about the remarks made more recently by Stephen Hawking. In *A Brief History of Time*, Hawking says that "the eventual goal of science is to provide a single theory that describes the whole universe" (12). Such a theory of everything, as it is called, will be the final triumph of mathematical physics—after which physics will come to an end because there will be no further need for it. This will be the ultimate triumph of human reason, Hawking tells us, "for then we would know the mind of God" (193). We can now recognize this as just another instance of the Platonism underlying mathematical physics. In fact, we could easily imagine remarks such as this being made by Galileo or Kepler. The content of the physics notwithstanding, there is nothing fundamentally new in the views of Stephen Hawking.

117. Koestler, *The Sleepwalkers,* 264.

118. Certainly Galileo thought so: see Burtt, 82.

119. Gurwitsch, *Phenomenology and the Theory of Science,* 51; "Galilean Physics in the Light of Husserl's Phenomenology," 84.

120. Strictly speaking, Descartes was not an atomist, but he was a corpuscularian. He believed that matter was indefinitely divisible, so there was no ultimate unit. But matter was corpuscular, and everything in nature was to be understood in terms of particles in motion. Gassendi, a contemporary of Descartes, adopted atomism. Robert Boyle treated atomism and Cartesianism as two expressions of the same corpuscular conception of nature, which he called the "mechanical philosophy" of nature. As he put it, the mechanical philosophy traces all the phenomena of nature to the "two catholic principles" of matter and motion—see Richard Westfall, *The Construction of Modern Science,* 41.

121. Tom Sorell, *Descartes* (Oxford: Oxford University Press, 1987), 57.

122. Ibid., 61.

123. Descartes, *Meditations,* Second Meditation.

124. What Descartes is really doing here is building in the division of man into mortal body and immortal soul, which was the doctrine of the Church at this time—the spirit having been denied to man by the Council of Constance in 869 A.D. This is one of the roots of Descartes's famous dualism—another, equally important, is his espousal of mathematics as the model for certainty in human

knowledge. What Descartes did was to reduce the soul to a purely thinking capacity. This, of course, is just the capacity needed for doing mathematical physics. This is all part of Descartes's hidden strategy to demonstrate that human beings, as understood by the Church, are ontologically constituted to be perfectly fitted to do mathematical physics. It is as if human beings had been designed by God for the very purpose of doing mathematical physics, so that, in doing it, they are fulfilling their nature and thereby doing God's will. The subtext to Descartes's text is really the key to the whole thing. His aim was to make it seem natural and right to replace Aristotelian physics with his new mathematical physics. As was mentioned in "Copernicus and the Moving Earth," in the later Middle Ages the Church had adopted Aristotelian philosophy in a thoroughgoing way, to result in Aristotelianized Christianity. Descartes was encouraged to think, by Mersenne and others, that his mathematical physics could replace that of Aristotle in a new synthesis of science and religion. So the *Meditations* was written for the purpose of laying the philosophical foundations for the new physics in a way which would be acceptable and attractive to the Church.

125. Descartes did not use the term "consciousness." It was introduced by Locke, but it has been used in connection with Descartes ever since. It is really nonsense to talk about "outside of consciousness," because consciousness is not spatial in Descartes's philosophy (or even apart from Descartes's philosophy!). This is just one example of the kind of insoluble difficulty Descartes gets into. Yet we find it very difficult to let go of this picture.

126. Steiner, *Goethe's World View*, 25.

127. Quoted in Heinrich O. Proskauer, *The Rediscovery of Color* (Spring Valley, New York: Anthroposophic Press, 1986), 106. See also Descartes, *Meditations*, Third Meditation.

128. Burtt points out that the effect of placing the secondary qualities within human beings is the "banishing of man" from nature— "Hence the real world must be the world outside of man" (89).

129. Westfall, 38.

130. See, for example, Antony Flew, *An Introduction to Western Philosophy*, rev. ed. (London: Thames and Hudson, 1989), 282.

131. See, for example, G.B. Madison, *The Hermeneutics of Postmodernity*; also the introduction to *After Philosophy*, ed. Kenneth Baynes, James Bohman, and Thomas McCarthy (Cambridge, Mass.: MIT Press, 1987).

132. Gurwitsch, *Phenomenology and the Theory of Science*, 55; Gurwitsch, "Galilean Physics in the Light of Husserl's Phenomenology," 87.

133. Ibid. This means that mathematical physics is to be understood as what is now called a research program.

134. Hübner, *Critique of Scientific Reason*, 48.

135. Quoted in Sepper, *Goethe Contra Newton*, 24.

136. Burtt, *The Metaphysical Foundations of Modern Science*, 81.

137. Ibid., 91, 98.

138. It is often said that time is "spatialized" in this process. But it should be noticed that space itself has been reduced to the form of quantitative space, and that it is really the form of quantity which is fundamental here.

139. On the very different approach of the medieval scientist to the qualities of nature, see Jeremy Naydler, "The Regeneration of Realism and the Recovery of a Science of Qualities," *International Philosophical Quarterly* 23 (1983): 155–72.

140. The complete text appears in Stillman Drake, *Discoveries and Opinions of Galileo* (New York: Doubleday, 1957).

141. Ibid., 274.

142. Democritus; quoted in Irwin, 49.

143. Quoted in Proskauer, *The Rediscovery of Color*, 140. Chaps. 6–9 of this book give an excellent account of the problems arising from the way that the senses are conceived in modern physics. Proskauer goes further than most treatments of this topic by indicating how the senses might be understood differently from this, and the influence which this could have on the science of color.

144. Burtt, 90.

145. Spinoza, *Ethics*, pt. 1, prop. III; Proskauer, 113.

146. The text of Newton's letter of 1672 to the Royal Society is given in Michael Roberts and E.R. Thomas, *Newton and the Origin of Colours* (London: Bell, 1934), 71–91. All quotations from this letter, as well as quotations from subsequent letters defending his new theory of colors, are taken from Roberts and Thomas. Ronchi points out that Newton began his experiments in the year following the publication of *De Luminae* by Grimaldi, and that "probably the mention of the 'celebrated phenomenon of colours' in the letter quoted above, was a reference to the investigation that Grimaldi made, and recorded in his book, into the behaviour of prisms and the nature of colours"—see Vasco Ronchi, *The Nature of Light* (London: Heinemann, 1970), 162.

147. Newton was wrong. The problem can be solved practically by making an achromatic doublet out of two lenses of different glass. This method was discovered by Chester Moor Hall, a London barrister whose hobby was making optical instruments.

148. The expression *experimentum crucis* is a misquotation of Francis Bacon's *instantia crucies*. See Alexandre Koyré, *Newtonian Studies* (Chicago: University of Chicago Press, 1965), 42, n. 3.

149. All quotations from Newton's letter to the Royal Society in 1672 have been taken from the text of this letter as it appears in Roberts and Thomas.

150. Casper Hakfoort, "Newton's Optics: The Changing Spectrum of Science," in *Let Newton Be!*, ed. John Fauvel, Raymond Flood, Michael Shortland, and Robin Wilson (Oxford: Oxford University Press, 1988), 84-89.

151. Newton discussed his distrust of hypotheses, and his insistence on experiment, in a further letter to Oldenburg (July 8, 1672):

> You know, the proper method for inquiring after the properties of things, is to deduce them, from Experiments. And I told you that the Theory which I propounded, was evinced to me, not by inferring 'tis this because not otherwise, that is, not by deducing it only from a confutation of contrary suppositions, but by deriving it from Experiments concluding positively and directly. The way therefore to examine it is, by considering, whether the Experiments which I propound do prove those parts of the Theory, to which they are applied; or by prosecuting other Experiments which the Theory may suggest for its examination.

152. Hakfoort, 85.

153. Cohen, *The Newtonian Revolution,* 138.

154. There is an interesting parallel in the case of Charles Darwin. In his autobiography he wrote "I worked on true Baconian principles, and without any theory collected facts on a wholesale scale . . . ." He also said, in the introduction to *The Origin of Species*, that "after five years' work I allowed myself to speculate on the subject and drew up some short notes." But his early notebooks, begun shortly after the voyage of the *Beagle*, tell a different story (cf. Newton's early notebooks). They indicate that Darwin became committed to an evolutionary viewpoint much sooner—"transformism," as it was then called, was all the rage in one form or another in the medical schools in London when he returned. Furthermore, in a private letter he expressed the non-Baconian view that "no one could be a good observer unless that individual was an active theorizer," and that ". . . all observation must be for or against some view if it is to be of any service."

As with Newton's publication of his new theory about light and colors, Darwin's account of evolution by natural selection, *The Origin of Species*, is really a careful exercise in rhetoric, arranged to persuade the reader while at the same time leading him or her to believe that the conclusions come directly from observations. What

Darwin presented was not a new factual discovery, or even a multitude of such discoveries, but a new organizing idea. The factual content is presented in the mode of this organizing idea, and hence it can easily seem that evolution by natural selection is a fact. Once again, we need to be aware of the distinction between the way of seeing and what is seen, while realizing that whereas these can be distinguished, they cannot be separated. We cannot have the content without the container, but we can stop confusing the two.

155. Goethe particularly disliked Descartes's mechanical philosophy:

> He employs the crudest analogies from the world of the senses to explain that which is intangible or even incomprehensible. Hence his various kinds of matter, his vortices, his screws, hooks and prongs are debasing to the mind.

Quoted in H. B. Nisbet, *Goethe and the Scientific Tradition* (London: University of London, Institute of Germanic Studies, 1972), 54, n.221.

156. Hakfoort, 98.

157. This happened with the development of quantum mechanics, when the threefold synthesis broke down because of difficulty with the theoretical component arising from the inapplicability of what Goethe called "analogies from the world of the senses" (note 155). Bohr referred to this as "the wish for sensuous presentation," which he and others (often as a result of Bohr's persuasion) believed it was impossible to achieve completely in any understanding of the atomic world. Bohr attempted to restore the theoretical component in a limited way by means of his principle of complementarity. Much has been written about this, especially in the last decade, but the fact remains that there is no consensus to this day.

158. For a history of the fundamental changes in optical science at the beginning of the nineteenth century, see J. Buchwald, *The Rise of the Wave Theory of Light* (Chicago: Chicago University Press, 1989).

159. Hakfoort, 81.

160. See all parts of "Making the Phenomenon Visible" in part II of this book.

161. See Richard E. Palmer, *Hermeneutics* (Evanston, Illinois: Northwestern University Press, 1969), 128. See also "The Depth of the Phenomenon."

162. Proskauer, *The Rediscovery of Color*, includes a prism and cards especially prepared for practical work.

163. This is described in detail in "The Primal Phenomenon of Color" in part II of this book.

164. The term "edge spectra" is appropriate because "spectrum" simply means "something to look at." However, an effort has to be made to disengage from the way that this term is now used in physics, following Newton, to mean the so-called spectrum of light. In this usage it is taken to mean the separation of colors which are already present *in* the light. We have explored this in some detail in the previous section, and should therefore now be able to recognize that this is an interpretation of the phenomenon derived from a theoretical perspective, and not a description of the phenomenon as such.

165. Quoted in Proskauer, 32. What follows, with reference to understanding Newton's observations, is based on the excellent practical account in chapter 1 of this work.

166. Sepper, *Goethe Contra Newton*, 27–38.

167. This procedure of dividing a visible object into point-like elements seems to have been introduced by the Arabian scientist who is known in the West as Alhazen (965?–1039). His work became known in Western Europe by a number of routes and eventually formed the conceptual basis of Kepler's book, *Ad Vitellionem Paralipomena* (1604), which itself formed the basis for the subsequent development of instrumental optics. The success of this science, in making the location of images calculable, for example, depends on the procedure of replacing a continuous source of light with a very large (infinite) number of point sources. For the contribution of Alhazen to the development of optics, see Vasco Ronchi, *The Nature of Light*. We have seen that Newton's interest in color was motivated by the wish to improve the quality of the image formed by the lenses in the refracting telescope.

168. See Proskauer, 14. It is interesting to notice that in this case the overlap color, ruby-magenta, is conceived as the mixing of red and violet, whereas in the case of the spectrum the color which occupies the equivalent position, green, is conceived as an elementary color (within the light) and not as the mixing of yellow and blue.

169. Ibid., 15.

170. It helps in this case also to use another figure, similar to the one considered here, except that the bright red rectangle is replaced by one which is white. The discussion given here is very compressed, and there are really many intermediate observations which should be carefully considered to bring out the phenomenon clearly. Space does not permit these to be described here, but full details will be found in Proskauer, *The Rediscovery of Color*, from which the account given here is taken.

171. Quoted in G. Daniel Goehring, "Newton's First Observation of Differential Refraction," *The School Science Review*, 59/207 (December

1977). The passage is cited in A.R. Hall, "Sir Isaac Newton's Note-book, 1661–5," *Cambridge Historical Journal* 9 (1948): 247–48.

172. Proskauer, 25.

173. Ibid.

174. Ibid., 25–26, for a description of this experiment.

175. The complete text of this essay appears in *Goethe: Scientific Studies* ed. D. Miller (New York: Suhrkamp, 1988).

176. Sepper, 70.

177. Ibid.

178. Ibid., 71.

179. Steiner, *Goethe the Scientist*, 189.

180. Miller, 310.

181. Taken from "The Experiment as Mediator between Subject and Object." See Miller, 16.

182. Indeed, this has been mythologized into an image of Faraday as some kind of empirically minded simpleton—a myth which has been used recently for political purposes in connection with the funding of scientific research in Britain. Fortunately, some excellent historical work has been done which shows that this myth is unfounded.

183. In the preface to the first edition of *A Treatise on Electricity and Magnetism*, Maxwell said:

> . . . before I began the study of electricity I resolved to read no math-ematics on the subject till I had first read through Faraday's *Experimental Researches on Electricity*. I was aware that there was supposed to be a difference between Faraday's way of conceiving phenomena and that of the mathematicians, so that neither he nor they were sat-isfied with each other's language. I had also the conviction that this discrepancy did not arise from either party being wrong.

Maxwell then went on to say:

> As I proceeded with the study of Faraday, I perceived that his method of conceiving the phenomena was also a mathematical one, though not exhibited in the conventional form of mathemati-cal symbols.

184. Proskauer, 38.

185. Goethe did not use the term *Urphänomen* in *Contribution to Optics* or in the essay "The Experiment as Mediator between Subject and Object," which was written shortly afterwards. He introduced the notion under this name in his *Colour Theory* (1810), but seems to have made use of the notion as early as 1793—see Sepper, 149. This is dis-cussed in "The Primal Phenomenon of Color" in part II of this book.

186. Quoted in Proskauer, 43.

187. Ibid., 84.

188. The way that refraction provides an occasion for the appearance of color is treated in detail by Proskauer in chapter 4 of *The Rediscovery of Color*. Although he maintains that "an exact work on the precise manner in which the processes in the prism take place has yet to be written" (85), Proskauer himself gives a very clear indication of the direction such a work would take.

189. See Lehrs, *Man or Matter*, 109. In "The Primal Phenomenon of Color," this was rendered as "exact sensorial imagination," whereas Lehrs translates it as "exact sensorial fantasy."

190. Hjalmar Hegge, "Goethe's Science of Nature," in *Goethe and the Sciences: A Reappraisal*, ed. Frederick Amrine, Frank J. Zucker and Harvey Wheeler, 196–99.

191. Dennis L. Sepper, "Goethe Against Newton: Towards Saving the Phenomena," in *Goethe and the Sciences: A Reappraisal*, 187.

192. Cf. Hegge, 205.

193. The distinction between analytic and empirical propositions is discussed at the end of "The Idea of Inertial Motion."

194. Hegge, 206. Hegge emphasizes that the way Goethe combines empirical observation with the discovery of apodeictic necessity (i.e., that which cannot be otherwise) in the phenomena, is the pattern for all his work in natural science. Goethe does not maintain that these connections can be derived from sense experience—"He is empirical, but not an empiricist." In fact an organ of perception, which he calls exact sensory imagination, has to be developed to perceive these necessary connections. These *inner* connections, which overcome the mutual separation of phenomena as they are first encountered, appear as the real nature of the phenomena. (External connections, on the other hand, try to overcome separation in an external way, which, paradoxically, has the effect of confirming it). It is important that this necessity is *within* the phenomena, and not behind the phenomena as in the two-world theory. Hegge emphasizes how much closer Goethe is here to the Aristotelian tradition in science than to the Galilean–Newtonian tradition (213).

195. Immanuel Kant, *Critique of Pure Reason*, translated by Norman Kemp Smith (London: Macmillan, 1964), *Bxii-Bxiv*, 20.

196. Miller, 39.

197. See "The Organizing Idea in Cognitive Perception" for a discussion of the active sense of organizing. The organizing act is an act which

is "organizing," so we refer to it here as "active-organizing." It was also pointed out at the end of that chapter that "organizing" is used to mean the primary act of "distinguishing which is relating,"and not the secondary operation of ordering what is already distinguished. The difficulty is always to "go upstream," to catch things in their coming-into-being instead of "downstream" at the finished product stage. But this is crucial to understanding the difference between thinking and thought. What is said here about the ontological manifestation of the active–organizing principle in the researcher's thinking activity depends on understanding this difference. There is a kinship between the *thinking* activity of the researcher and the intrinsic organizing activity in nature. We are reminded here of Parmenides' statement that "thinking and being are one, the same." This does not mean that the active–organizing principle is in nature *in the same way* that it *manifests* in human thinking. The failure to understand this results in the error of animism.

198. The key notion of the receptive will was discussed by Georg Kühlewind in a course of public lectures on "The Creative Power of the Human Being," given at Emerson College in May 1991. The difficulty we have in understanding this notion is that we think in terms of either/or, which in this case means either "active" or "not active," i.e., passive. But the receptive will is *not* passive. One way of looking at receptivity is to see it as the reconciliation of two opposites: activity and passivity. It is a third state, which is neither active nor passive, yet which includes both of these in such a way that each is transformed by the presence of the other. But this is a new condition, a third state, not a compromise or some kind of "average" of active and passive.

199. Cf. Goethe's views on the relationship between science and art, as he expressed them in his *Sprüche in Prosa*. See Steiner, *Goethe the Scientist*, chap. 18.

200. That is, the so-called Cartesian dualism. The problem here is that there is no possible way that the supposed correspondence of an idea in the mind with the outer world could be checked. Hence "knowledge" becomes problematic. No such difficulty arose for Aristotle, who would have found the Goethean cognitive participation in the phenomenon very familiar. Aristotle's theory of knowledge has by no means always been described correctly by modern writers. An exception is the brilliant book by Jonathan Lear, *Aristotle: The Desire to Understand* (Cambridge: Cambridge University Press, 1988). See chap. 4, especially section 4.3. See also Naydler,155–72.

201. In this respect, Goethe is in tune with premodern thought, i.e., prior to the dualistic theory of knowledge. Gadamer points out

"that knowledge incorporated in being is the presupposition of all classical and medieval thought" (*Truth and Method*, 458). But what this means for us now is that knowledge is not just a subjective state, but a state of the object which occurs in the subject. Goethe provides us with a practical way towards the experience of this involvement of being in knowledge, referred to by Gadamer, but in a manner which is appropriate for us today—i.e., after modern thought instead of before it.

202. Quoted in Easlea, 128.

203. Carolyn Merchant, *The Death of Nature* (London: Wildwood House, 1982), 168.

204. As well as describing the means whereby this could be done, Bacon was also concerned to show that (and under what circumstances) domination over nature is a legitimate aim for science to have. In the passage from the *Critique of Pure Reason* quoted earlier (see note 195), Kant says that Reason must devise experiments with which to "approach nature in order to be taught by it," but that it must do so in the manner "of an appointed judge who compels the witnesses to answer questions which he or she have themselves formulated." It seems likely that this very well-known statement of Kant's directly reflects Bacon's courtroom image of the experimental philosophy—especially in view of the fact that Kant extols Bacon, in the paragraph previous to the one quoted, for "his ingenious proposals."

205. In this respect Goethe was like Aristotle, who believed that, as well as the familiar enumerative induction from sensory particulars, there was a further kind of induction which entailed a direct insight into what is essential in the phenomenon (i.e., into what *cannot* be otherwise). It is interesting that this is not discussed in most books on the philosophy of science, which limit themselves to the enumerative induction favored by classical empiricism—and shown by Hume to be incapable of providing a basis for scientific knowledge.

206. Hegge, 215. See the discussion of exact sensory imagination, 209-15. See also Arthur G. Zajonc, "Fact as Theory: Aspects of Goethe's Philosophy of Science," in *Goethe and the Sciences: A Reappraisal*, 238-42.

207. Weinsheimer, *Gadamer's Hermeneutics*, 69.

208. Zajonc, 240.

209. This leaves aside the question of whether the genius of the artist could do this. The characteristic of this genius is that it can embody the nonsensible in the sensible, so that the nonsensible manifests

directly as appearance. The magic of the artistic transformation of matter is that it does the impossible—think of Cézanne painting the *existence* of apples! So we cannot preclude the possibility that a work of art could embody the unity of a plant, but we can say that this cannot be depicted by sensory representation, e.g., by a color slide.

210. Flew, 46.

211. *Meno*, 72 c and d (Penguin edition).

212. *Metaphysics*, 1078 b 13-35.

213. This refers mainly to philosophers in the continental tradition, whether they are in Europe or in America. There may well be other philosophers who disagree with this on the grounds that the two-world theory, as it developed in Western philosophy, is really a counterfeit form of metaphysics (and should therefore be thought of as pseudometaphysics) which obscures authentic metaphysics. Whether this is the case or not, the fact remains that this *is* what "metaphysics" has come to mean in the mainstream of Western thought, and this is what many contemporary philosophers now see as a deeply influential formative influence on Western thought. Western studies of Asian philosophy have begun to recognize that often this has not been understood because it has been seen through metaphysical spectacles by Western interpreters—this is particularly exemplified in Western studies of Taoism, for example. [See Roger T. Ames, "Putting the *Te* Back into Taoism," in *Nature in Asian Traditions of Thought,* ed. J. Baird Callicott and Roger T. Ames (Albany, New York: State University of New York Press, 1989)]. Whether we say that metaphysics *is* the two-world theory, and that what other traditions are doing is not metaphysics (as Heidegger does) or we say that what is called metaphysics in the Western tradition is only pseudometaphysics, and there is the possibility of a genuine metaphysics different from this—may well come down to simply two different ways of saying the same thing. However, those who adopt one or the other of these viewpoints may not feel strongly inclined to agree with this. The problem here may be, once again, a consequence of not seeing things sufficiently comprehensively.

214. Madison, *The Hermeneutics of Postmodernity*, 130. There remains the question of whether, and to what extent, Plato himself made the metaphysical separation. Certainly modern translations of the *Phaedo* and the *Republic* (two major texts for the theory of Forms) make it seem that he did. But then these are *modern* translations, and therefore inevitably read Plato through the spectacles of a long historical tradition, namely the metaphysical tradition. Heidegger strongly emphasized that the separation was present in Plato, and he saw the history of Western philosophy as the history of the

attempt to understand Being as "the Being of beings" beginning with Plato. Gadamer, on the other hand, who is a lifelong student of Plato, thinks the two-world interpretation of Plato is mistaken. He referred to this view as pseudo-Platonism, in a talk on "Unity in Heidegger's Thinking" given at the conference on *Heiddegger, Hermeneutics and Interpretation*, organized jointly by the Goethe Institute, London, and the British Society for Phenomenology (April 7–8, 1986).

Steiner referred to the two-world theory as one-sided Platonism. He saw it as a fundamental influence in the historical development of Western thought, and scientific thought in particular. He indicates in *Goethe's World View* that the two-world theory, with its ontological hierarchy (one *over* many) and distrust of the sensory, did not originate from a failure in Plato's understanding but from the way that he presented it, especially the way that he presented the relation between idea and sense experience. Heidegger also seems to have thought that the difficulty arose from the way that Plato presented his insight. Whatever the case may be, the fact is that it is one-sided Platonism, with its hierarchical two-world theory, which forms the basis of the Western metaphysical tradition according to which the sensory and the intelligible are conceived as existing separately. Aristotle's concern may have been not to reject Plato, but to correct the imbalance between the sensory and the intelligible, the many and the one, which arose in the way in which Plato presented their relationship. Steiner describes Plato's fundamental insight as being the recognition that reality cannot be attributed to the sense world *if this is regarded only by itself,* but only when it is "shone through by the light of ideas." If it is not shone through by the light of ideas, *then and only then* is it "a world of semblance." He describes Plato's error as follows:

> Plato did not stop short at emphasizing the knowledge that, in *human perception* the sense world becomes a mere semblance if the light of the world of ideas is not shone upon it, but rather, through the way he presented this fact, he furthered the belief that the sense world, in and for itself, irrespective of humanity, is a world of semblance, and that true reality is to be found only in ideas. (17)

This is what Aristotle tried to correct. What needs to be taken into account is the way that humanity itself is involved in the process of cognition. This is what we always forget: the way in which we ourselves are part of things. But Aristotle's attempt to correct Plato's distortion did not succeed. One-sided Platonism was carried forward historically through an alliance with Western (Roman) Christianity. This became the vehicle which carried it into the mainstream of Western thought. Aristotle himself was later misunderstood within this historical tradition, and often presented as if he had been in fundamental opposition to Plato. Approaching Aristotle in this way produces its own distortion—what could be called one-sided Aristotelianism.

215. H. Brady, " 257–300.

216. Copleston, vol. 4, 220.

217. Gerbert Grohmann, *The Plant*, vol. 1 (Kimberton, Pa.: Bio-Dynamic Literature, 1989), 26.

218. John Seymour, *The Countryside Explained* (London: Faber and Faber, 1977), 116.

219. By "external world" is meant the world in which externality is the primary feature, i.e., the bodily spatial world. It does not have the meaning which it usually has for our commonsense understanding, i.e., the world outside of ourselves.

220. Stephen J. Gould, *Ever Since Darwin* (Harmondsworth: Penguin Books, 1980), chap. 11.

221. Grohmann, *The Plant*, vol. 1, 25.

222. Steiner, *Goethe the Scientist*, 62: "The unity attains to reality in that which is perceived simultaneously with the manifoldness, as being identical with it."

223. Ernst Cassirer, *The Philosophy of Symbolic Forms*, vol. 1 (New Haven: Yale University Press, 1953), 155. Cassirer is concerned with the impact which the idea of the organic had on the understanding of language which was developed in Goethe's day by Herder and Wilhelm von Humboldt. He says further:

> For the philosophy of language this new conception of the universal meant abandonment of the quest for a basic, original language behind the diversity and historical contingency of the individual languages: it also meant that the true universal "essence" of language was no longer sought in abstraction from differentiation, but in the totality of differentiations.

It is interesting that the category of the organic was found to be so illuminating for the study of language and meaning at that time. The philosophy of language and meaning developed by Gadamer today also exemplifies the organic as a fundamental principle. An account of this is in preparation.

224. See part I of this book.

225. Stephen Edelglass, Georg Maier, Hans Gerbert, and John Davy, *Mind and Matter: Imaginative Participation in Science* (Hudson, N.Y.: Lindisfarne Press, 1992), show that this "choice" is grounded in the selection of one group of human senses as being more fundamental than others, namely, the senses of the body, such as touch.

226. The question which arises naturally at this point is whether it is in this perspective of "multiplicity in unity," the intensive dimension of One, that Plato's theory of Forms should be understood. If we look at what Steiner said about Plato, in note 214 above (see also note 112), we see that the emphasis is on the sense world being shone through by the light of ideas. Now it seems that if the sense world appears *in the light of ideas,* then this would be seeing multiplicity in the light of unity. Hence the perspective in which Plato can be understood correctly is inside-out with respect to the way that he is usually understood—"multiplicity in unity" instead of "unity in multiplicity." The theory of Forms takes on a new light when it is seen in the intensive dimension of One. If this is so, then it has some significance for the contemporary debate about the metaphysical tradition. It would mean that a distinction would have to be made between "counterfeit" and "authentic" metaphysics (cf. note 213). What has been called metaphysics hitherto in the Western philosophical tradition would now appear to be only a counterfeit form of metaphysics arising from an impoverished mode of unity. It seems possible that "authentic" metaphysics, grounded in the intensive dimension of One, may have been understood in the early Church, before the separation into Western (Roman) and Eastern (Greek) Christianity. Philip Sherrard has indicated how the Eastern Church was much more organic in its constitution and theology, whereas the Western Church became much more authoritarian—reflecting the (counterfeit) metaphysical separation of one-sided Platonism. See Philip Sherrard, *Church, Papacy and Schism* (London: SPCK, 1978). See also the same author's *The Eclipse of Man and Nature* (Hudson, NY: Lindisfarne Press, 1987)—but it should be noted that the views of Aristotle to which the author refers in this book belong more to the distortion and misunderstanding of Aristotle in the Middle Ages (fifteen hundred years after his death) than they do to Aristotle himself. Rudolf Steiner refers to the new interpretation given to Aristotle by the Christian philosophers and theologians of the Middle Ages in *Goethe's World View*, 22. Fortunately, a lot of work has now been done toward the rehabilitation of Aristotle—see, for example, Jonathan Lear's *Aristotle*, referred to in note 200.

The question of the universal and the particular which became central in medieval philosophy, and the associated argument between realism and nominalism, is also illuminated by seeing it in the perspective of "multiplicity in unity" instead of "unity in multiplicity." Many of the difficulties which arose concerning the universal and the particular disappear in the inside-out perspective of the intensive dimension of One, because they originate from the mode of unity associated with the extensive perspective. Referring to what is said about concepts in "The Organizing Idea in Cognitive Perception," one can ascertain that a concept itself has the form of "multiplicity in unity" and not "unity in multiplicity." Meaning is akin to life, not to solid bodies.

227. Steiner, *Goethe the Scientist,* 17.

228. Brady, 286.

229. Steiner, *A Theory of Knowledge Based on Goethe's World Conception,* 88. See also the same author's *Goethe the Scientist*, chap. 4, for an extended discussion of Goethe's notion of organic Type.

230. See Steiner, *Goethe the Scientist,* 60. Steiner gives a thorough account of this aspect of Goethe's scientific work in his essay "The Nature and Significance of Goethe's Writings on Organic Morphology," which appears in *Goethe the Scientist*, 50–86.

   See also Steiner, *A Theory of Knowledge Based on Goethe's World Conception*, chap. 16. The term "entelechy" was used by Aristotle, and it has often been taken in a teleological sense to imply the presence of purpose in living nature analogous to human purpose. Goethe rejected any such notion of goal-directed activity in nature, and it is important that we do not unwittingly read it into his work. See Brady, 288–89.

231. This is equivalent to suddenly introducing a statement about the dynamics of motion in a discussion in physics which, up to that point, had been restricted to the kinematics of motion. Something like such a jump from the descriptive level to the causal is made here when, instead of describing the mode of unity which pertains to the archetypal plant, a reference is made to the dynamics, i.e., the One *brings* the many out of itself. It is this jump from the descriptive to the causal which makes this statement jarring at the place where it occurs in the text above (264). But this was the step which Goethe was able to make in experience, i.e., he encountered the intrinsic dynamic of the archetypal plant.

232. Lehrs, 82.

233. In talks given at the International Academy for Continuous Education, Sherborne, Gloucestershire, in 1974.

234. Finished product thinking imagines that "invisible" means the same as "not visible" in which case we would imagine, for example, that the furniture in a dark room is invisible—whereas it is in fact merely not visible. The event of appearance, whereby something *becomes* visible, i.e., manifests, requires us to think in the dynamic mode of coming-into-being.

235. This is possible with participative consciousness but not with onlooker consciousness. Aristotle's philosophy of knowledge allows

this to be described. This is *not* intended to suggest that Goethe's way of science must be described in terms of Aristotle's epistemology. On the contrary, the suggestion is more that Goethe's way of science can provide a practical approach to understanding Aristotle's epistemology. A common mistake in describing Aristotle's philosophy seems to be to see it in the perspective of onlooker consciousness, as if he were a modern man. Careful accounts, on the other hand, which endeavour to be true to Aristotle, bring out the fact that he describes knowledge as it is for participative consciousness—see, for example, Lear (note 200). Lear does not use the term "participative consciousness," but it is clear from his account that this is what he is describing.

236. See Erich Heller, *The Disinherited Mind* (Harmondsworth, Middlesex: Penguin Books, 1961), 9.

237. Steiner, *Goethe the Scientist*, 61.

238. Steiner, *Riddles of Philosophy* (New York: The Anthroposophic Press, 1973), 144.

239. This is always a source of difficulty because we do not take into account the fact that we ourselves, i.e., as human beings, are an integral part of the process of the world. What appears in the light of consciousness manifests appearingly—in fact, it *manifests*. This is then its mode of being. But we believe that consciousness is separated from an already formed world, i.e., a world that is finished independently of humanity and is "just there," as it appears when seen, regardless of whether it is seen or not. Furthermore, we believe that consciousness is subjective, and hence that if something appears only in the light of consciousness, this would mean that it is only subjective. So it *seems* that the view being expressed here makes the appearance of the world subjective—which we would rightly reject. If we can just suspend the perspective of the onlooker consciousness, *then* we may catch a glimpse of just what an extraordinary thing the appearance of the world really is, and at the same time realize that we ourselves, i.e., as human beings, are intrinsically involved in the coming-into-appearance of the world. Without humanity the world could only be nonappearing.

240. Brady shows that it is the formative movement which generates forms, so that we must begin *from this movement itself* and not from a single form or some common underlying schema. Any single form is really an abstraction (a "snapshot") from this formative movement. The unity of the plant *is* this movement, not some underlying common form.

241. Steiner, *Goethe the Scientist*, 21.

242. Steiner, *Goethe's World View*, 81.

243. Cesalpino in the sixteenth century proposed that the various organs of the plant were modifications of the leaf—see Agnes Arber, *The Natural Philosophy of Plant Form* (Cambridge, Mass.: Cambridge University Press, 1950). Steiner mentions that the work of the English botanist Hill on the transformation of individual flower organs into one another, was well known in Goethe's time— see *Goethe the Scientist*, 23.

244. Grohmann, *The Plant*, vol. 1, 63, gives a photograph of a dandelion showing this abnormality.

245. See Brady, 272. Grohmann, *The Plant*, vol. 1, 43, gives diagrams of the transition from petal to stamen in the white water lily. See diagram in part II of this volume (82). See also Daniel McAlpine, *The Botanical Atlas* (Edinburgh, 1883; London: Bracken Books, 1989), 101.

246. *Natürliche Einstellung*—which would probably be better translated as "habitual standpoint." See Erazim Kohák, *Idea and Experience* (Chicago: University of Chicago Press, 1978), 31–32. Husserl is a difficult philosopher to understand in his original language, and even more so in English translation. This book is an outstandingly successful guide to Husserl's *Ideas towards a Pure Phenomenology and Phenomenological Philosophy, Book 1* (usually known as *Ideas 1*). Kohák's ability to present Husserl's fundamental insight in terms of examples taken from ordinary experience is particularly helpful for anyone who wishes to understand that insight for themselves.

247. The definition of "intentionality" which is often given is unhelpful at best, and at worst misleading, on account of the fact that it is too easily interpreted within the framework of the natural standpoint, which defeats Husserl's purpose. This is the definition of intentionality as the characteristic of experience that it is, and *must* be, experience *of* something—in the well-known formula "experience is always experience of —." The definition of intentionality in terms of the correlation of what is experienced with the way it is experienced is more comprehensive and informative.

248. Don Ihde, *Experimental Phenomenology* (Albany, New York: State University of New York Press, 1986), 42–43. See also Richard Kearney, *Modern Movements in European Philosophy* (Manchester: Manchester University Press, 1986), 13 ff.

249. Michael Hammond, Jane Howarth, and Russel Keat, *Understanding Phenomenology* (Oxford: Blackwell, 1991), 48. The unitary condition of the noesis–noema correlation comes *before* the separation into subject and object. This separation occurs subsequently due to the focusing of attention on the object of consciousness instead of the act of consciousness. The subject–object separation occurs as a

result of "falling" from the correlation into separation. But this is the level at which we are awake in the onlooker mode of consciousness. When the polarity is not recognized, the act of conceiving and what is conceived fall apart. The act is then imagined as the act of an entity—the subject—because this is how it must seem in the light of "separation." So we have the notion of a separate, independent entity, the subject (now conceived as an object), to perform the act. Similarly, what is conceived is now considered as being separate from the act of conceiving, and therefore as an independent entity, the object.

A widely held, but mistaken view of phenomenology sees it as a variety of subjectivism. According to this viewpoint, the correlation of the act of consciousness with the object of consciousness means that a structure is *imposed* on the world by consciousness. It should be clear that this presupposes a *separation* between world and consciousness which belongs to the stage of subject–object separation, and not to the stage of the noesis–noema correlation which is prior to this. In other words, talking about consciousness imposing structures on the world belongs to the very Cartesian dualism which phenomenology seeks to overcome. Phenomenology cannot be reduced to a variety of subjectivism.

It is well known that Heiddegger was critical of Husserl on the ground, that the latter's phenomenology did not succeed in overcoming Cartesian dualism. The basis of his criticism seems to have been that Husserl's mode of expression reinforced the very Cartesian dualism which it was supposed to overcome. Hence Heiddegger believed that Husserl's work was internally self-defeating, and he proposed the much more radical approach which he took in *Being and Time*. But Husserl should not be seen too readily through Heidegger's eyes. Gadamer has said that successful interpretation depends on goodwill, and that goodwill in interpretation is to take the other in his or her intention and not in his or her expression. If we approach Husserl in this way, then we do find it becoming quite clear that what he is concerned with is the nondualistic condition of cognition prior to the stage of separation into subject and object. In other words, we *can* encounter this through Husserl's work, notwithstanding any difficulties in the way of doing so arising from Husserl's mode of expression. An example of an interpretation which is grounded in goodwill, and which succeeds in taking the reader beyond the limitation of dualism, is the excellent work on Husserl by Erazim Kohák mentioned in note 246.

250. Edmund Husserl, *Cartesian Meditations* (The Hague: Martinus Nijhoff, 1960), 39: "Inquiry into consciousness concerns *two sides* . . . ; they can be characterized descriptively as *belonging together*

inseparably"—quoted in Hammond, Howarth, and Keat, *Understanding Phenomenology*, 49. Thus, in the phenomenological perspective, "noetic description describes acts of consciousness, but in so doing will make reference to *objects* of consciousness; noematic description describes the objects of consciousness, but in so doing will make reference to acts of consciousness" (ibid., 49).

Aristotle also described perception and cognition as *acts*, and in this philosopher, too, we find an inseparable "belonging together" of the two sides which Husserl refers to above. Thus, for Aristotle, perception is a single event with both a subjective and an objective aspect, which can be distinguished but not separated. In Aristotle's terminology, the actualizing of the agent and the actualizing of the patient are one and the same event. There is a single actualization in perception and cognition which has two sides, as it were, which we (not Aristotle) wrongly divorce into two separate entities, namely, subject and object, which we then imagine as independent existences which have, somehow, to be brought together in perception and cognition (hence the *problem* of epistemology). Aristotle's account of perception and cognition is lucidly described in Lear's *Aristotle*.

Looking back to "The Quantitative Way of Seeing," we can now recognize that the world of solid bodies is a noesis-noema correlation. It is not an object, i.e., the world external to and therefore separate from consciousness, existing independently in a bodily spatial manner. What we mean by the solid world is what appears in the light of the quantitative way of seeing—which could equally well be called the "solid" mode of cognition. What appears and how it appears, the way of seeing, are *necessarily* correlated. So the world of bodies, in all its aspects (separation, externality, quantity, fragmentation, identity, fixity, solidification, and mechanical causality) is a noesis–noema correlation, and not a realm of entities which is independent of the mode of cognition to which it appears (which does *not* mean the world of bodies is subjective). To think of the world of bodies as if it were independent of cognition is in fact a consequence of seeing cognition itself in the perspective of the world of solid bodies. When we think of the subject separate from the object, each what it is independently of the other, and the subject knowing the object in the manner of the causal theory of perception, then this very way of conceiving cognition is how it appears to be in the light of the "solid body" mode of cognition. There is no escape: we cannot stand outside the way of seeing. But what we can do is to become aware of the way of seeing as such, and thereby recognize the possibility of a change *within* the noesis–noema correlation, by means of a change in the way of seeing

251. It is a shift of attention *within* the original noesis–noema correlation itself. Gadamer has commented on what he calls the naïveté of reflection. This is the view that reflection is a new act of cognition, effectively constituting a new object of cognition, which in this case is the original act of cognition itself. He emphasizes that it is a feature of twentieth-century philosophy, especially phenomenology, to overcome this naïveté of reflection, which he sees as characteristic of earlier modern philosophy. Referring to the phenomenological perspective, Gadamer says:

> The kind of knowledge in question here implies that not all reflection performs an objectifying function, that is, not all reflection makes what it is directed at into an object. Rather, there is an act of reflecting that, in fulfillment of an "intention," bends back, as it were, on the process itself [Hans-Georg Gadamer, *Philosophical Hermeneutics* (Berkeley: University of California Press, 1976), 123].

There is in this nonobjectifying kind of reflection a consciousness of the perceiving as well as the perceived, which accompanies the consciousness of the perceived, "and by no means only as the object of a subsequent reflection" (ibid.). Whereas such a subsequent reflection is certainly possible—it is indeed what we usually mean by reflection—it is not the only possibility. There is also the possibility of a concomitant reflection accompanying perception, which is a simultaneous awareness of the perceiving along with the perceived. Gadamer points out that, as well as being fundamental to phenomenology, this perception which is "perception of the perceiving and of the perceived in one, and in no way contains 'reflection' in the modern sense" is described correctly by Aristotle.

The same redirection of attention is really the major characteristic of the new philosophy of science. This refocuses attention into the act of cognition instead of onto what is cognized. In other words, the new philosophy of science is characterized by a shift from the known to the knowing of the known. The recognition that the noesis–noema correlation is the invariant structure of all cognitive perception enables us to understand what the philosophy of science gives us that is different from science itself. It is the fact that it enables us to understand discoveries in science in terms of the way of seeing, instead of only in terms of what is seen, which makes the philosophy of science a different kind of cognitive activity from science itself.

252. Idries Shah, *The Exploits of the Incomparable Mulla Nasrudin* (London: Octagon Press, 1983), 26.

253. Illustrations of metamorphic series of foliage leaves appear in a number of works. See, for example, Grohmann, *The Plant*, vol. 1 chap. 3; Lehrs, chap. 5.

254. Lehrs, 81.

255. This expression was used by J. G. Bennett in seminars on modes of togetherness, at the Institute for the Comparative Study of History, Philosophy and the Sciences, Kingston-on-Thames, in 1964. Wittgenstein expressed this as "nothing, and yet everything, has changed"—quoted in Ray Monk, *Ludwig Wittgenstein* (London: Vintage, 1991), 533.

256. Brady, 276.

257. Ibid., 279.

258. Ibid., 274, translated by John Barnes, the complete text of this essay appears in Miller, 63-66. This essay forms the introduction to Goethe's journal *On Morphology* (1817–1824), which contains a collection of essays, one of which, *The Metamorphosis of Plants*, had appeared previously in 1790. The introduction consists of three parts, the second of which, entitled "The Purpose Set Forth," is the one quoted from here. This essay, together with the one which forms the first part of the introduction, was originally written by Goethe in 1807. He decided to use it as part of the introduction to his later writings on morphology because he had become concerned by the tendency of biologists and others to think in a direction which was opposite to the direction of his own thinking. Hence he felt, quite rightly, that his views on morphology would be misunderstood, because those who thought they understood what he was saying would not in fact have the appropriate way of seeing. This, it has turned out, is just what has happened. For the most part, Goethe's morphological work seems to have been interpreted as being in the Platonic tradition—no doubt the use of the term "archetype" encourages this misreading. In other words, those who interpreted Goethe in this way have read Goethe metaphysically. What we discover now is that this is far from being appropriate—in fact such an interpretation marches in the opposite direction to Goethe, instead of alongside him. As with his work on color, Goethe has been interpreted in a light which is not his own, and the potentiality of his way of seeing has been eclipsed. An exception to this is the philosopher Ernst Cassirer, who wrote of Goethe that "he did not think geometrically or statically, but dynamically throughout"—quoted in Brady, 274; see Cassirer, *The Problem of Knowledge* (New Haven: Yale University Press, 1974), 138.

259. Bergson, *Creative Evolution*, 322.

260. Ibid., 324.

261. Henri Bergson, *The Creative Mind* (New Jersey: Citadel Press, 1946), 190.

262. Ibid., 34.

263. Ibid., 147.

264. Ibid.

265. The discovery that there can be a unity of time, as well as a unity of space (Gestalt), is a fundamental discovery of Goethe's way of science. See Brady, 285.

266. Friedemann-Eckart Schwarzkopf, "The Metamorphosis of the Given," Dissertation for Doctor of Philosophy, San Diego, California, 1992, 480.

267. This apt phrase is used by Martha Nussbaum in connection with Aristotle's phenomenology. See Martha C. Nussbaum, *The Fragility of Goodness* (Cambridge: Cambridge University Press, 1986), 251.

268. Davy, *Hope, Evolution and Change,* 23–25. Davy emphasizes that "the plant world asks for a schooling of the imagination not towards 'objectivity' (the grasping of objects), but towards participatory movement (thinking with *processes*)." In this connection, he writes about "possibilities of conscious participation in nature . . . without demanding special states of awareness," and how "Nature herself offers us the schooling for those faculties which are available, still mainly undisciplined, as fantasy and imagination, but which are the germs of new, entirely 'scientific' (i.e., knowledge-bringing) faculties for the future."

269. This apt phrase is used by John F. Gardner in his foreword to Wolfgang Schad, *Man and Mammals* (New York: Waldorf Press, 1977), 2.

270. Goethe, quoted in Fritz Heinemann, "Goethe's Phenomenological Method," *Philosophy* 9 (1934): 73.

271. Heinemann, 73. The notion of enhancement (*Steigerung*) was introduced by Goethe in his account of the growth of the flowering plant. Here it is aptly applied to seeing. It is typical of Goethe's approach that what is found in nature will also be found in humanity. The difference is that what is done by nature, humanity must do for itself. So there is here the important notion that this very way of working to understand nature is simultaneously a process of self-formation (*Bildung*). This emphasis on the transformation of the scientist himself through his own scientific activity is central to Goethe's way.

272. See, for example, Margaret Colquhoun, "Meeting the Buttercup Family," *Science Forum* 8 (Spring 1989). Grohmann, *The Plant*, vol. 2, also contains many examples. See also Margaret Colquhoun and

Axel Ewald, *New Eyes for Plants* (Stroud: Hawthorn Press, 1996), chap. 7.

We have referred to the movement of metamorphosis in the organs up the stem, from the first stem leaves through to the stamens. But this can be extended to other organs of the plant. Goethe describes how style, stigma, and the carpel (seed vessels) can all be understood in terms of the metamorphosis of the "leaf" (*The Metamorphosis of Plants*, par. 67–81). See also Grohmann, vol. 1, 46–9; Colquhoun and Ewald, 151. Andreas Suchantke has shown how the roots can be understood as a further metamorphosis of the "leaf," in his essay "The Leaf: "The True Proteus," which is in Jochen Bochemühl and Andreas Suchantke, *The Metamorphosis of Plants* (Cape Town, South Africa: Novalis Press, 1995).

273. Schad (note 269).

274. Ibid., 218–19, 257–65. The account which follows is taken directly from Schad.

275. Ibid., chap. 2. See also "The Unity of Animal Organization," in part II of this book. In his discussion, Schad describes the way that these systems can be supplemented to become:

> *Nerve, speech and sense system.*
>
> *Respiratory-circulatory system.*
>
> *Metabolic, reproductive and limb system.*

Although there is no need to go into this here, mention of it will be useful in the discussion which follows.

276. Davy, 88.

277. It would be very naïve to suppose that this constituted "evidence" against Darwin's theory. Biologists have shown how this theory can accommodate the most unlikely facts, and even turn them to its advantage. Anyone who is familiar with the Darwinian style of thinking will know how skillful they can be in constructing arguments to do this. In the present case, it is not difficult to imagine that they would be able to show to their own satisfaction how this fact of progressive emancipation, far from contradicting Darwinism, cannot only be explained by it but in doing so also provides even better evidence for what a good theory it is. This is the way the rhetoric of science works. The point which is being made is simply that it has not been noticed that progressive emancipation has an evolutionary significance *in itself*, because the established theory of evolution focuses our attention in the opposite direction. But of course, if we do take progressive emancipation as being of fundamental significance in itself, then we may begin to consider the possibility of a different kind of theory of evolution.

278. Of course, Darwin did not propose that one animal transmutes into another one in a large-scale way. What he proposed is the *eventual* emergence of a different species as a result of many small-scale modifications. So the origin of a new species is really a statistical effect arising as a gradual shift in a population, and is not specific to individual organisms. In this respect Darwin's theory resembles the new statistical approach to the phenomena of heat (thermodynamics) later taken by Boltzmann.

279. The difference between these two approaches to evolution can be expressed also in terms of David Bohm's distinction between implicate and explicate orders. The Darwinian approach to evolution sees it in terms of the explicate order, whereas the Goethean approach sees it in terms of the implicate order. See David Bohm, *Wholeness and the Implicate Order* (London: Routledge and Kegan Paul, 1980) for an introduction to these two different kinds of order. See also P.H. Bortoft, "*A Non-reductionist Perspective for the Quantum Theory*," Birkbeck College, University of London, 1982, sections 6 and 7, where the relationship between the implicate order and the intensive dimension of the One is discussed, and it is shown how Goethe's holistic mode of perception of the organic world provides an instance of an intrinsic implicate order.

280. One of the few contemporary commentators on the theory of evolution to recognize the interest of this alternative to the route taken by mainstream evolutionary theory is the philosopher of science D.R. Oldroyd in *Darwinian Impacts* (Milton Keynes: The Open University Press, 1980), chap. 4. He recognizes that the process of *Entwicklung*, or progressive development, "though by no means the same as the doctrine of evolution by natural selection, entailed an evolutionism of a kind." Specifically with regard to the comparison between Goethe and Darwin, he says "thus can two utterly different approaches produce explanations of the same phenomenon."

Much light has now been thrown on Darwin as a result of the approach taken by what is often referred to as the new history of science. This is the view of science which sees it as being embedded within a social, political, cultural, and historical context. It recognizes that the fundamental ideas of science have a cultural–historical basis, and furthermore that sociopolitical factors can enter into the very constitution of scientific knowledge. It does not consider scientific ideas as if they were intellectual ghosts, existing in the pure realm of some "disworlded" intellect. In this respect, the new history of science is very much in tune with the continental tradition of hermeneutic philosophy. We have seen previously how both the move to Sun-centered planetary astronomy and the introduction of atomism into physics depended on the incorporation of ideas from schools of thought which were outside of science as such. We saw that the foundations of science are cultural–historical, and that science does not have intrinsic scientific foundations, i.e., it is not self-grounding. It has been shown by Hübner in *The Critique of Scientific Reason* that such ideas enter into the very form which the detailed results of science take, and do not just remain influential at a more overall but also more superficial level. In the case of Darwin, it has been shown by Adrian Desmond and James Moore in their magnificent biography *Darwin* (London: Michael Joseph, 1991), how the sociopolitical factor of the free market economy in early Victorian, Whig England entered into the very form of Darwin's theory of natural selection. The same point was made earlier, though without the same historical detail, in J.C. Greene, *Science, Ideology and World View* (Berkeley: University of California Press, 1981). Greene comments on the fact that several others who also came up with a theory of natural selection (Darwin acknowledged them in the "Historical Sketch" which he included in later editions of *The Origin of Species*) were also British, and he sees the style of thinking which this theory involves as fitting very well with the free market economics of the industrial capitalist society which was developing in Britain at the time. A key factor here is the way that the ideas of Malthus on population and competition were incorporated directly into Darwin's theory, influencing the very form of the mechanism (as he thought of it) for evolution which he proposed. Nature and free-trade society were both driven by competition and selection: organic and social evolution were fundamentally similar in Darwin's view. So Whig society and Whig-interpreted nature could be seen as being mutually supportive, the one appearing to confirm the rightness of the other. For example, the Whig reform of the Poor Law, whereby handouts to the poor were stopped, was now seen to be right because it was in accordance with the nature's own "Whig" procedure. See also Adrian Desmond, *The Politics of Evolution* (Chicago: University of Chicago Press, 1989) for a detailed account of all the political aspects of the idea of evolution in Britain in the decades before the publication of Darwin's book. The idea that the order of nature and the order of society can be twin aspects of a single whole—a "Cosmopolis" (i.e., *cosmos + polis*)—is developed in detail in the brilliant book by Stephen Toulmin, *Cosmopolis* (Chicago: University of Chicago Press, 1990). See 67–69 for the definition of "cosmopolis," which Toulmin uses to bring to light what he calls "the hidden agenda of modernity."

The very idea of evolution itself, regardless of any specific interpretation or suggested mechanism, was introduced *into* science (like Sun-centered astronomy and atomism) and not discovered *by* science. It was certainly not discovered by Darwin—he never claimed that it was, of course, but this misconception is still surprisingly common. Darwin embraced the idea of evolution, which was already under discussion in the world to which he belonged, and proposed a mechanism for it. His approach to this was based on a particular interpretation of evolution, namely, that it proceeds by procreational connections (what he called transmutation and descent), and not by the progressive development (*Entwicklung*) of an archetypal animal (*Urtier*) in the manner envisaged by Goethe. It was in constructing this idea of what the mechanism could be that political and economic factors entered into the form which his theory took. The claim which Darwin later made, in his autobiographical account, that he had reached the principle of natural selection by induction in the Baconian manner from countless observations, can only be looked upon as part of a scientific "public relations" exercise.

When we see the understanding of science which has emerged from the new philosophy and the new history of science, it is difficult to escape the conclusion that it is this kind of approach to science which needs to be taught in schools. If we are to have people who are educated to understand what science is, it surely makes more sense to introduce them to science as a cultural–historical enterprise than it does to subject them to the present approach of facts, experiments, and calculations torn out of their real context. On its own, the current approach to science education gives a distorted image of science which results in a pseudo-understanding. This distortion could now be corrected by complementing it with the approach taken by the new history and philosophy of science. Without the historical perspective, science is too easily reduced to scientism, and knowledge ceases to be such and becomes an idol. When this happens, science education becomes a pseudo-education in idolatory.

281. Monk, *Ludwig Wittgenstein,* 311 and *passim.* In this exceptional biography, Monk shows that Wittgenstein was profoundly influenced by Goethe. It is well known that Wittgenstein underwent a radical change in his approach to philosophy, resulting in what many have seen as a very different philosophy in his later period— although there are now some commentators who stress the continuity between Wittgenstein's earlier and later work, instead of the discontinuity. What has now become clear is that Wittgenstein's transition to a new approach was a result of his encounter with Goethe. At first this was Goethe as mediated by Spengler in *Decline of the West,* but from that first encounter Wittgenstein went on enthusiastically to embrace Goethe's morphological approach as this is exemplified in *The Metmorphosis of Plants.* He followed this in his own investigation of language, and he grasped the key point that this did not provide an alternative theory, but the means to

escape from any *need* for a theory. The "understanding that consists in seeing connections" replaces theory and explanation, and
this is why many (Bertrand Russell, for example) who had been
filled with admiration for his earlier work could not follow his
later philosophy and thought it to be trivial. What Wittgenstein
was doing was developing an entirely new method in philosophy
which had "no precedent in the entire tradition of Western Philosophy" (Monk, 216). Now this tradition, as Heidegger has made so
clear, is the Greek one which derives ultimately from Plato, i.e.,
what is now referred to as the metaphysical tradition. So, at the
same time as Heidegger, Wittgenstein was working in his own way
to overcome the metaphysical tradition. What is important about
his way is that it introduced a new method into philosophy based
explicitly on Goethe's way of seeing, and it is this *way of seeing*
that replaces metaphysics. This is further confirmation that
Goethe's way of seeing is not restricted to observations in natural
science, but is a radical alternative to the kind of thinking we have
become familiar with in modern science and the Western tradition
generally. What is particularly remarkable is that this is not just a
matter of an alternative in an intellectual sense, but entails the
concrete experience of a new kind of seeing.

One of the reasons why Wittgenstein became so opposed to mainstream science is because he saw it as the embodiment of metaphysics
(one-sided Platonism). However, he did not really grasp the fact that
Goethe's way showed the possibility of a new, different kind of *science* from the mainstream, and he seems to have considered that
Goethe was really offering an alternative *to* science. It is one of the
aims of the present work to show that Goethe offers an alternative to
metaphysics, but that this is not necessarily the same as an alternative
to science because it is possible for there to be a nonmetaphysical science—which is what Goethean science is, in fact.

282. Ibid., 308.

283. Ibid., 338. He also said that instead of wanting to say that things
which look different are really the same, as he believed Hegel did,
"My interest is in showing that things which look the same are really different" (537).

284. It needs to be remembered that "the senses" means what Kühlewind
refers to as "the conceptually-instructed senses"—see *The Logos-
Structure of the World*, 39-46. The point here is that if we see a chair,
say, then this is not the purely sense-perceptible experience it seems
to be, because it also entails the concept "chair." So what we usually
think of as sense perception alone is really a sensory–conceptual
coalescence.

285. Monk, 537.

286. Ibid., 531. Wittgenstein considers aspect-seeing in a wider context than visual figures which are puzzling or ambiguous in some way. He considers the ability to see a joke, to understand music, poetry, painting, and so forth. However, we can also consider it in the more restricted case of the gestalt figures discussed here—I came across someone who could not see the hidden human figure for several months!

287. "Significant Help Given by an Ingenious Turn of Phrase," in Miller, 39.

288. This and the three following quotations are taken from Goethe's account of his meeting with Schiller, "Fortunate Encounter," in Miller, 20. Monk refers to this meeting in connection with Wittgenstein (511–12).

289. We have seen previously that cognitive perception has the structure of what Husserl calls the noesis–noema correlation: what is seen and the way that it is seen are necessarily correlated. Wittgenstein's approach brings us to a very similar position, even though the manner in which it does so is very different. There is more fundamental agreement between Wittgenstein and the phenomenological tradition than has sometimes been recognized on either side. Wittgenstein is particularly concerned to dispel any notion that there is some kind of private mental *object*, as if when we see internal connections we are seeing such an object. This confusion effectively reduces all seeing to one kind: that kind of seeing which consists in seeing physical objects, i.e., sensory seeing. This is what Wittgenstein denies, and he sees the confusion as arising from our habit of carrying over the language which is appropriate to one kind of seeing into the way that we talk about another kind of seeing. Thus "object" *means* "physical object" in whatever context the term is used—e.g., mental object—even though superficially it may seem to be otherwise. So we carry over this way of thinking into other areas for which it is not appropriate. Hence we mistakenly introduce the concept "object" where what we have to do with is a way of seeing. As mentioned already, phenomenology leads to the same conclusion by a different route.

290. Barfield, *The Rediscovery of Meaning,* 123.

291. In a letter to Thomas Butts (1802), Blake wrote:

> Twofold always. May God us keep.
> From single vision, and Newton's sleep!

Quoted in Barfield, ibid., 113. See William Blake, *Letters*, ed. Geoffrey Keynes (New York: Macmillan, 1956), 79. For Blake, the notion of the twofold went beyond the orbit of the present essay. Nevertheless, although what we are concerned with here is only a restricted case compared with the vision of William Blake, the twofold structure of the experience is the same.

292. It is important to remember that the use of the term "imagination" here is very different from the way that it is commonly used. From all that has been said about the practice of exact sensorial imagination, it should be clear that the kind of imagination discussed here is a faculty which has to be developed by disciplined work. What we commonly call imagination—in daydreaming, for example—is the "material" out of which an organ of perception can be built, but which has not been organized. Hence it "runs wild," and the result is fantasy instead of perception.

293. Barfield, *The Rediscovery of Meaning*, 20.

294. As mentioned previously, there is a tendency to talk of the sensory aspect and the meaning aspect of the word as being on different levels. Although this can be a useful way of talking at times, it may be that it is really a consequence of the way that *we* experience language. In other words, the fact that two different kinds of perception are involved at the same time gets projected onto the phenomenon, where it appears as two different levels. Another way of looking at it, instead of in terms of levels, is in terms of coarser and finer aspects of the same phenomenon.

The claim that we see meaning directly, in the sense that it is meaning which is the focus of cognitive perception, is made very strongly by Brown in *Perception, Theory and Commitment*, chap. 6. Brown maintains that this is just what happens in our ordinary cognitive perception. For example, if we see a table or a chair, then what we are seeing in each case is meaning, for which the physical object itself (perceived through the senses) is the script. Consequently, our cognitive perception of the world about us is really an act of reading a script. Thus the world we know is a text, and not a set of objects as commonsense and naïve empiricism take it to be. This is a very persuasive view in the light of the account of cognitive perception given above in chapter 2.

295. Friedemann-Eckart Schwarzkopf, "The Metamorphosis of the Given," Dissertation for Doctor of Philosophy, San Diego, California, 1992, 454. I am greatly indebted to Friedemann Schwarzkopf for making his thesis available to me. My understanding of Goethe has been considerably improved by Appendix VIII, "Goethe—The Archetypal Phenomenon." Schwarzkopf bases his approach on the philosophy of the word developed by Georg Kühlewind in several books (which Schwarzkopf has translated), the one which is most relevant in the present context being *The Logos-Structure of the World*. I first encountered Kühlewind's fundamental insight into

the twofold nature of the word in a workshop which he gave on this theme in London (June, 1990). But I had not grasped just how *exactly* this fitted the Goethean way of seeing in science until I read the appendix in Schwarzkopf's thesis referred to above. I am considerably indebted to this, as well as to the particular work of Kühlewind's referred to above, in writing this section of the present essay—although it should be added that both these works go well beyond the confines of this essay.

296. Friedemann Schwarzkopf, 439. Goethe refers to reading the phenomena of nature in a letter written in 1785—see Lehrs, 95. Goethe also refers to this in *Wilhelm Meister* as follows (quoted in Friedemann Schwarzkopf, 75):

> But if I would treat those cracks and fissures as letters, and try to decipher and assemble them to words, and learn to read them, would you object?

297. Kühlewind, *The Logos-Structure of the World*, 30-31, 52-53, 64-65.

298. Helen Keller, *The Story of My Life* (London: Hodder and Stoughton, 1959), 23.

299. Kühlewind heads *The Logos-Structure of the World* with a quotation from Thomas Aquinas: "The reality of things is their light" (Commentary to *Liber de causis* 1, 6).

300. See, for example, the discussion of this in Gadamer, *Truth and Method*, section 3.3.A.

301. Martin Heidegger, *On the Way to Language* (New York: Harper and Row, 1971). The quotations from Heidegger which follow are taken from "The Way to Language," which is included in the above.

302. Kühlewind, *The Logos-Structure of the World*, 30.

303. Ibid., 31.

304. Kühlewind describes nominalism as follows:

> Immature reflection may draw the distinction between concept and word falsely—not between concept and word but between thing and word—not realizing that only its concept makes a thing this thing. Then nominalism arises. A thing is pictured without its concept, and the word is regarded as identical with the concept. Therefore, nominalism assumes that the concept is only a name, a way of naming an object. It is not noticed that we can only name something we have grasped conceptually. Nominalism introduced into the realm of human thought the idea that things could exist without concepts. (ibid., 34)

Nominalism is to language as empiricism is to knowledge. Both are instances of starting "downstream" with what is the end result of a process and trying to understand the process in terms of this by projecting the result back into the very process which produced it—trying to get to the milk by way of the cheese.

305. Ibid., 52. It is tempting to try to convey this by saying that it is the *experience* of language as *magical*, but this is so easily open to misunderstanding. Adults see the primal experience of language when it happens with their own children, but do not recognize it for what it is. Because the experience of language has become mundane for the adult (we cannot really say the adult consciousness *experiences* language), we miss what is happening with the child, and can even think the child is confused and mistaken when it seems as if he or she is attributing a property of concreteness to words. What we do not realize is that a consciousness is awakened here which is very different from the adult consciousness. In this state of consciousness it would be appropriate to refer to the self-referral of meaning (self-meaning) as the self-saying of the word (it says itself).

306. Notice here again how difficult it is to avoid dualism. We say that it appears *and* is seen. But the appearing *is* the seeing; it does not appear and *then* is seen. It is only by an effort of attention that we can become aware of the dualism which is there already in the way we automatically conceive things.

307. The recognition that this is so has given rise to much discussion in recent years, often arising specifically from widespread (if superficial) interest in the work of Derrida. We have heard talk about postmodernism, subjectivism, relativism, nihilism, and the end of philosophy. But it has to be said that much of this discussion rests on (1) failure to go into the question of language without becoming sufficiently aware of the way that we already set language in a dualistic context and (2) failure to understand the monistic stage of language in human development and how radically different this primary phase is from the secondary stage, where language is used for the purpose of communicating information. Some of Derrida's seemingly outrageous remarks take on a different aspect when these two factors are taken into account. Consider remarks such as "the thing itself is a sign," and *"il n'y a pas de hors texte"*—often weakly translated as " there is nothing outside of the text," whereas what is really being asserted is that there is no *hors texte*, i.e., there is no "outside." The failure to recognize the dualism in the way that we are accustomed to understand language, as well as the failure to recognize the monistic stage of language which is prior to dualism, has the consequence that we see these remarks of Derrida's as asserting that either (a) there is no reality or (b) there is a reality but it is forever hidden from us by the veil of language. In this case language appears as a prison in which we must spend a life sentence. But such

a dualistic picture is itself contrary to what Derrida is trying to say. There is an *hors prison*, but not an *hors texte*. So no matter how it may seem when we are pushed along by the dualism in our habitual thinking, it simply makes no sense in Derrida's terms to talk about being imprisoned in language. This itself is an instance of the very dualism which a less superficial understanding of language dissolves. The point is that, as Gadamer says, "reality does not happen 'behind the back' of language. . . . reality happens precisely *within* language" (*Philosophical Hermeneutics*, 35). This follows necessarily from the nature of language itself as saying–showing–seeing. When we recognize this, it transforms our understanding of language, and we can see immediately that the claim that there is no reality, or that if there is then it is hidden behind language and inaccessible, is fundamentally mistaken and unwarranted.

We also realize that the traditional categories of objectivism and relativism are confusing and need to be replaced by an organic perspective in which the world can be one and many at the same time. Such a perspective is provided by the notion of "multiplicity in unity," which enables us to understand how the world can be One without being one world. As with the ambiguous figure which can be a duck or a rabbit, each complete in itself but not comprehensive, so there can be many worlds which are One—which is *not* the same as many different views of one world. Many of the problems discussed in philosophy today, which arise out of the limitation of the traditional categories in which the discussion is conducted, can be transformed by Goethe's organic way of seeing. In particular, it can help us to understand that what is fundamental is not different perspectives of a single reality—different ways of looking *at* the world (i.e., the attitude of dualism)—but different worlds which are not extensively many (pluralism) but intensively One. [It is not my intention above to suggest that Gadamer is in agreement with Derrida, but only that there is some ground which they do share in common over the fundamental question of language. It is certainly more usual to give attention to the way that they differ radically from one another, which they certainly do. See Gadamer's *Truth and Method*, part 3, section 3(A), especially 447, for a succinct expression of his thinking on language and world. See also Joel Weinsheimer, *Philosophical Hermeneutics and Literary Theory* (New Haven: Yale University Press, 1991), 121-23, on the way in which Gadamer differs from Derrida].

308. This does not mean that words are atomic meanings. Words are not *separate* in their meanings, but mean themselves only in relation to other words. Language is holistic.

309. Gadamer, 474 (italics in the original).

310. Heidegger, *On the Way to Language*, 118.

311. Miller, 309.

312. Kurt Hübner, *Critique of Scientific Reason*, 124. What Hübner means by "a priori" here is to be understood as being historical and not transcendental. Thus, the Sun-centered cosmos, for instance, is not *necessary* in any other sense than the one we have discussed earlier (in chapter 3), in that it arose in a particular historical situation within which it functioned as an a priori element that guided research in advance of any empirical justification. Such historical a priori propositions constitute "the conditions of the possibility" of scientific experience (to adopt Kant's terminology), but they are in no sense absolute. The history of science shows us "that nothing is necessarily true, but rather that every position is dependent upon the particular conditions of its origin" (ibid., 89).

313. See Fernand Hallyn, *The Poetic Structure of the World* (New York: Zone Books, 1993), pt. 1, for a detailed account of the relation between Copernican astronomy and the Renaissance ideal in architecture and painting. Copernicus refers explicitly to symmetry and harmony as key features of his approach in his letter to the Pope, which he prefixed to *De Revolutionibus Orbium Caelestium*, and in the tenth chapter of the introductory First Book. See also Kuhn, 137-39, 141-43, 177-80.

314. This is described brilliantly by Adrian Desmond and James Moore in their biography, *Darwin*. They describe how Darwin considered that the mechanism of natural selection—which he referred to as nature's "manufactory of species"—had the effect of increasing the "physiological division of labour" among species in a way which he saw as analogous to the new production line factories. Darwin married a member of the Wedgewood family—one of his grandfathers was Josiah Wedgewood—who were among the first to introduce the production line in the organization of their pottery factories. Darwin himself was a heavy investor in industry, and so in the form which his theory took "Darwin put his mouth where his money was" (Desmond and Moore, 421). The result was, in effect, the ideological industrialization of nature. Here we can see quite clearly the way that cultural–historical factors enter into the very form which scientific knowledge takes.

315. Hübner, 114. See also the end of "The Metaphysics of Separation."

316. Gurwitsch, "Galilean Physics in the Light of Husserl's Phenomenology," 88; *Phenomenology and the Theory of Science*, 56.

317. "The thesis that nature is mathematical throughout can be confirmed only by the entire historical process of the development of

science, a steady process in which nature comes to be mathematized progressively" (ibid., 55 and 87).

318. The story of "The Blind Ones and the Matter of the Elephant" appears in Idries Shah, *Tales of the Dervishes* (London: Octagon Press, 1982), 25.

Bibliography

Part I: *Authentic and Counterfeit Wholes*

Arber, Agnes, *The Natural Philosophy of Plant Form*, Cambridge, Cambridge University Press, 1959. (23: 209)

Bergson, Henri, *Creative Evolution*, London, Macmillan, 1911. (13: ix)

Bohm, David, *Wholeness and the Implicate Order*, London, Routledge and Kegan Paul, 1980. (2: 149; 9: chap. 7)

Bortoft, P. H., "A Non-reductionist Perspective for the Quantum Theory," Birkbeck College, London University, 1982. (7: chap. 5; 8)

—, *Goethe's Scientific Consciousness*, Tunbridge Wells, Institute for Cultural Research Monograph, 1986. (38)

Burtt, E. A., *The Metaphysical Foundations of Modern Science*, London, Routledge and Kegan Paul, 1980. (15: 83)

Capek, Milic, *Bergson and Modern Physics*, Dordrecht, the Netherlands, Reidel, 1971. (13: 56, 69, 72-74)

Capra, Fritjof, *The Tao of Physics*, London, Wildwood House, 1975. (5: 313)

Cassirer, Ernst, *The Problem of Knowledge*, New Haven, Yale University Press, 1974. (29: 146)

Deikman, Arthur J., "Bimodal Consciousness," in *The Nature of Human Consciousness*, ed. Robert E. Ornstein, San Francisco, W. H. Freeman, 1973. (12)

Einstein, Albert, and Leopold Infeld, *The Evolution of Physics*, Cambridge, Cambridge University Press, 1947. (25: 33)

Gadamer, Hans-Georg, *Truth and Method*, 2d rev. ed., London, Sheed and Ward, 1989. (37: 474)

Gurwitsch, Aron, "Galilean Physics in the Light of Husserl's Phenomenology," in *Phenomenology and Sociology*, ed. Thomas Luckmann, Harmondsworth, Penguin Books, 1978. (18)

—, *Phenomenology and the Theory of Science*, Evanston, Northwestern University Press, 1974. (18: chap. 2)

Heidegger, Martin, *Being and Time*, New York, Harper and Row, 1962. (36: 58)

—, *Identity and Difference*, New York, Harper and Row, 1969. (27: 29)

—, *Kant and the Problem of Metaphysics*, Bloomington, Indiana University Press, 1962. (11: 206)

Hendricks, Gay, and James Fadiman, *Transperonal Education*, Englewood Cliffs, Prentice-Hall, 1976. (32: 33)

Jaspers, Karl, *The Great Philosophers*, vol. 2, London, Rupert Hart-Davis, 1966. (9: 129)

Kant, Immanuel, *Critique of Pure Reason*, trans. Norman Kemp Smith, London, Macmillan, 1964. (14: 20)

Kilmister, C. W., *The Environment in Modern Physics*, London, English University Press, 1965. (3: 36)

Lehrs, Ernst, *Man or Matter*, 3d ed., revised and enlarged, London, Rudolf Steiner Press, 1985. (19: 314; 21: 314; 26: 94, 109; 28: 123; 30: chap. 5)

Leith, T., and H. Upatnieks, "Photography by Laser," *Scientific American* 212, 1965. (1: 24-35)

Miller, Douglas, ed., *Goethe: Scientific Studies*, New York, Suhrkamp, 1988. (30)

Narlikar, Jayant, *The Structure of the Universe*, Oxford, Oxford University Press, 1977. (4: 250)

Nisbet, H. B., *Goethe and the Scientific Tradition*, University of London, Institute of Germanic Studies, 1972. (20: 39; 22: 36, n. 149; 25: 54)

Palmer, Richard E., *Hermeneutics*, Evanston, Northwestern University Press, 1969. (6: chap. 7)

Riegner, Mark, "Horns, Hooves, Spots and Stripes: Form and Pattern in Mammals," *Orion Nature Quarterly* 4, no. 4, 1985. (35)

Roberts, Michael, and E. R. Thomas, *Newton and the Origin of Colours*, London, Bell, 1934. (16: 60, 110)

Schad, Wolfgang, *Man and Mammals*, New York, Waldorf Press, 1977. (35)

Seamon, David, "Goethe's Approach to the Natural World: Implications for Environmental Theory and Education," in *Humanistic Geography: Prospects and Problems*, ed. D. Ley and M. Samuels, Chicago, Maaroufa, 1978. (34: 238-50)

Seidel, G. J., *Martin Heidegger and the Pre-Socratics*, Lincoln, University of Nebraska Press, 1964. (10: chap. 3)

Shad, Idries, *The Sufis*, New York, Doubleday, 1964. (17: xvi)

Stansfield, R. G., "The New Theology? The Case of the Dripping Tap," paper presented to the British Association for the Advancement of Science, September 1975. (31)

von Aesch, A. G. F. Gode, *Natural Science in German Romanticism*, New York, Columbia University German Studies, 1941. (24: 74)

Part II: *Goethe's Scientific Consciousness*

Abbott, Edwin A., *Flatland*, New York, Dover, 1952. (50)

anonymous, *The Times*, London, December 4, 1984. (10: 16)

Arbor, Agnes, *The Natural Philosophy of Plant Form*, Cambridge, Cambridge University Press, 1959. (59: 209; 67: 209)

Aristotle, *Physics*, Book III. (33)

Barfield, Owen, *Romanticism Comes of Age*, London, Rudolf Steiner Press, 1966. (97: 36)

—, *Saving the Appearances*, New York, Harcourt, Brace and World, 1965. (63; 98: chap. 13)

Barnes, Schofield and Sarabji, eds., *Articles on Aristotle, Vol. I: Science*, London, Duckworth, 1975. (85: 77)

Bastin, Ted, ed., *Quantum Theory and Beyond*, Cambridge, Cambridge University Press, 1971. (4: 321-34)

Bergson, Henri, *Creative Evolution*, London, Macmillan, 1911. (28: 169; 33)

Bochemuhl, Jochim, *In Partnership with Nature*, Wyoming, Rhode Island, Bio-Dynamic Literature, 1981. (59: 4)

Bohm, David, *Quantum Theory*, Englewood Cliffs, N.J., Prentice-Hall,. 1951. (31: chap. 8)

—, *Wholeness and the Implicate Order*, London, Routledge and Kegan Paul, 1980. (29: chap. 2; 31)

Bohr, Niel, *Atomic Theory and the Description of Nature*, Cambridge, Cambridge University Press, 1961. (41)

Bortoft, P. H., "A Non-reductionist Perspective for the Quantum Theory," Birkbeck College, London University, 1982. (31; 57)

—, "Counterfeit and Authentic Wholes," in David Seamon and Robert Mugerauer, eds., *Dwelling, Place and Environment: Essays Toward a Phenomenology of Person and World*, The Hague, Martinus Nijhoff, 1986. (55)

—, *The Wholeness of Nature*, Hudson, Lindisfarne Press, 1996. (61: Chap. 5)

Brown, Harold I., *Perception, Theory and Commitment*, Chicago, University of Chicago Press, 1977. (18: chap. 6; 70: chap. 6)

Brown, Spencer, *Laws of Form*, London, Allen and Unwin, 1969. (61; 86: chap. 7, esp. 105)

Cassirer, Ernst, *Substance and Function*, New York, Dover, 1953. (60: chap. 1)

—, *The Problem of Knowledge*, New Haven, Yale University Press, 1974. (53: 145; 90: 167)

Cohen, I. Bernard, *The Newtonian Revolution*, Cambridge, Cambridge University Press, 1980. (12: 205; 22: section 4.7; 23)

Collingwood, R. G., *The Idea of Nature*, Oxford, Oxford University Press, 1960. (44: 126)

Cottingham, John, *Rationalism*, London, Granada, 1984. (86: 115-20)

Darwin, Charles, *The Origin of Species*, Harmondsworth, Penguin Books, 1968. (80; 88: 90)

Deikman, Arthur J., "Bimodal Consciousness," and "Deautomatization and the Mystic Experience," in Robert E. Ornstein, ed., *The Nature of Human Consciousness*, San Francisco, W. H. Freeman, 1973. (34; 35: 76)

Descartes, *"Discourse on Method" and the "Meditations"*, Harmondsworth, Penguin Books, 1968. (92; 93: 107)

Dijksterhuis, *The Mechanization of the World Picture*, Oxford, Oxford University Press, 1969. (98: 148)

Einstein, Albert, and Leopold Infield, *The Evolution of Physics*, Cambridge, Cambridge University Press, 1947. (42: 33)

Feyerabend, Paul, *Against Method*, London, Verso, 1978. (23)

—, "Explanation, Reduction and Empiricism," in Paul K. Feyerabend, *Realism, Rationalism and Scientific Method*, Cambridge, Cambridge University Press, 1981. (23)

Flew, Antony, *An Introduction to Western Philosophy*, London, Thames and Hudson, 1971. (94: 300)

Gadamer, Hans-Georg, *Philosophical Hermeneutics*, Berkeley, University of California Press, 1976. (30: 66ff; 95: 119)

—, *Truth and Method*, 2d rev. ed., London, Sheed and Ward, 1989. (47: 474; 75: 474; 99: 416)

Galilei, Galileo, *Siderius Nuncius*, Chicago, University of Chicago Press, 1989. (22)

Gilson, Etienne, *The Spirit of Medieval Philosophy*, London, Sheed and Ward, 1950. (33: 66)

Goethe, Wolfgang von, review of Purkinje's *Sight from g Subjective Standpoint*, in Douglas Miller, ed., *Goethe: Scientific Studies*, New York, Suhrkamp, 1988. (58: xix)

—, "The Metamorphosis of Plants," in Douglas Miller, ed., *Goethe: Scientific Studies*, New York, Suhrkamp, 1988. (51; 52)

Goodwin, Brian, *How the Leopard Changed Its Spots*, London, Weidenfeld and Nicholson, 1994. (91: 122-3)

Grof, Stanislav, *Beyond the Brain*, Albany, New York, State University of New York Press, 1985. (58: 79)

Grohmann, Gerbert, *The Plant*, vol. I, Kimberton, Pa., Bio-Dynamic Literature, 1989. (56: 43)

Hanson, Norwood Russell, *Patterns of Discovery*, Cambridge, Cambridge University Press, 1958. (6: 13; 16; 43: chap. 1)

—, *Perception and Discovery*, San Francisco, W. H. Freeman, 1969. (14: 61)

Harre, R., *The Philosophies of Science*, Oxford, Oxford University Press, 1972. (24)

Heidegger, Martin, *Being and Time*, New York, Harper and Row, 1962. (46: 51; 58)

—, *Identity and Difference*, New York, Harper and Row, 1969. (26: 29)

Heller, Erich, *The Disinherited Mind*, Harmondsworth, Penguin Books, 1961. (66: 12)

Holton, Gerald, and Duane H. D. Roller, *Foundations of Modern Physical Science*, Reading, Mass., Addison-Wesley, 1958. (25: esp. chap. 13)

Hubner, Kurt, *Critique of Scientific Reason*, Chicago, University of Chicago Press, 1983. (101)

Hume, David, *A Treatise on Human Nature*, book 1, Glasgow, Fontana/Collins, 1962. (81; 82: 331)

Huxley, T. H., in *Nature* 1, no. 1, Nov. 4, 1869. (102: 10)

Kearney, Hugh, *Science and Change 1500-1700*, London, Weidenfeld and Nicholson, 1971. (2: 17-22)

Koestenbaum, Peter, introductory essay in Edmund Husserl, *The Paris Lectures*, The Hague, Martinus Nijhoff, 1975. (20)

Koestler, Arthur, *The Sleepwalkers*, Harmondsworth, Penguin Books, 1964. (23: 517)

Kolakowski, Leszek, *Positivist Philosophy*, Harmondsworth, Penguin Books, 1972. (24)

Kripke, Saul, *Naming and Necessity*, Oxford, Blackwell, 1980. (86)

Kuhn, Thomas, "Energy Conservation as an Example of Simultaneous Discovery" in *The Essential Tension*, Chicago, University of Chicago Press, 1977. (101: 97-100)

—, *The Structure of Scientific Revolutions*, Chicago, University of Chicago Press, 2d ed., 1970. (23)

Lehrs, Ernst, *Man or Matter*, 3d ed., rev. and enlarged, London, Rudolf Steiner Press, 1985. (7: 131; 11; 58; 64: 125; 65: 73-6)

Magnus, Rudolf, *Goethe as a Scientist*, New York, Collier Books, 1961. (1: 22; 54: 45)

Mason, Stephen F., *A History of Science*, New York, Collier Books, 1962. (101)

Merleau-Ponty, Maurice, *Phenomenology of Perception*, London, Routledge and Kegan Paul, 1962. (19)

Nasr, Seyyed Hossein, *Science and Civilization in Islam*, Cambridge, Mass., Harvard University Press, 1968. (58: 257)

Naydler, Jeremy, "The Regeneration of Realism and the Recovery of a Science of Qualities," *International Philosophical Quarterly* 23,1983. (103: 155-72)

Newton, Isaac, *Opticks*, New York, Dover, 1952. (9: 124)

—, "The Origin of Colours," in Michael Roberts and E. R. Thomas, *Newton and the Origin of Coulours*, London, Bell, 1934. (8: 71-91)

Nisbet, H. B., *Goethe and the Scientific Tradition*, University of London, Institute of Germanic Studies, 1972. (64: 39)

Ornstein, Robert E., *The Mind Field*, London, Octagon Press, 1983. (32: chaps. 2 and 3; 36: 52ff; 38: 24; 39: 26)

—, *The Psychology of Consciousness*, New York, Harcourt Brace Jovanovich, 1977. (27; 37: 184)

Palmer, Richard E., *Hermeneutics*, Evanston, Northwestern University Press, 1969. (30)

Scruton, Roger, *A Short History of Modern Philosophy*, London, Routledge and Kegan Paul, 1984. (96: 132)

Shad, Wolfgang, *Man and Mammal: Toward a Biology of Form*, New York, Waldorf Press, 1977. (71; 72; 73: chap. 11; 74: 30; 77: 118; 78: 11; 79: 153)

Shah, Idries, *The Perfumed Serpent*, London, Octagon Press, 1978. (13: 25)

—, *The Sufis*, New York, Doubleday, 1964. (83: 59; 84: xxvi)

Steiner, Rudolf, *Goethe the Scientist*, New York, Anthroposophic Press, 1950. (3: 15, 31; 5: 1; 100: 179)

—, *Riddles of Philosophy*, New York, Anthroposophic Press, 1973. (69: 183)

—, *The Philosophy of Freedom*, London, Rudolf Steiner Press, 1964. (49: esp. chap. 7)

—, *A Theory of Knowledge Based on Goethe's World Conception*, New York, Anthroposophic Press, 1968. (19: chap. 5)

Stuart, David, and Algis Mickunas, *Exploring Phenomenology*, Chicago, American Library Association, 1974. (20: chaps. 1 and 2)

von Aesch, A. G. F. Gode, *Natural Science in German Romanticism*, New York, Columbia University German Studies, 1941. (48: 74)

von Senden, Max, *Space and Sight*, London, 1960. (19)

Webster, G., and B. C. Goodwin, "The Origin of Species: A Structuralist Approach," *J. Social. Biol. Struct.* 5, 1982. (87: 29; 89: 16; 91: 42)

Whorf, Benjamin Lee, *Language, Thought, and Reality*, Cambridge, Cambridge University Press, 1964. (29; 30: 213)

Williams, L. Pearce, *The Origins of the Field Theory*, New York, Random House, 1966. (101)

Wittgenstein, Ludwig, *Philosophical Investigations*, Oxford, Blackwell, 1968. (17: 169)

Zolla, Elemire, *The Uses of Imagination and the Decline of the West*, Ipswitch, Golgonooza Press, 1978. (58: 29)

Part III: *Understanding Goethe's Way of Science*

Abbott, Edwin A., *Flatland*, New York, Dover, 1952. (43: final paragraph of "The Depth of the Phenomenon" in part II)

Abercrombie, M. L. Johnson, *The Anatomy of Judgment*, London, Hutchinson, 1960. (40: 35-8)

Agassi, Joseph, *Towards a Historiography of Science*, 'S-Gravenhage, Mouton, 1963. (68: cf. 23)

Ames, Roger T., "Putting the Te Back into Taoism," in *Nature in Asian Traditions of Thought*, ed. J. Baird Callicott and Roger T. Ames, Albany, New York, State University of New York Press, 1989.

Arber, Agnes, *The Natural Philosophy of Plant Form*, Cambridge, Mass., Cambridge University Press, 1950. (243)

Aristotle, *De anima*. (22: 425 a 25)

—, *Metaphysics*, (111: 991 b 1-3; 212: 1078 b 13-35)

Barfield, Owen, *The Rediscovery of Meaning*, Middletown, Conn., Weslyan University Press, 1977. (99: 162)

—, *Saving the Appearances*, New York, Harcourt, Brace and World, 1965. (23)

Baynes, Kenneth, James Bohman, and Thomas McCarthy, eds., *After Philosophy*, Cambridge, Mass., MIT Press, 1987. (131)

Bennet, J. G., (seminars on modes of togetherness), Institute for the Comparative Study of History, Philosophy and the Sciences, Kingston-on-Thames, 1964. (255)

Bergson, Henri, *Creative Evolution*, London, Macmillan, 1960. (104: *ix*; 259:322; 260: 324)

—, *The Creative Mind*, New Jersey, Citadel Press, 1946. (261: 190; 262: 34; 263: 147; 264)

Berlin, Isaiah, *The Age of Enlightenment*, New York, New American Library, 1956. (100: 18)

Berman, Morris, *The Reenchantment of the World*, Ithaca, Cornell University Press, 1981. (44: 62)

Best, David, *Feeling and Reason in the Arts*, London, George Allen and Unwin, 1985. (19: 23-4; 37: 25)

Blake, William, *Letters*, ed. Geoffrey Keynes, New York, Macmillan, 1956. (291: 79)

Bohm, David, *Quantum Theory*, Englewood Cliffs, N.J., Prentice Hall, 1951. (102: 170)

—, *Wholeness and the Implicate Order*, London, Routledge and Kegan Paul, 1980. (279)

Bortoft, P. H., "A Non-reductionist Perspective for the Quantum Theory," Birkbeck College, University of London, 1982. (279: sections 6 and 7)

Brady, Ronald H., "Form and Cause in Goethe's Morphology," in *Goethe and the Sciences: A Reappraisal*, ed. Frederick Amrine, Francis J. Zucker, and Harvey Wheeler, Dordrecht, the Netherlands, Reidel Publishing Company, 1987. (29: 282, 286, 287; 215: 257-300; 228: 286; 230: 288-89; 240; 245: 272; 256: 276; 257: 279; 258: 274; 265: 285)

Brannigan, Augustine, *The Social Basis of Scientific Discovery*, Cambridge, Cambridge University Press, 1981. (51)

Brown, Harold I., *Perception, Theory and Commitment*, Chicago, University of Chicago Press, 1977. (21: chap. 6; 56; 79: 116; 95: 105; 294: chap. 6)

Buchwald, J., *The Rise of the Wave Theory of Light*, Chicago, Chicago University Press, 1989. (158)

Burtt, E. A., *The Metaphysical Foundations of Modern Science*, London, Routledge and Kegan Paul, 1980. (72: 79; 118: 82; 136: 81; 137: 91, 98; 144: 90)

Butterfield, Hebert, *The Origins of Modern Science*, London, Bell, 1957. (84: 4)

Caird, Edward, *Hegel*, facimile ed., AMS Press, 1972. (103: chap. 7)

Cannon, H. Graham, *The Evolution of Living Things*, Manchester, Manchester University Press, 1958. (96: 116)

Cassirer, Ernst, "Einstein's Theory of Relativity Considered from the Epistemological Standpoint," supplement to *Substance and Function*, New York, Dover Publications, 1953. (81: 371)

—, *The Philosophy of Symbolic Forms*, vol. 1, New Haven, Yale University Press, 1953. (223: 155)

—, *The Problem of Knowledge*, New Haven, Yale University Press, 1974. (258: 138)

Clagett, Marshall, *Greek Science in Antiquity*, London, Abelard-Schuman, 1957. (65: 90)

Cohen, I. Bernard, *The Birth of a New Physics*, revised and updated edition, New York, Norton, 1985. (36: 188; 83: 117-25; supplement 8 (210))

—, *The Newtonian Revolution*, Cambridge, Cambridge University Press, 1980. (36: 212; 79: pt. 2; 153: 138)

Colquhoun, Margaret, "Meeting the Buttercup Family," *Science Forum* 8 (Spring 1989). (272)

Colquhoun, Margaret, and Axel Ewald, *New Eyes for Plants*, Stroud, Hawthorn Press, 1996. (272: chap. 7)

Copleston, Frederick, *A History of Philosophy*, vol. 1, pt. 1, New York, Doubleday, 1962. (109: chap. 20; 112: 195)

—, *A History of Philosophy*, vol. 1, pt. 2, New York, Doubleday, 1962. (109: chap. 20; 111: 35ff)

—, *A History of Philosophy*, vol. 4, New York, Doubleday, 1962. (216: 220)

Darwin, Charles, *Autobiography*, (154)

—, *Origin of Species*, (154; 280: "Historical Sketch")

Davy, John, Hope, *Evolution and Change*, Stroud, Hawthorn Press, 1985. (97: 8; 268: 23-25; 276: 88)

Descartes, Rene, *Meditations*, Third Meditation (123: Second Meditation; 124; 127:

Desmond, Adrian, *The Politics of Evolution*, Chicago, University of Chicago Press, 1989. (280)

Desmond, Adrian, and James Moore, *Darwin*, London, Michael Joseph, 1991. (280; 314: 421)

Drake, Stillman, *Discoveries and Opinions of Galileo*, New York, Doubleday, 1957. (140; 141: 274)

Easlea, Brain, *Witch Hunting, Magic and the New Philosophy*, Sussex, Harvester Press, 1980. (76: 59; 202: 128)

Edelglass, Stephen, Georg Maier, Hans Gebert, and John Davy, *Mind and Matter: Imaginative Participation in Science*, Hudson, N.Y., Lindisfarne Press, 1992. (225)

Feyerabend, Paul, *Against Method*, London, Verso, 1978. (48: 75)

—, "Explanation, Reduction and Empiricism" in *Minnesota Studies in the Philosophy of Science*, vol. 3, 1962. (79)

Flew, Antony, *An Introduction to Western Philosophy*, rev. ed., London, Thames and Hudson, 1989. (130: 282; 210: 46)

Gadamer, Hans-Georg, *Philosophical Hermeneutics*, Berkeley, University of California Press, 1976. (251: 123; 307: 35; 309: 474)

—, "Heidegger, Hermeneutics and Interpretation," seminar at Goethe Institute, London, April 1986. (112)

—, *Truth and Method*, 2nd revised ed., London, Sheed and Ward, 1989. (1: pt 1, section 1.I.B.(i); 8: 300ff; 22: 90; 24; 40: 92; 112: 481-82; 201: 458; 300: section 3.3.A; 307: part 3, section 3(A), esp. 447)

—, "Unity in Heidegger's Thinking," talk at *Heiddegger, Hermeneutics and Interpretation* conference, Goethe Institute, London, and the British Society for Phenomenology, 1986. (214)

Galilei, Galileo, *Siderius Nuncius*, trans. by Albert Van Helden, Chicago, University of Chicago Press, 1989. (35; 38: 64)

Gardner, John F., forward to Wolfgang Schad, *Man and Mammals*, New York, Waldorf Press, 1977. (269: 2)

Gaskin, John, ed., *The Epicurean Philosophers*, London, Everyman, 1994. (86)

Goehring, G. Daniel, "Newton's First Observation of Differential Refraction," *The School Science Review*, 59/207 (December 1977). (171)

Gould, Stephen J., *Ever Since Darwin*, Harmondsworth, Penguin Books, 1980. (220: chap. 11)

Greene, J. C., *Science, Ideology and World View*, Berkeley, University of California Press, 1981. (280)

Grohmann, Gerhert, *The Plant*, vol. 1, Kimberton, Pa., Bio-Dynamic Literature, 1989. (217: 26; 221: 25; 244: 65; 245: 43; 253: chap. 3)

—, *The Plant*, vol. 2. (272)

Gurwitsch, Aron, "Galilean Physics in the Light of Husserl's Phenomenology" in *Phenomenology and Sociology*, ed. Thomas Luckmann, Harmondsworth, Penguin Books, 1978. (114; 119: 84; 132: 87; 133; 316: 88; 317: 55 and 87)

—, *Phenomenology and the Theory of Science*, Evanston, Illinois, Northwestern University Press, 1974. (114: chap. 2; 119: 51; 132: 55)

Hakfoort, Casper, "Newton's Optics: The Changing Spectrum of Science," in *Let Newton Be!*, ed. John Fauvel et. al., Oxford, Oxford University Press, 1988. (150: 84-89; 152: 85; 156: 98)

Hall, A. Rupert, *The Revolution in Science*, 1500-1750, London, Longman, 1983. (92: 183ff)

—, "Sir Isaac Newton's Notebook, 1661-5," *Cambridge Historical Journal* 9, 1948. (171: 247-48)

Hallyn, Fernand, *The Poetic Structure of the World*, New York, Zone Books, 1993. (313: pt. 1)

Hammond, Michael, Jane Howarth, and Russel Keat, *Understanding Phenomenology*, Oxford, Blackwell, 1991. (249: 48; 250: 49)

Hanson, Norwood Russell, *Patterns of Discovery*, Cambridge, Cambridge University Press, 1958. (13: chap. 1)

Harris, Errol, *Hypothesis and Perception*, London, Allen and Unwin, 1970. (91: 120)

Hawking, Stephen, *A Brief History of Time*, New York, Bantam, 1988. (96; 116: 193)

Hegel, *Hegel's Logic*, Oxford, Oxford University Press, 1975. (103: section 119)

Hegge, Hjalmar, "Goethe's Science of Nature," in *Goethe and the Sciences: A Reappraisal*, ed. Frederick Amrine, Frank J. Zucker and Harvey Wheeler. (190: 196-99; 192: 205; 194: 206; 206: 215)

Heidegger, Martin, *Being and Time*, New York, Harper and Row, 1962. (27: 63)

—, *Introduction to Metaphysics*, New Haven, Yale University Press, 1959. (108: 106)

—, *On the Way to Language*, New York, Harper and Row, 1971. (301; 310: 118)

Heinemann, Fritz, "Goethe's Phenomenological Method," *Philosophy* 9, 1934. (270, 271: 73)

Heller, Erich, *The Disinherited Mind*, Harmondsworth, Middlesex, Penguin Books, 1961. (236: 9)

Hübner, Kurt, *Critique of Scientific Reason*, Chicago, University of Chicago Press, 1983. (6; 78: chap. 5; 134: 48; 280; 312: 124; 315: 114)

Hume, David, *A Treatise of Human Nature*, Glasgow, Fontana/Collins, 1962. (47)

Husserl, Edmund, *Cartesian Meditations*, The Hague, Martinus Nijhoff, 1960. (250: 39)

—, *The Crisis of European Sciences and Transcendental Phenomenology*, Evanston, Illinois, Northwestern University Press, 1970. (114: 23-59)

Huxley, Aldous, *The Art of Seeing*, Seattle, Montana Books, 1975. (20: 20)

Ihde, Don, *Experimental Phenomenology*, Albany, New York, State University of New York Press, 1986. (248: 42-3)

Irwin, Terence, *Classical Thought*, Oxford, Oxford University Press, 1989. (85)

Jeans, Sir James, *The Mysterious Universe*, Cambridge, Cambridge University Press, 1930. (116: chap. 5)

Kant, Immanuel, *Critique of Judgment*, (96)

—, *A Critique of Pure Reason*, trans. Norman Kemp Smith, London, Macmillan, 1964. (195, 204: Bxii-Bxiv, 20)

Kearney, Richard, *Modern Movements in European Philosophy*, Manchester, Manchester University Press, 1986. (248: 13ff)

Keller, Helen, *The Story of My Life*, London, Hodder and Stoughton, 1959. (298: 23)

Koestler, Arthur, *The Sleepwalkers*, Harmondsworth, Penguin Books, 1964. (61: 195; 62: 170; 66: 208; 78: pt. 4, chap, 6; 117: 264)

Kohák, Erazim, *Idea and Experience*, Chicago, University of Chicago Press, 1978. (246: 31-32; 249)

Koyré, Alexandre, *From the Closed World to the Infinite Universe*, Baltimore, Johns Hopkins University Press, 1968. (86: 278 n. 5)

—, *Newtonian Studies*, Chicago, University of Chicago Press, 1965. (148: 42, n. 3)

Kuhlewind, Georg, *The Logos-Structure of the World*, Hudson, New York, Lindisfarne Press, 1991. (20: 15; 30: 37; 32: 36; 33: 93; 297: 30-31, 52-53, 64-65; 299; 302: 30; 303: 31; 304: 34; 305: 52)

—, *From Normal to Healthy*, Hudson, New York, Lindisfarne Press, 1989. (25: 166-70; 51: 62)

—, *Stages of Consciousness*, Hudson, New York, Lindisfarne Press, 1984. (9; 25: 166-70)

Kuhn, Thomas S., *The Copernican Revolution*, Cambridge, Mass., Harvard University Press, 1957. (52: 157; 54: 109; 55: 114; 57: chap. 2; 58: 73; 59: 163; 60, 61: 169; 63: 139; 64: 142; 69; 70: 131 and 179; 71: 180; 74: 180; 88: 220; 90: 238; 313: 137-39, 141-43, 177-80)

—, *The Essential Tension*, Chicago, University of Chicago Press, 1977. (53: *xi-xiii*)

—, *The Structure of Scientific Revolutions*, 2nd edition, enlarged, Chicago, University of Chicago Press, 1970. (6; 7: 121; 41: 115; 42: 53-56; 79: 121; 101: 121)

Lear, Jonathan, *Aristotle: The Desire to Understand*, Cambridge, Cambridge University Press, 1988. (200: chap. 4, esp. section 4.3; 226; 235)

Lehrs, Ernst, *Man or Matter*, 3rd ed., revised and enlarged, London, Rudolf Steiner Press, 1985. (2: 100; 32:113-23; 189: 109; 232: 82; 253: chap. 5; 254: 81; 296: 95)

Madison, G.B., *The Hermeneutics of Postmodernity*, Bloomington, Indiana University Press, 1990. (105: 129; 106: 130; 131; 214: 130)

Maxwell, James C., *A Treatise on Electricity and Magnetism*, 1st ed., (183: preface)

McAlpine, Daniel, *The Botanical Atlas*, Edinburgh, 1883; London, Bracken Books, 1989. (245: 101)

Melling, David J., *Understanding Plato*, Oxford, Oxford University Press, 1987. (109: chaps. 10 and 11)

Merchant, Carolyn, *The Death of Nature*, London, Wildwood House, 1982. (203: 168)

Merleau-Ponty, Maurice, *The Phenomenology of Perception*, London, Routledge and Kegan Paul, 1962. (20)

Miller, Douglas, ed., *Goethe: Scientific Studies*, New York, Suhrkamp, 1988. (175; 180: 310; 181: 16; 196: 39; 258: 63-66; 287: 39; 288: 20; 311: 309)

Mitchell, David, *An Introduction to Logic*, London, Hutchinson, 1964. (94: 113-15)

Monk, Ray, *Ludwig Wittgenstein*, London, Vintage, 1991. (255: 533; 281: 311; 282: 308; 283: 338; 285: 537; 288: 511-12)

Naydler, Jeremy, "The Regeneration of Realism and the Recovery of a Science of Qualities," *International Philosophical Quarterly* 23,1983. (139: 155-72)

Newton, Isaac, (letter to Oldenburg, July 8, 1672), (151)

Nisbet, H. B., *Goethe and the Scientific Tradition*, London, University of London, Institute of Germanic Studies, 1972. (155: 54, n.221)

Nussbaum, Martha C., *The Fragility of Goodness*, Cambridge, Cambridge University Press, 1986. (267: 251)

Oldroyd, D. R., *Darwinian Impacts*, Milton Keynes, The Open University Press, 1980. (280: chap. 4)

Palmer, Richard E., *Hermeneutics*, Evanston, Illinois, Northwestern University Pres, 1969. (161: 128)

Penrose, Roger, *The Emperor's New Mind*, Oxford, Oxford University Press, 1989. (115)

Plato, *Meno*, Harmondsworth, Penguin Books, (211: 72 c and d)

—, *Phaedo*, (109: 74c ff)

—, *The Republic*, Harmondsworth, Penguin Books, (75: pt. VII, sec. 6, pt. VIII, sec. 2; 113: 510d)

Proskauer, Heinrich O., *The Rediscovery of Color*, Spring Valley, New York, Anthroposophic Press, 1986. (127: 106; 143: 140, chaps. 6-9; 162; 165: 32; 168: 14; 169: 15; 170; 172: 25; 173; 174: 25-26; 184: 38; 186: 43; 187: 84; 188: 85)

Redondi, Pietro, *Galileo: Heretic*, Princeton, Princeton University Press, 1987. (89)

Roberts, Michael, and E. R. Thomas, *Newton and the Origin of Colours*, London, Bell, 1934. (146: 71-91; 149)

Ronchi, Vasco, *The Nature of Light*, London, Heinemann, 1970. (146: 162)

Sacks, Oliver, *The Man Who Mistook His Wife for a Hat*, London, Pan Books, 1986. (20: part 1; 45: 89)

Schwartzkopf, Friedemann-Eckart, "The Metamorphosis of the Given," Dissertation for Doctor of Philosophy, San Diego, California, 1992. (295: 454, Appendix VIII; 296: 439)

Sepper, Dennis L., "Goethe Against Newton: Towards Saving the Phenomena," in *Goethe and the Sciences: A Reappraisal*. (191: 187)

—, *Goethe Contra Newton*, Cambridge, Cambridge University Press, 1988. (5: 94, 96; 135: 24; 166: 27-38; 176: 70; 177: 70; 178: 71; 185: 149)

Seymour, John, *The Countryside Explained*, London, Faber and Faber, 1977. (218: 116)

Shad, Wolfgang, *Man and Mammals*, New York, Waldorf Press, 1977. (269: 2; 273; 274: 218-19, 257-65; 275: chap. 2)

Shah, Idries, "The Blind Ones and the Matter of the Elephant," in *Tales of the Dervishes*, London, Octagon Press, 1982. (318: 25)

—, *The Exploits of the Incomparable Mulla Nasrudin*, London, Octagon Press, 1983. (252: 26)

—, *A Perfumed Scorpion*, London, Octagon Press, 1978. (11: 25)

Sherrard, Philip, *Church, Papacy and Schism*, London, SPCK, 1978. (226)

—, *The Eclipse of Man and Nature*, Hudson, N.Y., Lindisfarne Pres, 1987. (226)

Sorell, Tom, *Decartes*, Oxford, Oxford University Press, 1987. (121: 57; 122: 61)

Spinoza, *Ethics*, (145: pt. 1, prop. III)

Steiner, Rudolf, *Goethe the Scientist*, New York, Anthroposophic Press, 1950. (3: 48; 179: 189; 199: chap. 18; 222: 62; 227: 17; 229: chap. 4; 230: 60; 237: 61; 241: 21)

—, *Goethe's World View*, Spring Valley, Mercury Press, 1985. (85: chap. 1; 112: 17; 126: 25; 214: 17; 226: 22; 242: 81)

—, *The Philosophy of Freedom*, trans. by Rita Stebbing, London, Rudolf Steiner Press, 1988. (18)

—, *Riddles of Philosophy*, New York, The Anthroposophic Press, 1973. (238: 144)

—, *A Theory of Knowledge Based on Goethe's World Conception*, New York, Anthroposophic Press, 1968. (20: chap. 5; 229: 88; 230: chap. 16)

Suchantke, Andreas, "The Leaf: The True Proteus," in Jochen Bochemuhl and Andreas Suchantke, *The Metamorphosis of Plants*, Cape Town, South Africa, Novalis Press, 1995. (272)

Toulmin, Stephen, *Cosmopolis*, Chicago, University of Chicago Press, 1990. (280, incl. 67-69)

von Senden, M., *Space and Sight*, London, Methuen, 1960. (20)

Weinsheimer, Joel. C., *Gadamer's Hermeneutics*, New Haven, Yale University Press, 1985. (1: 67-72; 8: 181; 29: 100, 111, 112, 114; 207: 69)

—, *Philosophical Hermeneutics and Literary Theory*, New Haven, Yale University Press, 1991. (307: 121-23)

Westfall, Richard S., *The Construction of Modern Science*, Cambridge, Cambridge University Press, 1977. (82: 19; 120: 41; 129: 38)

Zajonc, Arthur, "Fact as Theory: Aspects of Goethe's Philosophy of Science," *in Goethe and the Sciences: A Reappraisal*. (206: 238-42; 208: 240)

Henri Bortoft has taught physics and philosophy of science for most of his career. His postgraduate research, which he did under David Bohm and Basil Hiley at Birbeck College, London, was on the problem of wholeness in the quantum theory. Subsequently, he worked with J. G. Bennett on problems of perception, language, and time. His monograph for the Institute for Cultural Research, "Goethe's Scientific Consciousness," included in this volume, has been published in German translation. Bortoft now lectures and gives seminars on Goethean science, as well as on the development of modern scientific consciousness. Married, with three grown children, he lives in England.